William Ewart

Juventus mundi

The gods and men of the heroic age

William Ewart

Juventus mundi
The gods and men of the heroic age

ISBN/EAN: 9783741163098

Manufactured in Europe, USA, Canada, Australia, Japa

Cover: Foto ©ninafisch / pixelio.de

Manufactured and distributed by brebook publishing software (www.brebook.com)

William Ewart

Juventus mundi

JUVENTUS MUNDI

THE GODS AND MEN

OF THE HEROIC AGE

BY THE RIGHT HONORABLE

WILLIAM EWART GLADSTONE

BOSTON
LITTLE, BROWN, AND COMPANY
1869

Ghc 2. n 5

Note. — In this edition, all the references to the poems of Homer have been carefully verified, and nearly two hundred errors corrected. No alteration has been made in the text, beyond the correction of a few misprints.

PREFACE.

In this work, which is mainly the produce of the two Recesses of 1867 and 1868, I have endeavored to embody the greater part of the results at which I arrived in the 'Studies on Homer and the Homeric Age,' 1858. Those results, however, are considerably modified in the Ethnological, and in the Mythological, portions of the inquiry. The chief source of modification in the former has been that a further prosecution of the subject with respect to the Phœnicians has brought out much more clearly and fully what I had only ventured to suspect or hint at, and gives them, if I am right, a highly influential function in forming the Greek nation. A fuller view of this element in its composition naturally acts in an important manner upon any estimate of Pelasgians and Hellenes respectively.

This Phœnician influence reaches far into the sphere of the mythology; and tends, as I think, greatly to clear the views we may reasonably take of that curious and interesting subject.

I have also greatly profited by the laborious and original treatise of Dr. Hahn, on Albanian Archæology and Antiquities, as well as manners; which, although published at Jena in 1854, was scarcely, if at all, known in this country in 1858.

But, further, I have endeavored to avoid a certain crudity of expression in some sections of the 'Olympos,' which led to misconceptions of my meaning with respect to the action of tradition (especially of sacred or Hebrew tradition) and invention respectively, in the genesis of the Greek mythological system.

In dealing with the Third portion of the 'Studies,' called Aoidos, I have contracted a great deal, but added and altered little.

The immediate purpose of the former work was to draw out of the text of Homer, by a minute investigation of particulars, the results that it appeared to me to justify. Many of them were more or less new, and the process of inquiry was therefore exhibited in great, perhaps in excessive or wearisome, detail. I have now felt warranted to give a larger space to deduction, and a smaller one to minute particulars of inquiry, in a work which aims at offering some practical assistance to Homeric study in our Schools and Universities, and even at conveying a partial knowledge of this subject to persons who are not habitual students. Of what appeared directly useful for this end, I have consciously omitted nothing.

I am anxious, then, to commend to inquirers, and to readers generally, conclusions from the Homeric Poems, which appear to me to be of great interest, with reference to the general history of human culture, and, in connection therewith, of the Providential government of the world. But I am much more anxious to encourage and facilitate the access of educated persons to the actual contents of the text. The amount and variety of these contents have not even yet been fully appreciated. The delight received from the Poems has possibly had some influence in disposing the generality of readers to rest satisfied with their enjoyment. The doubts cast upon their origin must have assisted in producing and fostering a vague instinctive indisposition to laborious examination. The very splendor of the poetry dazzles the eye as with whole sheets of light, and may often seem almost to give to analysis the character of vulgarity or impertinence.

My main object, then, in this, and in the former work, has been to encourage, or, if I may so say, to provoke, the close textual study of the Poet, as the condition of real progress in what is called the Homeric question, and as a substitute for that loose and second-hand method, not yet wholly out of vogue in this country, which seeks for information about Homer anywhere rather than in Homer himself.

In further prosecution of this purpose, I have begun,

and carried forward at such intervals as I could make my own, another task. With patient toil, which applied to most authors would have been drudgery, I have tried to draw out, and to arrange in the most accessible form, resembling that of a Dictionary, what may be termed the body, or earthy and tangible part, of the contents of Homer. To a dissection of such a kind, the ethereal spirit cannot be submitted. This analysis will be separately published, so soon as other calls upon my time may permit. It must not be supposed that so homely a production aspires to exhibit Homer as a poet. Yet it exhibits him as a chronicler and as an observer; it helps to give an idea of his power by showing some part at least of the copious materials with which he executed his great synthesis, the first, and also the best, composition of an Age, the most perfect 'form and body of a time,' that ever has been achieved by the hand of man.

Like Colonel Mure, I am convinced that the one thing wanted in order to a full solution of what is called the Homeric question is knowledge of the text. In an aggregate of 27,000 lines, as full of infinitely varied matter (to use a familiar phrase) as an egg is full of meat, this is not so commonplace an accomplishment as might at first sight be supposed. I have striven to attain it; yet, as I know, with very partial success. And I do not hesitate to say, with the productions of some recent writers and critics on the Poet in my mind, that the reading public ought to be very wary in accepting unverified statements of what is or is not in Homer. I eschew the invidious task of illustrating this proposition from the pages of others: possibly it might receive some illustration from my own.

I have felt great embarrassment, in common I suppose with many more, in consequence of the unsettled and transitionary state of our rules and practice with respect to Greek names, and to the Latin forms of them.

Upon the whole, not without misgiving, but not without consideration, I have acted upon the belief that we cannot permanently fall back into the system which we were content until half a century ago to follow, and which Mr. Mitford and Mr. Grote assailed in common; that we cannot well stand where we are; and that we should, if possible, in this as in all matters, try to make preparation for the future, and make approaches at least towards a durable system.

First, then, I follow many high authorities in adopting generally the names of the Greek deities and mythological personages, instead of the Latin ones.

Secondly, with respect to names which have in no way become familiar to our ears or been domesticated in the English tongue, instead of the Latin forms and terminations, I adopt commonly the Greek; and say Iasos, Acrisios, Eurumachos, instead of Iasus, Acrisius, Eurymachus : as also Achaioi, Hippemolgoi, Lotophagoi, Phaiakes, instead of Achaians, Hippemolgi, Lotophagi, Phæacians.

But I have usually followed the old custom in cases where Greek words have been, so to speak, translated, so that the English ear has become thoroughly accustomed to the rendering, whether it be effected by the Latin form, as Cyprus for Κύπρος, or by an English one, as Rhodes for Rhodos.

Yet a case like the first of these exhibits the practical mischief of a somewhat degenerate system; for the name Kupros would, more readily than Cyprus, have suggested the fact, that copper owes its name to that island, which first afforded to Europe and the Mediterranean a plentiful supply of so primitive and important a metal. In this matter of names I am less consistent than Mr. Grote; and less bold, for I have not the same title to expect obedience. I can only say that my practice is accommodated, as far as I am able, to a state of transition, and that I have no doubt it is open to criticism in detail, even from those who may accept the general rule.

Lastly, I have in many cases written a Greek word in Roman type. I know not whether it will or will not, at some time, be found practicable to serve the purposes of all languages by one and the same character. But the general knowledge of the relationship of tongues, and of particular languages, is increasing;

and it may be both of interest and of use to the English reader, though unacquainted with Greek, to know the form and body of the words discussed in the text, when this advantage can be given without seriously distorting the words themselves.

HAWARDEN, NORTH WALES,
October, 1868.

CONTENTS.

CHAPTER I.

INTRODUCTION.

	PAGE
Popular appreciation of the Homeric works	1
Viewed too much through later traditions	1
The Author unknown as a Person	2
Date at which he lived	3
Place of his birth and residence	6
The poetry of Homer historic	7
Theurgy of the Poems self-consistent	9
Important internal evidence as to the historic character of the Poems	10
Uncertainty respecting them	11
The 'Hymns'	12
Arguments of those who support a dual authorship discussed	14
Iliad and Odyssey compared	17
Text of the Poems discussed	18–26
Comparative antiquity of Homer and Hesiod	26
Evidence of Homer in relation to his age	28
Discrepancy between Homeric and Post-Homeric tradition	29
Conclusion concerning the Text of the Poet	30

CHAPTER II.

THE THREE GREAT APPELLATIVES.

The 'Greeks' of the Troica were Achaians	32
Pre-Hellenic races — Pelasgoi	32
Designations of the Greeks of the Iliad	33

	PAGE
Instances of chronological succession of Homeric names	34
'Argeioi' used as a national designation and in a local sense	35
The Danaoi	36
Derivation of Homeric national or tribal names	37
Homer's unwilling testimony to the foreign origin of Greek Houses	38
Genealogy of the race of Danaos	40
Post-Homeric tradition with regard to Danaos	41
Conclusions as to the Danaoi	42
Argeioi	42
Local use of the word	43
Poetic and archaic uses of it	44
Application of the territorial name Argos	45
Common term in three distinct territorial names	50
Four uses of in Homer	52
Derivation of Homeric names of countries and places	53
Uses of the word 'argos'	54
The derivative Argeioi	55
This name belongs properly to the commonality	59
The third Appellative: Achaioi	60
Epithets applied to the name Achaioi	62
Force of the word 'dios'	63
Instances of the use of the appellative Achaioi	64
The Myrmidons	66
Epithet 'Panachaioi'	70
Conclusion respecting the use of the Three Appellatives	71

CHAPTER III.

THE PELASGOI.

Classification of the Homeric testimony concerning the Pelasgoi	73
Wide extension of the Pelasgoi	73
'Pelasgic Zeus'	74
Thessaly a Pelasgic country	74
Thracians	76
Kaukones	76
Epithets given to the Pelasgians	76
The Larissa of Homer	77
Other heads of Homeric evidence concerning the Pelasgoi	78
Connection between Arcadians and Pelasgoi	79

	PAGE
The Ionians	81
Local, not personal, relation between Athens and Athene	83
Erectheus probably a Pelasgian	84
Evidence as to the Pelasgian character of Attica in early times (Ionians)	85
Pelasgian element in Thessaly	87
'Iason Argos'	88
Marks of a Pelasgian character in the population of Crete	89
The Five Races domesticated in Greece	90
Eteocretes and Kudones	90
The Leleges	91
Pelasgian occupation of Epiros	92
Etymology of the Pelasgian name	94
Difference of race and rank among the Greek population	95
The Pelasgian element in the Greek language	96
List of words (supposed to be of Pelasgian origin) common to the Greek and Latin languages	97
I. Objects of Inanimate Nature	97
II. Trees, Plants	98
III. Animated Nature	98
IV. Objects connected with Food	98
V. Related to Out-door Labour	98
VI. Navigation	98
VII. Dwellings	99
VIII. Clothing	99
IX. The Human Body	99
X. The Family	99
IX. Society	99
XII. General Ideas	99
XIII. Adjectives of Common Use	100
Scant stock of words relating to religion	100
Words relating (1) to war, (2) to navigation, (3) to metals	101
Distinction with regard to names of persons, &c.	103
Extra-Homeric evidence of the wide extension of the Pelasgoi	107

CHAPTER IV.

HELLAS.

The word 'Hellas' and its derivatives	110
Phthiê; the phrase 'Pelasgic Argos'	112
The designation 'Panhellenes'	114

CONTENTS.

	PAGE
Kephallenes	115
Hellol or Sellol: the Aspirate and Sigma interchangeable	116
Route of the Hellic tribes into Greece	118

CHAPTER V.

THE PHŒNICIANS AND THE EGYPTIANS.

Minos	119
His Phœnician character	120
Phœnician tongue probably spoken in Crete	121
Daidalos — Kadmos	123
Important works of art obtained from the Phœnicians	124
Dependence of the Greeks on the Phœnicians (ship Argo)	125
The Egyptian Thebes	129
Conclusion respecting the significance of the word 'Phœnicia' in Homer	130
Art of writing introduced by Phœnicians	131
Art of building with hewn stone probably introduced by them	132
The people of Scherië (Corfu) of Phœnician stock	133
Their games	133
Fine Art, in Homer, proceeded from a Phœnician source	134
Respective contributions of Pelasgians and Hellenes to the aggregate Greek nation	135
Possible personal medium between Greece and Phœnicia	136
Were the Aiolids Phœnician?	139
Achaian invasion of Egypt	145

CHAPTER VI.

ON THE TITLE 'ΑΝΑΞ ΑΝΔΡΩΝ.'

Substantial distinction between titles and epithets descriptive of station or office	151
Title 'Anax Andrōn,' to whom applied	153
I. Agamemnon	155
His extraction: passage concerning the Sceptre	155
Simultaneous rise of the Achaian race and of the House of Pelops	158
Tantalos	158
Niobe: Pelops	159

	PAGE
Achaians a Thessalian race	161
Title ('Anax Andrôn') anterior to the constitution of Achaian society	162
II. *Anchises*, and III. *Æneas*	163
Position of the Helloi and Dardanians severally	163
Why the title is applied to Anchises and Æneas, but not given to Priam or any of his family	163
Absence of Anchises from the Trojan Council; his sovereignty	164
Æneas: jealousy between him and the house of Priam	165
Pointed use of the phrase 'Anax Andrôn'	166
IV. *Augeias*	167
Ruled over Elis	167
His extraction and descent	168
Ephure, a town of Elis	169
V. *Euphetes*	170
King of Ephure: distinction between the towns so named	170
VI. *Eumelos*	171
Rules at Pheral; an Aiolid	171
Summing up of the Homeric evidence concerning the phrase 'Anax Andrôn'	172

CHAPTER VII

THE OLYMPIAN SYSTEM.

Homer the maker, not of poems alone, but of a language, a nation, and a religion	176
Contrast between Homer and the Hesiodic Theogony	177
Variegated aspect of Hellenic religion; reasons for this	178
Instances	179
Modes of reconciliation or adjustment	180
Debasement of the Olympian system	182
Its specific principle humanitarian	183
It wanted the supports of a hierarchy and of sacred books	183
Actual operation of the Hellenic Theo-Mythology	184
The later religion in relation to philosophers and legislators	184
Plato's reproaches against Homer's treatment of the gods unfounded; cases in point	187
Materials supplied as the base of Homeric religion	188
The five great deities	189

CONTENTS.

	PAGE
Homer's mode of dealing with the elder gods	189
Vestiges in the Olympian system of Elemental worship	190
Nature-gods generally treated as subterranean	192
River-worship local	192
Olympian system appropriates the materials of the older elemental one	194
Homeric mythology ought to be severed from the schemes of (1) Nature-worship; (2) Roman mythology; (3) scheme of classical Greece	195
Homeric polity framed on the human model	195
Instances of	196
Functions of the deities	197
Classification of the Olympian personages in Homer	200
Limitations and liabilities of the subordinate gods	201
Correspondence between certain features of the Olympian system and the Hebraic traditions	202
The Messiah	205
Theories as to the origin of heathen religions	208
Other Homeric correspondences with Hebrew tradition	209
The highest conception of deity does not exclude the element of fraud	211
Grand distinction between the Homeric and the later systems	214
Homer's wide notion of the gods as governing all mankind	214
Collective action of the Olympian deities	215
No instance of a married deity, save Zeus	216
Element of deontology; *will* and *ought*	217
Classification of the *Di majores*	218

CHAPTER VIII.

THE DIVINITIES OF OLYMPOS.

SECTION I. *Zeus*	221
Five different capacities ascribed to Zeus	222
1. *The Pelasgian Zeus*	223
2. *The Divine Zeus*	225
His universal supremacy	226
His limitations and liabilities	227
3, 4. *The Olympian Zeus, and the Lord of the Air*	228
Omnipotence not conceived of by Homer	230
Headship of Zeus; the arbiter among the gods	230

		PAGE
His sole and supreme responsibility	. . . .	232
Aristocratic character of the Olympian polity	. . .	233
5. *Zeus the type of Anthropomorphism*	. . . .	234
Individual character of Zeus of a low order	. . .	235
Not, however, devoid of affections	. . . .	236
The masterpiece of Homeric mythology with regard to the humanizing element	. . . .	236

SECTION II. *Herè* 236
  Of all deities the most national 236
  Special characteristics of; she disappears from the Odyssey 237
  Called 'Argeian Herè' 238
  Her rank in Olympos 239
  Interpretation of the myth of the deposition of Kronos . . 240
  The function of Herè as regulator of birth 241
  Vestige of the prerogative of Herè as a Nature-Power . . 243
SECTION III. *Poseidon* 243
  His position and rank 244
  Not an elemental deity; Nereus the true sea-god . . . 245
  Special functions of Poseidon 247
  Legends relating to him; their character 248
  His province in the Outer-World 248
  His supremacy in the Odyssey working, rather than abstract 250
  Prevalence of Poseidonian worship among the Phœnicians . 251
  The Trident; relation to some tradition of a Trinity . . 252
  Cyclops, children of Poseidon 252
  The Phœnician origin of Poseidon supplies a key to his position and attributes 253
SECTION IV. *Aidoneus* 253
  Probably a Nature-Power of an older Theogony . . . 254
  His character and functions 255
  The 'Zeus of the Underworld' 256
SECTION V. *Leto* 259
  Epithets given to her 259
  Her circumscribed action 260
  High ascriptions of her dignity 260
  Etymology of the name 261
  Probable record of the Hebrew tradition respecting the Mother of the Deliverer 262
SECTION VI. *Demeter* 262
  Homeric evidence respecting her 263
  Her share in the old tradition of Nature-worship . . . 265

	PAGE
SECTION VII. *Dionê*	265
A wife of Zeus; mentioned in one passage only	266
Testimony of Hesiod	266
A Nature-Power	267
SECTION VIII. *Athenê* and *Apollo*	268
Their position in Olympos a hopeless solecism, if viewed apart from Hebrew traditions	269
Relation of rank between Herê and Athenê	270
Dignity of Apollo	271
Correspondence of Homer with the Messianic tradition of the Logos and the Son of the Woman	272
Superior *sanctitas* of Athenê and Apollo	272
They are the two great Agents	273
Uniform identity of will between Zeus and Apollo	276
Apollo the defender of heaven and deliverer of the immortals	276
Functions of these two deities encroach upon the provinces of other divinities	277
Jointly invoked	279
No local limit to their worship	279
They are independent of limitations of place	280
Omnipresent; prayer addressed to them from all places	280
Exempt from physical infirmity or need in general	281
Attributes of bulk; locomotion	282
Apollo and Athenê administer powers otherwise referred to Zeus	283
Both exercise vast power over external nature	284
Both possess lofty moral excellence and purity	286
Distinctive functions of Apollo, severing him from Athenê	287
The ministry of death	287
Hellenic preservation of the element of Hebrew tradition	290
SECTION IX. *Hephaistos*	291
One of the seven astral deities of the East	291
Dual course of tradition relating to Hephaistos	291
The Charites	294
Matchless deity of Hephaistos	295
The architect of the palaces of the gods	295
SECTION X. *Arês*	296
'In point of strength divine, in point of mind and heart simply animal'	296

	PAGE
Represents the idea of raw courage	297
Instances of his action	298

SECTION XI. *Hermes* 301
   His part in the Iliad secondary 301
   Instances of his agency 301
   Idea of concealment inheres in his character 302
   His probable connection with the Phœnicians 303
   An agent rather than a mere messenger 304
   His name Argeiphontes 305

SECTION XII. *Artemis* 305
   In the main a reflection of Apollo 306
   Relation of, to the Moon-goddess 307
   Shares with Apollo the ministry of death 308
   Her agency ubiquitous in character 309
   Confers beauty (of figure) 310
   Epithet ἁγνή and its significancy 311

SECTION XIII. *Persephonê* 311
   Epithets applied to her 311
   Represents a mixture of Pelasgic and of Eastern traditions . 311
   Co-ruler with Aïdoneus 311
   Etymology of the name 312
   The Persian race 313

SECTION XIV. *Aphroditê* 313
   Her position and several functions in the Homeric mythology 313
   Local indications of her worship 317
   Etymology of the name 318

SECTION XV. *Dionusos* 319
   Obscurity of traditions concerning him 319
   No clearly divine act assigned to him 319
   Recital concerning Lucourgos 320
   Probable sign of his worship in the Odyssey 320
   Worship of Dionusos recent; and opposed on introduction 321
   He is placed within the Phœnician circle 322
   To be regarded probably as a deified mortal 322

SECTION XVI. *Helios, or the Sun* 323
   His personality 323
   His appearance in (a) the Iliad, (b) the Odyssey . . . 323

	PAGE
Theft of the Oxen of the Sun	324
This legend of Phœnician origin	324
The Sun an Eastern deity	326
Incorporation of the traditions of Apollo with those of the Sun	326
Section XVII. *Hebe*	327
Character of her offices	327
Expresses the idea of youth	328
Section XVIII. *Themis*	329
A member of the Olympian court	329
Signification of the name	330
Section XIX. *Paieon*	330
His function as healer	331
Relation between Paieon and Apollo	331
The pæan or hymn to Apollo	332
Section XX. *Iris*	332
Instances of her office as Messenger	333
The name of the rainbow; and the Hebrew tradition	333
Her agency	334
Section XXI. *Thetis*	335
Her origin elemental	336
Her vast influence	336
Her prayer to Zeus	337
Etymology of the name	337
Character of her marriage to Peleus	338
Pelasgian worship of Zeus; double relation of Thetis	339
Instances of her agency	340
The reconciler between the conflicting creeds	340
Her influence with the gods grounded on obligation	341
Principal particulars respecting her	342
Epithets applied to her	344
Later traditions appear but arbitrary comment	344

CHAPTER IX.

Further Sketch and Moral Aspects of the Olympian System.

I. *Various Orders of Preternatural Beings*	346
1. The Nature-Powers	346

	PAGE
2. The Minor Nature-Powers	847
3. Mythological Personages of the Outer or Phœnician Sphere	848
4. The Rebellious Powers	849
5. Ministers of Doom	849
6. Poetical Impersonations	850

II. *The Erinues* 850
   The three chief recognized descriptions of preternatural force 850
   Action of the Erinues 852
   Their functions 852
   Etymology of the name 856

III. *Atè the Temptress* 856
   Her place in Homer 857
   Character of her temptations 857

IV. *Fate or Doom* 858
   Distinction between the words conveying the idea — Kèr, Moira, Aisa, &c. 859

V. *Animal Worship* 861
   Sanctity attaching to the Oxen of the Sun 861
   Other traces of animal worship 862
   Animal Sacrifice 863

VI. *On the Modes of Approximation between the Divine and the Human Nature* 863
   Elements of the system of deification of mortals discernible in Homer 864
   Divine filiation 867
   'Zeus-born' princes 870
   Explanation of this title 871
   Four channels of approach between the human and divine natures 873

VII. *The Homeric View of the Future State* 873
   Three-fold division of the Future World 874

VIII. *The Olympian System in its Results* 877
   History of the human race before Christ is the history of a preparation for His Advent 877
   Character and vitality of the Olympian system 878
   A precursor of Christianity 880

CHAPTER X.

Ethics of the Heroic Age.

	PAGE
Section I. General outline of the moral character of the Homeric Greeks	381
Heracles	383
Moral force of Religion	384
Voice of Conscience	386
Homicide	387
The weak point of tenderness for fraud	388
Idea of sin implied in Homer	390
The Homeric view of patience	392
Virtue of justice	393
Virtue of self-restraint	394
The model spirit of moderation, the τὸ μέσον	396
Implacability regarded as unequivocally vicious	397
Extremest forms of depravity unknown	398
Domestic relations	400
The Poet's admiration for Beauty	402
The delicacy of Homer	403
Sketch of Greek life in the heroic age	405
Section II. Position held by women	408
No trace of polygamy	410
Concubinage	411
Relations of youth and maiden	411
Picture of Greek marriage	414
Employments of women	416

CHAPTER XI.

Polity of the Heroic Age.

Similitude between Homeric and British Ideas	417
Reverence for kings	418
No 'balance of forces'	419
The kings	420
Personal attributes of the king	422
His fourfold character	428

CONTENTS. xxv

	PAGE
Agamemnon a 'King of kings'	431
Transactions of the Army decided in the Assemblies	432
Ranks traceable in the army	433
Composition of the Council	434
Importance of Power of Speech	435
Majority and minority	439
The Τίς, or Public Opinion	441
Chief component parts of Greek society	442
Representation of the state of society in Ithaca	445
Absence of written 'law'—The Oath	447
The Xeinos or Xenos	447
Sources for supplying slaves	448
The medium of exchange	450
Leading political ideas of the Poems	451
Bonds cementing Greek society	453

CHAPTER XII.

RESEMBLANCES AND DIFFERENCES BETWEEN THE GREEKS AND THE TROJANS.

Double ethnical relation	455
Religion	456
Prevalence of Nature-worship in Troy	457
Sacerdotal institutions and ritual forms	460
Superior morality of the Greeks	462
Trojan tendency to sensual excess	464
Polygamy of Priam	466
Relation of Priam to subordinate countries	468
Trojan Assembly	469

CHAPTER XIII.

GEOGRAPHY OF HOMER.

SECTION I. The Catalogue	471
Genealogies of the Greek Catalogue	471
The Greek territory divided into three circles and a fourth irregular figure	472
Greek and Trojan Catalogues	473

	PAGE
SECTION II. The Plain of Troy	474
Leading topical points	474
Discussion of Homer's description	475
SECTION III. The Outer Geography	479
Data for an Homeric map of the Outer Geography	482
Indications of Homer's belief in a great sea occupying the heart of the European continent	484
Stages of the Voyages of Odysseus	488

CHAPTER XIV.

PLOTS, CHARACTERS, AND SIMILES.

SECTION I. The Plot of the Poems; especially of the Iliad	495
SECTION II. Some Characters of the Poems	500
1. Achilles	500
2. Odysseus	502
3. Agamemnon	506
4. Diomed and Ajax	508
5. Helen	509
6. Hector	513
7. Paris	516
SECTION III. The Similes of the Poems	518

CHAPTER XV.

MISCELLANEOUS.

SECTION I. The Idea of Beauty in Homer	521
Personal Beauty, and Beauty of Landscape	522
SECTION II. The Idea of Art in Homer	525
Works of Art	525
Material of Art	526
Homer's delineation of Art	528
Egyptian and Assyrian schools of Art	529

		PAGE
SECTION III.	Physics of Homer	530
SECTION IV.	Metals in Homer	533
SECTION V.	Measure of Value	538
SECTION VI.	Use of Number in Homer	540
SECTION VII.	The Sense of Color in Homer	544

INDEX 647

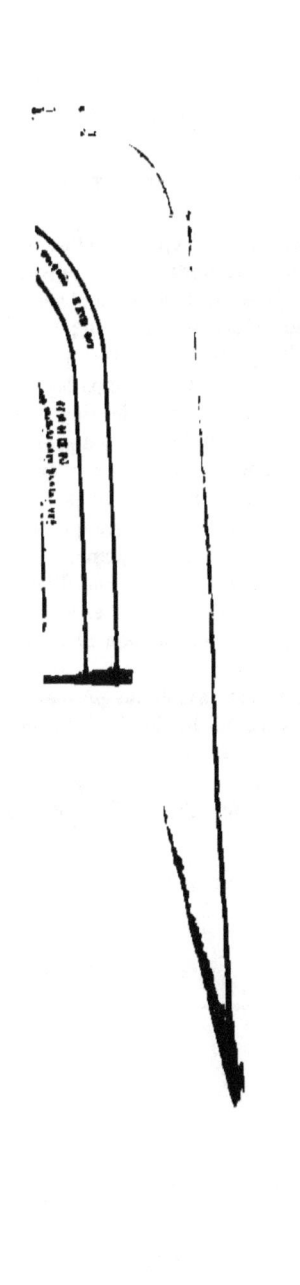

CHAPTER I.

INTRODUCTION.

If, as the general opinion holds, the Iliad and the Odyssey are the works of an individual poet (whom we term Homer), they are probably, as a connected whole, the oldest in the world; though a few of the Books of Scripture, and, in the opinion of some, a portion of the Vedas, may perhaps lay claim to a higher antiquity. They unquestionably contain a mass of information respecting man in a primitive or very early stage of society, which has not even yet been thoroughly digested, and such as is nowhere else to be found. They have also, through the intervention of the Greek and then of the Roman civilization, for both of which they form the original literary base, entered far more largely than any other book, except the Holy Scriptures, into the formation of modern thought and life.

A main reason, which has prevented mankind from profiting to the full by these invaluable works, appears to have been this; that, except for the purposes of purely poetical appreciation, they have been viewed far too much through the medium of later traditions, of

the productions of the classic ages of Greece and Rome,
and especially of the great epic of Virgil; and the
multiform features of the picture which he draws have
thus been confounded with the representations of much
later, and in many respects very different ages.

While the works of Homer have exercised an influence which has been greater than those of any other
poet, and which is rising apparently at the present
time, nothing is known of his person. His blindness,
but only in mature and late life, is allowably conjectured from the fact that he has drawn a careful and
sympathizing picture of the blind minstrel Demodocos
in Scherié[1] (now Corfû), and has made him more
conspicuous than any other Bard mentioned in the
Poems. Absorbed in his subject, the Poet never
refers to himself: in half-a-dozen passages the personal pronoun is used—'Tell me, O Musca,'[2] and the
like; but it is a mere grammatical form, never specially pointed to his own individuality. Of his character we can only judge as far as different passages of
the Poems may enable us to trace his personal sympathies in their tone and color. The conjecture as to
his blindness is indeed in accordance with a passage
which Thucydides[3] quotes as his from the Hymn to
Apollo, and which mentions it: but the weight of this
evidence depends much more on the beauty and pathos
of the verses, than on the fact that the great historian
treats it as by Homer; since he does not speak in the
character of a witness, and the reference to Chios as
the place of his residence is a circumstance calculated
to excite strong suspicion.

[1] Od. viii. 64.   [2] Od. i. 1.   [3] iii. 104.

INTRODUCTION. 3

With respect to the date at which Homer lived, nothing is known, except it be by recent and as yet scarcely recognized discovery,[1] from sources extrinsic to the Poems. Herodotus places him at four hundred years before himself, in the ninth century before Christ. This would bring him nearly to the epoch of Lycurgus. But the state of society and manners in Greece depicted by him is far anterior to all that is connected with the name of that legislator; and betokens not only priority, but long priority, to the historic period, which is commonly said to begin with the Olympiad of Corœbus, B. C. 776. The date of 1183 B. C. is fixed by Eratosthenes for the fall of Troy: but it has long been known to be no more than conjectural.[2] In my opinion, that event is quite as likely to have been older, as to have been more recent. But there are in reality no fully acknowledged measures of time applicable to the decision of the question. Homer alone seems to afford us, for his own age, any means of estimating, however rudely, the lapse of years. His only chronology is found in genealogies, given by him in considerable numbers, and in singular correspondence with one another. But this knowledge, if authentic, stands as an island separated from us by a sea of unknown breadth. We have as yet no mode of establishing a clear relation of time between it and the historic era.

The Poems afford, however, partial means of estimating the date of Homer, relatively to the War of Troy. He virtually states, that he was not an eye-

[1] See Chap. V. on Phœnicia and Egypt.
[2] Clinton, Fasti Hellenici, i. 123.

witness of the War.[1] Poseidon[2] prophesies that the grand-children of Æneas shall reign in Troas; and it is fairly argued that the Poet would not have ventured on the prediction, if he had not lived to see its entire or partial accomplishment. A grandson of Æneas may well have reigned in Troas within fifty or even forty years of the fall of the city; and a son within a much shorter period. Arguments for a greater interval have indeed been founded on the passages, in which the Poet contrasts the might of the Troic heroes with the lower standard of his own time. But a ready answer is surely found in the fact that Nestor, in the First Iliad,[3] draws a somewhat similar contrast between the heroes of his youth, and those of the Greek army before Troy. Figure is, in truth, the main element in all such comparisons. A third argument has been founded on the passage, in which Here observes to Zeus that he is free to destroy the cities she loves the best — Argos, Sparta, and Mycenæ.[4] Hence, it is thought, Homer must have lived after the Dorian conquest. But (1) we do not find that any of these cities were destroyed at that epoch; and (2) had Homer lived in an age posterior to that great revolution, he must have betrayed his knowledge of it not in one equivocal passage, but in many, and by a multitude of signs of later manners. (3) The Dorian conquest had the immediate effect of reducing Mycenæ to obscurity, while it left Argos and Sparta at the head of Greece; and it would be strange indeed that Homer, if he had witnessed it, should join the three in a single

[1] Il. ii. 486. [2] Il. xx. 307.
[3] Il. i. 260–272. [4] Il. iv. 51.

category, and take no notice of the distinction. From the manner in which the cities are mentioned, we may indeed rather say, that the passage affords an argument to show that the Poet lived before that epoch, and not after it. (4) It is urged also that Homer mentions riding on horseback, and the trumpet, as in use, but not as in use during the War. But in the Tenth Iliad, Odysseus and Diomed ride the horses of Rhesos; and the trumpet appears to be mentioned only as used to summon a beleaguered place on the arrival of the enemy.[1] On the other hand, Homer seems again to glance at his own case in the words addressed by Odysseus to Demodocos, respecting his Trojan lay: 'You have sung the Achaian woe right well, as if you had yourself been a witness, or else had heard it from one.'[2] The idea seems here to be conveyed with distinctness, that either actual experience or, at the least, the evidence of those who had possessed it, was a condition of true excellence in historic song. Again, the elaborate plan by which, in the Twelfth Iliad, Homer accounts for the disappearance of the defensive work of the Greeks, seems to show that the interval since the War must have been short, for if it had been long, natural causes would have done more to account for it.

A cardinal argument for placing the date of the Poet near that of his subject is, that he describes manners from first to last with the easy, natural, and intimate knowledge of a contemporary observer. He is in truth in visible identity with the age, the altering but not yet vanished age, of which he sings, while there is a very

[1] Il. xviii. 219, 220.   [2] Od. viii. 489–491.

broad interval of tone and feeling between him and the very nearest of all that follow him. And even the difference to be observed in the shade of style and of manner between the Iliad and the Odyssey, is just such as would be fairly due, in part to the difference of the subjects, and in part to the shock of those alterations, which were evidently caused in Greece by the absence of its kings and leaders, during a prolonged period, at the War. I conjecture, without pretending to do more, that Homer may well have been born before, or during, the War; and that he probably was familiar, during the years of his maturity, with those who had fought in it. For treating Homer as an Asiatic Greek, who lived after the migrations eastward, there is really neither reason, nor trustworthy authority.

As to the place of Homer's birth and residence, we are yet more in the dark than about his date. The testimony of the Poems is both slight and equivocal; and no other testimony is authentic. In one passage he says the Locrians dwell beyond, or it may mean over against, Euboea,[1] on the East of Greece; in another, the Echinades and Doulichion[2] are beyond, or over against, Elis, on the West of Greece. The second passage seems to destroy any such inference as Wood, in his ingenious Essay,[3] drew from the first. On the other hand, morning comes to Homer over the sea;[4] an expression which seems to contemplate a 'whereabout' on the West of the Ægean. The character given to Zephuros, the North-West wind, varies

[1] Il. ii. 535.
[2] Page 9. (First Ed. in 1775.)
[3] Il. ii. 625.
[4] Il. xxiii. 227.

according as it is a sea-wind, which it is in the description of the Elysian Fields; or a mountain-wind, when it is described as charged with snow:[1] and no inference can be drawn from it to show that Homer lived on any particular coast. Every line of the Poems bears testimony to the fact that Homer was not derivatively, but immediately and intensely, Greek. Contented with accumulated evidence of nationality in the highest sense, we must leave the question of the precise birthplace and dwelling of the Poet in the darkness in which we find it.

It cannot be too strongly affirmed, that the song of Homer is historic song. Indeed he has probably told us more about the world and its inhabitants at his own epoch, than any historian that ever lived.

But the primary and principal meaning of the assertion is, that he is historical as to manners, customs, ideas, and institutions: whereas events and names are the pegs on which they hang. It is with respect, not to the dry bones of fact, but to all that gives them life, beauty, and meaning, that he has supplied us with a more complete picture of the Greek, or, as he would probably say, Achaian, people of his time, than any other author, it might almost be said than any number of authors, have supplied with reference to any other age and people.

There are however very strong presumptions that Homer is also historical with respect to his chief events and persons. For, 1. It is the chief business of the Poet or Bard, as such, in early times to record facts, while he records them in the forms of beauty

---

[1] Od. iv. 566–568; xix. 206.

supplied by his art. 2. Especially of the Bard who lives near the events of which he professes to sing. 3. It is plain that Homer so viewed the Poet's office, from the nature of the lays which he introduces; from his representing to us Achilles engaged in singing the deeds of heroes;[1] and from his saying that the gods ordained the War of Troy that it might be sung to all posterity;[2] with other like sentiments. 4. The Poems were always viewed as historical by the Greeks. 5. If fictitious in their basis, they would have been far less likely to acquire and maintain such commanding interest. 6. The structure and tenor of the Poems throughout indicate the highest regard to national tastes and prepossessions: and these tastes were manifestly very strong as to all matters of tradition and hereditary fame. Of this we have an indication which may be taken by way of example, in the question usually put to a stranger, who are his parents? 7. The number and the remarkable self-consistency of the Genealogies given in the Poems, appear almost of themselves to prove an historic design. 8. The Catalogue in the Second Iliad implies a purpose with reference to the nation, much the same as that indicated by the Genealogies with respect to particular persons or families. 9. The Aristeia of the greater chieftains respectively, in the intermediate Books of the Iliad, are thought to load the movement of the Poem; but they receive a natural and simple explanation from the tendency of a Poet at once itinerant and historical to distribute carefully the honors of the War between the different States and heroes. 10. A con-

[1] Il. ix. 180-189.   [2] Od. viii. 579.

siderable number of the minute particulars given, especially in the Iliad, are of a nature to derive their interest wholly from recording matter of fact; such for instance as the small stature of Tudeus, the *mare* driven by Menelaos, and many more. 11. Homer often introduces curious legends of genealogy and race, in a manner which is palpably inopportune for the purposes of poetry, and which is, on the other hand, fully accounted for by the historic aim. These legends are not to be explained by the garrulity of Nestor; for, even if the character of Nestor admitted of a garrulity wholly apart from good sense, still these legends are not confined to him. Nor are they shared with him only by Phœnix, who is likewise in years; they are spoken by Æneas, Glaucos, and others, and this too even on the field of battle: and, by means of them, Homer has supplied us with a great mass of curious knowledge, highly interesting to his auditors, and eminently illustrative of the first beginnings of the Greek nation, as yet in embryo. His intermixture of supernatural agency with human events must be judged on its own grounds; but cannot by the laws of historical criticism be held of itself to overthrow his general credit.

We must not however attempt to define with rigor the limits, within which the Poems are to be considered historical. The free intermixture of the supernatural need not indeed constitute a serious difficulty. For the theurgy of the Poems is, so to speak, self-subsistent. It represents in the main a parallel and concurrent action, rather than a mere ornament, or a simple portion of one and the same narration with the War; and it lies upon the human and visible tissue like a continuous pattern of rich embroidery. But several points of the story are presented to us in a dress apparently mythical; for example, the distribution of the time into three periods, each of ten years: and many of the names of persons appear to have been invented, especially in cases where they carry an etymological meaning calculated directly to serve the purpose of the Poem. Again, if we suppose an historical existence for the persons indicated by the names, for example, of Achilles and Helen, it remains open to doubt how large a proportion of the remarkable and characteristic features, with which they are invested, may be due to the imagination of the Poet. In the case of Achilles, whose qualities everywhere border on the superhuman, this question is especially relevant. Nor is the circumstance to be overlooked, that a goddess is assigned to him as a mother, and is stated to have sat commonly, or oftentimes, as queen in his father's palace.[1]

It must also be fully admitted that, although the Trond may afford some physical indications favorable to the historic character of the Poems, yet the proof of that character chiefly, nay almost wholly, rests upon internal evidence.[2] But internal evidence, when carried to a certain point, is the very best we can desire in a case where we are obliged to travel back into the mist of ages, far beyond the limits of historical record.

Of all the features of the Homeric Poems, perhaps the most remarkable are the delineations of personal character which they contain. They are not only in a high degree varied and refined; but they are also marvellously comprehensive and profound. The proof

[1] Il. I. 396.   [2] Mure, Literature of Greece, vol. I.

of their extraordinary excellence as works of art is to be found in this, that from Homer's time to our own, with the single exception of the works of Shakespeare, they have never been equalled.

Homer is also admirable, when the specialties of his purpose are taken into view, in the arrangement of incidents: in keeping interest ever fresh: in his precise and copious observation of nature: in his power of illustration, his use of epithets; in the freedom, simplicity, and power of his language; and in a versification perfect in its application to all the diversified forms of human action, speech, and feeling.

It may probably have been the combined and intense effort of the Trojan War by which the Greeks first felt themselves, and first became, a nation. At any rate, from that epoch appears to date their community of interest and life. Homer, then, was hardly less wonderful in the fortune of his opportunity, than in the rarity of his gifts. In speaking of his theme, the two Poems may be taken as virtually one. He supplied to his country thenceforward, and for all periods, the bond of an intellectual communion, and a common treasure of ideas upon all the great subjects in which man is concerned. He was not only the glory and delight, but he was in a great degree the ποιητής, the maker, of his nation.

I have spoken of the darkness which, as far as direct testimony is concerned, envelops the person of the Poet. The same is the case with the Homeric Poems, distinguished from every other work of the first rank in these among other particulars: there is not one, of which so little has been told us by contemporary or early testimony; while there is not one which tells us so much. Of their origin, their date, and their first reception, we know nothing, except so far as we can gather it from themselves. The Cyclic Poems, 'which aimed at completing the circle of events with which they deal, never attained to an equal or competing fame, and have long ago perished. Periods of darkness, the length of which we cannot determine, both precede and follow the two great productions. At the dawn of trustworthy tradition, we find them holding a position of honor and authority among the Greeks, for which, with respect to works professedly secular, history affords no parallel.[1] The Greeks had no sacred books, properly so called: and it is probable that the Poems of Homer filled in some particular respects the place of Sacred Books[2] for that people.

By the Poems of Homer, I mean the Iliad and the Odyssey. I can find no adequate reason for assigning to him any other of the larger compositions of the early Greek Bards. Of the other works more or less reputed to be Homeric, not one can now be ascribed to him with confidence, or has been shown ever to have been so ascribed by the general and unhesitating opinion of the Greeks. The Hymns contain very few passages of such mark as even to allow the supposition that they could have proceeded from him. Nor do they carry, so to speak, his physiognomy. No writer of any period has borne stronger and more characteristic notes of style. We have seen that one beautiful passage is quoted from the Hymn to Apollo, by Thucydides. He describes that Hymn as a Hymn of Homer;

[1] The case which comes nearest to this is, perhaps, that of the Divina Commedia of Dante.
[2] Milman, Life of Horace, p. 1; Grote, Hist. of Greece, vol. 1.

and doubtless he represents a tradition of his day. There are also one or two fragmentary verses ascribed to Homer: one passage, in particular, is given by Aristotle,[1] and said to have been taken from a poem termed The Margites. It may be observed that besides their general inferiority, the Hymns in general embody mythological traditions, evidently of a later stamp than those of the two great Epics.

The Iliad and Odyssey give a picture of the age to which they refer, alike copious and animated, comprehensive and minute. The Iliad represents that age in its vigor; the Odyssey paints it in the beginning of its decline, when Greece had been unsettled and disorganized by the prolonged absence of its chiefs at Troy. The Iliad gives us what it had been; the Odyssey indicates what it was about to be. The delineations embrace jointly all the materials that human life and society could then in their simplicity supply: when writing was either unknown or unavailable, when civil rights had not begun to take the form of law, and when visible Art, in its higher sense, was an exotic not yet naturalized in Greece. In a manner chiefly incidental, there is supplied to us a mass of information on history and legend, religion, polity, justice, domestic life and habits, ethnical and social relations, the conditions of warfare, navigation, industry, and of the useful arts, exceeding in amount what has ever at any other period been brought for us into one focus by a single mind; except possibly by the philosophical works of Aristotle, if we possessed them entire.

[1] Eth. Nicom., vi. 7.

It has been doubted[1] at various times whether either Poem, and especially whether the Iliad, was the work of a single author; and also whether the two were due to the same hand. The Chorizontes, so called because they separate the authorship of the Iliad from that of the Odyssey, found themselves mainly,

(*a*) On supposed discrepancies in the mythology of the two Poems respectively:

(*b*) On differences of manners and institutions:

(*c*) On differences in the language.

Those who destroy the unity of the Poems, and especially of the Iliad, altogether, contend,

(*a*) That the art of writing did not exist at the time of their composition, and that poems of such length could not have been orally transmitted. This was the famous argument of Wolf.

(*b*) That there are such discrepancies, anomalies, and defects of plan, in the Iliad, as to preclude the belief that it could be the work of a single mind.

With respect to the argument of Wolf, it is now commonly admitted that no such art of writing existed, as could be available for the transmission of the Poems: but his second proposition, that they could not be transmitted orally, is also very commonly denied. Quintilian says, 'Invenio apud Platonem obstare memoriæ usum literarum.'[2] Even in the period when the exercise of the memory had become subject to this disadvantage, Niceratos, according to Xenophon,[3] stated that he knew the Iliad and Odyssey by

---

[1] See the account of the controversy from its earliest phase among the Alexandrian Critics, in Mure, Hist. of Greek Lit. vol. 1. ch. ii. iii. iv.

[2] xi. 2. [3] Sympos. iii. 5.

heart: and Athenæus[1] states, that Cassander, king of Macedon, could do nearly as much; he could repeat the chief part of the Poems. Even now, it would not be difficult to select youths, of strong memory, aided by poetic feeling, who, if they made it a profession, would be able to acquire by heart the whole of them: which however need not have been done by all those who recited them under a system apparently organized with a view to recitation in parts.

As respects the other heads of argument against the unity of the Poems generally, it may be sufficient for the present to reply as follows:—

(*a*) The plot of the Iliad (as will be shown) is admirably constructed for its purpose.

(*b*) Its internal discrepancies are both very few, and very insignificant.

(*c*) Some of the cases of alleged discrepancy are only such when the canons of modern prose are applied precipitately as the criteria of the oldest poetry.

As regards the arguments of the Chorizontes or separators of the authorship of the two Epics, let it be observed:—

(*a*) If the mythology of the Odyssey, in that region to which the voyage of Odysseus belongs, shall be shown to be Phœnician,[2] the whole argument from discrepancy in that mythology will thereupon disappear.

(*b*) The differences in manners or institutions are not greater than may be explained by the action of a revolutionary crisis, like the crisis caused by the pro-

---

[1] xiv. p. 620.
[2] See *infra*, Chap. V. on the Phœnicians; and Chap. VII. on Mythology, sect. Poseidon.

longed absence in Troas; and are really such as may
be taken rather for an evidence of unity in authorship
than the reverse.

(c) Some differences of language between the two
Poems is required by the different character of the
subjects: and the actual differences seem not to be
thought by scholars in general to betoken their belonging to different ages.

(d) A careful comparison of style between the Odyssey and the Iliad, and of a number of particulars of
turn and manner, will be found to supply a considerable amount of very specific evidence for the unity of
authorship. No such resemblances could be shown
to the works of any other author, or to the Pseudo-
Homeric compositions.

(e) Those characters of the Iliad, which are also
found in the Odyssey, reappear in the later Poem with
a perfect preservation of identity, confirmed, not impaired, by the altered shading which belongs to their
altered positions.

(f) The testimony of the Odyssey to facts, especially
those connected with the war, is in no case discordant
with that of the Iliad. For if the manhood of Neoptolemos[1] creates a certain amount of difficulty, we
should bear in mind that the adjustment of time with
reference to the Poem, appears to be one of the points
in which Homer has allowed himself a certain license,
with a view probably to poetical effect.

(g) But the overwhelming proof of the unity of authorship, both for each Poem, and as between the two,
is really supplied by the innumerable particulars of

[1] Od. xi. 506.

manners, institutions, and ideas, which pervade both the Iliad and the Odyssey with a marvellous consistency; and by the incommunicable stamp of an extraordinary genius which they carry throughout. If discrepancies exist, the difficulty they present is not only small, but infinitesimal, compared with the difficulty of that hypothesis which assumes that Greece produced in early times a multitude of Homers, and all of them with the very same stamp of mind. Whether in short we consider these works as poetry or as record, the marks of their unity are innumerable and ineffaceable. A part of their force is sensible to the ordinary reader; but it will be felt constantly and immensely to increase in proportion as the reader becomes the student, by virtue of a patient, constant, and thorough examination of the text.

Of the two Poems, it seems to me that, while both are wonderful, the Iliad is without doubt the greater. The plot of the Iliad, we shall find, is a marvellous combination of poetical skill with national spirit and practical prudence. The plot of the Odyssey, at first sight more organized and symmetrical, is in the first place of far easier construction, and in the second, is wound up in a manner which is feeble if not slovenly. The suspicions of the genuineness of the Twenty-fourth Book appear to me on the whole to be tolerably met by a general conformity of turn and handling, though with diminished force; and by many minute particulars of correspondence which, here as elsewhere, the text supplies. But they have perhaps been reasonably suggested by a perceptible inferiority of workmanship in this and, with some exceptions, in several Books preceding it. The vigor of the Iliad, on the other hand, continues quite unabated to the end. Again, in the Odyssey there is not a mere decline of vigor: the plan of the ending may be called degenerate and incomplete. The ends of some of the threads are dropped. If ever a peace was patched it is that which is announced in the closing passage. The intervention of Mentor, even though his exterior conceals a deity, is not what the dignity of the Sovereign or the grandeur of Odysseus would require. And the unexplained as well as unfulfilled prophecy[1] of the war, suggests that Homer had poetical intentions to which it was not permitted him to give effect.

Generally speaking, the Odyssey displays the same powers as the Iliad, but in less energetic manifestation. A faculty of debate, never surpassed if ever equalled in human history, is found in both; but though the flight of Odysseus in the Seventh Odyssey is, like that of the contention in the First Iliad, a lofty one, it cannot be compared with the wonderful speech of Achilles in the tent-scene of the Ninth. Again; no man but Homer could have reproduced in the Odyssey to the life the characters of the Iliad, or could have added the specific shading of their altered circumstances. But though Homer in each is stronger than any other of the Ancients, yet Homer of the Iliad is Homer at the height and maximum of his power in this transcendent quality; while in the Odyssey the great luminary seems to have just begun his descending course.

Next comes the question how far we may reckon on having substantially the same text as that of our

[1] Od. xi. 127; xxiii. 275.

author; not as to any minor detail, nor even so as
to exclude occasional interpolations, but as to the style,
diction, and language generally.

Mr. Paley[1] says (not that the Greek of the Iliad
is greatly different from that of the Odyssey, but)
that we find in the Poems two distinct and separate
phases of the Greek tongue: first, the language of
the earliest Trojan Epics, and secondly, the ordinary
Ionic of the time of Herodotus, with a mixture of
Attic idioms. The question is one evidently requiring minute examination; but it is beyond my compe-
tency to decide. I would observe, however,

(*a*) That in an author who composed at a period of
crisis, when all the elements of the Hellenic nation,
that was to be, were settling down, we should look for,
or at least should not be startled by, some mixture of
older and younger forms.

(*b*) That considerable changes of the minor order
might be made in the text of the Poems without
seriously affecting the substance, if there was a great
and constant anxiety to abide by the true sense of
Homer.

(*c*) That if we find the internal evidence as to manners, institutions, and facts, singularly self-consistent,
this goes far to show that alterations of the text have
been generally confined within merely verbal and narrow limits.

(*d*) The antiquity of the present text is not overthrown by the fact that the later poets in many instances have followed other forms of legend in regard
to the **Troica**: for they would necessarily consult the

---

[1] Athenæum, Aug. 10, 1867.

state of popular feeling from time to time; and tradition, which, as to religion, altered so greatly after the time of Homer, would, as to facts and persons, it is evident, vary materially according to the sympathies of blood and otherwise at different periods of Greek history. The displacement of the Achaians, and the rise of the Dorians and Ionians, must have occasioned great changes in this respect. It is also surprising, if such difference in the language really exists as is alleged by Mr. Paley, that it was not perceived by the Greeks of the classic period, who must surely be allowed to have known their own tongue.

There are passages of ancient writers, which tend to the disintegration of Homer. But they are late, and of small authority. Josephus[1] says it was reported, or thought, that from want of the aid afforded by the art of writing there were many discrepancies in the Poems. This was merely a current opinion, not of himself but of others, on the state of the text; an opinion which we can for ourselves see to have been erroneous. The Scholiast on Pindar[2] reports, and only reports, that Kunaithos and his school had made large interpolations. The Latin authors, such as Cicero or Paterculus, must be considered as giving their opinions, which cannot from the circumstances be of great critical weight, rather than as witnesses in the case.

The external evidence to a contrary effect, though fragmentary, is more considerable, and for the most part of much earlier date. Heraclides Ponticus[3] a

---

[1] Contr. Ap. i. 2.   [2] Nem. II. 1.
[3] Fragm. περὶ πολιτειῶν.

pupil of Plato, declares that Lycurgus obtained the Homeric Poems from the descendants of Kreophulos, and was the first to bring them into Peloponnesos. Ælian[1] makes the slight but material addition, that he brought this poetry in a mass (ἀθρόαν). Plato states in the Republic[2] that Kreophulos was a companion of Homer; Strabo,[3] that he was a Samian; Diogenes Laertius,[4] that Hermodamas, the master of Pythagoras, was his descendant. Plutarch[5] states that some portions of Homer were known in Greece before Lycurgus brought the whole from Crete.

Herodotus[6] states that Cleisthenes, the tyrant of Sicyon, when he had been at war with Argos, put a stop to the competitions of the rhapsodists in Sicyon, because the Homeric songs turned chiefly upon the Argeians and Argos (ὅτι Ἀργεῖοί τε καὶ Ἄργος τὰ πολλὰ πάντα ὑμνέαται). Also, that he sought to banish from Sicyon the memory of Adrestos, as being an Argive hero. Now the Iliad describes Greece not seldom under the title of Argos, and the Greeks frequently as Argeians; and it represents Adrestos as the first king of Sicyon, while at the same time it represents him as the father-in-law or grandfather-in-law, of Diomed the Argive chieftain.

From this passage it appears, —

(*a*) That there were at Sicyon, six centuries before Christ, State-recitations of the Homeric Poems, attended with prizes.

(*b*) That they are not named as peculiar to Sicyon,

[1] Var. Hist. xiii. 14.   [2] Rep. x. p. 600 B.
[3] xiv. p. 946.   [4] viii. 2.
[5] Lyc. p. 41.   [6] v. 67.

but rather as a customary institution, set aside in that place at a certain epoch on special grounds.

(c) That the recitations depended chiefly on the Homeric Poems; for they ceased when these were prohibited.

Dieuchidas of Megara, an author placed by Heyne after the time of Alexander the Great, is quoted by Diogenes[1] as stating that Solon provided by law for the recitation of the Homeric poems ἐξ ὑποβολῆς, one reciter taking up another; and therefore that Solon did more than Peisistratos to throw light upon the Poet. And Lycurgus the orator, who was contemporary with Demosthenes,[2] tells the Athenian people that their forefathers thought of him so highly as to provide by law for the recitation of his songs, and his alone, quinquennially at the Panathenaica; and such, he adds, was then the valor of their ancestors, that the Spartans took Tyrtæus[3] from among them to be their general.

Hence it appears that —

(a) According to Lycurgus, Homer was recited at Athens in the time of Tyrtæus, nearly seven centuries before Christ.

(b) Just when Athens begins to rise, Solon appoints by public law competitive recitations of Homer, to be taken in turn by the reciters.

(c) And of Homer alone.

(d) It appears negatively that probably there were recitations at Athens before Solon, but without regular turns.

[1] Diog. Laert. i. 57.   [2] In Leocritum, 104-8.
[3] Smith's Dict., art. Tyrtæus.

(e) If public authority thus established the recitation of the Poems, we may rest assured that care was taken, as far as possible, to preserve their text from corruption.

(f) The vanity or carelessness of a particular rhapsodist would tend to corrupt them; but the matches were free and competitive, and each reciter would be watched and checked by the vigilant jealousy of his rivals. This element of competition would in all likelihood have a highly conservative effect, before the art of writing had come into use. And it is plain, from Il. ii. 594-600, that the practice prevailed from before the time of Homer himself; as he tells us that Thamuris had challenged the Muses to compete with him, and was punished accordingly for his audacity. Hesiod witnesses to the matches, and says that in Aulis he himself won a tripod.[1] Thucydides also finds proof of them in the Hymn to Apollo.[2]

(g) In a word, while there were at work what may be called centrifugal forces, tending to impair and vitiate the text of the Poems, there were also centripetal forces tending to restore it; in the rivalry of States as well as of Bards, in the intense love of the song of Homer felt by every Greek, and in the great value set by the whole people upon it as a record.

When we come down to the historic period, we find in it full evidence of the standing anxiety both of States and persons to preserve the text of Homer. It appears probable that a common text was more or less recognized, while many even of the Greek Colonies had their public or State Recensions. Individuals of

---

[1] Opp. 651-657.   [2] Hymn Apoll. 140-150, 166-173.

eminence, or of literary taste, had their editions also. The Venetian Scholiast constantly refers to these two descriptions of copies, and while the references prove that there were in this, as in every ancient document, many variations of text, they also show that such variations were confined within narrow limits, and did not affect the body of the work. The State editions were called αἱ πολιτικαί, αἱ ἐκ τῶν πόλεων, αἱ ἀπὸ πόλεων: those prepared for individuals αἱ κατ' ἄνδρα: and a third class, got up apparently for public sale, and of very variable quality, were αἱ κοιναί, αἱ δημοτικαί, αἱ δημώδεις.

Among the public or State Recensions, we hear of those of Crete, Argos, Sinopè, Marseilles, Chios, Cyprus; the Aiolis or Aiolikè, a name which may perhaps indicate the recognized text of what is called Homer's Æolian Greek; the Recension of the Mouseion, or depository near the School at Alexandria; and the Kuklikè, which is supposed to mean an edition wherein Homer appeared with other poems of the Cycle.

It seems very probable, that the work of Peisistratos was in substance a critical recension of the text effected by a comparison of different versions, and a complete publication by authority of the several portions of the Poems in the order in which we now have them; in fact that it was an early and notable example of the reactive tendency to preserve the text by recurrence to a standard, and to check its variations, which I have mentioned as the natural counterpoise to disintegrating agencies.

We have no clear account of the proceedings of Peisistratos; but we know that when, at a later period, the Alexandrian School of Zenodotos, Aristophanes, and Aristarchos brought the best critical power of the time to bear upon the Poems, they found comparatively little to question. Nor have the suspicions they entertained of particular passages since received any thing approaching to an unanimous approval.

As to more general reconstructions, it is allowed that the Odyssey does not admit of them; and such as have been proposed with regard to the Iliad have manifestly failed to obtain any sensible, much more any permanent, amount of assent.

But the strongest argument for the soundness of the text, as well as that for the unity of the Poems, hangs upon internal evidence. I do not hesitate to say that no work known to me presents, in any degree equal or approaching to these Poems, the proof, in kind among the strongest of all, which arises out of natural unstudied self-consistency in detail. The particulars in which the text confirms at one point what it conveys at another may be counted by many thousands: those where it appears to be inconsistent are but a few units to be reckoned by the primitive process of Proteus upon the fingers. Errors undoubtedly there must be. Still, if they were very serious, it is impossible but that a far greater number of them must have been tracked out, and their detection established to the general satisfaction of cultivated men. On one portion only of the Forty-eight Books, namely the close of the Odyssey, has there been thrown what may be termed grave or recognized doubt; and even here doubt is all that can be reasonably sustained. Indeed, over and above correspondence of tangible particulars, there is what I must call an unity of atmosphere in the Poems, such as I believe has never been achieved by forgery or imitation.

In this chapter I have not relied upon the tradition according to which Lycurgus, the great Spartan lawgiver, brought the Poems into use in Lacedæmon, because it is one belonging to the Roman rather than the Greek period. On the other hand I cannot attach great weight to the statement in the Hipparchos,[1] which assigns to that Sovereign the original introduction of the Poems into Attica. It appears simply incredible that the Poems should have been unknown in Attica, when we learn from Herodotus that they had long before been recited in Sicyon.

On the whole, then, we are not in every case dogmatically to assert that each line of the Poems as they stand is the work of Homer; but while fairly weighing the evidence in the comparatively few cases where doubt sustained by argument has been raised, we may, as a general rule, proceed to handle the text with a reasonable confidence, that the ground is firm under our feet; a confidence, which experience in the work will, I think, be found progressively to confirm.

Thus far we have seen reason to suppose that the Iliad and the Odyssey are the work of a Poet who lived at a date that we are unable to define otherwise than by its nearness to the Trojan War; an event which, if we attempt to measure its distance from the historic era by manners and institutions, we must hold to be of a high antiquity.

At times it has been questioned, whether Homer or Hesiod was the older poet. We know of Hesiod that while the reputed authors of the Cyclic Poems belong to the historic era,[2] he is pre-historic; and we must

[1] Sect. iv.   [2] Mure, Lit. of Greece, ii. 282.

seek, therefore, in his works, as in those of Homer, for the means of estimating his probable 'whereabout' in the deep mist of ages. He gives us no sign that the instrument of writing had become available at his epoch for the preservation of poetry; and if his compositions, as being much shorter, taxed the memory more lightly, on the other hand we have no reason to believe that they were watched with the same jealous care to preserve, or to recover, the genuine text. But if the episode of the Five Ages be genuine, they are decisive of the question. For the composer of it had been witness to an iron age; and iron, as compared with copper, had in his time come to be the inferior, that is to say the cheaper, metal. The use of it therefore must have grown common, as from remains still extant, it had evidently come to be common in Assyria at a period supposed to be about the eighth century before Christ. Homer lived at a period, as defined by œconomic laws, much earlier; at a time when the use of iron was but just commencing, when the commodity was rare, and when its value was very great. This argument appears to me so conclusive as to the comparative dates, that I forbear to dwell on other particulars, or upon the considerable difference in the manners of the Hesiodic, as compared with the Homeric, Poems.

We have also seen that in the state of primitive society it was essential to the business of the Epic Bard to commemorate, in poetic forms, actual events; and that the works of Homer prove how he kept this property of his art constantly in mind.

Viewing then his position in human history and his profession, we find that he is an original and a solitary, as he is also a most copious, witness to the condition of mankind, and especially of the Greeks, at a period to which we have no other direct literary access. Traditions there are in abundance, reported by Apollodorus in mass, or scattered here or there through the works of earlier writers; and these traditions may, in any given case, contain matter relating to the age of Homer, or to what preceded him, and may even in some cases be true, or nearer the truth than his. But they carry as a general rule no attestation; and their confused and promiscuous nature marks them as a miscellany gradually accumulated in many ages and from many lands. I submit then that we ought to make the evidence of Homer, in relation to his age and to what had gone before, a separate study, and to assign to it a primary authority. The testimony of later writers should be handled in subordination to it, and in general even tried by it as by a touchstone, on all the subjects which it embraces. It will be seen, as we proceed to deal with the contents of the Poems, that this is a proposition fruitful of important results as regards the religion, the polity, and the manners of early Greece.

In asking for the testimony of Homer a primary authority, I refer only to those cases where it stands in competition with other, and in truth inferior, literary evidence. The evidence of fact, whether in geography and topography, in language or in archæology, stands upon its own ground, and Homer, like every other author, must yield, if a conflict arise, to its more cogent authority.

I will give a single example of the discrepancy between the Homeric, and the later, representations of the early Greek ethnology. According to a tradition founded in part upon Apollodoros,[1] in part upon a fragment ascribed by Tzetzes to Hesiod,[2] Deucalion was the son of Prometheus, and a certain Hellen was the son of Deucalion. Hellen had three sons, Aiolos, Doros, and Xouthos; and Xouthos again had two sons, Ion and Achaios.

It is impossible not to be struck with the convenient adaptation, speaking generally, of this tradition to the reputed descent and succession of the various Greek races, so as to give to each its share of fame and its order of seniority. All Greeks were Hellenes, so Hellen is made the father of them all. The oldest among these names in the Greek tradition is Aiolos; so an Aiolos is made the eldest son of Hellen. The great dominant race of the first historic ages of Greece was the Dorian; accordingly, Doros is the second son of Hellen. The Ionians, represented by Attica, came later to their repute and power; so they, and the Achaians to whom they gave a refuge after the Dorian conquest, appear as the children of the third and youngest son. This tradition may be properly viewed as a pretty piece of joinery. But Mure[3] has with justice observed that the name Hellen bears witness against itself, being apparently derived from the territorial name Hellas, and that in its turn from the Helloi. When we bring this tradition, thus discredited by internal evidence, to the bar of Homer, we find him in discord with it on every point. Of Hellen as a person he knows nothing: the name would to all appear-

---

[1] Lib. vii. 2, 3.   [2] Fragm. xxviii. ap. Tzetz. ad Lyc. 284.
[3] Lit. of Greece, vol. i. p. 39 n.

ance have meant in his car most properly an inhabitant of Southern Thessaly. Aiolos, if named by him at all, is named as a foreigner; while only particular families, not a tribe descended from him, are indicated as having borne or bearing rule in parts of Greece. Doros is wholly unknown to him; and the Dorians are a portion, apparently an obscure portion at the time, of the inhabitants of Crete. Of Xouthos we have no trace whatever; in fact this whole family is, as such, utterly non-existent. There is no Ion; and the Iaones who appear as settled in the Attica of Homer, are without any tribal eponymist. Again, there is no trace of an Achaios; but the name Achaioi is the dominant name of the period, and the crown of its celebrity.

Such, exhibited by an example, is the contrariety between Homeric and post-Homeric tradition. We shall see in due time what materials the text of Homer can contribute towards the construction of the ethnology of Greece in the heroic age.

In the following pages I endeavor to give to the testimony of Homer what I have described as its due place. They are based upon a wide collection of particulars from the text. And, as far as possible, I have supplied the reader with means of judging where it is Homer that speaks, and where it is an illustrative tradition, or an indication drawn from some other than a literary source; as also of distinguishing in all cases between evidence, and the inference or conjecture which I may have presumed to found upon it.

Upon the whole, I trust enough has been said to show that in the text of the Poet we may find solid materials to work upon for the handling of the Homeric question. With this encouragement, let us commence our inquiries.

CHAPTER II.

THE THREE GREAT APPELLATIVES.

THE name of Greeks, as the modern equivalent of the several appellatives by which Homer describes the army engaged in the siege of Troy, is too firmly established to be changed. But it is not a correct name. The Greek equivalent of the word is Γραικοί. The name Γραῖα[1] is found in the Iliad, but it is only a local name of a settlement of Boiotoi or Bœotians. The name applied to themselves by the Greek people throughout the historic times, as at the present day, was not Graikoi, but Hellenes. And even this name, as Thucydides[2] observes, had not come into vogue in the time of Homer. It was indeed, as we shall find, creeping, so to speak, into use: but the standing appellations of the army in the Iliad are those three, Danaoi, Argeioi, and Achaioi; and it is sufficiently plain that the most proper national name for the Greeks of the period was that of 'Αχαιοί, Achaians. We call them Greeks conventionally: but with no more accuracy than we should render the Galli of Cæsar by the word 'French.' We should bear in

[1] Il. ii. 498.   [2] i. 3.

mind, then, that in strictness the Greeks of the Troica were Achaians.

We find in Homer traces, as of a religion, so of a race, or group of races, who inhabited the Greek peninsula before the Achaians, or any other tribe of the blood afterwards classed as Hellenic. These inhabitants passed in different places under a variety of designations; of which the most comprehensive and wide-spread[1] appears to have been Pelasgoi. They seem to have formed the base of the Greek army, and of the people subject to the sway of Achaian and other great families.

There is no trace in the poems of their having used a language different from that of their superiors in station, although the tradition of a difference in blood subsisted down to the historic time, and although the Pelasgian language, where the people using it had not been blended with the Hellenes, had then come to be accounted as a distinct, if not a foreign, tongue.

The relation between this older race and the Hellenic tribes leads to the conclusion that both were alike derived from the Aryan stem. And there is no reason to believe that there were any earlier occupants of the Greek, or of the Italian Peninsula,[2] than the group of tribes that was called Pelasgian. Neither of these countries presents us with remains belonging to what is called the stone period of the human race, when implements and utensils were made of that material, and the use of metals was unknown. The first emigrants from the East may probably have worked their way by

---

[1] Thirlwall, Hist. of Greece, vol. i. chap. ii.
[2] Mommsen, Hist. of Rome, chap. i.

land to and along the comparatively level and easy countries of Central Europe, and seem not to have penetrated through the masses of mountain, which inclose on their northern sides both Greece and Italy. The boast of autochthonism, or birth from the soil, so rife in the historic ages of Greece, was therefore not irrational, if we consider it to betoken only the claim to first occupancy. And it seems to have been principally in vogue among the people of Attica and Arcadia, the former of which had long been impressed with a markedly Pelasgian character, while the latter retained that character even through the historic period. The particulars which have been embraced in this slight survey are partly suggested by, and are in all cases accordant with, the Homeric testimony.

The Greeks of the Iliad are ordinarily called by Homer

1. Danaoi.
2. Argeioi.
3. Achaioi.

They are also called

1. Panhellenes, Il. ii. 530.
2. Panachaioi, Il. ii. 404; vii. 73, 159, 327; ix. 301; x. 1; xix. 193; xxiii. 236. Od. i. 239; xiv. 369; xxiv. 32.

With respect to the three first, which may be called the Great Appellatives of Homer, it is manifest that the Poet frequently uses them as interchangeable and synonymous. Yet, upon examination, important distinctions will be found to exist between them.

The various legends interspersed through the Poems carry back the Homeric tradition to a period several generations earlier than the War of Troy: which War, together with the attendant group of circumstances, I shall commonly call the Troica. But we shall find that Homer does not also carry backwards the use of these appellatives indifferently through the pre-Troic period: and thus we shall obtain pretty clear evidence of a chronological succession among them.

This rule applies likewise to other Homeric names. For example; when reference is made, in the narrative of the Iliad, to the soldiers belonging to the country afterwards called Bœotia, he describes them as Boiotoi. But where Agamemnon and Athené introduce the legend[1] of Tudeus, which touches the people of the same district at a prior epoch, they are called not Boiotoi but Kadmeioi and Kadmeiones. Moreover, in this same legend appear the people of Argos and the people of Mycenæ. They are both called Achaioi, a name never given to the Kadmeioi.

In the legend of the birth of Eurustheus,[2] the scene is laid in Ἄργος Ἀχαιϊκόν. This name we shall find still attached perhaps to the Peloponnesos, and certainly to the Eastern Peloponnesos, in the time of Homer. Its inhabitants, who are described, as we have seen, in the time of Tudeus, that is to say one generation before the War, as Achaioi, are called, in the time of Eurustheus, and therefore before the period of the Pelopids, not Achaioi but Argeioi.[3] It seems impossible to treat these very marked usages as accidental.

About the same period Proitos, whom the post-Homeric tradition represents as a brother of Eurustheus, expelled Bellerophon from Ephuré.[4] The text,

[1] Il. iv. 385-398; v. 800-807. [2] Il. xix. 95 seqq.
[3] Il. xix. 122, 124. [4] Il. vi. 158.

true to itself, describes the people over whom Proitos ruled, not as Danaoi or Achaioi, but as Argeioi. In the same manner the Poet here describes as Ephurè what in the Catalogue he calls Corinth.[1]

Homer then appears to point to Argeioi as the more ancient, and Achaioi as the more recent, name. But, moreover, he uses the two designations with marked respect to place as well as time.

In the Eleventh Iliad,[2] Nestor details to Patroclos the legend of the war between the Pulians, and the Epeians who inhabited Elis. He calls the Pulians distinctively Achaians, where he is speaking of them as the conquering party. He seems to withhold that name from the conquered: and he gives it to the Pulians at a period which must have been within the life and reign of Eurustheus, that is to say, the period when the name of Argeians was attached to those who inhabited the ruling quarter of Greece, or the Eastern Peloponnesos.

But the word Argeioi, used freely by Homer as a national designation, has also a marked local sense in the poems. It is a standing epithet, in the singular, of Helen, and this too in the mouth of Greeks, and of deities, whose use of it gives it a force quite different from that which it might have had among the Trojans. The purely national name would in such a case have been void of distinctive meaning; but now we naturally interpret the epithet as referring to the part of Greece with which Helen was especially connected. According to the post-Homeric tradition, confirmed by the Iliad, which makes Lacedæmon the country of

---

[1] Il. ii. 570.   [2] Il. xi. 670-701.

Castor and Poludeukes,[1] Tundareos, her father, was king of Sparta. Till the Pelopid House acquired it, and thus the Achaian sway began, this would be an Argeian kingdom; and thus Helen, though the wife of Menelaos, represents by her descent an Argeian title to it, so that the epithet thus acquires a full significance.

Thus far I have cited some examples to illustrate the practice of Homer. Let us now consider the leading particulars connected with the use of the three Great Appellatives.

The name Danaoi is used in the Iliad 147 times: in the Odyssey thirteen. Once it is combined with Argeioi, in Od. viii. 578, and appears to serve as an epithet. It is never used in the feminine. It is never used in the singular; and never locally. It seems never to signify the people inhabiting the Greek peninsula and islands, nor their ancestors in prior history: but invariably and only the Greeks of the army. It has therefore all the appearance of being an heroic and poetical rather than an historical appellation, and thus it is well adapted to describe men engaged in a military expedition surrounded with the most romantic associations.

Accordingly, the epithets applied to Δαναοί are exclusively of a military character. They are

1. ἥρωες, Il. ii. 110, 256; xv. 733 (heroes).
2. θεράποντες Ἄρηος, Il. vii. 382; xix. 78 (comrades of Ares).
3. φιλοπτόλεμοι, Il. xx. 351 (war-loving).
4. αἰχμηταί, Il. xii. 419 (spearmen).
5. ἀσπισταί, Il. xiii. 680 (shielded, heavy-armed).

[1] Il. iii. 244.

6. ἰφθιμοι, Il. xi. 290 (stalwart).
7. ταχύπωλοι, Il. viii. 161 (of swift steeds).

It being then plain that Danaoi was not the proper contemporary name of the Greeks, it is also plain that it could not have been applied to the Greeks as an army before Troy, unless it had had some root lying deep in the history or legends of Greece.

National or tribal names in Homer usually come

1. From an eponymist or founder of a state, directly as Dardanoi or Troes, or Kadmeioi; or indirectly, when they proceed from the name of a country, which name has been acquired from an eponymist. Such is Ithakesioi from Ithakē, Ithakē itself being derived from Ithakos, who is mentioned in Od. xvii. 207.

2. In like manner a name may come mediately from a race instead of an individual. Thus it seems that Hellas is derived from Helloi, and is in its turn the source of the great national name Hellen.

3. From the physical character of the country inhabited, as Threkes (Thracians), from θρῂξ, describing a rough highland country:[1] or Aigialeis, from Αἰγιαλός, the district of coast to the south of the Gulf of Corinth.

4. In the single case of the Athenians, we find the name of a population derived from that of a deity.

Besides the Homeric names which can be traced to one or other of these sources, there are names of which the connection with any of them is not established, or even where it is improbable.

The text of Homer affords very slender aid for

---

[1] Cf. Od. ix. 27.

tracing the name Danaoi up to its source. But we
must combine the fact of its application, limited as it
is, to the nation, with the negative evidence afforded
by this fact, that Homer nowhere uses the name as a
domestic name, either for his own or for the immediately preceding generations. This seems to throw
back the origin of the name to a period comparatively
remote.

And when we reach such a period, we find at least
a clue. In Il. xiv. 319 we hear of the amour of Zeus
with a beautiful Danaë, of the royal house of Acrisios,
from which union sprang Perseus and his line. The
presumption then arises, that this Danaë, being the
daughter and mother of princes, was of the lineage of
a Danaos, that this Danaos was himself a real or reputed prince of celebrity, and that he gave his name
to the people with whom, and among whom, he effected
a settlement in Greece.

This may be the proper place to observe that, on the
subject of the foreign origin of Greek races or houses,
Homer is what is termed an unwilling witness. Intensely national in feeling, he represents the first form
of that peculiar sentiment which, in the historic period,
divided mankind into Greeks and Barbarians; much
as the Hebrew race, upon grounds of a more definite
character, made their division of the world into Jew
and Gentile. There can be little doubt that Homer
could, if he would, have told us much respecting im-
migrations and settlements in Greece, which now remains the subject of comparatively dark conjecture.
But it may be broadly laid down that he systematically
eschews tracing either a family or a tribe to an origin
abroad. It seems to be his intention that we should

assume all Greek families and races, and further all Greek manners and institutions, to have sprung out of the soil. The sources of silver and copper and some other commodities, and moreover of works of art, he is willing, or even careful, to point out. But not so as to man and his highest operations. Though he tells us sometimes of foreign persons and events, he never, I think, consciously supplies, but seems habitually to keep back, the link between them and his own beloved Greek nation.

All this seems to be comformable to the course of natural feeling. Arrivals from abroad, in the earliest periods of the life of a nation, usually indicate either the conquest, or at least the superiority, in one form or another, of foreigners over natives, of what is strange to the soil over what is associated with it. In this there is some violation of that feeling of simple reverence for the past, which is so conspicuous among the Greeks of Homer, and which is jarred by the memory of all disturbances of its even tenor. It can hardly be that, in any country, such narratives should be popular at or near the time of the events. Even the process by which Hellenes mastered Pelasgians, or by which Pelopids put themselves in the place of Perseids, is nowhere disclosed to us by Homer: whose purpose it was to unite more closely the elements of the nation, and not to record that they had once been separate.

When Homer tells us of descendants of a Tantalos, or an Aiolos, and of a people called Kadmeiones, but gives us no clue to the extraction, or to the habitation, of any of these personages themselves, we may conclude, without much risk of error, that none of them were native Greeks, and that their names mark the point of transition from a foreign to a Greek domicile for their respective families. He never even names the connection of Kadmeiones with Kadmos, or of Pelopidai with Pelops; both these great personages are only named by him incidentally, in remote portions of the Poems; and as to Aiolos, the ancestor of the Aiolids, it has not yet been generally recognized that the Poet names him at all.

Without, then, calling in the aid of extraneous traditions, it appears highly probable that the Danaoi bore the same relation to a Danaos, as the Kadmeioi obviously bear to a real or imaginary Kadmos.

It is also probable, that Danaë stands in the generation next to Danaos. For Danaë herself stands, as we shall see, in the sixth generation before the Troica; and the knowledge and traditions of Homer nowhere go back beyond the seventh generation. But as Danaë is the daughter of Acrisios, not of Danaos, it is probable that Acrisios was a younger brother of Danaos; and that the genealogy stands as follows:

1. Danaos = Acrisios.
   2. Danae.
     3. Perseus.
       4. Sthenelos.
         5. Eurustheus.   Contemporary with Herakles and Pelops.
                           6. Atreus = Thuestes.
                                  7. Agamemnon = Aigisthos.

It will here be perceived that the text of Homer is altogether at variance with those later legends, which throw back the first Greek dynasties into a very remote comparative antiquity. There is, I apprehend, an intrinsic improbability in such legends as affect to trace prolonged lines of sovereigns through ages of darkness and barbarism, not possessed of the ordinary means of record; but there is also this strong presumption in favor of the Homeric text, that his genealogies, gathered indiscriminately as they are from different parts of the Poems, are in singular, if not absolutely unvarying, accordance with each other.

According to the post-Homeric tradition, Danaos was an Egyptian, and was brother of Aiguptos. He migrated into Greece, and became king of Argos. Proitos was his great-grandson; and as, according to the legend of the Sixth Iliad,[1] Proitos stands at two or two and a-half generations before the war, there is here an apparent agreement with Homer; but as Acrisios also is made the brother of Proitos, a much greater antiquity is in effect claimed for the immigration of Danaos. So far, however, as respects his personality, the seat of his kingdom, and his being of foreign origin, the later tradition sustains the presumptions arising from the text of Homer.

The early disappearance of the name from the roll of tradition would be easily accounted for by that change of the dynasty in the male line which takes place at the time of Danaë.

From what country Danaos came, we shall hereafter have occasion to consider. For the present we may take him to have been one of the personages who arrived in Greece as a stranger, and who there founded such a dynasty, among the primitive or Pelasgian population, as became naturalized. This foundation seems to have taken place at the very commencement of what we may call the traditionary, as opposed to the

[1] Il. vi. 158.

merely mythical, period, about two hundred years before the Trojan War.

Even this is considerably older than the date of any family which we can connect with the Achaian name, or with the Hellenic stock. It seems, however, quite possible that Perseus and his race may on the father's side have descended from an Hellenic ancestry, and that the fable of Zeus and Danaë may be no more than a veil employed to cover the transition, and to dignify the origin of the incoming family.

Hesiod[1] terms Perseus both Danaïdes, and son of Danaë and states that Danaos relieved Argos from drought. Æschylus in the Supplices[2] represents the whole Greek Peninsula as having been originally subject to one and the same sway under Pelasgos. Euripides[3] says that Danaos changed the name of the Peloponnesians from Pelasgiotai to Danaoi. These reports are in no way at variance with the Homeric text.

Upon the whole, then, the probable conclusions are:

1. That the Danaan name was dynastic.
2. That the dynasty was pre-Hellenic.
3. That it stands next in chronological succession to the Pelasgic time; and
4. That it makes its appearance at about two centuries, more or less, before the War of Troy.

We have next to deal with the name Argeioi. And first as to the facts connected with its use in the Poems.

It is found 177 times in the Iliad, and seventeen

---

[1] Fragm. 58, and Scut. Herc. 216, 229. [2] v. 262.
[3] Ar. Fr. ii. 7.

times in the Odyssey. I speak of the plural form. The singular is also used eleven times in the Iliad, and seventeen times in the Odyssey.

Of the seventeen passages in the Odyssey, not one refers to the Greeks as a nation, or as contemporary with the action of the Poem. In two of them, Od. iii. 309 and xv. 240, the word signifies the inhabitants of Argolis or the North-Eastern Peloponnesos. In the other fifteen, it is always applied to the Greek army before Troy.

In the Iliad, we have certain cases of the local use. Proitos,[1] who was nearly contemporary with Eurustheus, ruled over Argeians. From the text it would seem as if he were a neighbor to Sisuphos, of Ephurè or Corinth: and if so, his subjects may have been Argives of Argolis, taken largely; of the Eastern, or Eastern and Northern, Peloponnesos. Such is evidently the meaning of Argeioi in the legend of the birth of Eurustheus.[2] On the other hand, the name of Proitos was attached to one of the Gates of Thebes. It was plainly therefore a Phœnician name. It is far from clear that he reigned in Thebes; but, if he did so, then the name Argeioi is applicable to the inhabitants of Bœotia. This slender probability is the only presumption afforded us of the use of the name Argeioi beyond the limits of the Perseid or Pelopid dominions in Peloponnesos, except as a designation for the army before Troy. Again, in the chariot race of the Twenty-third Iliad, Diomed is described as Ætolian by birth, but as ruling among Argeioi.[3] These, it seems plain, must be the Argives of Argos,

[1] Il. vi. 159.   [2] Il. xix. 122.
[3] Il. xxiii. 471.

who formed his contingent. Still, upon this local
name there had supervened, since the accession of the
Pelopid dynasty, as we shall find from the legend of
Tudeus, the paramount and wider name of Achaioi.[1]

The name of Argeioi, then, appears to stand partially in the same category with Danaoi, as a name
rather poetic and archaic, than actually current; and
as one of which the common application to the Greeks
in general, at any period, is uncertain; but which had,
several generations before, been the proper designation
at least of the inhabitants of the ruling portion of the
peninsula.

This name is, on the other hand, so far unlike the
Danaan name, that we find it in the singular number
and the feminine gender. But it is only thus applied
to two persons; Helen, and the goddess Herè. It is
plain, as we have seen, that, for the former, it means
not Greek Helen, but Argive Helen. It is but twice
given to Herè: both times where she is acting with
Athenè in the fourth and fifth Iliad;[2] in the first passage Zeus cites them as helpers of Menelaos, in the second, as having restrained and baffled Arès on the field.
The meaning of Argeiè, when applied to a goddess,
according to analogy, must be, 'worshipped in Argos,'
as Aphroditè is called Kuthereia, and Apollo Smintheus.
The local worship of Herè continued, as is well known,
to characterize Argos throughout the historic period.
It was to this local point in particular that her tenacious attachment was constantly directed. It survived
dynastic changes; watched over Eurustheus; reappeared in hatred of Heracles; and protected Agamem-

---

[1] Il. iv. 384; v. 803.   [2] Il. iv. 8; v. 908.

non. Three cities, we know, she loved beyond all others:[1] Mycenæ, Argos, and Sparta; and her attachment to the Greeks in the War possibly may have its root in this more special and local affection; or may, on the other hand, be due to the representative character of that district as the political centre of the whole of Greece.

If in one point of view, as has been suggested, the use of the Argeian name by Homer was poetic and archaic, on the other hand, we may compare this employment of the designation of the ruling part to signify the whole with the cases of more extended empires. All the races, that served under Xerxes and Darius in their expeditions against Greece, were regarded as Persians. The Roman name was applicable to the people of Campania or Calabria, as forming parts of the Roman dominion; while in any domestic or Italian matter their local name would naturally revive. So it may be that, while all the Greeks of Homer are Argeians on the field of Troas, a portion of them may also be Argeians in the local sense afterwards given to Argives; with regard, like Kadmeians, Ætolians, Arcadians, or Locrians, to their own local habitation.

We have thus traced back this, the second of the Great Appellatives for the Greek army, to a more ancient and also more limited use for the inhabitants of the ruling part of Greece; but we have still to ask, how came it originally to be so applied in either way, and what is the root and meaning of the name?

Plainly its root is that of the word Argos; and

[1] Il. iv. 51.

plainly also, as we shall find, the application of the territorial name Argos is wider than that of its derivative.

There are several forms of geographical expression under which Homer appears to signify the entire territory inhabited by Greek races, or subject to Greek sway.

(*a*) The only word which manifestly, without addition of any kind, suffices with the Poet for this purpose is Achaiis. It is used either substantively, or adjectively with γαῖα or αἶα, in eight passages. It will suffice to quote one in which Nestor describes the gathering of the army, a process that manifestly included the whole dominion:

λαὸν ἀγείροντες κατ᾽ Ἀχαΐδα πουλυβότειραν.[1]

In a line twice used, indeed, it is combined with Argos:

Ἄργος ἐς ἱππόβοτον καὶ Ἀχαιΐδα καλλιγύναικα.[2]

But there is no reason why in this line the word should not follow what we have seen to be the ruling sense, Argos meaning the more famous part, and Achaiis meaning the whole.

(*b*) A second and compound form of expression, evidently conveying, as a compound, the same sense, is found in the combination of Argos with Hellas:

ἀνδρός, τοῦ κλέος εὐρὺ καθ᾽ Ἑλλάδα καὶ μέσον Ἄργος.[3]

The meaning of the line plainly is, a reputation reach-

---

[1] Il. xi. 770. 'Collecting an army through fertile Achaiis.' Cf. Il. i. 254; vii. 124.

[2] 'Horse-feeding Argos and Achaiis with beautiful women.'

[3] Od. i. 344. 'Whose fame extends through Hellas and mid-Argos.'

ing over all Greece. It is not conceivable that Penelope, who uses the phrase more than once, could mean to assign to her husband's fame a limit narrower than the Greek nationality. But we shall find that the name Hellas evidently has a special affinity with the north of Greece. Presumably, then, this line may mean,

'Through Northern and through Southern Greece.'

(c) But we find also a third form of expression, in which the word Argos, with the affix παν, appears to cover the whole, at least, of continental Greece, and thus to be equivalent, or nearly so, to Achaiis, and also to Hellas combined with Argos:

πολλῇσιν νήσοισι καὶ Ἄργεϊ παντὶ ἀνάσσειν.[1]

For this line, joining Argos with the islands, describes the range of the whole empire, or (to use a modern phrase) suzerainty, of Agamemnon.

(d) Next it appears that we have the word Argos, with particular ethnical or tribal affixes, used distributively for each of the chief parts of Greece.

In the Catalogue, after Homer has enumerated all the contingents drawn from the Islands, as well as from Southern and Middle Greece, he opens a new division with the line:

Νῦν αὖ τοὺς ὅσσοι τὸ Πελασγικὸν Ἄργος ἔναιον.[2]

And he then proceeds to reckon nine contingents, all of which were drawn from Greece north of Mount Othrus, or, in other words, from Thessaly.

[1] Il. ii. 108. 'To rule over many Islands and all Argos.'
[2] Il. ii. 681. 'But now (recount) those, as many as inhabited Pelasgian Argos.'

It appears, then, that by Pelasgic Argos Homer meant Thessaly.

(e) Next we have an Achaiic Argos mentioned in five passages.

In the first[1] (of which the words are repeated in the second), Agamemnon is speaking of the return to Greece. While the phrase therefore might carry the sense of that country at large, it may also very properly mean the seat of the Pelopid power, or the Eastern Peloponnesos.

In the third, Here goes to Achaiic Argos[2] to hasten the birth of Eurustheus. The meaning appears to be that she went to the kingdom of Sthenelos his father, which again will mean the Eastern Peloponnesos.

In the fourth, Telemachos asks where was Menelaos whilst Aigisthos was engaged in the work of treachery and murder. 'Was he away from Achaiic Argos, and travelling abroad?'[3] Here, while Sparta only might (as far as the meaning goes) be signified, the sense of 'Eastern Peloponnesos,' or the 'Pelopid dominion,' is perfectly suitable, and appears to be the true sense of the phrase.

(f) Further we find an Iason Argos. Eurumachos, the suitor, pays a compliment to the beauty of Penelopè by saying, 'You would have more suitors than you now have,' i.e. than these islands yield you:

εἰ πάντες σε ἴδοιεν ἀν' Ἰασον Ἄργος Ἀχαιοί.[4]

He evidently goes beyond the dominions of Odysseus. But then he probably speaks only of the territory lying nearest to them, and in habitual intercourse with them.

---

[1] Il. ix. 141, 283. [2] Il. xix. 115. [3] Od. iii. 249.
[4] 'If all the Achaians of Iasian Argos could see you.' Od. xviii. 246.

Now this was Western Peloponnesos: as we know from the limited range of Greek navigation; from the direct testimony of the Poems, which tell us of the journey of Odysseus to Ephurè,[1] and of the debt which Odysseus went to Messenè[2] to recover; and (not to mention other circumstances) from the apprehension of the Suitors that Telemachos would at once repair to Elis, or to Pulos,[3] for aid. In the same manner the relations of Crete were with Eastern Peloponnesos; and therefore Helen at Troy easily recognizes Idomeneus, because, as she says, she has often seen him in Sparta.[4] So far, then, Iasian Argos would seem to consist of Western Peloponnesos, including therein the dominions of Elis, Pulos, and perhaps parts at least of Messenè.

We have other means of connecting the name of Iasos with Western Peloponnesos. For Amphion, the king of the Minueïan Orchomenos, was the son of Iasos. He was also the father of Chloris, whom Neleus married, and who became queen of Pulos. Now there was a river Minueïos[5] between Pulos and Elis; and not only is there an Orchomenos included in the places which supplied the Arcadian contingent,[6] but also Agamemnon asks of Odysseus, in Hades, whether his son Orestes is at Orchomenos, or at Pulos, or at Sparta;[7] as if it were some considerable seat of power where a prince might find refuge. Thus Amphion, the son of Iasos, is placed in close connection both with Bœotia and with Western Peloponnesos.

Further, Homer acquaints us that he and his brother

[1] Od. I. 260.
[2] Od. xxiv. 431.
[3] Od. xxi. 15.
[4] Il. iii. 212.
[5] Il. xi. 722.
[6] Il. ii. 606.
[7] Od. xi. 459.

Zethos first founded and fortified Thebes; for, says the Poet, not even they could hold it unfortified.[1] As his daughter married Neleus, this fortification must have been effected from four to five generations before the Troica. But he founded no dynasty in Thebes. On the contrary, we find from Homer that Œdipus ruled there, apparently in succession to his father, two generations before the War.[2] And, according to tradition, he was the descendant of Kadmos, who had colonized Thebes from Phœnicia. It seems very possible that Amphion, like so many others,[3] was expelled from the fat soil of Bœotia; that he passed into Western Peloponnesos; and that he carried thither both the names of Orchomenos and Minueïos, which we find undeniably existing in that region, and the name Iasos, which thus receives a probable and natural application.

Iasian Argos then is the Western Peloponnesos.

And thus moreover we find Argos, with adjuncts, running over the three most famous portions of Greece. It is the common term in three distinct territorial names, as if it meant 'a settlement,' and as if they respectively signified

1. Thessaly, the settlement named from the Pelasgoi.
2. Eastern Peloponnesos, the settlement named from the Achaioi.
3. Western Peloponnesos, the settlement named from Iasos.

(*g*) Further, it is incontestable that Argos sometimes means the city known in history by that name, or rather that city with its immediately contiguous terri-

---

[1] Od. xl. 264.   [2] Od. xi. 273-276.   [3] Thuc. l. 2.

tory: for example, in the Catalogue,¹ where it is mentioned with Tiruns and other places, as making up the contingent of Diomed; and where it is named with Mycenæ and Sparta as being together the favorite cities of Here (πόλιες). The word polis does not indeed invariably include a district; for in certain cases we find it used for the town, in opposition to agros, the country.² But this seems to be the only case where the word is applied to Argos. We have a similar use, when, as Telemachos is quitting Sparta, he is joined by Theoclumenos, 'a fugitive from Argos.'³

On the other hand, the signification, though still local, must be enlarged where Agamemnon says that Briseis shall pass her life at his palace 'in Argos,'⁴ since the city of Argos was under the sway of Diomed, and the residence of Agamemnon was at Mycenæ. The same will hold good of the passage in which Ephure, afterwards Corinth, is described as situate in a nook of horse-feeding Argos, μυχῷ Ἄργεος ἱπποβότοιο.⁵

The epithet 'horse-feeding' has the effect of showing that the country designated is a plain country. Thus the island of Ithaca is described as a goat-feeding⁶ spot, and more beautiful than a horse-feeding district. Of course the phrase is to be understood by comparison.

(b) Lastly, there are one or two passages in which the name Argos may be held to stand alone for Greece at large: as when Nestor declares it shameful for the army to return to Argos ('Ἄργοσδε ἰέναι⁷) before the mind of Zeus is known. And Poludamas, speaking

---

¹ Il. ii. 559. ² Il. xxiii. 832, 835; Od. xvii. 182.
³ Od. xv. 224. ⁴ Il. i. 80. ⁵ Il. vi. 152.
⁶ Od. iv. 606. ⁷ Il. ii. 348.

of the possible destruction of the Greek army in Troas, thus describes that contingency:

νωνύμνους ἀπολέσθαι ἀπ' Ἄργεος ἐνθάδ' Ἀχαιούς.[1]

Paris, too, says he brought home property from Argos. This may mean from Sparta as part of the Pelopid dominion; or it may mean from Greece at large. But perhaps we cannot be sure that in these passages Argos stands for more than a description of the whole by its capital part.

Argos, then, with Homer has these four uses:

1. It may be held to mean, alone or with πᾶν, Greece at large; but, if so, it is rarely thus used.

2. It may mean the Pelopid dominions, or, taken roughly, the Eastern Peloponnesos.

3. It may mean the city of Argos, with the immediately surrounding district attached to it. In this sense it accepts the epithet πολυδίψιον: and the epithets ἱππόβοτον, πολύπυρον, and οὔθαρ ἀρούρης, appear to apply to it both in this and in the last-named sense.

4. When joined with distinctive epithets of an historical, not a physical, character, it seems to be applicable to most portions of Greek territory, as if a radical signification, such as settlement, or colony in the original sense of the word, still adhered to it.

When we proceed to examine the etymology of the word, we find that, as it is but once combined with polis, so the epithets attaching to it (as above), all of them indicate a tract of country; like 'land' among the Scotch, as in the expression 'landward parishes.' And again, on comparing it with agros, the proper

---

[1] Il. xii. 70. 'That the Achaians perish inglorious away from Argos.'

term for describing a rural tract, this latter appears to be the very same word with the middle consonants transposed. So far, then, the meaning may be that of a tract of land suited for, or brought under, cultivation.

The Homeric names of countries and places, as far as we can trace them, appear to be derived —

1. From an individual founder: as Ithakè from Ithakos, Dardaniè from Dardanos.[1]

2. From a race in occupation or in ascendancy: as Achaïis from Achaoi, Cretè or Cretai, from Cretes.[2]

3. From a race in occupation, which race has itself derived its name from features or circumstances of the country: as Threkè from Threkes, Thracians; the race in turn taking a name related to the rough character of a highland country, and probably proceeding from the same root with τρηχύς. So again, Aigialeia from the Aigialeis, these being named from Aigialos, the strip of coast afterwards called Achaia.

4. From these local features or physical incidents directly, like Aigialos: or like Euboia, which apparently signifies the adaptation of that fertile island to tillage; an adaptation which afterwards made it the granary of Athens.

It is plain, negatively, that the word Argos has no connection with any of the three first-named sources. The suggestion already made would attach it to the fourth. It would then apply to Argos of the Eastern Peloponnesos, as the Argos κατ' ἐξοχήν.

The word argos is used adjectively by Homer for

[1] Od. xvii. 207; Il. xx. 216. [2] Od. xiv. 199.

dogs, Il. i. 50; for oxen, Il. xxiii. 30; and for a goose, Od. xv. 161. And we have these compounds into which it enters:

1. ἀργὴς (κεραυνός).
2. ἀργικέραυνος.
3. ἀργεστὴς (Νότος).
4. ἀργεννοί ὄϊες, ὀθόναι.
5. ἀργινόεις (Κάμειρος).
6. ἀργιόδοντες (ὕες).
7. ἀργίποδες (κύνες).
8. Ποδάργη, a horse of Achilles.

The sense of whiteness or brightness may apply to every one of these uses, both primitive and derivative: but whiteness or brightness could only be applicable to such districts of country as might be chalky or sandy; and this sense therefore will in no way assist us towards an explanation of the territorial name Argos with its very wide application.

If Argos have a connection with ἔργον, then it at once admits the sense of an extent of land tilled or suitable for tillage, a sense nearly akin, though not similar in etymology, to that of the word 'lowlands.' For ergon in Homer, while it is applicable to industrial operations generally, is primarily and specially applied to agriculture.[1]

We can, then, conceive how, out of many districts, all fitly described as lowlands, in one, from being merely a description, it would become a proper name; and how, at the next stage in the process, it would give a designation to its inhabitants. In accordance with this supposition, we have more than one Argos in Homer: and in the historic period we have Argos of Orestis in Macedonia, Argos of Amphilochia in Western Greece, and Argos near Larissa in Thessaly. But only one Argos is inhabited by Argeioi. Just as there

[1] Od. vi. 259.

are Highlands of Saxony no less than of Scotland, but only the Scotch mountaineers acquired the name of Highlanders, as a standing and ordinary name.

In referring Argos to a common root and significance with ἔργον, we are not bound to hold that it attains its initial vowel by junction with the particle α in its intensive, or in any other, sense. For we have the word ergon, and also its derivatives, in this form, handed down from very ancient Greek. Among the four tribes of Attica, which subsisted until the time of Cleisthenes, one was that of the husbandmen, called Argades. And in the Elian Inscription, supposed to date about the fortieth Olympiad, or more than six hundred years before Christ, we have the word ergon, in the form argon with the digamma, as follows —

αἴτε fεπος αἴτε fοργον.[1]

Another probable example of the exchange of these vowels is in ἀροῦ, to plough, compared with ἐρα, the earth. In the Latin tongue we find both forms preserved, in aro, to plough, and sero, to sow, respectively.

We need not here inquire what is the common root of ἔργον and of Argos. But, if labor be the idea conveyed, this may perhaps suggest a meaning for the Homeric adjective argos and for all its compounds. The groundwork of that meaning may be conveyed by the word 'strenuous.' Sometimes this takes the form of keenness, and then follows the idea of swiftness: sometimes it takes the form of a persevering patience, and then slowness is not less appropriately suggested.

---

[1] Museum Criticum, i. 536; and Marsh, Horæ Pelasgicæ, p. 70.

The labor of a dog is swift, that of an ox is patient: hence we have laborious oxen, moving slow; laborious dogs, moving fast. The sense of whiteness legitimately attaches to the effect of rapid motion on the eye. This explanation will perhaps be found to suit all the diversified phrases which have been cited above.

And (reverting to the fountain-head), we perceive that the notion of strenuous labor will adapt itself to other uses of Argos. We may consider the name of the ship Argo as meaning possibly 'swift,' but preferably 'stout,' able to do battle with the waves, as we now say a good or a gallant ship. Again, this sense suits, far more fully than the mere idea of speed, the noble dog Argos of the Odyssey; for whom mere whiteness would be a vapid description. Once more, we have in the Ἀργειφόντης of Homer a glimpse of the tradition of Argos the spy, to whom we naturally ascribe a strenuous vigilance. The epithet ἀργαλέος, 'hard or difficult to cope with,' follows in the train: while the later word ἀργοῦντες,[1] 'idle,' takes up the idea of slowness at the point where it passes into inertness.

When we turn from Argos to its derivative Argeioi, we find subsidiary evidence to the effect that the word properly meant a husbandman, a rustic. In Suidas[2] we have the proverb Ἀργείοις ὁρᾷς, 'You see Argeioi,' with the explanation παροιμία ἐπὶ τῶν ἀτενῶς καὶ καταπληκτικῶς ὁρώντων.[3] Now we know nothing of the Argives as inhabitants of Argolis, which would lead to the belief that they stared hard, or conveyed alarm by their looks. But if the word Argeioi meant husband-

[1] Soph. Fr. 288.   [2] Suid. in voce.
[3] 'A proverb concerning people who stare hard and whose looks cause alarm.'

men, then, as the population, instead of living dispersedly in hamlets (κωμηδόν) gathered into towns, the rural part of the community would gradually become also the ruder part, and from this point the transition is easy to the sense of a wild and savage aspect.

The Latin word agrestis stands to ager as Argeios, according to the foregoing argument, stands to Argos. The agrestis, or countryman, was opposed to the urbanus, or townsman. The latter, with its Greek correlative ἀστεῖος, came by degrees to mean a person of polished manners; but agrestis, following the movement I have supposed in the case of Argeios, came to mean coarse, wild, barbarous. Thus Ovid says of the River Achelous, when mutilated by the loss of his horn in the combat with Heracles,

'Vultus Achelous agrestes
Et lacerum cornu mediis caput abdidit undis.'[1]

And Cicero, after describing the battles of the Spartan youth, carried on with nails and teeth as well as fists and feet, asks, 'Quæ barbaries Indica vastior atque agrestior?'[2]

Again, Suidas gives us the expression Ἀργεῖοι,[3] which he says is used for sheer villains, because the Ἀργεῖοι are held up in plays as noted thieves; for which he refers to a lost play of Aristophanes. According to the view I have given, the word may well mean robbers, since theft in the early stages of society always frequents solitary places.

Again, Æschines[4] charges Demosthenes with gross

[1] Ov. Met. ix. 96.   [2] Cic. Tusc. Disp. v. 27.
[3] In voc. 'Ἀργεῖοι Φῶρες.   [4] De Falsâ Legat. p. 41, l. 14.

offences, which had brought upon him disparaging nicknames. One of these was Argas; which Suidas and Hesychius explain as the name of a snake, signifying sharp and crafty. But Æschines say she was called Argas, each of his guardians having suits against him to recover money. So that the meaning would be 'crafty in getting hold of the money of others,' *homo trium literarum*, a sharper.

Once more. Hesychius on the name Argeioi says, ἐκ τῶν Εἱλώτων οἱ πιστευόμενοι οὕτως ἐλέγοντο, ἢ λαμπροί, 'those Helots distinguished for fidelity are so called.' Why was it that select and confidential Helots thus received the name of Argeioi? That name may have retained its local force, as applicable to the whole Pelopid dominion, long after Homer: and it may also, apart from its use as a proper name, have borne the meaning of a free or ordinary agricultural settler. The Helot was a serf by the fortune of war; but he was a serf whose forefathers had, according to this view, been Argeioi. If then a Helot made himself conspicuous, and acquired the confidence of his lord by fidelity and smartness, it would seem a very natural reward to efface from him the brand of his captivity, and give him the old name of the free countryman of that part of Greece. In this case Argeios might mean a libertus, without a defined *formula* of emancipation.

It is worth remark that the cognate word *agrios* appears to have gone through the same process as *agrestis* and Argeios. For there was an Ætolian prince Agrios,[1] a grand-uncle of Diomed, two generations before the War of Troy. In the contemporary

[1] Il. xiv. 117.

language of the Poet, Agrios had come to mean savage and cruel, and is so applied to Poluphemos.[1] The intermediate meaning probably was that of a dweller in a wild and unsettled place. The word is never used to describe the passion, or the cruelty, of Achilles.

It should also be noted that Argeioi, where applied to the Greeks at large, never means the chiefs, but always the mass; whereas the word Achaios has, as we shall see, in many places a decided leaning towards the aristocracy. Epithets are scarcely ever given by Homer to the Argeian name. Only in four passages do they appear. In Il. iv. 242 they are ἰόμωροι and ἐλεγχέες, 'dishonored;' in Il. xiv. 479 ἰόμωροι,[2] and ἀπειλάων ἀκόρητοι. These are, in each case, not descriptive epithets attaching to or indicating general character, but reproaches growing out of the occasion. In Il. xxi. 429 they are θωρηκταί, clad in breastplates, which, from the context, seems to do no more than state a fact: the phrase is equivalent to 'the Greeks in arms.' In Il. xix. 269, the Argeioi are called φιλοπτόλεμοι, lovers of battle; and this appears to be the sole passage in which an epithet of description, properly so called, is attached to the word. But the Danaan name, though more rarely used, has epithets in twenty-two passages; and the Achaian name in nearly 130. This circumstance tends to show, that the Argeian name properly belongs to the commonalty or masses, rather than to the chiefs.

We have assumed above, in accordance with the

[1] Od. ix. 215, 494.
[2] I render ἰόμωροι, not archers, a sense neither suited to the passage nor to the general armament of the Greeks, who were not, as a rule, archers; but braggarts, loud talkers, in close harmony with the sister-phrase ἀπειλάων ἀκόρητοι = insatiate of boasts.

general Greek tradition, that the Pelasgoi were the
first agricultural settlers of the peninsula; but that
their name, and any other cognate names, were sup-
pressed or thrown into the shade by the dynastic name,
which a Danaos probably gave to his people. That
name, again, naturally disappearing with the accession
of another line to his throne and dominions, the name
Argeioi, taken either from the occupation of the
people (like Argades), or from the settlement they
had made, would take its place with great propriety,
in lieu of reverting to the Pelasgic name, which would
silently pass out of use, as that of a race conquered and
therefore comparatively depressed.

The third and most weighty of the Great Appellatives is Achaioi.

The evidence of the Poems will I think suffice to
show —

1. That this is the most familiar designation of the
Greeks of Homer.

2. That the manner of its use indicates, among the
Greeks of Homer, the political predominance of an
Achaian race over other races ranged by its side in the
War, and composing along with it the nation which
owned Agamemnon for its head.

3. That, besides its national use, the name of the
Achaioi has a local use in many parts of Greece.

4. That the manner of this local use points out with
sufficient clearness, that the rise of the Achaian name
was contemporary with that of the family of Pelops.

The first proposition may be at once settled by the
rude, but not inconclusive, test of numbers. While
the Danaan name is used about 160 times, of which
thirteen are in the Odyssey; and the Argeian 205

times, of which twenty-eight are in the Odyssey; the Achaian name is used about 597 times in the Iliad, and 117 in the Odyssey, making 714 in all. This frequency of use in the two poems of itself goes far to determine that the Achaian designation was the most modern of the three.

It is also worth observing, that in the opening of the Iliad the word Achaioi is used five times, before Danaoi or Argeioi are introduced at all.

We have seen that the Danaan name is never used in the singular; and that the Argeian name is so used only in its local sense. But the Achaian name, and that only, is used in the singular to designate an individual as belonging to the nation; with the reserve, however, of a separate shade of meaning, sometimes[1] tending to attach it to a class. So the Poet uses Ἀχαιός; ἀνήρ[2] for a Trojan or a Dardanian.

Again, Homer has worked this name into the female forms Achaiides, Achaiiades, Achaiai, to signify the women of Greece; but has made no such use of the Danaan or Argeian[3] names.

Also the phrase υἷες Ἀχαιῶν, sons of the Achaians, has no correlation with the Danaan or Argeian names, and further helps to show the predominant familiarity of this designation. What the patronymic was to the individual, this form of speech was to the nation — an appeal to a standard of honor, an incentive under the form of an embellishment.

Epithets are given to the name Achaioi in 130 places, besides eight or ten more in which they are used either for the women, or for the word in its territorial sense. And the familiar use of the word

---

[1] Il. iii. 167, 230. [2] Il. ii. 701. [3] *Supra*, pp. 30, 44.

Achaiis for the country is a proof of the prevalence, ascendancy, and familiarity of the name, which was thus applied on its own merits, so to speak, and not, like Argos, because it was the proper designation of the most eminent part of the country.

When we look to the character of these epithets, we find them such as point to the Achaians in the character of a dominant race or aristocracy.

In one or two cases we have epithets of reproach, such as were addressed to the army at critical moments: ἀνάλκιδες, Il. xv. 326; ἀπειλητῆρες, Il. vii. 96, and in the same passage Ἀχαιΐδες. In a few others we have them as simple descriptions of circumstances of the moment.[1] But the pointed epithets, descriptive of character, are as follows: —

1. δῖοι, worthy or noble: Il. v. 451; Od. iii. 116, *et alibi*.
2. ἑλίκωπες, from the rapid motion of the eye giving brightness: Il. iii. 239, *et alibi*.
3. ἐϋκνήμιδες, stoutly-greaved: Il. iii. 304; Od. iii. 149, and in thirty-two other places.
4. ἥρωες, heroes: Il. xii. 165, *et alibi*.
5. καρηκομόωντες, with flowing or abundant hair: Il. ii. 11; Od. i. 90, and in twenty-seven other places.
6. μεγάθυμοι, high-spirited: Il. i. 123, 135; Od. xxiv. 57.
7. μένεα πνείοντες, ardent: Il. iii. 8.
8. χαλκοκνήμιδες, with greaves of χαλκός or copper: Il. vii. 41.
9. χαλκοχίτωνες, with armor for tunics: Il. i. 371; Od. i. 286, and in twenty-two other places.
10. ὑπερκύδαντες, exulting: Il. iv. 66, 71.
11. ἀρηΐφιλοι, lovers of war: Il. vi. 73; xvi. 303; xvii. 319.
12. φιλοπτόλεμοι, lovers of battle: Il. xvii. 224.

[1] Il. xii. 20; xiii. 15; xv. 44.

These epithets are very marked in character; they describe courage, personal beauty, well-made and well-finished arms, or excellence generally.

The epithets given to D a n a o i are exclusively those of a soldiery: those of A c h a i o i are more extended, and seem to extend to nobility of race.

The epithet d i o s is, in my opinion, wrongly translated 'divine;' and much confusion arises from the attempt to apply that sense to the various uses of the word. But if we understand it to mean a limited or special excellence, excellence in its own kind, we have no difficulty in understanding how Eumaios[1] and Clytemnestra[2] can both receive it, the one for his trusty character, the other, the sister of Helen, for her beauty. There is, however, one other sense which might be given to it, that of high-born, well-descended, which perhaps would not be less adapted to all the cases of its use.

In the plural, Homer applies it to Achaians and Pelasgians only. This rare use supplies a presumption of some peculiar meaning; and it may be thought that the Achaians are δῖοι because both of their blood and of their power and predominance, the Pelasgians because of their antiquity.

It is Thersites, who in the Second Iliad attempts to stir up the soldiery by calling them Achaiides, or she-Greeks. It is to be noted, that in his short speech, of which an inflated presumption is the principal mark, the Achaian name is used five times within nine lines, and neither of the other names is used at all. In two of these cases, the speaker pointedly calls himself an Achaian. Probably the upstart and braggart uses this

---

[1] Od. xiv. 48, and in ten other places.   [2] Od. iii. 266.

name only because it was the most distinguished or aristocratic name, as an ill-bred person always takes peculiar care to call himself a gentleman.

There are, however, numerous single passages, in which the simple term Achaioi appears from the context to have a special, sometimes perhaps even an exclusive reference to the chiefs and leaders, or to the officers and higher class, of the army. And if this be so, then we must consider the national use of the name as derivative like that of Argeioi, the whole being named from the prime part; but with this difference, that in the case of Achaioi it is the prime blood of the country, in that of Argeioi the prime seat of power.

The injured priest, Chruses, solicits all the Achaioi, and most of all the two Atridai. All the Achaians assent, except Agamemnon.[1] There is no sign that he solicited the army. In truth, this could only be done in an Assembly; and there was no Assembly. It follows, that the Achaioi here mean the chiefs. But when Chruses invokes the vengeance of the god upon the army at large, the phrase alters to Danaoi.[2]

The actual division of booty is, from the nature of the case, a matter that must have rested principally or wholly in the hands of the chiefs. When this matter is referred to, Agamemnon says, Do not let me, alone of the Argeians, that is, of all the Greeks, go without a prize;[3] and Nestor uses the same word, when he stimulates the army at large by the hope of booty.[4] But Achilles replies to Agamemnon that the Achaians have no means of compensating him[5] there and then, since they hold no common stock in reserve. The

[1] Il. 1. 15, 22, 26–32. [2] Il. 1. 42. [3] Il. 1. 118.
[4] Il. ii. 350–356. [5] Il. 1. 123.

phrase is the same in subsequent passages.¹ So far then the Achaian name seems to fall especially to the chiefs.

The same leaning may be observed, when reference is made to other governing duties. Achilles, in his adjuration by the staff or sceptre, the symbol of governing power, describes it as borne by the sons of the Achaians, obviously the kings, chiefs, or persons in authority.

When Priam on the wall of Troy inquires from Helen the names of two prominent commanders, he both times asks, who is that Achaian?² and in the second case, the king describes him as out-topping the Argeians by his head and his broad shoulders. Here the Achaian seems to mean the prince or noble; the Argeians, the soldiery at large. Indeed, the words are hardly susceptible of any other construction; and they seem almost to warrant of themselves the conclusion that the Achaian name is properly that of a dominant race, grown, generally speaking, into a class, and possibly including others of that class, although not of Achaian descent.

In the historic ages of Greece, the Achaian name acquired a local force, similar to that of the Argive name, in exclusive, or almost exclusive, connection with one particular district. We cannot say that it has in this sense, if strictly taken, a local use in Homer. Yet we find the Achaians in many parts of Greece mentioned in such a way, as to distinguish them from other

---

[1] Il. i. 135, 162, 392; ii. 227. In Il. ii. 250, the giving is by the ἥρως Ἀχαιοί. The passage has the obelus; but it is not out of harmony with my argument.

[2] Il. iii. 167, 226.

inhabitants of the country, either in the same or in neighboring tracts.

1. We have already seen that the name Achaioi had come into use among the people of Mycenæ and of Argos a generation before the War; and that it is used of them in contradistinction to the Kadmeioi of Bœotia.[1] At earlier epochs they are called Argeioi; but we are not to suppose that this name had fallen into local desuetude, even though the other might be more in vogue. We shall see that the Myrmidons of Achilles afford us an example of a race, or body, who bore more names than one.

2. It has also been shown that, in the legend of the Eleventh Iliad about the Epeian War, the Pulian party are called Achaians at the period of the youth of Nestor; and this in apparent contradistinction to their opponents, who therefore were not Achaian at all at that time, or not Achaian in the same eminent sense.

3. The troops of Achilles, always called Myrmidons among the other divisions of the army in the field, inhabited, as we find from the Catalogue, Hellas and Phthie,[2] and bore, evidently with some distinctive force, the name of Hellenes, and likewise that of Achaioi.[3] In the Ninth Iliad, Achilles describes the women of the same tract of country as Achaiides.[4] On the origin of the name 'Myrmidon,' which this division of the army had wholly to itself, Homer throws no light. Hellenes they were, as inhabitants of Hellas[5] in the special sense of the word. And as

[1] Il. iv. 384; v. 803; vi. 223.　　[2] Il. ii. 683.
[3] Il. ii. 684.　　[4] Il. ix. 395.
[5] See *infra*, Chap. IV.

the Achaian name in Homer is not territorial, we must suppose them to have borne it in virtue of their blood, the Myrmidons being probably a subdivision of the great Achaian family.

4. Of the five races [1] who inhabited Crete at the time of the Troica, four were named Eteocretes, Pelasgoi, Kudones, and Doricis: the fifth, which is named first, perhaps by reason of political predominance, was Achaian. The appearance in this passage of the Dorian name, together with the Achaian, subdivides, more pointedly than any other passage in the Poems, the Hellenic family.

5. Again, a portion of the force of Diomed is described as composed of those 'who held Ægina and Mases, Achaian youths.' [2] The site of Mases appears to be unknown. But tradition, according to Pausanias, gave the name of Pelops to the small islands off the coast of Troizen.[3] Such a tradition corresponds remarkably with the indirect testimony of the verse I have quoted, if there be a relation, as I suppose, between the rise of the family of Pelops and the predominance of the Achaians.

6. On turning to the dominions of Odysseus, we find that three names are used to describe their inhabitants: Kophallenes, Ithakesioi, and Achaioi.

The first is used four times in the Odyssey,[4] and is the distinctive name in the Iliad of the military contingent led by Odysseus. We shall find that it appears to indicate the predominance of the Hellenic element.[5]

---

[1] Od. xix. 175–177. [2] Il. ii. 562.
[3] Paus. II. 34. 4, p. 191. [4] Od. xx. 210; xxiv. 354, 377, 428.
[5] *Infra*, Chap. IV.

The suitors[1] are ordinarily called Ἀχαιοί, never Ἀργεῖοι or Δαναοί. They constituted the aristocracy of the islands. It appears that either they were an Achaian race, or else they were called Achaian because they were an aristocracy.

The sway of Odysseus appears to have depended upon his personal qualities. Like his father Laertes,[2] he was both a conqueror and an economist. Accordingly, his long absence is fatal to his power; though Menelaos, after an absence almost as long,[3] resumed his throne without impediment. When Odysseus reappears, his final proceedings against the Suitors are attended with precautions, evidently dictated by his fear of the people. And in the Assembly of the last Book, whilst more than one half take up arms against him,[4] the rest simply remain neutral: he has no positive aid to rely on, except that of his father, his son, and a mere handful of immediate dependants. During his absence the Suitors are ruining him, but are not said to oppress the people. All this looks as if his family was perhaps of foreign or extraneous origin, and in any case had recently attained to power.

Autolucos, the maternal grandfather of Odysseus, resided at Parnesos in Phokis:[5] Penelopê has no trace of connection with Southern Greece: her sister Iphthimê was married to Eumelos, heir-apparent of Pherai in Thessaly.[6] Of Arkeisios, the father of Laertes, with whom the genealogy begins, we have no trace in Ithaca. But we do hear of an eponymist or founder, Ithacos,[7] who, with Neritos the eponymist of

[1] Od. ii. 51; xvi. 122.
[2] Od. iv. 82.
[3] Od. xix. 394.
[4] Od. xxiv. 205-207, 377.
[5] Od. xxiv. 463.
[6] Od. iv. 798.
[7] Od. xvii. 203-207.

the chief mountain of the island, and Poluctor, constructed the fountain, from which the city was supplied with water. A descendant of this Poluctor, probably his son, by name Peisandros,[1] appears, with the title of anax, among the leading Suitors. He may not impossibly have represented a family, displaced by Laertes from the sovereignty of this island dominion. I say by Laertes, because if Arkeisios had founded the sovereignty in Ithaca, it appears probable that Odysseus would have taken his patronymic from that personage, and not from his father.

But, apart from the question to what root the family of Odysseus is to be referred, it seems plain that either the Suitors, being the aristocracy, were Achaian in blood; or, because they were the aristocracy, they fell under the designation of Achaians.

When the mass of the people are gathered in Assembly, they are invariably addressed, not as Achaioi, but as Ithakesioi.[2] And when, instead of the inhabitants of the island, the subjects throughout the dominion are spoken of, they are called Kephallenes, the name always given to the military division in the Iliad.[3]

When the Suitor Eurimachos expresses a misgiving lest, in lieu of Penelope, it should prove he would have done more wisely in courting some other dame, he says there are many (other) Achaiides[4] in Ithaca, and in the other territories. This must surely refer to women of noble birth.

It is true that, in the Second Odyssey, Telemachos summons 'the Achaians' to the Assembly.[5] But we

[1] Od. xviii. 299. [2] Od. ii. 25, 161, 229; xxiv. 453, 531.
[3] Od. xxiv. 354. [4] Od. xxi. 251. [5] Od. ii. 7.

find in Scherié that principal persons only seem to have been summoned man by man,¹ though all classes usually attended. Again, in the Ithacan Assembly of the Twenty-fourth Book, Eupeithes complains of the harm Odysseus has done the Achaians.² The Suitors, whom he has slain, were (he says) far and away, the ἄριστοι, the aristocracy, of the Kephallenes. This is exactly conformable to the view I have taken. When Eupeithes ceases, we are told that pity seized all the Achaians.³ This seems to mean the party of the Suitors, those allied with them by blood or interest, or near them in station. For, shortly after, the Assembly divides, part taking arms against Odysseus, and part, by the advice of Halitherses, remaining neutral.

We have also to consider the word Panachaioi. It is used eleven times in Homer. We cannot take it for a mere synonym of Achaioi. Seven times out of the eleven, it appears in the expression ἀριστῆες Παναχαιῶν. In conformity with the sense of the word πᾶς, we may assign to the compound a cumulative and collective force: so that Panachaioi would mean the entire body of the Achaians, or all classes of the Greeks. In the other passages⁴ where the word occurs, this sense is very suitable, and especially in the passage of the Iliad where Odysseus, interceding with Achilles, says, 'If you do not care for Agamemnon, yet pity the Panachaioi,' or the Greeks at large.⁵

I have now collected the particulars connected with the use of the three Great Appellatives in Homer, and presented them to the reader sufficiently, as I hope,

---

¹ Od. viii. 10. ² Od. xxiv. 426. ³ Od. xxiv. 438.
⁴ Il. ix. 301; Od. i. 239; xiv. 369; xxiv. 32. ⁵ Il. ix. 300.

for certain purposes. These purposes are, first to establish in their due order the succession of the periods at which they had respectively obtained some root in the country: next to show that the most proper national name of the Greeks at the time of Homer, the name most nearly approaching to what we mean by a national name, was that of the Achaioi: thirdly, to exhibit, as the specific shades of meaning attaching to the three Appellatives respectively, (1) for Danaoi, the soldiery, the people in warfare; (2) for Argeioi, the masses, the people engaged in tillage; (3) for Achaioi, the chiefs or aristocracy, the people regarded through the governing class.

This class, and the race that formed it, appear to me to be entitled to a more separate and concentrated attention than it has as yet received in the investigation of Greek history. It forms a distinct type of Hellenic character, the earliest in time, and certainly not the least remarkable in grandeur or in completeness. The Greek of Homer is neither the man of Athens nor the man of Sparta: he is neither cast in the Dorian nor in the Ionian pattern: he is the Achaian Greek. Simple, and yet shrewd; passionate, and yet self-contained; brave in battle, and gentle in converse; keenly living in the present, yet with a 'large discourse' over the future and the past; as he is in body 'full-limbed and tall,' so is he in mind towering and full-formed. His portrait could never have been drawn but from the life: and, disregarding what I conceive to have been the figments of the first *renaissance* after the wild and rude Dorian revolution, I set down Homer himself as the Achaian painter of his own kith and kin.

It will however be requisite to inquire,

1. What light can be thrown on the origin of the Achaian name through the growth of the power that brought it into vogue.

2. How it was superseded; and what place the three Appellatives respectively occupy in the later tradition and literature.

But this will best be done after we have examined and illustrated, as far as may be, the Homeric use of other national and tribal names, especially four of them, which, though of much rarer occurrence, are of an importance scarcely second to the names already discussed. These are—

1. Pelasgoi.
2. Hellenes.
3. Phoinikes.
4. Aiolidai.

We may then sketch in outline the relative position of the families or races respectively embraced by these Appellatives, and consider what they severally contributed to the formation of the great Greek nationality.

CHAPTER III.

THE PELASGOI.

RESPECTING the Pelasgoi, we have some direct and some indirect testimony from Homer. And we have also certain supplements to this Homeric information —

(1) In the later Greek and classical tradition;
(2) In the results of modern ethnological and archæological research.

The direct testimony of Homer establishes —
The wide extension of the Pelasgoi.

The country afterwards called Thessaly bears in the Iliad the name of Pelasgic Argos.[1] It furnished to the Greek army nine contingents, and 280 ships, or about one fourth of the entire fleet. And this seems to be the only name which it bears as a whole. The line, in which this name is given, is evidently prefatory to the great Thessalian division of the Catalogue.[2] Pelasgic Argos appears to be included with other countries in the wider name of Hellas; a name which probably may also have had an especial application to the part

[1] Il. ii. 681.   [2] Studies on Homer, vol. I. pp. 100-106.

of Thessaly ruled by Peleus, and inhabited by the Myrmidons.

It further appears, from the Odyssey, that the Pelasgoi were one of the five nations of Crete.[1]

And we learn from the Trojan Catalogue in the Second Iliad, that the Pelasgoi of Larissa served in the War among the allies of Troy.[2]

The facts thus exhibited, though few and simple, indicate the wide extension of the Pelasgoi, who thus appear on both sides, in a war which draws the armies engaged in it from so considerable an extent of country.

But further; Zeus, the Zeus of Dodona, the Zeus served by Hellic interpreters of his will, is, in the most solemn invocation of the Iliad, addressed as Pelasgic Zeus[3] by Achilles, the greatest representative of the Hellenic mind and life.

This was at a period of complete and well established Hellenic predominance. The name Pelasgicos is, then, evidently an archaic name of Zeus; and it is not easy to see how he could have received it, unless the inhabitants of the country from Dodona, at least as far as the kingdom of Peleus, had been known as Pelasgoi. The concurrent evidence of this passage with that of the line in which all Thessaly is called Pelasgic Argos, appears to demonstrate that Thessaly had formerly been known as a country of Pelasgoi, and that these Pelasgoi were worshippers of Zeus.

Accordingly, of the nine Thessalian contingents, seven are described by the places they inhabit, without any national or tribal name. It is probable that in

[1] Od. xix. 177.   [2] Il. ii. 840.   [3] Il. xvi. 233.

these districts the Pelasgian name had not yet been superseded by any other designation for the purposes of familiar use. The only territorial name used in this part of the Catalogue, besides Pelasgic Argos, is in the case of the eminently Hellenic dominions of Peleus.

When Homer names the Pelasgoi of the Trojan Catalogue, he describes them as those Pelasgoi who inhabited the deep-loamed Larissa.[1] He therefore distinguishes them from other Pelasgoi. But he cannot possibly mean, in composing for a Greek audience, to distinguish them from the only other Pelasgoi mentioned by him, those of Crete, who are not named in the Catalogue or in the Iliad at all. It is likely, then, that he refers to other Pelasgoi of the Trojan army; of which the two contingents immediately preceding this one are described without any national or tribal designation.

Again, the Poet does not simply say, 'Hippothoos led Pelasgians,' but, 'he led tribes (φῦλα) of Pelasgians,' thus pointing again to a variety of tribes comprised under that name. This has been observed by Strabo.[2]

If in general the Achaians were paramount, and the Pelasgoi were subordinate members of one and the same community, it is not difficult to see why Homer should nowhere apply the Pelasgian name to any portion of the Greek army; and again, why the same scruples should not bind him as to a portion of the Trojan force.

He has pursued an exactly similar course with

[1] Il. ii. 811. [2] xiii. 3, p. 620.

respect to the Thracians. He mentions them in the Trojan Catalogue, and again in the Trojan army.[1] They have no recognized place among the Greeks, and yet Thamuris, evidently a Greek, is described as Thracian.[2] And the word Threx seems to mean Highlander, in opposition to Pelasgos as Lowlander. Probably Thracians existed diffusively, like Pelasgians, among the Greeks; but were absorbed in designations more prominent and splendid.

We have yet a third example. The Kaukones appear in the Tenth Iliad as part of the Trojan force.[3] They are nowhere found in the Greek host, or in the Greek Catalogue. But in the Odyssey, where there was no reason for keeping the name in the background, as the same national distinctions did not require to be kept in view, Homer mentions the Kaukones apparently as a people dwelling on the west side of Greece, for the Pseudo-Mentor[4] is going among them from Ithaca to claim payment of a debt. They were probably, then, near neighbors. He distinguishes them as high-spirited μεγάθυμοι: which reminds us of the reverence he has shown for the ancient possessors of the country by calling the Pelasgians d i o i.

Again, Homer, in the three passages where he names Pelasgians, names them each time with a laudatory epithet; a circumstance deserving some notice, when we observe to how small a proportion of his national or tribal names epithets are attached.

Once he calls them ἐγχεσίμωροι,[5] addicted to the spear. He elsewhere uses this epithet but thrice; once for the Arcadians,[6] whom, in the only other place where they are

[1] Il. ii. 844; x. 434. [2] Il. ii. 594–600. [3] Il. x. 429; xx. 329.
Od. iii. 366. Il. vii. 134. [6] Il. ii. 611.

named, he describes as skilled in fight; once for two royal warriors individually;[1] and once for the Myrmidons.[2] This epithet then is of high rank as describing valor.

On the other two occasions he calls the Pelasgians dioi.[3] This epithet implies, sometimes, perhaps a narrow, but always a special and peculiar excellence. And it is one which Homer allows to no race except only the Pelasgians and Achaians.[4] There is no difficulty in explaining the latter use of it. The former is also appropriate, if we suppose the Pelasgoi to be the ancient and primary base of the Greek nation.

The leaders of the Pelasgoi before Troy are themselves the sons of Pelasgos, who was the son of Teutamas.

Only then in five places altogether does Homer give us traces of this name or its derivatives. But this affords no presumption averse to the hypothesis that the Pelasgians were the base of the Greek nation; because it is his uniform practice to throw into the background whatever tends to connect the Hellenic race with foreign origin or blood; and the currency of the Pelasgian name beyond the limits of Greece, and among its foes, evidently had this tendency in a marked degree.

The Larissé[5] mentioned in the Trojan Catalogue appears once more;[6] and on both occasions it has an epithet denoting fertility. The tendency of this epithet is to show that the Pelasgoi were an agricultural and settled people. Of this we shall find other signs.

When we come to the historic age, we find many

---

[1] Il. ii. 692.   [2] Od. iii. 188.   [3] Il. x. 429; Od. xix. 177.
[4] Il. v. 451, et alibi.   [5] Il. ii. 841.   [6] Il. xvii. 301.

Larissès;[1] and the mere name is commonly believed to indicate a seat of the Pelasgians. But in Homer we have only one Larissè. A possible explanation is, that Larissè was properly the name of a fort or place of refuge, somewhat like the bell-towers of Ireland and other countries, to which the people of the district betook themselves for refuge on an emergency, from their dwellings in the surrounding country. Around these forts, as happened in our own country about the feudal castles, towns would gather by a gradual process. And so the application of the word Larissè to the town conjointly with the district,[2] of which we seem to have this single example in Homer, might by degrees become common. That which was an Argos, or settlement for tillage, in the original or Pelasgian stage, might, afterwards had taught the necessity of defence, become in some cases a Larissè; while in others the old name might continue: or the one name might be applied to the part for habitation, the other to the part for defence. This hypothesis is supported by the fact that the citadel of the historic Argos, which stood upon an eminence, was called Larissè.[3]

Such are the direct notices of the Pelasgoi in Homer. They are scanty in amount. But there are three other heads of Homeric evidence relating to them.

1. The signs of alliance between the Pelasgoi and the inhabitants of particular parts of the country:

2. The signs of a difference of race, pervading the population, and more or less running parallel with differences of rank:

[1] Cramer's Greece, vol. iii. p. 244.
[2] Comp. Ἀργέϊος Ὀδύη, and the passage Od. xi. 260-265.
[3] Strabo, viii. 6, p. 870.

3. The signs of an occupation of the country prior to that by the Hellenic tribes:

Independently of another head of inquiry, to be dealt with at a later stage, namely the relation of the Trojan to the Greek race:

And, again, independently of evidence supplied by the later tradition.

1. The Arcades [1] of Homer show signs of connection with the Pelasgoi.

In the Catalogue the Arcades are described as ἀγχιμαχηταί, or heavy-armed,[2] and we are also told that they had no care for maritime pursuits. In both respects, their relation to the people of Troas is remarkable. Homer nowhere else uses the epithet except for the Dardanians, whose position in Troas resembled that of the Arcadians in Peloponnesos. And the Trojans were so destitute of vessels, that the shipwright who built for Paris is mentioned as on that account a notable character.[3] Nor do we hear of a Trojan ship in any case but his. Heavy-armed troops are furnished by a settled peasantry, light-armed by a population of less settled habits. The absence of maritime pursuits tends to imply a pacific character, in an age when enterprise by sea was so intimately connected with kidnapping and rapine. Arcadia was not a poor country. In historic times it was, next to Laconia, the most populous province of Peloponnesos.[4] In the Troica it supplied sixty ships with large crews.[5] All this is accordant with Pelasgian associations.

[1] Niebuhr, Hist. of Rome, vol. i. p. 29, sets down as Pelasgian the Arcadians, the Argives, probably all the original inhabitants of Peloponnesus, the Ionians, and the people of Attica and Thessaly.
[2] Il. ii. 604, 614.
[3] Il. v. 59–64.
[4] Xen. Hell. vii. 1. 23 ; Cramer, iii. 299.
[5] Il. ii. 610.

Again, the Arcadians were commanded by Agapenor[1] the son of Ankaios. But Ankaios was of Ætolia. Ships supplied by Agamemnon,[2] and a chief not indigenous, tend to mark the Arcadians as politically subordinate, therefore as Pelasgian.

At the funeral games of Amarunkeus there were present Epeians, Pulians, and Ætolians;[3] that is to say, all the neighboring tribes except the Arcadians. Now the Homeric indications respecting the origin of games, in a marked manner tend to connect them, as we shall find, with sources other than Pelasgic.[4]

In the Seventh Iliad, Nestor relates that in his youth the Pulians and Arcadians fought, near the river Iardanos. The former seem to have been victorious; which accords with the military inferiority of Pelasgoi to an Hellenic force. Clearly, when Nestor killed their king Ereuthalion,[5] it was by the aid of Pallas; and Pallas, we shall find, is always a Hellenising deity against Pelasgians. The Pulians, as we have seen, are Achaian in a special degree.

In marked accordance with this indirect testimony, the later tradition places Lucaon son of Pelasgos in Arcadia; represents the people as autochthonous; and makes the district compete with Argolis for having given them their first seat in Peloponnesos.

We have here, too, some aid from philology. The Arcadians called themselves Προσέληνοι, which is commonly rendered 'anterior to the moon.' Now it is difficult to see why the moon, which continually waxes, wanes, and disappears, should be selected as the type

---

[1] Il. ii. 609; xxiii. 630–635.   [2] Il. ii. 612.
[3] Il. xxiii. 630–635.   [4] See *infra*, Chap. V.   [5] Il. vii. 154.

of stability and longevity among natural objects. But if we refer the origin of the word to πιό and Σιλλοί or Σιλλητες, then it becomes the appropriate form in which the Arcadian, or Pelasgian, people assert their priority in the Peloponnesos to the Hellic or Sellic races.

Until very late in the historic period, the Arcadians remained an undistinguished people. But they were the Swiss of Greece; and they supplied a hardy soldiery to any state in want of mercenary assistance, without reference to attachments of race as between Dorian and Ionian. With the Lacedæmonians they invaded Attica: with the Thebans they invaded Lacedæmon:[1] in the great siege of Syracuse, one contingent fought by the side of the invaders, the other along with the besieged.[2]

2. The Ionians (Iaones) are but once mentioned in Homer. They are one of five divisions appointed, in the Thirteenth Iliad,[3] to meet the attack of Hector, when that attack is destined to prevail. The others are the Locrians, Phthians, Epeians, and Boiotians. The same spirit of nationality, which prevents Homer from allowing any eminent Greek chieftain to be slain or wounded in fair conflict with the Trojans, apparently leads him in this place to select, (perhaps with the exception of the Epeians,[4]) some of the less distinguished portions of the army to resist the Trojans, on an occasion when the resistance is to be ineffectual. The Myrmidons are of necessity absent: but he might have placed in the post of danger those troops whom

[1] Xen. Hell. vii. 1. 23. [2] Thuc. vii. 57. [3] v. 685.
[4] They have laudatory epithets in Il. xi. 732 and xiii. 686. They were, however, worsted by the men of Pulos.

he pointedly commends, the troops of Agamemnon, or the Abantes.[1] Our finding the Ionians among undistinguished contingents tends to fix upon them a like character.

Further, they are called ἑλκεχίτωνες,[2] men with long flowing tunics. As Homer has nowhere else used the epithet, he gives us no direct aid in illustrating it. But it clearly has more or less of disparaging effect, since such an habiliment is ill-suited for military purposes. And it is in direct contrast with the epithet ἀμιτροχίτωνες of the valiant Lukioi or Lycians, whose short and spare tunic required no cincture to confine it.

These Ionians were, as it would seem, the ruling class of the Athenians, the Ἀθηναίων προλελεγμένοι;[3] or, it may be, their picked men. The praise awarded to Menestheus in the Catalogue, even if the passage be genuine, is only that of being good, to use a modern phrase, at putting his men into line.[4] The Athenian soldiers, indeed, are declared in Il. iv. 328, to be valiant, μήστωρες ἀϋτῆς; but the character of the commander is less than negative. Though of kingly parentage, he nowhere appears among the governing spirits of the army, nor is he called one of the kings, although his father Peteos had enjoyed the title;[5] and on the only occasion when we find him amid the clash of arms, namely, when the brave Lycians are threatening the part of the rampart committed to his charge, he shudders, and looks about him for aid.[6] The inferiority extends to the other Athenian chiefs, Pheidas,

---

[1] Il. ii. 542, 577.   [2] Il. xiii. 685.   [3] Il. xiii. 689.
[4] Il. ii. 554.   [5] Il. iv. 328.   [6] Il. xii. 331.

Stichios, Bias, and Iasos;[1] of whom all are undistinguished, and two, Stichios and Iasos, are 'food for powder,' slain by Hector and Æneas respectively. Here then there seems to have been bravery without qualities for command; and all this tends to exhibit the Athenians as in a marked degree Pelasgian at this epoch, stout but passive, without any of the ardor or the μένος[2] of the Hellenic character.

Something will hereafter be added to this evidence from an examination of the etymology of names in Homer.

The close relation between Athenê and Athens, however, is a sign that seems to tell in the opposite direction. But upon examining into it, we perceive that it is a local and not a personal relation. Ever active in the protection or guidance of Achilles, Agamemnon, Diomed, Odysseus, Athenê says and does nothing whatever in the War for any Athenian. Yet Athens has the epithet 'sacred,'[3] the unfailing mark in Homer of special relation to some deity; and, as far as Athenê has any favorite place of earthly residence or resort, it appears to be Athens, to which, seemingly as matter of course, she repairs from Scheriê,[4] in the Odyssey. There is something remarkable, and not easy to explain, in this combination of strong local connection with a total absence of personal care and patronage.

It is to be borne in mind that Athenê appears to have been a deity of universal worship.[5] She was regularly adored by the Trojans,[6] whom she labored to ruin.

[1] Il. xiii. 691; xv. 329, 332.   [2] Od. xi. 308.   [3] Od. xi. 823.
[4] Od. vii. 80.   [5] Infra, Chap. VIII.   [6] Il. vi. 300.

On both the occasions when Athens is placed in direct connection with the goddess, the name of Erechtheus is introduced: in the Catalogue he is stated to have been nursed by Athene, and he was the child of Aroura.[1] She (probably Athene) set him in Athens, in her (or his) rich or well-endowed temple (ἑῷ ἐνὶ πίονι νηῷ).

It is impossible wholly to shake off the apprehension of forgery in dealing with this passage, which falls short in the grammatical clearness usually so notable in Homer. On the other hand, the objections which have been taken to it seem insufficient to condemn it; to condemn at any rate the part of it I have cited, which remarkably corresponds with Od. vii. 81: there she enters the well-built house (πυκινὸν δόμον) of Erechtheus.

Erechtheus appears in the Catalogue to be described as an autochthon; and therefore probably as Pelasgian. The wealthy temple may perhaps mean a temple with a τέμενος or glebe for a priest, which we shall find to be a sign, not of Hellenic, but of Pelasgian nationality. On the whole, we cannot ignore the existence of Pelasgian signs, while we cannot find in the text of Homer any full explanation of the fact that Athene is the eponymist of Athens.

The type of Athene, however, is far too high to allow us to view her as a deity merely national. She is not circumscribed by any limits either of blood or place. This does not exclude specialities of attachment; but her special attachment to the Greeks is one apparently having reference to great qualities of mind and char-

[1] Il. ii. 547–549.

acter. The Pelasgianism of the Trojans does not, before the great quarrel, cut them off from her. She singularly loved Phereclos, who built the ships of Paris;[1] and she aided the Trojans in erecting the rampart which sheltered Heracles from the pursuing monster.[2]

There is, however, very powerful evidence outside the text of Homer to show the strongly Pelasgian character of Attica in early times. Her subsequent greatness was evidently connected with a remarkable mixture of blood, arising from her having been, during long periods, a place of refuge for fugitives, and for the worsted party expelled from other portions of Greece.

Thucydides[3] states that, from early times, Attica was inhabited by one and the same race, because the poverty of the soil offered no temptations to an invader. Hence it is, without doubt, that we find the Athenians of history ever claiming the character of autochthons. But this is in effect to call them Pelasgians.

Herodotus[4] declares the Athenians to have been Ionian, and the Ionians to be Pelasgian. Having been Pelasgians, he says, the Attican people became Hellenic, apparently by the reception of immigrants, and by a gradual amalgamation. Evidently, according to this historian, the change did not take place by an arrival of Ionians, for he declares that which Homer only suggests, that the Ionians were Pelasgian.

Some conflict, however, there was, apparently, between the urban and the rural population. The Pe-

[1] Il. v. 59–61.   [2] Il. xx. 146.   [3] l. 2.   [4] l. 56.

lasgians complained, said Hecatæus,[1] that the Athenians drove them from the soil, which they had improved in such a degree as to excite envy. The Athenians alleged that their children, when they went forth to draw water, were insulted by the Pelasgians. The Dorian San, Herodotus[2] adds, was the Ionian Sigma.

Thucydides[3] says the Athenians were the first among the Greeks to lay aside the custom of bearing arms, and to cultivate ease and luxury. We may naturally connect this fact with the undisturbed condition and pacific habits of the people: and perhaps it is partially indicated by the word ἑλκεχίτωνες, 'tunic-trailers,' already cited.

The Hesiodic tradition of Hellen and his sons does not mention Ion. It is remarkable that Euripides does not represent Ion as Hellenic, but as the adopted son of Xouthos, the real son of Creusa, an Erechtheid; in entire conformity with what, as I conceive, the text of Homer suggests.

Peisistratos and his family claimed a Neleid, that is, a non-Pelasgian descent; recognizing as it were the difference of the ruling blood.

According to Herodotus,[4] there remained in the Athens of history a portion of the wall called Pelasgic, and the primitive Athenians were called Pelasgoi Cranaoi, and were reputed to be autochthonous.

Eleusis, in Attica, was the chief seat of the worship of Demeter—a deity, as we shall find, of eminently Pelasgian character and associations.

[1] As quoted in Herod. vi. 137, 138.   [2] l. 139.
[3] L 6.   [4] l. 56; v. 64; viii. 44.

Strabo declares that ancient Attica was Ias, with an Ionian people, who supplied Asia Minor with the colonists of the Ionian migration.[1]

The careful researches of Dr. Hahn in Albania have accumulated much evidence of the Pelasgian character of the population. It includes remarkable coincidences with the institutions of Attica: for example, the fourfold division of the tribes.[2]

To us the origin of the Ionian name remains in great obscurity. It is probably related to the Pelasgian stock. It certainly appears not to be Hellenic.

3. In the Thessaly of the Greek Catalogue, not only does the paucity of tribal names leave us to suppose that the population of the districts generally had not yet distinctly emerged from what may be called Pelasgianism, and not only is this supposition confirmed by the name of Pelasgic Argos, but there are other confirmatory signs.

One of them is the worship of the River Spercheios;[3] which, though offered by Achilles for a special purpose, was also practised by Peleus, and is probably due to a strong local tradition of a Pelasgian character. His τέμενος, or glebe, also connects him with the Pelasgians.[4]

Another sign is the τέμενος or sacred glebe of Demeter at Purasos.[5] Possibly the name may be related to πυρός, wheat. Apart from this, the associations of Demeter in Homer are never Hellenic.[6] The ap-

[1] Bk. viii. p. 333.
[2] Hahn, 'Albanesische Studien,' Abschn. II. pp. 43–40, and note 19, p. 130.
[3] Il. xxiii. 144.
[4] See *infra*, Chap. VII.; also p. 106.
[5] Il. ii. 696.
[6] See *infra*, Chap. VIII.

pearance of a τύμπος in this case is also a Pelasgian sign.

The historical growth of the Graian[1] (Greek) name out of the Greek settlements in Italy connects it with communities highly Pelasgian. In Homer we find that name only in Boiotia, a land of rich cultivation, like the Italian colonies. But Aristotle[2] places the Graicoi in the ancient Hellas, a portion of Thessaly, about Dodona and the Acheloos, which, he says, was inhabited by them and by the Selloi. Thus the Graian name serves further to associate Thessaly with the Pelasgoi.

4. The name Iasos has an early and important place in the Homeric tradition.

(a) The phrase 'Iasou Argos,' which means Western Peloponnesos,[3] appears to indicate a dynasty, or dominion, of an Iasos in that country.

(b) Demeter (in Crete, according to Hesiod) gives way to her passion for Iasion,[4] a son or descendant of Iasos, in a tilled field.

(c) Demetor Iasides, a son, or rather a descendant, of Iasos, is represented by the pseud-Odysseus as reigning in Cyprus[5] at the period of his return to Ithaca, and as being in xenial relations with Egypt, the people of which, he says, made a present of him to Demetor. This clearly shows that there had been an Iasid dominion in Cyprus.

(d) Amphion and Zethos, who first founded and

[1] The name Graicos, according to K. O. Müller, came back into use with the Alexandrian poets, through the old common tongue of Macedonia. — Müller's Orchomenos, p. 119.
[2] Meteorol. l. 14.   [3] See above, Chap. II. p. 48.
[4] Od. v. 125.   [5] Od. xvii. 442.

walled in the city of Thebes, were Iasids:[1] Amphion at one time (ποτε) reigned in Minyan Orchomenos.

(e) Iasos,[2] son of Sphelos and grandson of Boukolos, was one of the Athenian commanders, and fell by the hand of Æneas; this too without any commemoration: from both which circumstances we perceive that he was in no great esteem, and was most probably not of Hellenic, but of Pelasgian blood.

The attachment of Demeter to Crete was plainly connected with the Pelasgian period. The secondary place given to Iasos in the war, and the etymology of the names of his ancestry, seem to establish his Pelasgian extraction. If Amphion and Zethos were, as it appears probable, displaced from Bœotia by Kadmos and the Phœnicians, they were probably of a Pelasgian family: and indeed it would be very difficult to give evidence of any Hellenic race or family at their epoch, which is between four and five generations before the Troica. Lastly, Cyprus, distant as it was from Greece, was evidently in some position of qualified subordination to its ruling house; because, when the expedition to Troy was meditated, Kinures,[3] its ruler, sent a beautiful gift to Agamemnon, probably more as an apology for non-appearance, than as a disinterested token of good-will.

All the several indications then converge upon this point, that the name of Iasos appears to bear no Hellenic character. It has certain points of contact at least with some of the races that dwell in Egypt; and likewise with Phœnicia through the city of Thebes, and through the indubitable presence of a Phœnician

---

[1] Od. xi. 262, 283. [2] Il. xv. 337. [3] Il. xi. 19–23.

influence in Cyprus. Anterior to, and apparently reaching beyond the Hellenic name, its most marked associations appear to be Pelasgian.

5. There are abundant marks of a Pelasgian character in the population of Crete.

We know that the ruling family in Crete was Phœnician; but the wealth of the hundred-citied island[1] was just what might be expected to arise from the early combination of Phœnician enterprise with Pelasgian industry.

There were many races in Crete, and there was a mixture of tongue.[2] This appears to indicate the presence of the Phœnician element in considerable force with its Semitic form of speech, as we have no reason to suppose, among the races actually named, any radical difference of language. In this passage the speaker is addressing Penelope, and it is in accordance with the uniform usage of the Poems, that he should mention only races which had been domesticated in Greece.

Those races are, 1. Achaioi, 2. Eteocretes, 3. Kudones, 4. Dorieis, 5. Pelasgoi. Of these, the first and fourth may at once be classed as Hellenic. With respect to the Eteocretes, we may most naturally suppose them to have been part of the Pelasgian family, whose date of arrival was more remote, in relation to whom all the other races had thus been strangers, and to whom therefore is given a name that is the equivalent of autochthons. The Kudones appear to be of similar origin. They lived on a Cretan river Iardanos.[3] This was the name of the river in

---

[1] Il. II. 649. In Od. xix. 174, ninety.
[2] Od. xix. 175. [3] Od. iii. 292.

Peloponnesos, on the banks of which the Pulians fought the Arcadians. The battle,¹ as being one between Achaians and Pelasgians, was probably on Arcadian ground; and the name of *rapid* Keladon, given to the stream, also shows that it was on the high land.

This Pelasgian population, with its less warlike, possibly also less energetic, habits, appears to have sunk at a later period into servitude. According to Ephorus, as quoted by Athenæus,² there were in Crete festivals of the slave population, during which freemen were not permitted to come within the town walls, while the slaves were supreme, and were competent to flog the free. These festivals were held in Kudonia, the city of the Kudones.

Fifthly, the name of Pelasgoi speaks for itself.

6. The Leleges have a place on the Trojan side, apparently more important than that of the Kaukones. They appear, with the Kaukones and Pelasgoi,³ as part of the force which was encamped upon the plain during the period when the Greeks were shut up within their entrenchment. Priam had for one of his wives Laothoo, daughter of their king Altes.⁴ He calls them lovers of battle. Æneas says⁵ that Pallas 'incited Achilles to make havoc of Trojans and Leleges.' Homer can hardly mean, under the name of Leleges, to speak of the whole body of allies, which included both Pelasgians and his favorite Lycians. The name may be one covering some of the allied contingents; or it may signify the fourth and fifth divisions of the

---

¹ Il. vii. 134; xi. 735-752(?).   ² vi. p. 263.
³ Il. x. 429.   ⁴ Il. xxi. 85.   ⁵ Il. xx. 90.

Trojan army, which appear in the Catalogue[1] without any national or tribal designation, immediately before the Pelasgoi and the rest of the allies.

We have abundant instances in Homer of double names attaching to the same population. The people of Elis are Eleioi and Epeioi. The Dolopians are included under the Phthians; perhaps under Achaians and Hellenes.[2] Five races in particular are named as inhabiting Crete; but all, possibly with others, are included in the Cretes[3] of the Second Iliad. The Ionian name, with that of the Kaukones, and of Leleges, not to speak of the Temmikes, Aones, Huantes, Telebooi, of whom we do not hear in Homer, are most probably subdivisions of the great Pelasgian category. On the whole, it seems safest to adopt the conclusion of Bishop Thirlwall, that in all likelihood 'the name Pelasgians was a general one, like that of Saxons, Franks, or Alemanni; but that each of the Pelasgian tribes had also one peculiar to itself.'[4] The evidence directly deducible from Homer tends to this conclusion; and it is powerfully sustained, as we shall see, by more copious indirect testimony.

The work of Dr. Hahn affords ample evidence of their occupation of Epiros, which was also recognized by the tradition of the ancients.[5]

The belief that the Pelasgoi were the original inhabitants of Greece, appears to be held undoubtingly by the modern Greeks, if we may trust the recent work of Petrides[6] upon the ancient history of his country.

---

[1] Il. ii. 828–839. [2] Il. ii. 683; ix. 484; xvi. 186.
[3] Od. xix. 175; Il. ii. 645. [4] History of Greece, vol. i. ch. ii.
[5] Strabo, bk. v. p. 221. Leake's Travels in Northern Greece, vol. iv. p. 174. [6] Chap. i. pp. 2, 8 (Corfu, 1830).

We are in no way obliged to suppose that tribes of so wide a diffusion came into Greece by a single route. The prevailing opinion[1] of the ancient writers was that their first seat was in the Peloponnesos. Homer gives abundant signs of them in Thessaly, but also in Crete and in Cyprus. It seems probable that they may have arrived both by the landward route of the Thracian coast, and by the stepping-stones, so to speak, which the southern islands afforded them.

If there has been presented reasonable ground for the conclusion that the Pelasgians formed the base of the Greek nation, it is interesting to observe, by the light of history, how the most durable vitality of a people resides in the mass, while the energies of mere class, or of any branch socially separate from the trunk, are liable to exhaustion if they are not refreshed by popular contact; as water taken from the sea grows foul, while the sea itself is ever fresh. The astute Aiolid, the high-souled and fiery Achaian, the Dorian with his iron will and unconquerable tenacity — each for a time enjoys ascendancy and disappears; and the districts which successively attain to military pre-eminence in the later historic ages, are Bœotia, Macedonia, Arcadia, Epiros, none of which had been the early depositories of powerful Hellenic influences. Lastly, Achaia emerged into a late celebrity. It is probable that we ought to consider this name, not so much in connection with the old and famous Achaian race, as with the party worsted in the great Dorian conquest: and if this be so, we shall be safe in concluding that, in all likelihood, the province had retained throughout a dominant Pelasgian character.

[1] Cramer's Greece, I. 17.

The etymology of the Pelasgian name has been long and variously discussed without any conclusive issue. Some draw it from Peleg of the tenth chapter of Genesis, a name said to mean 'partition,' that is, of the earth: this opinion is questioned by Marsh,[1] and rejected by Clinton.[2] Again, it has been derived from pelargoi, the Greek name for storks. This, according to some, because the Pelasgians were wanderers, and the stork is migratory. But the periodical movement of the stork seems to have no great correspondence with an irregularly roving habit in a people. Aristophanes[3] appears undoubtedly to make the name of storks a vehicle for a jest on the Pelasgian origin of the Athenians. Another plea seems to me more plausible. The stork is a social bird: in the East it settles on the roofs of houses; it freely follows the ploughman along his furrow; and its habits thus, in both points, supply links of association with the first appearance of a people of husbandmen. The stork was one of the sacred birds of the Egyptians.

Some have derived the name from pelagos, a word used in Greek for the sea. And this, either because the Pelasgians came by sea, or because they came from beyond sea. It seems doubtful, however, whether 'sea' was the proper or only the second meaning of pelagos. We have the phrases, ἅλος ἐν πελάγεσσι (Homer), πόντιον πέλαγος (Pindar), ἁλὸς πελαγία (Æschylus), πέλαγος θαλάσσης (Apollonius), all of which seem to show that pelagos, like aequor, may mean 'a plain,' and may thus come to mean the expanse or level of the sea. Strabo tells us of a people called

[1] Horæ Pelasg. c. 1. sub fin.   [2] Fasti Hellenici, 1. 97.
[3] Aves, 1354.

Pelagones in Macedonia, and in Homer we find the names Pelagon and Pēlegon. Hesychius renders the word πέλαγος as meaning greatness or depth, or the breadth of the sea. If the name of Pelasgoi be related to the word pelagos, it may be either because they were great and numerous, or because they were settlers upon plains. So Thrēx, its counterpart, akin to τρηχύς, meant the inhabitant of a rough or rocky place, a mountaineer.[1]

Of the signs of a difference of race among the Greek population more or less in correspondence with a difference of ranks, some have been exhibited in the examination of the Achaian name, which appears properly to have designated an aristocracy formed from a conquering or dominant race, and placed amid a population of distinct and less aspiring blood.

Yet the difference must not be overstated. By common consent we are dealing with different branches from the Aryan stem: and the distinction of Hellic and Pelasgic finds a correlative classification in the Italian races, where the Oscans hold the place of the Helloi. It is represented indeed in our country by the distinction among Normans, Scandinavians, Saxons (or the group of tribes collectively so called with no great propriety), and Celts; though it may be more or less doubtful at which point of division we should draw the line among these several races.

I shall endeavor to show that the Trojan War may in some sense be considered as the conflict of Hellic with Pelasgic elements. But it is remarkable, 1. that

[1] K. O. Müller (Orchomenos, p. 110), assuming Pelasgos to be identical with Pelargos, derives the word from πέλω, ' to be,' ' to be wont to be,' and so ' to frequent ' or ' inhabit,' together with Ἄργος.

Homer nowhere represents the Trojans as speaking a tongue different from that of the Greeks; 2. that the Trojan soldiery are nowhere represented as generally inferior to the Greek force; it is the superiority of the chiefs which determines the fate of battle throughout the Poems.

With respect indeed to tongue, Homer tells us that the Trojan public called the son of Hector by the name of Astuanax, which is of Greek etymology; and we have in Troas[1] examples of that double nomenclature which is commonly interpreted as referring to the epochs of two different nationalities, the second of them corresponding, for all we know, with the contemporary Greek tongue, though we are made aware that a variety of languages were spoken among the allies of Troy.[2] A long list of names, common to Greek and Trojan personages, may be drawn out from the Poems.

But while we greatly lack positive information in the case of Troas, we possess it in the case of Italy. Care indeed must be taken to exclude from any comparison those words which were transported bodily out of the Greek into the Latin tongue after literary communion had begun, and according to the practice which Horace[3] has described and recommended.

Niebuhr[4] laid down these propositions, which appear to be reasonable.

1. That the words truly common to the Greek and Latin languages are Pelasgian:

2. That they chiefly relate to tillage and to peaceful life:

[1] Il. ii. 813; xx. 74. [2] Il. iv. 438; x. 420.
[3] De Arte Poet. 53.
[4] Hare and Thirlwall's Transl. vol. i. p. 65.

3. That, accordingly, the Pelasgians were given to peace and to husbandry:

4. Conversely, that the words in which the two tongues differ are due to another race, and indicate its pursuits.

Speaking generally, those words of the Latin and Greek which most closely correspond, are

1. First elements of the structure of a language, such as pronouns, prepositions, numerals.

2. Words relating to the commonest objects of perception, and the primary wants of life, and forms of labor.

Under the second head the following lists are presented, by way not of exhaustion, but of example.

1. OBJECTS OF INANIMATE NATURE.

ἀήρ	aer	νέφος	nebula
αἰθήρ	æther	(νίξ) νιφάς	nix
ἅλς, θάλασσα	salum	νύξ	nox
ἄντρον	antrum	πεύκη	pix
ἀστήρ	astrum	πόλος	polus
αὔρα	aura	πόντος	pontus
Διός (Ζεύς)	dies	ῥῖγος	frigus
δρόσος	ros	σελήνη	luna
ἔαρ	ver	σκόπελος	scopulus
ἐνιαυτός, ἧνις	annus	σπέος, σπήλαιον	spelunca
ἔρα	terra	(ὕδωρ)	sudor
ἕσπερος	vesper	ὑετός	{ fluvius, pluvius }
ἥλιος	sol		
καῖλον	cœlum	ὕλη	sylva
λᾶας	lapis	φῦκος	fucus
λάκκος, λάκυς	lacus	φύλλον	folium
		χαμαί	humus
λίσσω, λίπη ἐν λικάβας	lux	χειμών	hyems
μήν	mensis	ὥρα	hora

7

II. TREES, PLANTS.

ἴον . . . . . viola	φηγός . . . . fagus
ῥόδον . . . . rosa	

III. OF ANIMATED NATURE.

ἀλώπηξ . . . . vulpes	κύων, κυνός . . . canis
ἀμνός . . . . agnus	λέων . . . . . leo
βοῦς . . . . . bos	λύκος . . . . lupus
ἔγχελυς . . . anguilla	ὄϊς . . . . . ovis
θήρ . . . . . fera	οὖθαρ . . . . uber
ἵππος . . . . equus	πῶλος . . . . pullus
ἰχθύς . . . . piscis	ταῦρος . . . taurus
κάπρος . . . aper	ὗς . . . . . sus
ἀρνός . . . . aries	ὠκύπτερος . . . accipiter

IV. OBJECTS CONNECTED WITH FOOD.

ἄμπελος . . . . panipinus	μέλι . . . . . mel
γάλα, γάλακτος } . lac, lactis	μῆλον . . . . malum
γλῆος . . . . }	οἶνος . . . . vinum
λαῖς . . . . . dapes	σῖτος . . . . cibus
ἐλαία . . . . olea	σῦκον . . . . ficus
ἔλαιον . . . . oleum	τρύγη . . . . fruges
κάλαμος . . . calamus	ἀ-τρύγετος . . . triticum
καινή . . . . coena	ᾠόν . . . . . ovum
κρέας . . . . caro	

V. RELATED TO OUTDOOR LABOR.

ἀγρός . . . . ager	ζεῦγος } . . . jugum
ἄροτρον . . . aratrum	ζυγόν }	
ἄρουρα . . . arvum	κῆπος, σηκός . . sepes
	ὄρχατος . . . hortus

VI. NAVIGATION.

ἄγκυρα . . . . ancora	λιμήν . . . . limen
ἐρετμόν . . . remus	ναῦς . . . . navis
κυβερνήτης . . gubernator	πούς . . . . pes

VII. DWELLINGS.

αἰθάλη	favilla	θύραι	fores
αὐλή	aula	κληΐς	clavis
δόμος	domus	λέχος	lectus
ἔδος	sedes	οἶκος	vicus
θάλαμος	thalamus		

VIII. CLOTHING.

ἐσθής	vestis	χλαῖνα	læna

IX. THE HUMAN BODY.

γόνυ	genu	μηρός	femur
δείκνυμι	digitus	μυελός	medulla
ἕλκος	ulcus	ὀδούς	dens
ἔντερον	venter	ὀστίον	os (ossis)
ἧπαρ	jecur	παλάμη	palma
καρδίη } κῆρ }	cor	-πέζα (comp.) } πούς }	pes, pedis
κεφαλή	caput	ὠλένη	ulna
κόμη	coma	ὦμος	armus
λάξ	calx	ὤψ	os (oris)
λάπτω	labrum		

X. THE FAMILY.

γένος	gens, genus	φρήτηρ } φρήτρη }	frater
ἑκυρός	socer		
μήτηρ	mater	χήρη, } χηρωστής }	heres
πατήρ	pater		
υἱός	filius		

XI. SOCIETY.

ἐλεύθερος	liber	τέκτων (στέγω) }	tectum / tego
παλλακίς	pellex		
ῥέζω (ῥέξω)	rex	φώρ	fur

XII. GENERAL IDEAS.

αἰών	ævum	λήθη } λήτω }	letum
ἄλγος	algor		

ἄνεμος	. . . .	animus
αὐδή	. . . .	audio
βίος	. . . .	vita
βίοτος	. . . .	victus
γεύω, γεύσις	. .	gustus
δόσις	. . . .	dos
δῶρον	. . . .	donum
εἴδω	. . . .	video
θεός	. . . .	deus
θιγγάνω	. . . .	tango
θυμός	. . . .	fumus
ἴς	. . . . . .	vis
κνίσση	. . . .	nidor

μένος	. . . .	mens
μόρος	. . . .	mors
μορφή	. . . .	forma
νεύω	. . . .	numen
νόος	. . . .	nosco
ὀδμή	. . . .	odor
ὀδύνη	. . . .	odium
ὄνομα	. . . .	nomen
ῥώμη	. . . .	Roma, robur
ὕπνος	. . . .	somnus
φάτις, φατόν	. .	fatum
φήμη	. . . .	fama
φυγή, φύζα	. .	fuga

XIII. ADJECTIVES OF COMMON USE.

ἀγκός	. . . .	uncus
ἄλλος	. . . .	alius
βραδύς, βαρδύς	.	tardus
βραχύς	. . . .	brevis
γενναῖος	. . . .	gnavus
γραῦς	. . . .	gravis
γυρός	. . . .	curvus
δεξιός	. . . .	dexter
ἐρυθρός	. . . .	ruber, rufus
ἡδύς	. . . .	suavis
κυρτός	. . . .	curvus
λεῖος	. . . .	levis
λεπτός } λεγύς }	· ·	{ lentus { levis
μάσσων	. . . .	major

μέγας	. . . .	magnus
μείων	. . . .	minor
νέος	. . . .	novus
ὅλος	. . . .	solus
ὀρθός	. . . .	ordo
παῦρος	. . . .	{ parvus { paucus
παχύς	. . . .	pinguis
πικρός	. . . .	acris
πλατύς	. . . .	latus
πλέος	. . . .	plenus
πυρρός	. . . .	furvus
τέρην	. . . .	tener
ὕπτιος	. . . .	supinus
χύος	. . . .	cavus

For such a people as we have supposed the Pelasgians to be, here is no inconsiderable equipment of words. But there are exceptions.

1. In regard to religion, the stock is scanty. We have deus related to θεός, numen to νεύω, rex to ῥέζω, in virtue probably of the sacrificial office of a primitive king: and we may add, as correlatives, λοιβή to libo, and ἀρύομαι, ἀρυτήρ to ara, orare, orator. But this is

THE PELASGOI.

little: and there is a great lack of correspondence in the principal words, such as, on the Greek side, ἱερός, ἅγιος, θύω, βωμός, νηός, ἄγαλμα, τέμενος, εὔχομαι, and on the other, sacer, sanctus, pius, templum, preces, vates, macto, mola. In one case, or in both, there must have been a great displacement of the Pelasgic vocabulary. And as the Roman religion was far more Pelasgian than the Greek, it is probable that this displacement, if it occurred in one only of the two peninsulas, occurred in Greece.

2. The words relating to war are almost without exception irreducible to agreement.

αἰχμή	cuspis, mucro, acies	ἀλωαί	castra
		κνημίς	ocrea
		κολεός	vagina
Ἄρης	Mars	κύκλος	rota
ἅρμα, δίφρος	currus, rheda	κυνέη	galea
		μάχη, ὑσμίνη	pugna, proelium
ἀσπίς, σάκος	scutum, clypeus	ὀϊστός, ἰός	sagitta
βέλος	telum	πόλεμος	bellum
βιός, τόξον	arcus	ῥυμός	temo
ἔγχος, δόρυ	hasta	σάλπιγξ	tuba, classicum
θώρηξ	lorica		
ἀλωή[1]	tabernaculum	φάσγανον, ξίφος	ensis

Here the most striking correspondence is that of Arês with Mars, both used to signify war itself, as well as to mean the god of war. But Arês, though he is not easy to trace, appears to be a deity whose origin would assign him exclusively neither to the Pelasgian nor to the Hellenic family.[2] The relationship of βέλος

---
[1] Caesar, De Bell. Civil. b. iii. c. 96.
[2] See infra, Chap. VIII.

to telum appears clear enough. Except a rather faint similarity of πόλεμος to bellum, and of θώρηξ to lorica, there is no apparent connection between any other words in the list.

It is also worth observing that, while the Greeks derive the important ethical words βέλτερος, better, from βέλος, and ἄριστος, best, from ἄρης, the Latins are content with optimus, obtained from a common root with opes, wealth; possibly, however, as we, not much to our honor, say that one man is *worth* more than another.

With respect to the terms belonging to navigation, it is remarkable how they bear upon rowing, its rudest form, and do not include the names for mast, yard, or sail.

Again, the use of metals is slight in the earliest stage of society. Even with the Greeks of Homer only one, χαλκός, or copper, was at all common; and we may observe a great want of correspondence between the Greek and the Roman names for these invaluable commodities.

1. χρυσός . . . aurum	4. σίδηρος . . . ferrum
2. ἄργυρος . . . argentum	5. κασσίτερος . . . stannum
3. χαλκός . . . æs	6. μόλιβος, μόλυβδος plumbum

The Greek δοῦλος, again, is in marked contrast with the Latin servus. We might on the whole plausibly suppose that slavery was not a Pelasgian institution at the time when the Greek and Italian branches of the race parted company. War and maritime adventure were the chief feeders of that institution; and the Pelasgians, as we see, were not of themselves addicted to either, however good the materials they afforded for soldiery.

Nearly all those Greek words which are in close affinity with the Latin are found in Homer.

It seems, then, in sum, that the Pelasgian tongue supplied both peninsulas with most of the words relating to the primary experience, and to the elementary wants and productions, of life; but not with those of a more arduous range, such as war, art, policy, and song. And the religious vocabulary of the Greeks was probably supplied from Hellenic sources.

There is also a very traceable distinction in the names of persons throughout the Iliad. I am far from contending, that we are to suppose them to be in general authentic. But the elements, out of which Homer has constructed them, will indicate a marked difference of character and pursuits. Homer gives his Phaiakes names generally connected with nautical habits, in accordance with his picture of the people. It is probable that he proceeds on a similar principle in other cases. The evidence which names, analyzed according to this hypothesis, will supply, tends to show the strength of the Pelasgian element — 1. among the Trojans; 2. in the inferior class of Greeks; 3. particularly in certain portions of Greece; while 4. the Lycian names, though on the Trojan side, appear to fall into an opposite class.

The test of a Pelasgian leaning in the names I suppose to be their connection with rural, pacific, or industrious habits, and the like. The opposite class express ideas belonging to glory, policy, mental powers, martial vigor and operations.

We must not apply the rule too closely to slaves: such as Eumaios, Eurucleia, Eurumedousa, Alkippé;

for high-born slaves were frequently obtained by policy and by the chances of war.[1]

It is also to be observed that the names etymologically related to the horse are almost exclusively on the Trojan side. Such are Hippasos, Hippothoös, Hippolochos (Lycian), Hippodamas, Hippodamos, Hippocoon, Hippomachos, Hippotion, Melanippos, Euippos, Echepolos. Hippodamos, too, will be remembered as one of the stock or staple epithets of Hector. On the other side I have only noticed Hipponoos.[2] In Homer, the horse-feeding country is the plain country.[3] And Thessaly had already begun to obtain the pre-eminence in its breed of horses, which distinguished it in the historic period; for the two best teams 'by far,'[4] in the Greek army, were Thessalian. This may perhaps be the link of association between the horse and our Pelasgian lowlanders.

Again, the names connected with gates are generally of the Trojan party. There are Pulaios, Pulon, Pulartes, and Pulaimenes. Of the Greeks we have Eurupulos. But all these appear to be the names of leaders or prominent personages.

Among Attic names we find Pheidas, Stichios, Spheolos, Boucolos. These names belong to prominent personages. But an etymology relating to such ideas as parsimony and tillage is such as we do not find among the Hellenic races in a corresponding rank.

Among Trojans slain, without much note of distinction, we find Amphiteros, Echios, Puris, Polumelos, Argeas (compare Argeioi), Dresos, Opheltios, Bouco-

[1] Od. xv. 418.   [2] Il. xi. 303.
[3] Od. iii. 263.   [4] Il. ii. 763, 770.

lion, Melanthios (compare Melanthios and Melantho of the Odyssey, both servants). Many of the names accompanying these are of doubtful etymology: comparatively few relate to high qualities or pursuits.

In the Eleventh Iliad, Hector slays in a mass nine persons,[1] who are called ἡγεμόνες, or leaders, as opposed to the πληθύς or common soldiery. But as none of these are anywhere else even mentioned, and as Homer never allows Greeks really distinguished to fall wholesale by the Trojan sword or spear, we cannot render this as meaning more than that they were officers. Accordingly we find a mixture of names; Aisumnos, Autonoos, Agelaos, are of the Hellenic class: Dolops, Opites, Opheltios, Oros, and perhaps Hipponoos, of the Pelasgic. Dolops, however, is the son of Clutos, a name belonging to another order.

When we turn to the Lycians, whose affinities are plainly not Pelasgian,[2] we find that Odysseus slays in succession Koiranos, Alastor, Chromios, Aleandros, Halios, Noemon, Prutanis. These names are all probably of the Hellenic class; for Halios means maritime, and we find no presumably Pelasgian names which point to maritime pursuits (Astualos[3] is simply local); while Chromios seems to mean bright-colored (χρῶμα), i.e. beautiful. All the others are clearly of a patrician cast.

We find in the Iliad ten legitimate sons of Antenor, and one bastard. Eight of the ten have names palpably of the Hellenic order: Agenor, Acamas, Archilochos, Demoleon, Echeclos, Iphidamas, Laodamas, Laodocos. Nor can the other two, Coon and Helicaon,

[1] Il. xi. 304. [2] Il. v. 677. [3] Il. vi. 29.

be referred to the Pelasgian class. The bastard is Pedaios, Il. v. 70: he was brought up on the same footing as the rest.

It will be remembered that Homer expressly declares the Myrmidons to be Hellenic and Achaian. Now we have named among them Patroclos, Menoitios, Menesthios, Eudoros, Peisandros, Maimalos (μαιμάω), Alkimedon, Laerkes, Automedon. Every one of these names is of what I have described as the Hellenic character.

Upon the whole, and without any allegation of a rigid uniformity, indeed with a confessed inability to assign an etymology for many of the Homeric names, still it may be held that, where we have already on other grounds found reason to presume Pelasgian blood, there the names are frequently related to peace, industry, wealth, and are not of a soaring character: whereas in cases of high station generally, and of clear Hellenic blood, they refer to valor, fame, command, mental power, and the like.

The chief of all the Homeric signs that Greece had been occupied, before the Achaian period, by a non-Hellenic race, is to be found in the sphere of religion. I will not anticipate what there will be an opportunity of unfolding in detail hereafter.[1] It may suffice for the present to observe, that while the genius of the Olympian system of Homer is intensely human or anthropomorphic, we can trace, especially outside of that system, but partially as adopted into it, the remains of a religion of a different order, based, principally, at the least, upon the worship of Nature-Powers,

---

[1] *Infra*, Chap. VII.

that is to say, of the powers discerned in material and sensible nature.

I now turn to glance at some of the extra-Homeric evidence of the wide extension of the Pelasgoi at an early period.[1]

Besides associating Dodona both with Hellic and Pelasgic races, Hesiod may be interpreted as personifying Pelasgos: a testimony legendary in itself, but betokening the importance of the race.[2]

Asios, a very ancient poet, as quoted by Pausanias, represents Pelasgos to have been the child of Earth, born upon the mountains that he might be the father of men.[3] Æschylus, in the Supplices,[4] makes him the son of the earth-born Palaichthon; from him the Pelasgians take their name: his dominion reaches from the Strumon northwards to the Peloponnesos. In the reign of this Pelasgos, Danaos comes to Greece. Of Pelasgos, Argos in the historic period professed to show the tomb. Arcadia held the tradition that he taught the use of dwellings and clothes, and to eat chestnuts instead of roots, grass, and leaves.[5] Thessaly had its separate tradition of him.

According to Herodotus, Greece was anciently called Pelasgia: the Peloponnesian women under Danaos were Pelasgiotides: the Arcadians and people of Aigialeia (afterwards Achaia) were Pelasgian: the case of Attica has already been mentioned: recollections of the Pelasgian worship were preserved in his day at Dodona: the Pelasgian race subsisted in Samothrace and Lemnos, and in Plakiè and Skulakè, settlements on

---

[1] See Bishop Marsh, Horæ Pelasgicæ, Cambridge, 1815.
[2] Hes. Fragm. x. 2.   [3] Paus. viii. 1. 2.   [4] v. 247.
[5] Paus. viii. 2. 2.

the Hellespont.¹ He writes² that they use a foreign tongue; and at this we need not wonder, when they and the Pelasgians of the Greek peninsula had moved for so many generations on separate and diverging lines.

Thucydides places the spot, or building, called Pelasgicon, under the Acropolis at Athens; and states that the Pelasgian race was the race principally diffused over Greece in early times. He also calls the Pelasgians of his own day barbaroi; the name then applied by Greeks to everything not Greek. He adds that they were of the same family, the Tursenoi, who anciently occupied Athens.³

Theocritus, early in the third century before Christ, describes the Pelasgians as the principal race in Greece before the Troïca; and Apollonius, two generations later, calls Thessaly their country. The Scholiast on this passage quotes Sophocles in the Inachos as declaring that Pelasgoi and Argeioi were the same: which, for those within the limits of Greece, is very nearly the conclusion suggested by the text of Homer as a whole.⁴

Strabo states that the Pelasgoi were the earliest lords of Greece; that the oracle of Dodona was a Pelasgian foundation; that Thessaly was called Pelasgic Argos; that, according to Ephorus, Pelasgia was a name of the Peloponnesos; and he gives us the fragment of Euripides, which reports that Danaos changed the name of its inhabitants from Pelasgiotai to Danaoi.⁵

¹ Herod. i. 146; ii. 52, 56, 171; vii. 94.
² Herod. i. 57.   ³ Thucyd. I. 3; v. 100.
⁴ Theocr. Idyll. xv. 136-140; Apoll. Argonaut. i. 580; and Schol. Paris.   ⁵ Strabo. vii. p. 327; v. p. 221.

Dionysius looks upon Peloponnesos as the first seat of the race, and affirms that it was Hellenic: meaning, probably, that it entered into the composition of the Hellenic body.[1]

Niebuhr[2] shows the wide range of Pelasgian occupancy in Italy: Cramer, in Greece and Asia Minor.[3]

[1] Dion. Halic. l. 17.
[2] Hist. chap. iii.
[3] Geogr. of Ancient Greece, vol. I. p. 15.

CHAPTER IV.

Hellas.

The name which the Greeks have given their country for a period approaching three thousand years, and which foreign countries have incorrectly rendered by the term Greece, is Hellas. It has a secondary place in Homer; and yet there are indications of its coming greatness. With Hellas as a territorial name, we meet not unfrequently in Homer; but we likewise have the derivatives of that word,—

1. Hellenes, Il. ii. 684.
2. Panhellenes, Il. ii. 530.
3. Kephallenes, Il. ii. 631 *et alibi*.

And we have also the primitive tribal name from which it is itself derived, Helloi, or Selloi, Il. xvi. 284.

We first make acquaintance with the Hellas of Homer in the Catalogue. He takes unusual pains to fix in his picture, as it were with fast colors, the contingent of Achilles. In four lines he represents them,—

1. As occupying a part of Pelasgic Argos or Thessaly.
2. As occupying Alos, Alopé, Trechin, with Phthié

and Hellas. The three places named are probably the chief or only towns.[1]

3. As bearing the designations (1) of Myrmidons, (2) of Hellenes, (3) of Achaioi.

In Homer, great part of Greece is wholly without territorial names; and, when such names appear, we must not at once assume that they are employed with the same precision as in later times, when they came to signify districts of fixed and known delimitation.

Hellas is named ten times in the Poems; four times together with Argos, in the set phrase καθ' Ἑλλάδα καὶ μέσον Ἄργος,[2] 'throughout Hellas and mid-Argos:' four times obviously in the same sense as in Il. ii. 683; and three of the four times in immediate connection with Phthiè, and with reference to territory under the dominion of Peleus.[3]

But, in Il. ix. 447, Phœnix says that he left Hellas to enter the dominions of Peleus, and in Il. ix. 478, that he left Hellas, and entered Phthiè. Yet the Catalogue, and three other passages, show us, that a part at least of the dominions of Peleus was called Hellas; and the Myrmidons were also called Hellenes, and are indeed the only people to whom that designation is expressly given.

Now, when Phœnix thus took refuge, he was flying from his father Amuntor, who dwelt in Eleon;[4] and this Eleon, as we find from the Catalogue, was in the land of the Boiotoi.[5] Consequently the name Hellas, besides designating at least a part of the kingdom of

---

[1] See the Catalogue, Il. ii. 603 seqq., 615 seqq.
[2] Od. i. 344; iv. 726, 816; xv. 80.
[3] Il. ii. 683; ix. 395; xvi. 595; Od. xi. 490.
[4] Il. x. 266.   [5] Il. ii. 500.

Peleus, embraced the country as far as to include Bœotia.

Accordingly, it must have included the country of the Locroi, afterwards called Locris. So that, when Homer says the Oilean Ajax excelled, in the art of casting the spear, 'the Panhellenes,' that is, all the Hellenes, 'and the Achaians,' it is pretty plain that the name Hellenes in his view embraced the Locroi.

We find, then, that the two passages, where Hellas is named by Phœnix in contradistinction to Phthiê, are in general harmony (according to the results of our previous inquiry[1]) with those where it is mentioned with Argos; and that, in both, it is, without any rigid definition of boundary, a general name for the parts of Greece north of the Peloponnesos.

And the four passages, in which the name Hellas is applied to territory under the sway of Peleus, do not compel us to give a second sense to the term; for they do not imply that Peleus ruled all Hellas, but only that his dominions extended beyond the territory specially called Phthiê, and included part of what had Hellas for its ruling appellation.

Phthiê itself is remarkable as the only territorial name, denoting a district of country without reference to a town, which we find in the Greece of Homer north of the Isthmus of Corinth. We may regard it as carved out of Hellas, and so distinguished from it when mentioned alone; yet included in it when Northern Greece is named as a whole. The phrase 'Pelasgic Argos' is hardly an exception, since that appears rather to be a description given by the Poet of the great Pelasgian

[1] *Supra*, Chap. II.

Lowlands, than a recognized and current title. So 'the plain of York' is a descriptive phrase, not an established territorial name.

It is plain that Phthié was the principal part of the dominions of Peleus, since it is used for the whole of them,[1] like England for the United Kingdom. It was a rich and fertile country.

Yet its inhabitants are never called Phthioi. This name is given to two other Thessalian contingents, the second under Podarkes, and the fourth under Medon.[2] And here we have a remarkable indication of the distinction between the Hellenic and the Pelasgian races. We cannot doubt that the kingdom of Peleus had been inhabited by Phthioi, since they had given it the name Phthié. We have no reason to suppose these Phthians were displaced by the Myrmidons, since we find Phthians and Myrmidons side by side in the same army. But the more distinguished title effaces the more obscure; and while the Phthian name continues to attach to the population of other less Hellenized parts of Thessaly, in Phthié itself the people have in lieu of it the three designations of Myrmidon, Hellene, and Achaian; Achaian, as a great and leading branch of the illustrious Achaian family; Hellene, as inhabiting a country included under the overriding name of Hellas; and Myrmidon, probably as a subsept of the Achaians.

It is plain, that Homer has made use of special means to mark the Hellenic and Achaian character of the kingdom of Peleus, and to exclude it in a marked manner from the category of Pelasgian influences. This

---

[1] Il. I. 155, 169; ix. 363; xix. 299.
[2] Il. xiii. 686, 698; cf. Il. ii. 704, 727.

observation, however, opens up another subject, to which we may revert.

The word Panhellenes, though only once used, in the description of the Oilean Ajax, is of great importance. 'In spear-casting he excelled the Panhellenes and Achaians.'[1] These two names cannot refer to the inhabitants of different territories. Even if they did, the former would include the inhabitants of all Hellas, that is, of all Northern and Middle Greece. But we know (1) that there were Achaians there; (2) that these Achaians were also, in the case of the Myrmidons, called Hellenes. Homer may seem, then, to designate, though not as by absolute and well-understood synonyms, but rather with a certain vagueness, substantially the same persons, namely all the Greeks; but to give them both their territorial name, and their blood-name.

Though Thucydides[2] is right in saying Homer does not call the Greeks Hellenes, yet it thus appears not improbable that, once at least, he calls them Panhellenes. Yet the verse ought hardly to attract suspicion on account of the word, since independently of it we have sufficient proof that the territorial name of Hellas might be applied without impropriety to describe the range at least of Northern and Middle Greece. Nor do I broadly deny that this may be the meaning of the word Panhellenes. If such be the true construction, then the use of Panhellenes and Achaians to signify all Greeks, may be compared with the use of 'Hellas and the breadth of Argos' in the Odyssey to describe all Greece. It is also just possible that, as the Achaian

[1] Il. ii. 530. [2] i. 3.

name has a leaning to the dominant class or aristocracy, the Hellenic name may in this passage have a similar leaning, and may, like the other, be used to denote the community, as the part supposed more excellent often is used to denote the whole.

There is another designation in Homer which seems probably, if not certainly, to be a derivative from the same stock — the name Kephallenes, a name still engraved on the island of Cefalonia. This word is used in the Iliad to describe the subjects of Odysseus. It, however, appears but twice. It might be expected to recur frequently in the Odyssey. But it is employed only five times, and never for the inhabitants of Ithaka, taken alone, who are always called either Ithakesioi, or Achaioi. In Od. xx. 210 it refers especially to those who inhabited the continental pasture lands of Odysseus. In Od. xxiv. 354, 377, 428, it seems to be capable of no meaning except the subjects of Laertes and those of Odysseus generally, as in the Iliad. Generally, I mean, as opposed to any narrower territorial limitation; for I do not exclude the belief that the name of Kephallenes may imply the better blood of the community. It may moreover be conjectured that this was a word, like Hellenes, creeping into use, but not as yet fully established.

It appears to be formed from the word Hellenes, with the prefix κεφ-, meaning 'head,' which appears in κεφαλη, in the Sanscrit kapâla, the Latin caput, and the German kopf,[1] not to mention other words.

Let us now ascend to the word from which Hellas itself is derived; since it obviously means, according to

---

[1] Donaldson, New Cratylus, p. 291.

a regular Greek formation, the country which had been occupied by, and which had come to be named from, the Helloi. These Helloi appear to be the Selloi of Il. xvi. 234. They seem also to be a people of the rudest habits, dwellers in the mountains; having prophets or interpreters, it is said, not priests, of Zeus, and being especially devoted to him in that capacity. We have other vestiges of this race in Homer; in the name of a river Selleeis, which we find in or near Troas,[1] as well as (probably) at more than one point in Greece; and especially in the name Hellespontos, which in Homer means not the narrow strait merely, but the whole sea between Troas and Thessaly at the least, or the northern Ægean.[2]

Independently of the grammatical connection between Helloi, Hellas, and Hellene, there can be little doubt that in his solemn invocation, Achilles, himself described as a Hellene, means to invoke Zeus by the tie of race. This, then, is signified in the recital concerning the Selloi, or Helloi, the *sigma* and the aspirate here representing one another as in many other cases; for example, hex, hepta, hudor, hus, and sex, septem, sudor, sus. The one form reappears in Selleeis, and in the Proselenoi[3] of Arcadia; the other in Hellespont, and in the Hellopia of Hesiod.

The Scholiast on the Birds of Aristophanes[4] informs us that braggarts were called Selloi; and that the word σελλίζειν meant to vapor or brag. He derives this sense of the word from Sellos, the father of one Æschines, satirized by the dramatist. Now it seems very little probable that the name of the obscure father of an

[1] Il. ii. 839. [2] Il. ix. 360.
[3] See *supra*, Chap. II. p. 80. [4] v. 824.

obscure man should thus have given by metaphor a word to the Greek tongue; and again, that the explanation should have been handed down from the time of Aristophanes to that of the Scholiast. Such words as 'hectoring' and 'rhodomontading' presuppose a great celebrity in the personage on whose name they are based, as without this they would not be intelligible. But if we refer this phrase to the ancient Selloi, the explanation is easy. In Greece, and especially in Attica, to be autochthonous or indigenous, and consequently to be of a very ancient race, was notoriously matter not only of credit but of vainglory, and thus to play the Sellos would be a natural and effective way of describing the manners of a vainglorious person.

The great Greek chieftains of the war are supplied as follows: Achilles, from a district of which the whole military class is expressly described as Hellene and Achaian; Idomeneus, from Phœnician ancestry; Odysseus also, from a region in which the upper class is Achaian; Agamemnon, Menelaos, Diomed, Nestor, from districts in which Pelasgianism is wholly submerged. The greater Ajax is the near kinsman of Achilles, and we must therefore suppose the Telamonian race to be strongly marked with Hellenism.

It may reasonably be asked, how it happens that if Southern Greece, meaning the Peloponnesos with the adjoining islands, thus abounds in Hellenic elements, we should be entirely without traces of the name of Hellas in that portion of the country.

We find indeed its kindred there; the name Selloeis for a river, and Kephallenes for a people. But these are not very prominent. The proper answer seems to be that, as the name Hellas took a natural precedence over names of Pelasgian associations, so the Achaians were probably the flower and the ruling order of Hellenes. Consequently, their name, where they were largely spread, might tend to suppress that of Hellas; or to prevent its formation, by filling already the place it would occupy with the territorial name Achaiis. This Achaian name is here found prevailing in the dominions of Agamemnon, of Diomed, of Nestor, of Odysseus: the same must be presumed of those of Menelaos. And at least much the larger part of the Peloponnesos seems to be included in the Achaic Argos, besides that the word Achaiis unquestionably includes the whole country from north to south.

There may however be an inference drawn from the local concatenation of names. Beginning at or near Troas, and moving towards the west, we have Selleeis, Hellespont, Helloi, Hellenes, and (from Hesiod) Hellopia. Probably we have here an indication that the route of the Hellic tribes into Greece was by the Hellespont and the northern extremity of the country. They were not, like the Pelasgians, an essentially lowland people, as we perceive from the brief description in the Invocation of Achilles. The name Trechin, as one of the settlements in the kingdom of Peleus, allied as it is with Threx, or Thracian, affords a similar indication. Again, Thamuris, the Bard who attended the solemn public competitions of song, and challenged the Muses, and whom I suppose, like those competitions themselves, to be Hellenic, was a Thracian. There is therefore less difficulty in assigning this route unequivocally to the Hellic than to the Pelasgian race.

CHAPTER V.

THE PHŒNICIANS AND THE EGYPTIANS.

Direct Notices.

1. MINOS, who is stated by Thucydides[1] to have been the first known founder of a maritime empire, appears in Homer as the greatest and most important of his archaic personages. The achievements of Heracles are personal, indeed corporal; but the name of Minos, whether mythical or not, is a symbol of political power, of the administration of justice, in a word, of civilization. He is the only person, indeed, lying so far back in time as three generations before the War, about whom Homer has supplied us with any details of real and historic interest.

Minos had Zeus for his father, and the daughter of a distinguished Phœnician[2] (such appears to be the most probable interpretation, but in substance there is little doubt about the meaning) for his mother. At nine years old he received revelations from Zeus,[3] and

---

[1] i. 4.   [2] Il. xiv. 321.   [3] Il. xiii. 450–453; Od. xix. 178.

reigned over all Crete, at that early age, in the great city of Knossos,[1] named first among the Cretan cities in the Catalogue. He was the father of Deucalion, and the grandfather of Idomeneus,[2] who, at the period of the War, was passing from middle life into old age,[3] and had begun to feel its effects in failure of the organs of sense. After death, the Cretan sovereign exercised the office of a ruler in the realm of Aïdoneus, and administered justice among the dead,[4] as a king does among his subjects upon earth. His brother Rhadamanthūs,[5] hardly less distinguished, has the custody of the Elysian Plain. Him the Phaiakes conveyed (by water from Scheriê[6]) to Euboea, on his way to Panopeus of the Phokes, for the purpose, apparently, of his passing judgment upon Tituos, son of Gaia, who had offered violence to Leto, as she was on her way (probably from Delos) to Putho or Delphi.[7] The presumption arising upon these passages is, that Rhadamanthūs was acting for his brother Minos, and that the authority of that sovereign prevailed not only in Scheriê but in Phokis; in other words, that he bore sway over a considerable dominion, both maritime and continental, in Greece.

This connection with Scheriê confirms his Phoenician character: and the signs of an authority extending to the mainland of Greece, and to the islands on its western coast, appear to be plain. It may be as a relic of this dominion, that we find in Ithaca a harbor of Phorcūs,[8] who is a maritime god of the Phoenicians.

[1] Il. ii. 646.   [2] Od. xix. 180.   [3] Il. xxiii. 469, 476.
[4] Od. xi. 569.   [5] Od. iv. 564.
[6] See the Outer Geography, infra, Chap. XIV.
[7] Od. vii. 321–324; xi. 576–581.   [8] Od. xiii. 96.

General tradition reports that Minos laid a tribute upon Attica.[1] Of this we have no direct evidence from Homer; but the fact that Theseus went to Crete to seek Ariadne the daughter of Minos to wife,[2] indicates a political relation between them, and in this way partially sustains the tradition.

Minos is in the last named passage called ολοόφρων.[3] This is a word confined by Homer to the circle of Phœnician personages. The epithet seems to imply in some form a formidable if not injurious craft. It may apply to the character of the Phœnicians as astute and tricky merchants, who acted at times as kidnappers and pirates: but as it is applied to great personages,[4] Atlas, Aietes, and Minos, it may probably refer to what is politically formidable; and, if so, it may well be a trace of a former supremacy in Greece, standing in connection with the Phœnician name.

It may even be doubted whether Homer does not mean to describe the Phœnician tongue as still spoken in Crete; for he says[5] that in that island there is a mixture of languages. This with him is a significant and rare expression. It is difficult to suppose that he would have used it merely because the island contained Pelasgian as well as Hellenic races. For he speaks of the mixed tongue of the Trojan army, not in connection with the people of Troas, who probably spoke the same or nearly the same language with the Greeks, but with the allies,[6] of whom he distinctly calls the

---

[1] See the Dialogue Minos, ascribed to Plato, 16, 17.
[2] Od. xi. 322.
[3] Ολοός is applied to an adverse divinity. See Il. iii. 365; xxii. 15.   [4] Od. i. 52; x. 137.
[5] Od. xix. 175.   [6] Il. ii. 803, 804.

Carians barbarophonoi.[1] He applies the phrase allothrooi[2] to the people of Temesd in Cyprus, who were probably Phœnician. If the Phœnicians gave Crete its name, then the Eteocretes of this passage of the Odyssey may be a Phœnician race, amidst the other four, which are apparently Hellenic and Pelasgian. This conjecture is in some degree supported by the fact that the Poet calls them megaletores, or haughty; an epithet suited to a race in possession of political ascendancy, much in accordance with the oloophrōn already cited, and yet more closely with another of his Phœnician epithets, agauos.[3]

It is possible that the Deucalion whom the later tradition connects with Thessaly, may have been the son of Minos; and that his appearance there ought to be taken as another indication that the power of Minos reached to that region. Thucydides[4] states that this personage appointed his children to be hegemones or rulers; which implies a dominion distributed in provinces, and also Asiatic in some of its features.

If this be so, then, on finding Minos installed as a ruler in the Underworld, we reasonably conclude that he is not so placed by the arbitrary choice of the Poet, but that he governs below the same persons, of the same countries, which he had governed upon earth. In short, that his office there is a testimony to the existence of a bygone Phœnician dominion, exercised in Greece from Crete as a centre. The great wealth of Crete is eminently in harmony with this hypothesis.

Bishop Thirlwall[5] has explained the position of Minos, as it is defined by general tradition. Again,

[1] Il. ii. 867.   [2] Od. I. 183.   [3] Od. xiii. 272.
[4] I. 4.   [5] Hist. of Greece, I. 5.

the existence of an empire connected with his name best explains the partial introduction of Cretan institutions into Laconia. I have elsewhere[1] ventured on the conjecture that the mnoia, or public slavery, of Crete was an institution of Minos, and is named after him.

Herodotus repeats, that Minos expelled his brother Sarpedon from Crete; and that Sarpedon colonized Lycia, which, even in the time of the historian, was governed by laws partly Cretan. If the royal house of Lycia was thus connected with that of Crete, and with the man who made the first recorded effort to bind Greece together in civil order, it gives a satisfactory explanation to the remarkable partiality which the poet always shows in the Iliad for the Lukioi or Lycians, far above all the other portions of the Trojan force.

Again, Homer places Daidalos in Crete; and says that he wrought there for Ariadne, in metal, a dance, which formed the model of that wrought by Hephaistos on the shield of Achilles.[2] He could not more distinctly have connected the Crete of Minos with the Phœnicians than by placing there the great traditional producer of works in metallic art, from whose name was taken the verb δαιδάλλειν, to embellish.

Next to Minos we may consider the case of Kadmos in connection with the Phœnician name and race. Homer gives us conclusive evidence of the migration of such a person into Greece, by calling the inhabitants of Thebes, one generation before the Troïca, by the

[1] Studies on Homer, vol. I. p. 179.
[2] Il. xviii. 592.

names of **Kadmeioi** and **Kadmeiones**. His proper name is only mentioned in the Odyssey as the father of Leukotheê,[1] once a mortal, now deified in the Sea-region, who appears to Odysseus after the wreck of his raft on the way from Ogugiê, and provides him with a girdle for his preservation from the angry flood. There could hardly be a more distinct intimation of the Phœnician extraction of Ino than her deification, not in Greece, but in the Sea-sphere, and her appearing to Odysseus before he had regained the threshold of the Greek world.

We learn from general tradition that the Thebes of Kadmos had seven gates, which were in correspondence with the sevenfold planetary worship of the East. And Homer[2] calls the Thebes of the Kadmeioi seven-gated. But Kadmos was not the first founder of the city; its first founders were Amphion and Zethos:[3] and Homer, when he mentions the foundation by them, does not call it seven-gated, but champaign, from the character of the country, conformably to the description given by Thucydides.

In the Underworld of the Odyssey we find a great proportion of persons having Phœnician associations. Again, the name Phoinix had, at the epoch of the War, been variously naturalized in Greece. Besides being a Greek proper name, it also meant a Phœnician, a palm-tree, and a purple dye.[4]

The most important works of art named in the poems are obtained from the Phœnicians. Not only was this the case with works in metal, but it was from Sidonia that Paris brought the beautifully wrought

---

[1] Od. v. 333.   [2] Il. iv. 406.   [3] Od. xi. 263.
[4] Od. xiv. 288; vi. 168; Il. iv. 141.

tissues which were so prized by the royal family of Troy.[1] And all navigation, except that of the coasts and the Ægean, appears to be, at the Homeric period, practically in the hands of the same people. The Taphians, who carry iron to Temesè[2] in Cyprus, and mean to bring back copper, appear clearly to be a Phœnician colony. Odysseus, feigning that he had escaped from Crete to Ithaca,[3] speaks, as if it had been a matter of course, about the ship's company who brought him, as Phœnicians. In his second fiction,[4] and here again as if it were a matter of course, it is a Phœnician rogue who inveigled him in Egypt, carried him to Phœnicia, and then intended to take him to Libya and sell him for a slave. When Odysseus represents himself in another of his fictions as a practised navigator, he is a Cretan, but he is one of the highest station, and represents himself as having been the colleague of Idomeneus in the Trojan command; therefore, probably, as like him of a Phœnician family.[5] Eumaios, telling of his own home in the distant Surië,[6] describes how the Phœnicians came thither for trade or kidnapping, and how a Phœnician woman was a domestic in his father's house.[7] Alone among the races of the epoch, the Phoinikes, with their imagined counterparts, the Phaiakes, are called nausiclutoi,[8] 'ship-famous.'

The immense fame acquired, and the mythical character assumed, by the single great Achaian voyage of the traditionary fore-time, that of the ship Argo to the Euxine, combine with all the other negative evidence of the Poems to prove to us how

[1] Il. vi. 289.   [2] Od. i. 184.   [3] Od. xiii. 272.
[4] Od. xiv. 290–300.   [5] Od. xiv. 230, 237.   [6] Od. xv. 403.
[7] Ib. 417.   [8] Od. xv. 415; vii. 39; xvi. 227.

completely the Greeks of the Homeric age were dependent on the Phœnicians for their ordinary intercourse with the outer world; and the outer world here means everything beyond the Greek Peninsula, with the islands coasting it to the south of the Corinthian Gulf, and with the islands and coasts of the Ægean.

Besides the name Phoinix, we have in the poems the names of Marathon, Turo (Tyre), and Danae,[1] which are all apparently represented in Phœnician names still traceable on that coast.

The direct notices of Egypt in the Poems are much narrower than those of Phœnicia; and the name Aiguption,[2] borne by an Ithacan noble, is perhaps the sole positive trace which we find of an Egyptian influence within the limits of Greece.

Egyptian Thebes was known as a city of vast wealth, with twenty thousand persons possessed of chariots, and with an hundred gates.[3]

In the Odyssey we learn that Menelaos, driven by the winds, visited the Aiguptioi.[4] In the palace of Menelaos,[5] one of the attendants of Helen carried her silver basket,[6] given her by Alkandrê, wife of Polubos, who dwelt in Egyptian Thebes. Helen had likewise the drug of marvellous effects, which may have been opium. This drug had been presented to her by the Egyptian Poludamna, wife of Thon.[7] It grew in Egypt, which abounds in drugs, and where all the inhabitants are unrivalled physicians, being of the race of Paieon.[8]

---

[1] See Renan's Phœnicie.
[2] Il. ix. 381-384; Od. iv. 127.
[3] Od. iv. 87.
[4] Od. iv. 227-232.
[5] Od. li. 15.
[6] Od. iii. 800.
[7] Od. iv. 125.
[8] See Paieon, infra, Chap. VIII.

In this region Menelaos was detained by the gods for neglecting to offer the proper sacrifices, at Pharos,[1] a day's sail from the mainland. There he had his interview with Eidothoë, and his conflict with Proteus, the servant of Poseidon.[2] By Proteus, after his victory, he was directed to return to the mouth of the river Nile, which, as well as the country, was called Aiguptos. At that point he was to make his offerings, which he did. And there he erected a funeral mound in honor of Agamemnon, 'for his eternal fame.'[3] This passage seems to show either that Agamemnon was already known in Egypt, or that the memorial would make him famous because it was in so famous a country. In either sense, particularly in the latter, the recital savors of some tradition which exhibited Egypt as a great centre of power.

In the fiction where Odysseus pretends to be a Cretan, and the bastard son of Kastor, he relates that he sailed to Egypt with a crew, who in spite of him began to lay waste the exceeding fine fields (pericalleas agrous) of the Egyptians,[4] and to assail the inhabitants. Next morning the Egyptians gather in great numbers and drive off the marauders, killing many, and reducing the rest to slavery. As being their chief, he besought the king's mercy. He was treated with exceeding kindness both by the king, and, after the first excitement, by the people. In this passage[5] Homer calls Egypt 'the well-watered.'

In another fiction Odysseus relates that he went with free-wandering pirates, probably meaning Phœni-

---

[1] Od. iv. 351 seqq.   [2] Od. iv. 386.   [3] Ib. 584.
[4] Od. xiv. 249–287.   [5] Ib. 257.

cians, to Egypt, and the very same circumstances are repeated; but this time, instead of his applying to the king, and obtaining mercy, he reports that they made him over to Demetor, the lord of Cyprus.[1]

We have no such thing as a voluntary voyage to Egypt by a pure Greek, or as any voyage to Greece by an Egyptian. The sea which separates them is so wide, that the very birds can traverse it but once a year.[2]

And yet, though Homer knew little of Egypt, he had informants who told him of what lay beyond it. Most strange it is to find that his account of the Pugmaioi or Pigmies,[3] so long regarded as pure fable, has been found, according to recent travellers, to be founded in fact.

Such are the direct Homeric notices of these two countries. But eight Books of the Odyssey (v–xii) describe the adventures of the hero on his way home. From the time when he leaves the Kikones, whose country is his very first halting-place, and passes Cape Malea, the scene of these adventures is in an outer world, evidently foreign to Greek experience. They are made up from materials just such as the tales of daring seamen would supply, with the double resource of strange fact and of embellishment at will: and, in all probability, also with a tendency to give to places and persons an aspect not too inviting to the Greeks, who might have seemed capable of becoming, as indeed they did become, their competitors in a lucrative pursuit.

---

[1] Od. xvii. 424–444.   [2] Od. iii. 318–322.
[3] Il. iii. 6. See in the Revue des Deux Mondes for Oct. 1855, Review of the work of the German missionary, Dr. Krapf, pp. 886, 904. These Pigmies are ' hauts d'un metre à un mètre trente centimètres.'

Among the reasons for supposing the materials of this part of the Odyssey to be Phœnician, come first these two, that Greek experience could not have supplied them, and that the Phœnicians could.

Thirdly, we are brought into contact, while the scene is laid in this region, with an altered mythology. Most of the Olympian deities retire, for the time, from the stage. On the other hand, the prerogatives of Poseidon are enhanced; and we even find him apparently presiding at an Olympian meeting.[1] A new deity, faintly glanced at in the Iliad as having Trojan sympathies, comes forward in full personality and with distinct attributes. Poseidon's sway seems to lie towards the west and north: it is as we move eastward that we encounter Helios, the Sun. He appears as a recognized member of the Court of Immortals: he has descendants, and satellites, and an island on earth especially consecrated to him. Here, too, we trace the strongest marks of the sacredness of the ox, an idea wholly alien to the Hellenic mythology. And, in these Books of the Poem, both sea and land are peopled with new and strange half-human races, and with a fresh series or cycle of personages properly mythological, who stand in no relations to the most familiar of the Greek deities, but only to Poseidon and Helios. Nay a change even of diet confronts us; and, as we get clear away from the Hellenic world, the ox ceases to be used as food, his place being taken by sheep and swine. In short the evidence is full and thick, to the effect that we have passed into a new and foreign world.

[1] Od. viii. 322, 344.

When such evidence has reached the point of sufficiency for a legitimate induction, it gives us authority to pronounce Phœnician, from the company in which we find it, even what may not of itself and directly bear the stamp: and further, when reflected on the Hellenic world, it enables us to discern and identify many notes of Phœnician influence, which, but for this clue, we should have been unable to detect.

And the consequence is, that we find the debt of Greece to Phœnicia to be very large: so large as to be inexplicable, until we bear in mind that, if the Phœnicians were the only foreigners at that time in ordinary contact with Greece, it is highly probable that all, which the Greeks knew or received through the arrival of Phœnician vessels, would with them commonly bear the Phœnician name. It may indeed well have happened that the name Phœnician should, for the Greek people of that day, become the synonym or representative of 'foreign;' so that whatever came from Syria, Assyria, or Egypt, would sound as Phœnician to the Homeric ear, much as in later times every foreigner in the Levant was a Frank, and as in Abyssinia (we are told), a foreigner is, at this our own epoch, termed an Egyptian.

Phœnicia, so understood, comes to mean for Homer, when taken in its widest sense, the East: and the conclusion to which I am led, as the probable result of an inquiry much too large to be here set out in detail, is no less than this: that, under cover of the Phœnician name, we can trace the channels, through which the old parental East poured into the fertile soil of the Greek mind the seeds of civilization in very many (to speak moderately) of its most conspicuous provinces.[1]

To begin with Greek commerce and navigation. Both these pursuits were in Phœnician hands at the epoch of the Poems. Ever since the time of Minos, without doubt, the Greeks had been their apt pupils: but, even at the epoch of the Troïca, they were far behind their masters. From what Homer says of the Arcades,[2] I conclude that the Pelasgian tribes were not apt to acquire nautical habits.

It is on general tradition that we must in a great degree rely for showing that Greece owed to Phœnicia, by the immigration of Kadmos, the gift of letters: and these were probably at first rudimentary symbolical signs, rather than a regular alphabet. For, had an alphabet been conveyed to Greece several generations before the War, we must surely have perceived more of its results. But the general tradition, thus understood, receives both direct and indirect support from the text of Homer. Proitos, ruling over, or, as it might well be rendered, mightier than, the Argeioi,[3] sends by Bellerophon a fatal message, couched in signs which were intelligible, not to the bearer, but to the receiver. Now one of the seven gates of Thebes bore the name of Proitos.[4] He is spoken of as one who had come in and acquired a sovereignty in Greece by strength or talent.[5] On the one side, he is in relations with the family of Sisuphos, which we shall find reason

---

[1] The argument is partly stated in the Quarterly Review for January, 1868, art. 'Phœnicia and Greece.'
[2] Il. ii. 614. [3] Il. vi. 157.
[4] Paus. ix. 8. 4; Æsch. Sept. 360; Eurip. Phœn. 1109.
[5] Il. vi. 159.

to suppose Phœnician; on the other side, with the
royal house of Lycia, as to which we have already
found similar presumptions.[1] And these facts date
from a period of two generations before the War. Yet,
in the ordinary dealings of the Greeks, we find nothing
like written memorial or record. It appears, then, as
if an art of writing, but one of rude and ill-developed
contrivance, remained in Greece as an occult art, the
privileged possession of a few Phœnician families.

The Pelasgians have been sometimes supposed to
have brought the art of building with hewn stone into
Greece. And yet the rival name, commonly given to
the ancient remains of this class, is Cyclopian. But
what is Cyclopian is, as we see from the Odyssey, immediately related to Poseidon and to the cycle of Phœnician tradition. Now I think we may lay down this
rule: that wherever Homer mentions solid building,
or the use of hewn or polished stone, we find it always
in some relation to the Phœnicians. Tiruns is 'the
well-walled.'[2] But Apollodorus, Strabo, and Pausanias[3] report (in no conflict with Homer) that it belonged
to Proitos, and was built for him by the Cyclops. The
wall of Troy,[4] which so long defied the Greeks, was
built by Poseidon[5] the Phœnician god: that is to say,
by Phœnician artisans. The same supposition will
apply to another Trojan edifice, the palace of Priam.[6]
Again, there were polished stones in the mansion of
Kirkè;[7] a Phœnician goddess. There was a court

---

[1] Il. vi. 153, 168. [2] Il. ii. 559.
[3] Apollodorus, D. ii. c. 2; Strabo, viii. p. 872; Paus. II. 16. 4; Pind.
Fragm. 642.
[4] Il. xxi. 516. [5] Il. xxi. 440.
[6] Il. vi. 242, 243. [7] Od. x. 211.

before the cave of the Cyclops[1] built with hewn stone; and the Agorè or market-place of Scheriè[2] was constructed in like manner; both scenes belonging to the Outer or Phœnician world.

That the Phaiakes, the people of Scheriè, now Corfù, were Phœnicians, has been argued by Col. Mure[3] from their name and their pursuits. There are abundance of confirmatory arguments; such as the worship of Poseidon as their chief god;[4] the descent of their royal house from him;[5] the return of Athenè from Scheriè to Athens by Marathon,[6] a place which was out of her way, but which appears, from a comparison of the word with the Marathus of Phœnicia,[7] to have been a Phœnician settlement. Now we observe, that these Phaiakes prided themselves especially on their skill in games: in boxing, wrestling, leaping, running:[8] and Odysseus gained immense honor by his successful cast of the quoit.[9] The games in Scheriè are the only games regularly described in Homer, besides those of the Twenty-third Iliad. They do not include the horse or the chariot race, nor is the horse mentioned anywhere in Scheriè. But they appear to give us a clear indication that the use of these competitive matches in feats of bodily strength was derived from the Phœnicians. And if so, then, taken in connection with the absence of the horse from Scheriè, they suggest a natural explanation of what I for one have found a most difficult subject, namely, the close connection between the horse and the god Poseidon, by the following hypo-

---

[1] Od. ix. 185.   [2] Od. vi. 267.
[3] History of Greek Literature, l. 510.   [4] Od. vi. 356.
[5] Od. vii. 56.   [6] Od. vii. 80.   [7] Renan, Phénicie, pp. 20, 97.
[8] Od. viii. 100–108, 158–164.   [9] Od. viii. 235, seqq.

thesis. That the institution of games, being Phœnician, was under the god Poseidon. That the legend of the Centaurs, and the immense preponderance of interest attaching to the chariot-race in Il. xxiii., warrant us in the belief that the Hellenic tribes, much given to horsemanship, introduced the horse into the institution of the Games. And lastly, that the horse, by his introduction into the Games, which (from Il. xi.) we know to have taken place at least two generations before the Troïca, came under the special care and patronage of Poseidon.

With respect to fine art, it seems impossible to resist the clear and ample evidence of the Homeric text, to the effect, first, that works well deserving that name in all essentials existed in the time of Homer;[1] and secondly, that they are exhibited to us as proceeding from a Phœnician source.

Lastly, there is reason from Homer to suppose, that not perhaps the vital spark of poetry, but yet the use and art of music came to Greece from those whom he calls Phœnicians. In the first place, it is only in the palace of Alkinoos that Homer has presented us with the Bard actually at work; not only as one regularly installed in the household, but with his successive lays given at length. In the palace of Odysseus, the Poet only mentions, and that but once,[2] the subject of the lay: in the palaces of Menelaos and Nestor, which afforded admirable opportunities, we do not hear of the Bard at all. Again, when we enter the mythologic circle of the Phœnicians, we have all the beings of the highest order, whom it contains, engaged in music:

[1] See 'Hephaistos' and 'Art,' *infra*, Chap. VIII. sect. ix.; and Chap. XIV. sect. ii.   [2] Od. I. 326.

the Sirens, who may be called goddesses of the chant; Calypso and Kirkè, who have no special connection with the art, but both of whom are found singing in their respective abodes.[1]

If these reasonings be well founded, it may be asked what contributions were made by Pelasgians and Hellenes to that marvellous aggregate which we know as the Greek nation. The answer, I presume, would be this. That the Pelasgian races brought into Greece the pursuits of agriculture, and the habits of a settled life. That the practice, or discipline (it was more than a sport), of hunting, which had so powerful a hold on the mind of Homer, and that a high political genius, together with an extraordinary excellence in war, were rather due to the masculine habits, both mental and bodily, of the Hellenic tribes. But that the main question is not the actual possession of this or that accomplishment, of this or that institution; it is the possession of the quality, in soul or body, which is adapted first to receive the gift as into a genial bed, and then so to develop its latent capabilities as to carry them onwards, and upwards, to its perfection. Among all the gifts of the great nations of modern Europe, how many are there which we can affirm to be, in each case, absolutely original?[2]

But then follows the just demand of a sound criticism, that for such gifts as it may seem that the East may have conveyed to Greece at the time when its energies were beginning to expand, we ought to be able to point out an adequate personal medium, through

[1] Od. v. 61; x. 221.
[2] It seems to be admitted that the very bagpipe of the Highlander is a comparatively modern introduction.

which the communication was effected. It would be much to lay all this honor upon Minos, whose empire, whatever it was, had passed away, and the more enduring fruits of whose political achievements do not seem, for the time, to have reached beyond the bounds of Crete; or upon Kadmos, whose influence, whatever it had been, certainly had not made the Thebes of the Troic period an 'eye of Greece' or a recognized centre of its civilization, as it ought to have done had he supplied the channel through which were so largely transmitted by his mother-country the gifts of civilization: not to mention, that with respect to each of these personages it is questioned whether they were real, or only mythical. Minos, indeed, stands near the period of the War. But Kadmos is more remote; and I learn from distinguished authority that his name signifies simply one coming from the East. Either way, it may justly be urged that a channel should be indicated for those most fruitful communications, which I suppose to have taken place. To this reasonable demand I propose to suggest a reply.

But here our path must be a little circuitous. In my Studies on Homer I have endeavored to point out, that we have no warrant from the Poems for speaking of an Æolic dialect of the Greek tongue, or of supposed Æolians as the prevailing race of Greeks at the Troic or the Homeric period. Nor is Homer merely silent on the subject; for while he tells us nothing of the existence of the Æolians as a tribe, he tells us of Aiolid houses, and gives us to understand that from this stock proceeded a considerable proportion of the reigning families of Greece during and before his time. From him we hear of Sisuphos reigning in Corinth, descended from Aiolos: of the Neleids in Pulos, of Pelias, of Aison, Pheres, Amuthaon, all similarly descended: of Augeias reigning in fertile Elis, to whom tradition gives a similar extraction. The question arises, were these Aiolids Phœnician?

If they were, we have to add to them, first, Kadmos and Minos, already reckoned; then the great house of the Actoridai, which is described as being descended from Poseidon; then Proitos, who made himself King of the Argeioi; and, lastly, there is every reason to suppose that Danaos was a Phœnician. That in the later tradition he stands for an Egyptian is not to be wondered at, when we consider how the two countries melted into one another, in the view of the early Greeks, like a concave line of bays upon a coast trending towards a distant horizon; and while Phœnician vessels were the channel of communication, Phœnicia itself was, before the time of the Troïca, deeply charged with Egyptian elements. M. Renan has found a district in the neighborhood of Tripoli called Dannié,[1] or Dyanniyeh. So in the old Irish histories we find that the third recorded invasion of the island was effected by the Tuath-de-Danaans, who are stated to have been a Greek people.[2] No doubt they are set down as Greek, because of the connection established in Homer between Greece and the Danaan name. But we see at once, so far as the Irish tradition is concerned, how much more appropriate it becomes, if the name Danaan be of Phœnician extraction. Again: Pausanias tells us[3] that there stood at the reputed

[1] Phénicie, p. 123.
[2] The Irish before the Conquest, by M. C. Ferguson, p. 7.
[3] II. 16. 4.

landing-place of Danaos, on the Argive coast, a temple of Poseidon Genesios, an association which at once assigns to that personage a Phœnician origin.

I return, then, to the question of the Aiolids. And, first, as to Troas. We have found signs that in Ilios, Troy of the plain, the Phœnicians themselves, or the Phœnician worship of Poseidon, had been cast out; and this ejection is probably represented in the poetic or traditionary fiction, that the god Poseidon had become bitterly hostile to the city of Priam. Not so in Dardania; for Poseidon specially protects Æneas, the heir to that sovereignty, and rescues him, at the critical moment, from the attack of Achilles.[1] This at once betokens a relation between Poseidon and the Dardanian branch of the royal house of Troas.

Here history comes in to our aid. Pausanias[2] and others assure us that, in the historic period, there were Æolians at a place called Assos in Troas, and that an Æolian race held what was reputed to have been Troy. And the general connection of Æolians with the worship of Poseidon may, I believe, be taken as an uncontested fact.

Everything combines to raise the presumption thus obtained, about the Phœnicianism of the Aiolids, to the rank of a rational conclusion. Take, for example, the fact that Homer never mentions Aiolos himself in conjunction with his Aiolids. Considering their illustrious position, this reticence demands observation; especially as in almost every case Homer names the person who stands at the head of one of his genealogies. If Aiolos were a Greek, either born or natural-

[1] Il. xx. 318–340.   [2] vi. 4. 5.

ized, it seems wholly inexplicable. But if Aiolos were an immigrant who never lost his foreign character, or if he were the famous foreign siro or ancestor of men who acquired sovereignties in Greece; or, thirdly, if he were only a mythical formation, representing the foreign paternity of a group of distinguished men who had cast their lot in that country, then nothing can be more in keeping with the general method of the Poet than that, just as he cuts the thread which connects the Pelopids with Tantalos (and, in the preternatural order, the thread which connects Demeter with Persephone), so he should cut the thread which connects the Aiolids with Aiolos.

Again, observe the link supplied by horse-breeding, and by the introduction of the horse into the Games. Two generations before the Troïca, Augeias, a reputed Aiolid, holds Games in Elis,[1] probably at what was afterwards Olympia: and at these Games there were chariot-races: and it is in direct connection with Games that all which relates to horses is placed under the sanction of Poseidon,[2] whom tradition so long connected with the Olympian contests.[3] Eumelos, an Aiolid, has the finest mortal horses of the army.[4] The Trojans, who had Æolian relations, are famous for their horses. Sisuphos, an Aiolid, reigns in Corinth:[5] and this is one of the districts where Poseidon strives against another deity for the sovereign worship,[6] and obtains it as far as the low ground is concerned.[7]

[1] Il. xi. 699-702.
[2] Pindar, in the Olympic Odes.
[3] Il. vi. 158.
[4] Il. xxiii. 681-585.
[5] Il. ii. 763.
[6] Pind. Ol. xiii. 4.
[7] For a large collection of particulars about Poseidon, see Gerhard, Ursprung, &c., des Poseidon, in the Berlin Transactions; and Preller, Gr. Mythologie, vol. I. p. 452.

If then Aiolos was foreign, and was connected with Poseidon, he could hardly be other than Phœnician. We turn then to those books of the Odyssey which we have found to have been constructed out of Phœnician materials. And here we meet him, exactly such as we might have anticipated, in consonance with the foregoing *data*. If Aiolids, settled in Greece, had brought the use of the horse into the Games, nothing could be more natural than that Homer should mythically connect Aiolos with the horse: accordingly, even in this foreign region, and upon this sea-girt isle, Aiolos is the son of Hippotas,[1] a name of Greek etymology. If the Aiolids were sea-borne to Greece, so Aiolos dwells in a sea-island, and is the guardian of the winds. If they were a large variety of houses from one ancestor, either real or supposed, so we find him supplied with six prolific pairs of children: brothers and sisters, coupled together in a way which was alien to Greek manners, but which we may, reasoning from analogy, suppose to have been much more agreeable to Phœnician customs and ideas. If the actual or ideal person represented in Greece by the name of Aiolos was popularly taken to be connected with the ruling houses of Greece, and with Troy, then it is quite natural that he should feel an interest in the Trojan War. Accordingly, the Aiolos of the Odyssey inquires minutely of Odysseus about both Troy and the Greeks:[2] which, be it observed, neither Kirkê nor Calypso does, nor does any other of the foreign personages encountered by Odysseus in his tour.

I suppose, then, that the Aiolos of the Tenth Odyssey

[1] Od. x. 1-4.   [2] Od. x. 14-16.

is the ancestor, real or reputed, of the Aiolid houses of Greece named in Homer; and I remark with some confidence, that if he is not this, he is a personage wholly unaccountable and unintelligible.

This somewhat lengthened though inadequate statement will, I hope, appear to be justified, when it is remembered that the historical question, which under the legendary veil invites investigation, is one of extreme interest: it is the question of the amount, the nature, and the channels of the earliest powerful Semitic influence upon an Aryan or Japhetic people.

And this leads me to my concluding point in the present argument. It may naturally be asked, is there anything in the name Aiolos, which is a Greek name and perhaps a mythical one, to account for its being applied by Homer to Phœnician or Semitic families? This question has been considered by Dr. Hahn,[1] who offers his solution of it. He observes that, among many nations, warriors have been tattooed, to make them look terrible: and that a tattooed man might very well be called Aiolos, or 'variegated.' He thinks, therefore, that the name Aiolos, which ran, as we see, wholly in the ruling class, meant a warrior.

Without denying the ingenuity of this hypothesis, I offer another: for I feel that Dr. Hahn's interpretation is scarcely applicable to the Greeks of Homer. Among them we hear nothing whatever of tattooing; nor is the name Aiolos, with its derivatives, particularly attached to warriors; nor have we reason to suppose that the Phœnicians were in any manner superior to Hellenes in war, however they may have acted

[1] Hahn, Alb. Stud. p. 247.

as teachers, or as forerunners, in arts and knowledge.

I lean to another explanation of the name, which appears to me very simple and sufficient. I find it in a fact stated incidentally by Professor Rawlinson.[1] He tells us that, among the Persians, dresses were not often patterned, but depended generally for their effect on make and uniform color only. And he adds, ' In all these respects we observe a remarkable contrast between the Aryan and the Semitic races, extreme simplicity characterizing the one, while the most elaborate ornamentation was affected by the other.'

If this were so, then nothing could be more natural than that when a few prominent and conspicuous persons from a Semitic country came to settle in Greece, and especially when they held there a position and attitude of superiority, they should bring with them the customs and dress of their country, and that to them, in respect of the style of their habiliments, the name of Aiolos, meaning patterned or variegated, should attach.

Let our line of thought now enter upon a somewhat wider field.

If an empire, connected with the Phœnician name, had already weighed upon Greece within the memory of man ; if Phœnicians, very probably officers of that empire, had penetrated the country at a number of points, and had usually been able, wherever they appeared, to obtain the ruling power ; we can have no cause to wonder that Homer should have regarded them as a great power in the past, even if to the Greeks of his day they were chiefly known as merchants or as freebooters. Hence we can be at no loss

[1] Ancient Monarchies, vol. iv. p. 320.

to comprehend how it is that his epithets for them, oloophrones, olophoïa eidotes, agauoi, go much beyond what was necessary to describe the astute man of business, or even the daring kidnapper.

The detection, if it be a real one, of these powerful Semitic influences, both in the Greece of Homer, and as they had operated before his time, opens a new perspective into the ancient history of the world. The knowledge of this history has recently much advanced, through research of many kinds in various quarters, and especially through the interpretation of the Egyptian hieroglyphics. Before this region of knowledge was unbarred to us, the poems of Homer were justly regarded, even by those who appreciated the evidences for their unity of authorship, as might have been some isle of Delos floating on the sea of time, without possessing root or anchor visible to human eye, and without affording us any *data* whereby we might measure the distance of the extraordinary phenomenon from the continuous and solid ground, the true ἤπειρος, or continent, of history. But now the case is altered. Men of learning think themselves to have obtained means of computation, whereby they can follow the annals of Egypt, and, in a degree, of the countries related to it, upwards, for thousands of years before the Advent, along the stream of time. So far as I understand the matter, modern Egyptology adopts in general the chronological computations of the priest Manetho, as sufficiently corroborated by the deciphered records of the country. For myself, I do not understand by what certain criterion Manetho could distinguish, at the period when he wrote, between the contemporaneous and the successive dynasties of the far olden time. It seems that he attempted it, and in some cases refrained accordingly from heaping together in series all the years of all the recorded reigns. He may not have been very far wrong: but how can we know that he was right? To me the constant changes[1] of the chief seat of government, which are allowed to have taken place, suggest the suspicion that there may be more of contemporary and less of successive power than is supposed, and that the gross figures of the chronology may be exaggerated. But I take them as very rough approximations to the truth, which doubtless lies, not beyond, but within them. And, so viewing them, it appears to me that the period perhaps has arrived when the Poems of Homer may, for the first time, be regarded as becoming gradually susceptible of chronological handling, and when attempts may not be hopeless to give them their approximate if not exact place in relation to the main chain of events, which marks for those ancient times the central movement of the history of man.

And this with reference firstly to Phœnicia; secondly and principally to Egypt; which, as I have shown, the Greeks of that early day could hardly have the means of distinguishing from Phœnicia with regularity or precision.

It is plain, from both the Poems, that, at the epoch of the Troïca, Sidon was in its vigor. The Sidonians are mentioned apart from Phoiniké, in the list of the countries which Menelaos visited.[2] Here, as we find, were produced the noblest works of metallic art;[3] here the richly embroidered robes.[4] From the king of Sidon (who has the poetical name of Phaidimos)

[1] Le Normant, Histoire Ancienne de l'Orient, Paris, 1868, vol. 1. p. 187.
[2] Od. iv. 84.   [3] Od. iv. 617.   [4] Il. vi. 290.

Menelaos receives a noble gift.[1] And some of Homer's Phœnician personages are also called Sidonian.

Now the period of the Sidonian supremacy closed, as we are told, with the razing of that city by the Philistines in the year 1209 B.C.[2] Then began the supremacy of Tyre; a city of which we have no indication throughout the poems, unless we may be thought to find one in the name of Turo,[3] the grandmother of Nestor. From many signs it appears that Turo must have been Phœnician. But Homer tells nothing, knows nothing, of a Tyrian. It seems pretty clear, then, that the epoch of the War, and probably of the Poems, must have been antecedent to the fall of Sidon, reputed to have taken place in 1209 B.C. I do not here attempt to enter into the complicated questions with reference to the succession, juxtaposition, and intermixture of races in Phœnicia, where all the three great families of Noachian man seem to come in turn upon the stage; but I simply treat their influence as a Semitic influence, on the evidence of their Semitic tongue, and in conformity I believe with the general judgment of persons entitled to authority.

Now with respect to Egypt. Ample proof is afforded by the verse of Homer that the Greeks of the Troic period had for their proper national name the name of Achaians. We also see very clearly that it had come into vogue but one or two generations before the Troïca. We know that it lost its hold as a national name at, if not before, the conquest of the Heracleidai, two or three generations later.

[1] Od. iv. 617; xv. 117. [2] Le Normant, vol. II. p. 280
[3] Od. xi. 235.

At the end of the nineteenth Egyptian Dynasty,[1] and with the reputed date of the fourteenth century before Christ, under Merephtah, successor of Rhamses II or Sesostris, it appears from the inscriptions that the people of Libya and of the North, who had formerly succumbed to the Egyptian power, effected an invasion of that country in return. In this invasion participated, among others, Achaians of the Peloponnesos, and Lakonians. They made great havoc in the country; but a great battle was fought, in which they were entirely defeated, and their enterprise was broken up.

It seems in a high degree probable, that this invasion occurred during the period which I have described as defining the prevalence of the Achaian name, and the duration of the supremacy of that noble race of Greeks.

It is much more likely that the effort was made before the War of Troy, than after it; for the condition of Greece was then less impaired by exhaustion and by internal revolutions. We have no means of saying whether, so far as Greece was concerned, it was a national, or only a local effort. It is probable that Crete may have been its base: that island was nearest to Egypt; it had a strong Phœnician element, and probably a considerable marine; and in one of the fictions of the pseud-Odysseus, when representing himself as a Cretan of high rank, he declares that he undertook a voyage to Egypt,[2] an effort in navigation of which we hear in no other quarter.

We need feel no surprise at the silence of Homer with respect to this daring enterprise. The Poet, fre-

[1] Le Normant, ii. 280.   [2] Od. xiv. 246.

quent and even copious in his allusions to the minor
legends of his country, seems almost jealous of the
greater ones. The ship Argo is mentioned but once
in the Poems;[1] the allusions to the war of Thebes are
slight. But if little careful to mix with his own great
theme the records of what he might deem rival histories, in a case like this invasion, another and more
powerful order of motives would come into play. He
sang for the glory of Greece; and as on this occasion,
sharing the disastrous fate of their Libyan allies, his
countrymen were utterly worsted by the foreigner, it
was no fit subject for his minstrelsy. Yet it is very
remarkable that in the fictitious narrative just made,
the expedition takes the form of an invasion. Great
havoc at first takes place.[2] But the Egyptians are
roused; a battle is fought; the invaders are slain or
taken; a pretty exact counterpart, although in miniature, of the history of the actual invasion, as it appears in the Egyptian records.

Under Thouthmes III,[3] of what is termed the eighteenth dynasty, and at a date taken to be about 1600
B.C., the military power of Egypt reached its zenith.
The Empire extended east and northwards over Mesopotamia, Syria, Phœnicia, and even into Armenia.
This military dominion was so constructed as to recognize the local governments, under the suzerainty of the
Pharaohs. Among the supports of its power was a
fleet,[4] which established its supremacy in the Mediterranean waters. There can be little doubt that this
fleet was, both in its men and material, Phœnician.

[1] Od. xii. 70.
[2] Od. xiv. 263.
[3] Le Normant, ii. 239.
[4] Le Normant, ii. 240.

An inscription at Karnak[1] shows that it conquered Crete, the islands of the Archipelago, and portions of the coast, at least of Greece and Asia Minor. It penetrated into the Black Sea; and it acted on the populations of the Libyan coast. Centuries appear to have passed away before this empire, probably not too stringent in its action, crumbled into fragments. But it subsisted amid much vicissitude. In 1462 B.C. the nineteenth dynasty is reckoned to commence. It seems doubtful whether the maritime supremacy, which there was no native marine able to maintain, had not already dwindled to nothing. The second monarch of this dynasty, Seti I., was a great warrior; but he made no effort to retrieve the dominion of the sea.

Here I may venture conjecturally on the following observations. The Egyptian history of the maritime conquests of Thouthmes III, if we are allowed the almost inevitable assumption that the nautical instrument for creating the supremacy was Phœnician,[2] reads like an account in other words of what Thucydides has slightly but firmly sketched from general tradition, and what we are enabled to gather with a considerable amount of proof from Homer, respecting the empire of Minos in Crete, over the Archipelago, and on the continent of Greece.

But the empire by sea soon vanished; while the empire by land, extending it appears into Asia Minor, continued, though in varying phases, to subsist. There

---

[1] Le Normant, II. 247.
[2] In much later times we find Phœnicia performing much the same office for the Persian king. Herod. iii. 19; vii. 44.

is at least one indication gathered from Homer and the general tradition jointly, which would lead to the conclusion that the War of Troy took place after the fall of the first, but before the disappearance of the second, portion of the Egyptian power. The Poems are altogether opposed to any idea that a maritime Egyptian empire still existed. Crete, apparently its old head-quarter, was not at the Troic period the centre of prevailing power that it had been before. But Memnon was among the allies of Troy;[1] and all tradition reports that Memnon was Egyptian. It may perhaps be worth noting, that the Memnon of Homer is gifted with the highest personal beauty, and that this honor would not have been awarded by the Poet, who above all things admired the lighter hair and complexion, to the swarthy, nay tawny, natives of the Egypt of our geography. Is it not also highly improbable that Priam, whose list of allies in the Catalogue stops at Lycia and Caria, should have been able to draw an auxiliary force from so great a distance? But if the political Egypt, the Egyptian supremacy or empire of that day, reached as far as Armenia or Asia Minor, the difficulty disappears at once; from such a region Memnon might have come, and the account of Homer, together with the later tradition, becomes natural and intelligible.

In the year 1311 B.C., which is considered as a date astronomically ascertained,[2] Rhamses III, the last great military monarch of Egypt, came to the throne. Mesopotamia, however, was under Egyptian rule as late as 1150 B.C.

---

[1] Od. xi. 522.   [2] Le Normant, p. 200.

The time may be at hand, when, from further investigations, it will be possible to define with greater precision those periods of the Egyptian chronology to which the Homeric Poems, and their subject, thus appear to be related.

In the mean time it may reasonably be pointed out[1] that the discoveries already made tend to show that those inquirers have not been wrong, who have assigned the greatest measure of antiquity, and of historical character, to the works of Homer.

[1] Le Normant, p. 802.

CHAPTER VI.

ON THE TITLE 'ANAX ANDRŌN.'

There is a substantial distinction between titles, and epithets descriptive of station or office. Titles are in effect that class of descriptions which have been gradually accepted by society and established in common usage for the purpose of indicating a certain rank or function, just as a given weight and form of the precious metals is appointed by law or custom to indicate a certain value. In both cases the symbol, becoming familiar to the minds of all, is accepted in common use without examination.

By titles, and also by epithets, I understand, for the present purpose, either adjectives or substantives, as the case may be.

Epithets, or descriptive phrases, may by degrees grow into titles: and it is probable that all titles, properly so called (I do not now speak of those denoting relationship), may begin in descriptive phrases.

One sign of a title is, that it can either be combined with the name of the person to whom it belongs, or substituted for it.

In Homer, the substantives hegemones, aristees, and the adjectives skēptouchoi (of kings), theioi (of bards), are epithets or descriptive phrases. Again, with respect to individuals, echephron (for Penelope), pepnumenos (for Telemachos), polumetis (for Odysseus), are descriptive phrases. But Basileus, Basileia, for king and queen, are titles. Anax sometimes means ruler or lord, somewhat vaguely, as a title; sometimes noble, as a class; sometimes lord, as a master or proprietor, for example, of slaves or animals. It differs from Basileus in these particulars: first, that it is more rarely used as a title; secondly, that, while both indicate a superiority, the idea conveyed by anax leans to ownership and absolute command, while the Basileus is a ruler not an owner, a ruler of freemen organized under the social bond, and limited by civil right which he is himself bound to observe.

As a designation of dignity, Basileus is the higher, as well as the more definite. The word nearest to it is koiranos; but this has hardly, in Homer, settled down into a title. The ruling office is also more vaguely indicated by the expressions $κρείων$, and $ποιμὴν λαῶν$, shepherd of the people. Basileus is well rendered by 'king:' anax by 'lord,' a word at once wider, more absolute, and less elevated in the sense it conveys.

But we find in Homer the remarkable phrase anax andrōn, lord of men; and this is used, not descriptively, but, beyond all question, as a title. Now, as the word anax has no reference to reciprocal rights and duties, it is very remarkable that we should find it thus used with regard to relations towards men, and evidently freemen, in a title enjoyed by certain individuals. The physiognomy of the phrase, so to speak, is not that of Hellenic society; for Hellenic society was already founded in *rights*. It suggests therefore a history of its own, and a character either foreign, or archaic, or both.

The facts relating to the use of this phrase are as follows: —

It is applied to Agamemnon forty-four times in the Iliad, and twice in the Odyssey.

It is also applied to

Æneas, Il. v. 311.   Augeias, Il. xi. 701, 739.
Euphetes, Il. xv. 532.   Eumelos, Il. xxiii. 288.
Anchises, Il. v. 268.

Thus then anax andrōn is a stock or staple phrase for Agamemnon. Yet it is applied to five other persons, all of them sovereigns; but none of them at all approaching Agamemnon in point either of personal eminence, or of power. It is not therefore on account of his personal eminence or of his power that the title is bestowed on Agamemnon.

But again. While it is given thus frequently to Agamemnon, it is given but once to four of the other five, and but twice to Augeias. One of these personages, Euphetes, is named but once in the Poems,[1] and then he is named with the title. Augeias (except once in a patronymic) is only mentioned twice,[2] in the legend of the Eleventh Iliad; and twice with the title. Eumelos has the title once, out of five passages in which he is named. Anchises once only, out of thirteen. But Æneas is very frequently named in the

[1] Il. xv. 532.   [2] Il. xi. 700, 738.

Poem, and yet never with the title except once. He appears to hold it as heir-apparent to his father's throne; and his possession of it marks its hereditary character under such circumstances.

It is to be noticed, that all the six names to which Homer annexes the title are virtually of the same metrical value in the place of the verse where it is almost invariably so annexed. The same observation applies to the word Atreides joined with it in Il. i. 7. At first sight, then, it might appear that metrical convenience had prompted the use of the phrase. But then,

1. Two of the six names, in their simpler forms, Aineas and Augeas, are modified into Aineias and Augeias in order to fall in with the title.

2. It cannot be metrical convenience which gives it so very frequently to Agamemnon, and so rarely to the others.

3. There are at least from thirty to forty names of equivalent metrical value in the Poems, including many princes, heroes, and notable persons, which never receive the title. Among these are, of the living, Patroclos, Sarpedon, Antenor, Diomedes, Agapenor, Menelaos, Aigisthos; and of the dead, Amphion, Herakles, Eurusthous, Adrestos, Rhadamanthos, Meleagros.

Homer never inflects the title, giving it always in the nominative. He never severs the phrase by tmesis, except once only, through inserting the copulative particle τε. Once, in Il. i. 7, it lies between the second and fourth foot of the verse; in every other case it is found between the third and fifth. Some of these particulars may be held, according to the laws of Homeric use, to add dignity to the title. In illustration of this

proposition, I will observe that, conversely, in the few
instances where the Poet introduces himself into the
verse, he never once uses the nominative. Again,
Enosicthon is used for Poseidon forty times; thirty-
nine of them in the nominative. Diogenes is found
in the nominative and vocative only. The masculine
kudistos is used sixteen times, all in the vocative.
Eurucreion twelve times, only in the nominative.

The phrase anax andrōn entirely disappears from
use after Homer.

Let us now look to particulars connected with the
application of the phrase to each of the six names
severally, in order to discover the thread, if there be
one, on which in common all are hung.

I. AGAMEMNON.

The sovereign of all the Greeks is nowhere described
by personal epithets of pointed characteristic force.
Eight times he is called by the epithet dios, which
indicates some specialty of excellence, and which was
fairly due to his prominence whether among rulers or
among warriors. Generally he is marked either by the
patronymic, which is simply historical, or by what may
be called official epithets, creiōn, eurucreiōn, poi-
mēn laōn. But the staple or stock phrase is anax
andrōn.

I have already given a reason why this cannot be on
account of his great power and sway. Again, the passages which most forcibly describe these are the lines
about the Sceptre in Il. ii. 100-108, and that which gives
him his place in the Catalogue, Il. ii. 576-580. In
these he is not called anax andrōn, but creiōn.
In two other passages of the Poem he is personally

glorified: as to his appearance in Il. ii. 477–483, and as to his arming in Il. xi. 15–46. In neither of these is he anax andrōn. Neither corporal distinctions, then, nor official position thus far appear to supply a basis for the phrase. Yet the very emphatic use of it after the proper name in the prefatory passage of the Poem, which contains so much, as well as its frequent reiteration, prove its general dignity and importance. Again, therefore, it seems likely that we are to look somewhere in the past for the secret of its meaning.

Unfortunately, in the case of this great family of the Pelopidai, the past at a certain point, and that too one soon reached, becomes obscure.

All that Homer desires or intends us to know of the extraction of Agamemnon is contained in the famous and very significant passage of the Sceptre, Il. ii. 101–108. Here we are informed that

1. Hephaistos fashioned it.
2. He gave it to Zeus.
3. Zeus gave it over to Hermes Diactoros, the Agent, or Go-between; or Ambassador.
4. Hermes gave it to Pelops, 'the driver of horses.'
5. Pelops gave it to Atreus, shepherd of the people (δῶκε).
6. Atreus dying left it (ἔλιπε); it remained or passed over to Thuestes, rich in flocks.
7. From Thuestes in like manner it was left to Agamemnon (λεῖπε).
8. It conveyed suzerainty (at the least) over all Greece and its numerous islands.

The first question is, what are we to say to the theotechny or preternatural machinery here introduced? If we are to give it an ethnological meaning, the names of Hephaistos and of Hermes give it a color foreign, and such as I have called Phœnician. Little stress could be placed upon this, if it were an isolated phenomenon. But the sphere of the art of Hephaistos, and of the general activity of Hermes, lies so completely beyond the limits of Greece, that I cannot but attach weight to their names as indicating that, before Pelops, the family had been foreign, and probably Asiatic. The passage also demonstrates that the starting-point of the house is one at which it had attained to princely rank.

Next, the epithet given to Pelops tends to support the tradition, which places him in relations with the Olympian Games, and with the god Poseidon.

Further; Atreus first appears in the Pelopid time as 'shepherd of the (or a) people.' There is something in this phrase which seems to point him out as the first head, in the Pelopid line, of a settled and consolidated Greek sovereignty. The same inference may be drawn from the fact that his name supplies the standing patronymic; as Neleus supplies it to Nestor. There is also some more direct evidence. Heracles may be reckoned as living one generation and a half before the War, since he has in it both a son and grandsons; and Eurustheus, who was his contemporary, reigned in Achaic Argos, which afterwards became the seat of the Pelopid power. There seems to be only room, therefore, in the natural course, for one generation of sovereigns in Achaic Argos after Eurustheus and before Agamemnon.

To this generation probably belong both Atreus and Thuestes, the father of Aigisthos. In the change of phrase from δῶκε, 'gave,' to ἔλιπε and λεῖπε, Homer may seem to glance at a departure from the common line of direct succession, and a return to it. Thuestes, then, not being in that line (or, if we were to suppose him in it, being in it only as the brother of Agamemnon), we have but two generations of ancestry, and but one of established sovereignty, given for the house of Agamemnon; Pelops having probably founded the power of the house, but not placed it in its fixed seat, or obtained for it the full measure of acknowledgment and positive authority.

We see plainly, from this circumstantial account of the derivation of the Sceptre, that the Pelopids did not simply subvert, or succeed to, a prior dynasty; but that they held a new dominion, legitimated, in poetic phrase, by the gift of Zeus. And we know, from the comparison of dates and particulars already made, that this was the great Achaian dynasty, having the old Argeian dominion for its centre, but reaching much beyond its bounds, with an undefined though acknowledged supremacy over Greece and its whole coronet of islands.

The joint and simultaneous rise of the Achaian race, and of the house of Pelops, is well and clearly founded in the facts of the text: which, however, carries us but little farther. Tradition asserts that Pelops was the son of Tantalos, and Tantalos the king of a race of Phruges. Homer introduces him to us in the Underworld, together with a variety of personages, all of whom have relations, in one form or other, with Greece. Placing him among such persons, he still conforms to his rule by not naming him in the passage of the Sceptre; since he never, on any occasion, deduces a Greek dynasty from a confessedly foreign ancestor.

The nature of his punishment, pointing to some form of greed as his offence, is also well assorted with the tradition which represents him as the last holder of his inherited power, and his son as an immigrant in a foreign land.

We have no means of determining, from the Poems, whether Tantalos was reputed to be of divine descent; but it is far from improbable, since most of those among whom he appears in the Odyssey were so descended.

Post-Homeric tradition makes Niobè the daughter of Tantalos. The tradition of Niobè herself is recited by Achilles,[1] and from this we may infer, first, her dignity and fame; next, her having relations with Greece. The theotechny, too, of the tradition exhibits her as one of the great of the earth; and the term laous,[2] applied to those who were vicariously punished for her offence, evidently means her subjects. Very possibly, the epithet ἠΰκομος, commending the beauty of her hair, may indicate that the Poet regarded her as a Greek, either born or naturalized.

Homer places the mourning Niobè on Mount Sipulos, near the Acheloos; and Pausanias found the reputed tomb of Pelops on the summit of the hill. The Phruges of Tantalos are reputed to have been a Thracian people.[3] Their name[4] appears even in Attica; and a harbor in Elis was called after Tantalos.[5]

Pelops is commonly said to have gained the hand of Hippodameia, and the throne of Elis, by success in the chariot-race. Local traces of him remained. He was worshipped in a sanctuary hard by the temple of

[1] Il. xxiv. 602.
[2] Il. xxiv. 611.
[3] Strabo, xii. p. 579; xiv. p. 680.
[4] Thuc. ii. 29.
[5] Paus. V. xiii. 1–4.

Zeus Olympios;[1] and revered there among heroes, says Pausanias, as Zeus was among gods. He is the reputed founder or restorer of the Games who raised them to their historic celebrity. Another tradition brings him from Olenos into Elis; no improbable indication of his route from the north. Nine islands off the coast of Methana were called the islands of Pelops in the time of Pausanias;[2] and we have already noticed in that quarter traces of the Achaian name.

That the Achaians were Hellenes, and that they rise to pre-eminence with the Pelopids, are circumstances which lead us to look for further traces of the connection. Now Strabo[3] seems to attach a great value to a tradition which he repeats, that the Achaians of Phthiotis came with Pelops into the Peloponnesos, occupied Laconia, and gave it the name of Achaic Argos; and subsequently, when the Achaians were driven out of Laconia, they drove out an Ionian race from Aigialos, and gave their name to that region. This account of the journey of the race, and of Pelops, is in accordance with the traces we have found in Homer and elsewhere of the passage of the family of Pelops towards the south, and with the emergence of the dynasty of Atreus. It is also in marked accordance with the emphatic application of the Achaian name to the inhabitants of Phthié, and with the prominence that the Poet gives to that district in the War, through its Myrmidon soldiery and its illustrious chief, who are thus placed in near relations with Agamemnon and his adherents. Although we have found in many places vestiges of the local use of the Achaian

---

[1] Paus. V. xiii. 5.   [2] ii. 34.   [3] Bk. viii. 5, p. 365.

name, this is one of only two where it is expressly and directly assigned to the inhabitants of a district as such. The other is in Crete; and there no such great importance attaches to the statement, which exhibits them in conjunction with Dorians and other races.

History at this point comes in to our aid. Down to the late era of Polybius, the connection of the Achaian name with Phthiè still subsisted. There were always Achaians of Phthiotis; and in the year 205 B.C. Quintius, the Roman general, recognized the Achaians, upon inquiry, as the Thessalian race.[1]

And the close relation of this race to the Pelopids is in no respect more clear than in this, that as they rose, so they fell, with that particular dynasty. In the post-Homeric literature, all of which follows the Dorian conquest, the Achaian name has ceased to be a current designation for the Greeks.

We are not entitled, however, to carry the connection backwards in time beyond Pelops. We may reckon with confidence that, if Tantalos had been recognized as a Greek, he would have been named by Homer in the line of the ancestry of Agamemnon.

Yet not even the Heracleid victors in the struggle could afford to let slip the repute and credit of the Achaian sovereignty. So although Tisamenos, their representative in blood, had been expelled, and had betaken himself with his followers to Aigialos, his tomb in aftertimes was shown at Sparta; and hard by it the feast of Pheiditia was kept: with an explanatory tradition that their fathers, admonished by an oracle, had fetched the remains of the last Pelopid

---

[1] Polyb. xviii. 30–37.

sovereign from their home at Helikê, in Achaia. On the other hand, the Achaians had now set up a legendary ancestor, Achaios by name, whose image they professed to exhibit; and along with it they cherished a tradition, that the family of Tisamenos had continued to reign among them down to the time of Ogygos, in the third century before Christ, when their league was formed upon the basis of democratic institutions. In neither quarter do we see any such honor paid to the yet older dynasty of Danaos or of Perseus. All this seems to enhance the dignity of this Achaian sovereignty, to which the title of anax andrōn was attached, as if it were possessed of some peculiar attribute which it had not received, and which it did not transmit.

We have now examined the proper import of the phrase, and its use in the case of Agamemnon. We have found that its groundwork does not lie either in his personal qualities or in his position as general-in-chief or as king. It appears to point backwards to a state of things anterior to the constitution of Achaian society; which, as we find it in Homer, though immature in its forms of administration, was profoundly penetrated with a political spirit, and had completely possessed itself of the substance of civil right, though not in the form of law. It suggests, then, a chieftaincy or hereditary superiority, older than the settlement of the family in its present form and power, and, whether founded in blood or otherwise, having reference to an origin in time and place beyond the limit of Greek history, even in that wide sense of the phrase in which we apply it to the chronicles of Homer.

Let us now see what further lights can be supplied from the cases of the five personages who share this title with Agamemnon.

II. ANCHISES, and III. ÆNEAS.

If the strong sense of nationality in Homer has led him everywhere to keep back from his hearers what he may have known or heard of a foreign origin for any Greek race or family, it seems plain that least of all would he be disposed to lift the veil in the case of a people whom the Greeks had conquered, and whose great chieftains especially he exhibits throughout in marked though skilfully softened and disguised inferiority.

As the Helloi are first introduced to us in the mountains above Thessaly, so the Dardanians appear in the recesses of Ida, above the Ilian plain. Dardanos is expressly declared to be the son of Zeus; as Agamemnon may probably have been his reputed descendant. On the one side we have Zeus, with the Helloi for his prophets: on the other, Zeus of Ida, Zeus Idaios. The term anax andrōn applied to a father and his son, both living, shows the derivative and more than hereditary character of the title, and supports the hypothesis that it springs from some remote fountain-head. But why is it that, given both to Anchises and Æneas, it is not given to Priam or to any of his family? Here there is opened to us a curious field of inquiry.

Certain facts are on the face of the Poems.

Priam[1] had, before the war, been a potentate, excelling all in that vicinity. Besides the Allies, and besides his own troops under the command of Hector, who are described in terms somewhat like those applied to the troops of Agamemnon in the Greek army, the

[1] Il. xxiv. 543–546.

Dardanians appear as a separate contingent; and there are three other military contingents,[1] one certainly, but perhaps all, included under the name of Tröes, forming the third, fourth, and fifth divisions of the army. The King of Troy, then, probably held a position less powerful indeed, yet resembling that of Agamemnon in having, besides his immediate subjects, various princes under his suzerainty.

There was at Troy an Union or Chamber of δημογέροντες,[2] which occupied the same relative place as the βουλή or Council among the Greeks. It was composed of royal and princely persons; yet Anchises appears neither in this body, nor anywhere upon the scene of the poem. It is not directly stated that he was alive; yet it seems to be assumed.[3] If he lived, his absence from the Council is remarkable, as his dominions were engaged in the war, and Æneas, before he came to Troy, had only been rescued by Poseidon from the hands of Achilles.[4] This prince is never spoken of as in possession of his inheritance.

The sovereignty held by Anchises was the older of the two; for Dardania was built by Dardanos,[5] Troy apparently by his grandson Tros, or his great-grandson Ilos. Priam was the great-grandson of Tros through Ilos and Laomedon, Anchises through Assaracos and Capūs. We cannot judge with certainty from this genealogy, the longest and most detailed in the Poems, whether the branch of Ilos or that of Assaracos was the younger. But the presumption arising out of his removal from the original seat into the plain seems to be

[1] Il. II. 824–839. [2] Il. iii. 146–148. [3] Il. xx. 240.
[4] Il. xx. 90–93; 128–131. [5] Il. xx. 215–240.

against Ilos. It is true he is named before Assaracos: but in Il. vi. 76 we have Æneas named before Hector by Helenos; and here likewise he gives precedence to his own birth. Again, Æneas takes no part in the councils of Hector; and his personal qualities are very faintly marked. Yet, like Hector, he is honored as a god;[1] and the special protection given him by Poseidon marks him as a most important personage. His name is combined with that of Hector[2] in a way which almost implies a parity of military command. Moreover, there is jealousy between him and the house of King Priam. He hangs on the outskirt of the battle,[3] and cherishes resentment, because he does not receive due honor from the monarch. Yet the character of Priam was genial and kindly. Again, Æneas is taunted by Achilles[4] with entertaining the hope of succeeding to the throne of Troy. In answer to this taunt, he utters no contradiction of it, but simply gives his genealogy. This seems very like an assertion of his title, which, if it existed, could only rest on seniority.

Æneas does not thwart Hector in counsel like Poludamas: so that there could be no umbrage taken on that ground.

Zeus had presented Tros with certain horses, in compensation for the loss of Ganymede. These horses remained with Laomedon in the plain. But Anchises[5] brought his mares to them surreptitiously, and got possession of the breed. And it is here that this prince is called anax andrōn, as though to say, in virtue of his being the lineal representative of the elder branch, he

[1] Il. xi. 58; cf. v. 467. [2] Il. vi. 75, 77. [3] Il. xiii. 459.
[4] Il. xx. 179-183. [5] Il. v. 268.

thus asserted his claim to the use of a gift which had been presented to Tros the common ancestor.

I have said, that the import of this title seems to carry it back to a period anterior to the political organization of society which we find in Greece. Are we then to suppose, that it also came into the family of Dardanos before his settlement on Mount Ida? I reply that first there is not the same cogency of reason for supposing it: for the relation of the Asiatic king to his people was far more accordant than that of the Greek to the idea implied in anax andrōn. But neither need it be rejected on the ground that Dardanos is the son of Zeus. For, in these remote ascriptions of Divine origin[1] to royal houses, possibly little more in substance is intended than is less pointedly conveyed in the peculiar and exclusive ascription to Kings of the epithets Diogenes, Zeus-born, and Diotrephes, Zeus-nurtured. Certainly they are to be distinguished from cases of nearer mythological parentage; and they can hardly mean more than something of special dignity as among kingly houses, or else a simple attribute of the class. But in truth the case of Dardanos and his family will, if I mistake not, be found to fall in with the general course of the argument.

The use of this title is a remarkable sign of affinity between the Trojans and the Greeks: but here is not the place most convenient for examining into the general signs of that affinity.

We have seen that, in the case of Anchises, the title anax andrōn is employed as if to justify him in an act of aggression in virtue of this dignity. Again, in

[1] Il. xx. 215.

the case of Æneas, we are told at a great crisis, 'and now would have perished utterly the anax andrōn Æneas, had not Aphrodite perceived his plight.'[1] As if to say, 'great though he was, it would have been all over with him.' There will be occasion to notice in other cases, how pointedly this phrase is used in connection with some striking act or crisis, and by no means as an otiose or merely ornamental epithet.

IV. AUGEIAS.

The Elian contingent is sent to the War under four separate leaders; of whom one is Poluxeinos, son of Agasthenes. He is termed a prince or lord, and (by patrohymic) descendant of Augeias.[2]

In the Nestorian legend of the Eleventh Iliad, we are told that Neleus[3] sent to Elis a four-horsed chariot to contend in the Games; but Augeias, who is here termed anax andrōn, laid hands on the horses, and detained them. Hence the invasion from Pulos, effected by Achaians, under the guidance of Athenè. Agamodè, the daughter of Augeias, was profoundly versed in drugs.[4] And she was married to Molios, a descendant of Poseidon through Actor; who resided at court, and was slain by Nestor in the Pulian raid.[5]

We may justly suppose that Augeias ruled over Elis, because the noble Actorid family were attached to his court as the court of a superior. Whereas at the time of the Troïca, when the unity of the Elian State appears to have been broken up, the Actorids of the

[1] Il. v. 311. [2] Il. ii. 615–624. [3] Il. xi. 670 seqq.
[4] Il. xi. 741. [5] Il. xi. 738, 740, 741.

time command distinct military divisions, upon a footing of equality with the descendant of Augeias. It is probable that Elis, like Bœotia, had already undergone revolutions; and for the same cause, namely, its fertility.

Other circumstances enhance the presumption of the great position and high descent of Augeias; especially, his presiding over the Games. To these Games, as we see, the neighboring States, some half-century before the war, already sent their chariots to compete. To these it seems probable that Thamuris[1] was on his way, when he met with the calamity which deprived him of the gift of song; for we find he had reached the Alpheos, at a distance from his own country, and from the court of Eurutos, to which he apparently belonged.

With respect to the descent of Augeias, Homer is silent, and we must look for the aid of general tradition. He was reputed to be the son of Salmoneus, and thus a descendant of Aiolos. In this manner he comes within the circle of the Phœnician traditions. And though Aiolos is of divine descent, like Bellerophon,[2] the text of the Odyssey supports this tradition[3] (1) by giving him the epithet of amumōn, which appears to be used by Homer not as an epithet of character, but most commonly as one indicating a divine descent, of the same class as that of the Dardanids; (2) Because the name of his daughter Turo points to Tyre; (3) Because she is called εὐπατέρεια,[4] an epithet only used in two other places,[5] and both

---

[1] Il. ii. 594–600.   [2] Il. vi. 191.   [3] Od. xi. 235 seqq.
[4] 'daughter of a noble sire.'   [5] Il. vi. 292; Od. xxii. 227.

times with respect to Helen, who is treated as the daughter of Zeus, Διὸς ἐκγεγαυῖα.[1]

Tradition also places in Elis one of the ancient towns called Ephurè. The text of Homer, without directly confirming the tradition, is more than probably in accordance with it. For Odysseus visited Ephurè to obtain poison for arrows.[2] And it was feared that Telemachos might pay a like visit.[3] Now it is certain (1) that this must have been an Ephurè on the west coast of Greece; therefore probably in Peloponnesos, for intercourse does not appear to pass northwards beyond the Gulf of Corinth; (2) that it could not be the Ephurè of Sisuphos, since this to all appearance had now become Corinth, and is so named in the Catalogue.[4] Furthermore, in both cases Ephurè was a place where the use of drugs was studied; and in this use the daughter of Augeias, as we have seen, was skilled. We may, then, reasonably assume that Augeias dwelt at Ephurè, though at the period of the Troïca the place was not significant enough to be named in connection with the force from Elis; but few towns or settlements of which, however, are recited in the Catalogue.

In the case of Augeias, as of Anchises and Æneas, we may observe the very emphatic use of the phrase. The anax andrōn detained the mares: i.e. he kept the mares, as if presuming upon his dignity of anax andrōn.

---

[1] Il. iii. 199, 418, et alibi. Cf. Od. iv. 569.
[2] Od. i. 259.
[3] Od. ii. 828.
[4] Il. ii. 570.

V. Euphetes.

Euphetes is named but once by Homer. Meges, a Greek chieftain, is saved from the spear-stroke of Dolops by the stoutness of his many-layered breastplate,[1] brought by his father Phuleus from Ephurè, hard by the River Sellecis, where it was given him by his host the anax andrōn Euphetes.

Euphetes, then, is manifestly the king of Ephurè: and is at once brought within the circle of those traditions to which the name belongs.

The question, over which Ephurè Euphetes reigned, is at first sight less important than the relation established by the name itself. Strabo[2] reckons, besides Corinth, an Ephurè in Elis, one in Thesprotia, one in Thessaly, and five others, which had fallen to the condition of mere villages. In Homer, we hear (1) of the Ephurè of Corinth, (2) indirectly of that of Elis, (3) of the Ephurè from which Heracles carried off Astuocheia, the mother of Tlepolemos, after a destructive raid. This would appear to have been in Thessaly; since Tlepolemos comes from Rhodes, and we have other examples of connection between Thessaly and the southern islands in the persons of the descendants of Heracles;[3] but none between those islands and the west of Peloponnesos.

According to Strabo,[4] Euphetes was the son of Augeias. If so, nothing can better accord with the Homeric text, which makes Meges[5] the commander of a contingent from the coast over against Elis; which

[1] Il. xv. 530. [2] p. 832. [3] Il. ii. 670-680.
[4] p. 459. [5] Il. ii. 627.

places him in battle at the head of the Epeian troops;[1] and which states that Phuleus, his parent, had emigrated on account of a feud with his own father.[2] Phuleus is not condemned on account of this feud, but on the contrary is commended as dear to Zeus. It was in every way fit, then, that he should continue to be united by the ties of guestship with the lord of Elis. And as to the use of the title anax andrōn, the case of Euphetes may thus in all probability fall under that of Augeias. It appears indeed possible, though I will not now venture to dwell upon it, that the name Ephurē may of itself be a sign of Phœnician relations.

VI. EUMELOS.

Eumelos commands before Troy the forces of his father Admetos. The seat of his throne seems to have been at Pherai, a name not improbably akin to Ephurē.[3] And here we find it holding the same relation to the anax andrōn Eumelos, as Ephurē holds to two other bearers of the same title, namely Augeias and Euphetes. Further, we have seen that the name Ephurē is also connected with the Aiolid line in the person of Sisuphos. Now we find from Homer that Alcestis the mother of Eumelos was the daughter of Pelias, and that Pelias was the spurious child of Poseidon, by Turo afterwards the wife of Cretheus the Aiolid: while in the male line, which would govern the descent, the family was descended from Pheres,[4] and Pheres was one of the legitimate sons of Cretheus.

[1] Il. xiii. 692.
[2] Il. ii. 711-715; Od. iv. 798.
[3] Il. ii. 629.
[4] Il. ii. 703.

Eumelos therefore is an Aiolid, and as such is sprung from Zeus.

He is mentioned six times in oblique cases, either of his own name or of his patronymic Pheretiades, and five times in the nominative; but only once as **anax andrōn**.[1] This again is on the only occasion that called for the use of an emphatic phrase, since his only conspicuous action in the Poems is that, being possessed of the finest horses,[2] and excelling in their management, he springs up much more rapidly than any other chieftain, to accept the challenge of the chariot-race in the Twenty-third Iliad.[3]

The Homeric evidence then, gathered from various parts of the Poems, and slightly aided by the filling in of blanks from tradition, may be summed up as follows:—

1. The employment of this phrase seems not to be accidental or to be meant for mere ornament; but to rest upon a common character attaching to those who bear it.

2. It is borne only by ruling princes, or their heirs.

3. But though a title of peculiar dignity, it does not indicate a present superiority of power or prerogative to other contemporary rulers.

4. In the cases of the Dardan princes, and of Eumelos, the text shows expressly that it accompanies descent from Zeus, at a remote date, and without the name of a mother.

5. In the cases of Euphetes and Augeias, tradition states, and the text indirectly but strongly supports, a similar descent.

[1] Il. xxiii. 288.   [2] Il. ii. 763.   [3] Il. xxiii. 288.

6. In the case of the Pelopids, all direct indications fail us; but even here, Pelops, or his reputed father Tantalos, would appear to be a personage standing relatively to Greek history in much the same position as Aiolos, that is, as the foreign head and founder of a ruling race; a character, which also apparently attaches to Dardanos in Troas.

7. In each and all of these cases, the ancestor appears upon the scene of Greek tradition as already a prince; and always at a period antecedent to the formation of anything like polity in Greece.

8. It is in this attitude that we are justified in believing Homer presents to us those archaic characters in Greece, whose prior history and descent were foreign, so that if distinctly unfolded they would have broken his uniform rule by representing leading elements of Greek society and nationality as derived from foreign sources.

9. The nature of the phrase anax andrōn meaning nearly, as it does, 'master of men,' seems to bear a foreign rather than a Hellenic color, and is probably drawn from a state of civil society, which may be called either more patriarchal, or more Asiatic, than that of the Hellenes: a state where power was more absolute, and right less distinctly recognized, than they were respectively in the Greece of Homer. It is a title which, whatever be its lingering glories, has not in it any savor of liberty.

10. The name is nowhere found in connection with Pelasgian associations; but it attaches strongly to what had been all along the ruling element in Greek society from its first recorded formation, whether in connection with the Achaian or with the Phœnician

name; namely, a primitive chiefship or superiority, linked to something which, as to time and place, lay beyond the Greek horizon proper.

11. Under these conditions, it is not difficult to see that the title of anax andrōn could not apply (for example) to Achilles or Odysseus, whose families were not the representatives of these ancient sovereignties: or to Nestor, whose descent from Poseidon was veiled by spurious birth, and who was connected with Aiolos only in the female line: or to Sarpedon, who is directly affiliated to Zeus: neither do any of them, nor does Diomed or Ajax, stand in any relation to the characteristic name of Ephurē, or of the Selleeis.

12. Nor is it difficult to understand why this title of sovereignty and honor, alone among those employed by Homer, passes away with him.

We cannot say whether it was accompanied with any prerogatives of a substantive character, as it evidently was with a peculiar form of dignity. Those characters and families, who had not risen by effort and degree, of whom no human memory bore record that they had at any period been less than the leaders and the lords of men, and whose names were associated with the earliest guidance lent to Greece in her first struggles for civilization, might well remain as bright luminaries adorning the past of the race, until either a great lapse of time, or, more probably, a breaking up of the social and political system they had taken a lead in creating, should bring about their extinction. And it is change of this kind, on the brink of which Homer leaves us, as he disappears from us in the distance. In soft music, he sings out the heroic age of heroes: and after him, as Hesiod tells us, a ruder and a darker age is sung in with a wilder music. The traditions, and the families, of the older time are submerged by the flood of Dorian conquest. The noble and refined Achaian succumbs to the half-savage Heraclid. The Hellenic world is resolved into a chaos, which devours its ancient ideas and institutions: though the spirit of life still breathes over the formless mass, and gradually moulds it into a new and more organized and splendid, if not a more pure and healthful civilization.

CHAPTER VII.

THE OLYMPIAN SYSTEM.

HOMER was the maker not only of Poems; but also, in a degree never equalled by any other poet,

1. Of a language;
2. Of a nation;
3. Of a religion.

The common tradition of Greece recognized the poets, as having had a large share in the formation of the religion of the country. These poets were in particular Homer and Hesiod, as represented by the works ascribed to them. But the difference is immense between the work performed by the author of the Iliad and Odyssey, and the author of the Theogony respectively. The latter, at a date very early without doubt, though sensibly later than that of Homer, placed upon record, and arranged, the mythological legends of the portion of country, supposed to have been Bœotia, within which he lived; and the late position, given in the poem to the gods of the Olympian dynasty, is in accordance with all the indications of the Homeric productions. But the mythology of Homer, instead of being a chronicle or a catalogue, is a supreme work of art, that lives, breathes, and moves, like the metallic statues of his own Hephaistos. And it is precisely the contrast between this wonderful performance and the Theogony of Hesiod, which enables us to conceive in some degree the immense power with which the imagination of Homer operated in shaping the characters of the Olympian gods, in adjusting their relations to one another, and in fixing the conditions of their government of the world, and of their intercourse with the children of men. On these great matters, a poem like that of Hesiod could have no other influence, than a register of births and deaths could have upon the social and political fortunes of a community.

In the supernatural world of Homer, we find deities not only of different ranks and attributes, but marked with very great varieties of moral character and tone; bearing marks of connection with different places, countries, races of men, and celestial dynasties, or theogonies, with very different degrees of respect paid to them; and these again varying with races of men and local situations.

At the same time, these beings have a head, a central place of habitation, a system and polity among themselves; to which, however, the various members of the supernatural order are very variously related.

In a word, we appear to see a great mass of heterogeneous materials having reference to the unseen world, which, as they were probably settling down in the world of fact, from their recent contact, into more stable and normal relations, so, in the world of poetry,

12

they receive from the hand of the master an unity fitting them to constitute that intellectual and ideal whole, which we know as the Hellenic religion. In this process of construction, the actual belief, traditions, and tendencies of the people could not but be the chief determining force. But the potent mind and imagination of the Poet, in all likelihood, exercised an influence in modifying the stages and fixing the consummation of the process, which, if secondary and subsidiary only with reference to the powers before mentioned, may still be justly supposed to have been far greater than any ever wielded by any other Greek, whether legislator, poet, or philosopher.

There is nothing contrary to reason in the supposition that the condition of religion in Greece, at the epoch of Homer's existence, may have offered remarkable opportunities for the formative influence even of an individual mind.

In a nation of one blood, which claims to be autochthonous or indigenous, because, since first the migration of the primitive tribe was arrested, it has never changed its seat, we may look for a religion based upon the predominance of some single idea, and invested with great uniformity of color.

But where, as in Greece, the nation itself is compounded out of a variety of factors, the religion will naturally assume a variegated aspect.

Each race or family of immigrants arrives *cum Penatibus et magnis Dis;* brings with it its own conceptions and names of deity. These they set down for themselves upon ground already occupied by the religion of the former inhabitants, and by their traditional conceptions. These conceptions will be in many cases representatives of the same original ideas; and though diversely modified, after the separation of the races, according to the genius and associations of each branch, they will often claim the same attributes, and the respective worships will tend to compete and even clash together.

Of this clashing we find the mark in Homer, when two deities have the same function. Thus Athenè is even more supreme over war than Arès. A Paieon has to do with healing as well as Apollo. Poseidon is god of the sea; but beneath him, yet in independence of him, is Nereus, inhabiting the depths; and the sea is affected by the agency of Zeus, or Here, or Athenè,[1] or Apollo, with respect to breeze, and storm, and shipwreck, as well as by his own agency.

The same kind of competition is represented in Homer by the deposition, and relegation to a distance, of the older gods of the Nature-system, and by the legends of the youth, or infancy, of Hephaistos and Dionusos.

Also this conflict of religions, growing out of the relations and conflicts of races, is powerfully exhibited in Homer by the division of Olympos into two factions during the Trojan War, and by the bold and effective, if to us incongruous, conception of the Theomachy, or Battle of the gods.

In the later tradition, this clashing comes to be represented by the legends of contests between two deities for a given territory. Poseidon contends with Helios (the Sun) for Corinth; and with Athenè for Athens. A variety of other cases may be cited.

---

[1] Od. v. 108, 109.

Had the Poet worked up his mythological scheme out of Greek materials alone, we may be sure that the relations of subordination among the gods would have been at least as well defined, as those subsisting among the leaders of the army, or perhaps even the members of a well-ordered family. Whereas now we find first that Okeanos, as the head of an older though superseded dynasty, stands aloof, and is exempt from attendance at the Olympian court;[1] and that the position of Zeus among its members reminds us of the position of the kings of France before Louis XI among their great feudatories. Poseidon, even singly, is not without pretensions to an equality of force: Athenê, without proceeding to physical resistance, does not hesitate to oppose in debate, as well as in veiled action, the councils of her father: and a combination of these two with Herè had once proved too much for his solitary strength.

When the various worships thus met in competition on the same soil, the result could not but be, either that the objects of them were amalgamated; or that some of them were expelled; or that by division of functions, that is a compromise, their differences were adjusted.

Of amalgamation we observe an example in the first deity of the Homeric poems. The Zeus of Dodona, and of the Pelasgians, becomes also the Zeus of the Hellic tribes.

Of permanent expulsion we have examples in the Okeanos, and also in the Kronos, of Homer, with their followings respectively.

Of the resistance to a new worship, and of its tem-

[1] Il. xx. 7.

porary exile, we have an instance in the driving of Dionusos into the sea by Lukourgos.

But the great principle of the Homeric mythology is, adjustment by distribution of offices. And the anthropomorphic idea greatly favored the application of this principle; since it gave to the Poet all the varied functions and orders of humane society, both domestic and political, as a framework after which to arrange his Olympian personages.

And thus it is that Homer, from living in the midst of an intermixture and fusion of bloods continually proceeding in Greece, acquired a vast command of materials, and by his skilful use of them exercised an immense influence in the construction of the Greek religion.

It became with him, what it probably had never been before, and what it was not in the works of any later writer, a most gorgeous and imposing, and even in a certain sense a highly self-consistent, whole: containing in itself, without doubt, many weak and many tarnished elements, but yet serving in an important degree the purpose of a religion to control the passions and acts of men.

The Olympian system of Homer is eminently what Horace describes as

'Speciosa locis, morataque recte
Fabula.'

It is wrought out with pains and care, full of character and individuality, marvellous alike in the grandeur and the weaknesses of its personages — a work, in the very highest sense that is applicable to any human production, of true and vast creative power.

Even without the attestation of Plato, we might have been able to judge that it was in all likelihood a main instrument in establishing the dominant features of the Hellenic religion, such as we know them from the historic ages. Partly it reduced to unity the competing elements of the true Hellenic tradition, of the old Pelasgian Nature-worship, and of the Phœnician, Syrian, and Egyptian mythologies: partly it cast them into the shade of local, as opposed to national, devotion. In the poems of Hesiod, it appears to us as the latest form of Greek religion; but, more artfully compacted than the rest, it acquired and retained a real supremacy among them, although the diversity of aspect never was effaced.

Yet its character continually altered; and altered for the worse. It has features which are sublime, and features which are debased. But the sublime features of the Olympian characters became, with the lapse of generations, less and less observable. The debased ones grew more and more prominent. And the profoundly interesting specialties of the several deities, indicating their respective origins, at length became apparently imperceptible even to the Greeks themselves. No one can closely and carefully examine the system of Homer without a deep interest: no one can find much ground for such an interest in the theological part of the religion of the historic period. Only its ethical ideas, and the highly poetic ideas connected with destiny, retain any attractive power; and from the mythology these ideas are, in the later stages of the Olympian system, almost wholly dissociated.

The wonder indeed is, not that the Olympian religion should have failed to resist the corrosion of change, but that it should have been able in any manner to retain its identity. Devoid as it was of all authority, and even of the allegation of authority, for its origin, and not only unsustained, but belied, by the witness of surrounding nations, it probably had little else of unity than such as it derived from the great Bard of the nation, and from its imaginative splendor; while it had none of the guarantees, real even if partial, which are afforded either by Books known and recognized as sacred, or by a compact and permanent hierarchy, dating, or professing to date, from the beginning of the system. If the Homeric poems stood in the place of the former, yet we can perceive for them no avenue to the mind and heart of man, except that of the poet, and the delight he gives;

ἣ καὶ θέσπιν ἀοιδὸν ὅ κεν τέρπῃσιν ἀείδων.[1]

And as respects the latter, neither was the priest, as such, a significant personage in Greece at any period, nor had the priest of any one place or deity, so far as we know, any organic connection with the priest of any other; so that if there were priests, yet there was not a priesthood. Its strength lay, then, in its beauty; a beauty which, surviving the death of the subject in which it resided, had power to ravish the mind of Goethe, one among the greatest of modern poets; and probably we could not name in all human experience a more signal instance of the vast power of the imagination, than is to be found in the long life, and the extended influences, of the Greek religion.

It found a way to the mind of man through his sympathies and propensities. Homer reflected upon

[1] Od. xvii. 385.

his Olympos the ideas, passions, and appetites known to us all, with such a force, that they became with him the paramount power in the construction of the Greek religion. This humanitarian element gradually subdued to itself all that it found in Greece of traditions already recognized, whether primitive or modern, whether Hellenic, Pelasgian, or foreign. The governing idea of the character of deity in Homer is a nature essentially human, with the addition of unmeasured power. It is at once obvious, then, that the elements of a profound corruption abound in his Olympian Court, although they affect very variously the personages who fill it. And the principle upon which it is constructed makes but too copious a provision for further deterioration.

Such accordingly was the actual working of that Hellenic Theo-mythology, of which we must regard Homer as the great founder. With the progress of time it became more and more debased, and the distinctions originally perceptible among its elements being worn away, it likewise fell into such a state of complexity as approached to chaos.

But, while the popular creed thus degenerated, the intelligence and the speculative mind of the Greeks became more and more estranged from it. With the lapse of time we must learn to regard it, not as in Homer, under a single aspect, but under three: as a religion of philosophers, a religion of legislators, and a religion of the people. By the philosophers, the abstract idea of deity was greatly purified and reformed; but the sense of personality connected with it became feebler and more remote. In Aristotle, the most profound and powerful mind of Greece in the classical ages, as well as perhaps among the purest which the country produced, it is reduced, as a practical principle, to zero. Still, the lofty sentiments, thus elaborated in the abstract, again acquired much of the warmth of life in the writings of some at least of the dramatic poets; and may thus have exercised influence in a wider sphere than that supplied to the few by the thoughtful studies of the Schools.

Meantime the mythology, with its constant development and deterioration, continued to be accepted by the people; while with a view, as must be supposed, to public order, all its institutions had the steady countenance of the ruling authorities.

It may then be believed that there resided among men, six, eight, or ten centuries after Homer, a much purer intellectual conception of deity than can be collected from his poems; while, as a first necessity of wealth and civilization, a defined but narrow morality of property, so to call it, arose; both in a form more determinate than any known to the Poet, and also sustained by the machinery of law and public policy.

But, notwithstanding all this, a great real declension in other, and perhaps yet graver, respects had taken place. For the mass of the population, the abuses and corruptions of the older creed 'did not pass, but grew.' Not perhaps against society, which had learned to take care of itself, but against the unseen Ruler of the world, and against the sanctity of human nature, sins and loathsome abominations had come in, and were flourishing in a rank and foul luxuriance, which seem to have been unknown to the Greece of Homer. For the religion of his day had not ceased to be a power. Variously and imperfectly, but truly, men were commanded and restrained by it. It presented a system of rewards and punishments, intelligible to its votaries, and operative, as it appears, to no small extent upon human conduct. And whatever may have been, as it is represented, the personal practice of the Homeric deities, their system of government was addressed in the main to good ends. It exhibited, generally speaking, though in an imperfect, yet in a real manner, superior power, armed and active on behalf of truth, justice, and humanity. This could not but be an engine of great good. That it was so, we may learn from a tone of general character, which certainly did not afterwards improve, and from the absence of the horrors already named, which afterwards abounded even in the more refined regions and in the educated classes of society.

It may seem strange that the two processes of a speculative ascent and a practical decline, a mental discipline of the few and a general dissoluteness of life, should be simultaneous. But so it was, even to the day of the last dying throes of paganism. Never was the heathen creed, on its intellectual side, in a condition so sublimated, as when it perished under the blows of the Christian apologists and the influence of the Church. But also, never had its practical power, as a religious system elevating or constraining action, fallen so low, as in the days when its votaries were habitually content to deify even monsters in human shape, if they wore the imperial purple.

To say, then, *simpliciter*, either that the Greek religion as it grew old improved, or that it degenerated, would be to use equivocal and misleading language. By its side, and never in any degree taking its place in the minds of the many, there grew up a speculation, which was hardly a belief, but which put aside a mass of fables, and in many points approximated to the truth, concerning the nature of God. But as a living creed it worsened; and as an instrument for the government of conduct, it more and more lost its power.

The reproaches of Plato against Homer, for the unworthy treatment of the gods, can have little influence on our minds in the light of such knowledge as we now possess. It would appear, from the Cratylus for example, that Plato had little knowledge of the origin of the Hellenic mythology; and the personages, who filled the chief places in it, had in his day assumed a sameness of color and position, which they had not in the time of Homer. In order to comprehend the method of the Poet, we must bear in mind (1) that many deities, afterwards completely naturalized, were in his day only making the first steps of their way into Greece; (2) that deity is with him a most elastic idea, susceptible of infinite diversities, in point of both virtue and power; (3) that he has a vivid conception of intercommunion between the two natures, divine and human, which was probably lost in the time of Plato.

If Arès and Aphroditè are exhibited by Homer in lights which are even ridiculous, we have to observe that nothing can be more profound, more entire, than the reverence of his mortals for Apollo and Athenè, nay often for Poseidon and Herè. This difference is not casual; it is in the whole manner of treatment: and what we seem to learn from it is, that among the Hellenes of his time, Arès and Aphroditè had as yet no regular recognition, no established worship. There is not a single indication of either in the Poems; though it appears from them that these deities were worshipped in Thrace and in Cyprus respectively.

Apart from this, Homer's system of thought included a number of beings, whom he calls divine, but in whom the divine attributes are minimized. The Gigantes, who rushed to their own ruin; the Kuklopes, who exhibit a perfectly brutalized humanity; the Phaiakes, who in all manly qualities are represented as much below the Greek level; all these were kinsfolk of the gods.

A slight circumstance shows us how, in Homer, the divine idea could be reduced to the smallest dimensions of power. When the comrades of Odysseus ate the oxen of the sun, Lampetiê, his daughter by Neaira, expressly called a goddess,[1] carried the news of the deed to her father. Obviously, then, she had not herself sufficient power to prevent or punish this offence, committed by a mere handful of exhausted mariners. Neither could the Sun, who is called all-beholding, see the act from his pathway in the heavens, without her intervention as a messenger.

The principal materials of religion which Homer found ready to his hand were, so far as appears, supplied by

1. The Pelasgian or other archaic races, which had had possession of the peninsula prior to the Hellenes.
2. The Hellic families and tribes.
3. The Phœnician immigration.
4. An Egyptian and oriental influence which we trace (a) in obscure traditions, and (b) in the actual remains of a worship clearly proceeding from this origin, which

[1] Od. xii. 131-133.

endured down to the time of Pausanias. This was probably brought to Greece through the Phœnician vehicle.

The Zeus of Homer is equally Pelasgian and Hellenic.

The Apollo, the Athenè, and the Herè appear to belong especially to Hellenic traditions. But the two first carry marks, which can hardly be mistaken, of an affinity, probably dating from a very early period, to the Hebrew traditions, recorded in the sacred Scriptures.

The Poseidon of Homer is manifestly Phœnician. This deity waives as it were his supremacy on coming into Greece, in deference to the paramount force of the religion of the major number, and to the ruling influences. Yet the character and worship of Poseidon may occasionally in Greece, as well as elsewhere, have been preserved under the name of Zeus.

These five are the five great deities of the Poems. But it may be convenient to consider first the mode which Homer has devised for dealing with the elder gods.

It is in a far-distant perspective that he places the Elemental or Nature powers; which are thus removed from inconvenient contact with the actual governors of the world, and yet are subjected to no indignity.

At the head of these is Okeanos; whom Homer regards as the source (not the father, that title being reserved for Zeus) of all the gods. He is not invested with anthropomorphic attributes, a circumstance which indicates the distinctness of the race which had worshipped him. But Homer, paying a marked respect to his dignity, does not summon him to the great Olympian Assembly of the Twentieth Book,[1] where, if he

[1] Il. xx. 7.

had appeared, he must have been second to Zeus. It is possible even that the relations of this deity to mankind were pre-Pelasgic; as Zeus appears to have been in the Pelasgian system, and Okeanos could hardly have been there except as its head.

In no case is the Homeric treatment more artful, than in that of the sea or water god Nereus. He is completely invested with the anthropomorphic character; for he is blessed with an abundant progeny of daughters. But his place was wanted for Poseidon: he is therefore confined to the sea-deep; and he is in no manner or degree an object of worship in the Poems.

While the Olympian system generally is to be regarded as alien to elemental worship, and as founded on a different basis, it is important to trace nevertheless such vestiges of the elder religion as are to be found among the Greeks of Homer.

1. In the Pact of the Third Iliad, the original terms were[1] that the Greeks should offer a lamb to Zeus; the Trojans two, the one black, the other white, to Gaia and Helios, the Earth and the Sun. This appears to draw the line pretty clearly between some leading ideas of the worship of the two countries; which nevertheless had, as is plain, many points of contact.

When we come to the actual Invocation, Agamemnon officiates on behalf of both parties.[2] Accordingly he first invokes Zeus (but as ruling from Ida); then the all-seeing, all-hearing Helios; and then he inserts, before Gaia, the Rivers; and he adds the deities (without naming them) who dwell beneath, and who punish perjurers in the Future State, or Underworld.

[1] Il. iii. 103.   [2] Il. iii. 276–280.

2. In the Nineteenth Iliad we have an oath and Invocation purely Greek;[1] and on comparing it with the former we find

a. That Zeus is invoked without any mention of Ida.
b. The Earth is next named.
c. The Sun is invoked without any special words of personification.
d. The Erinues, strictly ethical personages, are named as the deities below, unnamed in the previous Invocation.
e. The Rivers do not appear.

3. We also have, in the Ninth Iliad, another imprecatory Invocation; that of Althaia, mother of Meleagros. She addresses herself to (a) the Earth, (b) Aïdoneus, and (c) Persephonè: and her prayer is heard, and evidently granted as well as heard, by the air-stalking Erinūs. The offence here was not perjury, but the slaying of her brother by her son.

We thus perceive, from the first Invocation, either that the Earth and Sun stood to the Trojans as Zeus did to the Greeks, or that, when all were to be addressed, the Earth and Sun fell to the Trojans from some greater affinity to their creed. But when we come to an Invocation affecting the Greeks alone, in the Nineteenth Book, the Sun is less prominently named, and the purely ethical element is introduced in the Erinues, avengers of perjury in the nether world.

In the mixed Invocation the Erinues are not named, but are evidently the personages glanced at as avengers beneath the earth and after death.

[1] Il. xix. 258-260.

We also find it clearly established by these passages, that the Nature-gods in general were treated by Homer as subterranean: though this did not absolutely and invariably exclude them from the Olympian family. And the office generally assigned to them is not a share in the ordinary government of the world, but is the infliction of punishment, both for perjury and also for other offences, in a future state.

Hence it is that Achilles, a lock of whose hair had been promised by his father Peleus to be dedicated to the River Spercheios on his return home, deposits such a lock, at the time when he knows he shall not return home at all, in the hands of the dead Patroclos; that his spirit may carry it to the River-god, in the Underworld.[1] Here we have the clearest evidence that the Underworld, into which Patroclos was about to find entrance, was the ordinary residence of the River-gods.

Nor is this the only case of River-worship in the Poems. The Pulians in the Epeian even sacrificed a bull to Alpheios,[2] when they reached his banks; and Odysseus likewise invokes the unnamed River of Scherié, at whose mouth he touches the shore.[3] These two, it will be observed, were plainly acts of worship with reference to some immediate result, and implied the exercise by the Rivers respectively of some present prerogatives. On the other hand we may notice their strictly local character, as well as that of the act done by Achilles.

To the great Olympian Assembly of the Twentieth Book, which is to prepare the way for a decisive issue

---

[1] Il. xxiii. 144-151.   [2] Il. xi. 728.   [3] Od. v. 445.

to the war, Themis summons the Rivers (except old Okeanos) and the Nymphs who frequent or inhabit the groves and fountains. These latter, both here and elsewhere, are evidently conceived under the conditions of the human form. A like process had been begun with the Rivers; because Poseidon[1] accomplishes his purpose with Turo in the form of the River Enipeus. Others, too, of the Rivers have human sons. Nay, they even sate on the burnished chairs of the Olympian Hall.[2]

Nor let it be thought strange, that while the worship (except for imprecation) of the greater deities of the old Pelasgian system had been superseded, that of smaller ones had thus survived. For the Dii majores of that system, by reason of their very greatness, had no one exclusive residence. But the River-worship was strictly local; and it is the nature of this local worship, in whatever age, and in connection with whatever creed, to take a deep hold, and live a tenacious life. Of this there can be no stronger proof than the great number of temples recorded in Pausanias as having been erected in honor of deities, whose existence is hardly traceable in the public and national religion of historic Greece. Just so it was that the heathen system, when it was slowly and reluctantly yielding its ground to Christianity, lingered long in the villages and remoter districts, and thus gave us, as if by caprice, the singular name of Paganism for the religion, which had blazed with such extraordinary splendor in the Forum of Rome, and on the Acropolis of Athens.

[1] Od. xl. 241. [2] Il. xx. 11.

There is another form of relation between the older and the younger scheme. While the anthropomorphic spirit of the Olympian religion repels the counter-system of elemental worship, it nevertheless appropriates its materials, and even exhibits occasionally traces of its form. Thus, while the air- or sky-god becomes Zeus, the rainbow becomes Iris: and, as the rainbow in nature belongs strictly and exclusively to the sky-region, so Iris remains in the closest adherence to Zeus. She is his messenger, not the messenger of the gods in general; and even when he sits on Ida, she is in attendance on him, and available for a mission.[1] And as we may suppose that Ida was the habitual resort of Zeus when the armies were on the field, we can thus understand, not only why it is Iris who informs the Trojans about the Greek array,[2] but how she is at hand to prompt Helen's going to the Wall,[3] and to take Aphrodite out of the turmoil, and drive her, in the chariot of Arès, to Olympos.[4]

In like manner, Here appears to be constructed out of the old traditions which treated the Earth as a divine power: Demeter from a like source: and Hephaistos from an elemental god of fire.

If the local cultus thus survived in fact long after the central system had been eclipsed and superseded by one founded on ideas of greater vigor and elevation, then Homer, who of course had to exercise his plastic powers as a poet upon traditions which he found ready to hand, could not wholly extinguish the representation of those minor nature-powers in his Olympian system. And the ultimate form of recon-

[1] Il. viii. 399. [2] Il. ii. 786.
[3] Il. iii. 121. [4] Il. v. 858–869.

ciliation for the two systems was not in the ejection of the minor powers, but in the establishment of their assumption of human form, and with it the presidency over the object in which they at first inhered, as the condition of enlistment, so to speak, in the popular religion. Such was the basis of compromise, so to call it, which secured to Rivers, Fountains, Hills, and Woods, in each case their proper place in the Olympian system.

To obtain a right view of its nature, the Homeric mythology must be carefully severed, not only from the bygone schemes of Nature-worship, but likewise from (1) the Roman mythology, and (2) the mythology of classical Greece; from this classical system even as we have it in the poets, and much more as we draw it from the later writers.

We then find that the Homeric formation consists of a Polity, framed on the human model, with a king, an aristocracy, and even a people or multitude; and that its seat is on Olympos. The king is Zeus. The aristocracy consists of a number not precisely defined. Somewhere about eight or ten deities take actual part in the debates of Olympos. The ordinary meetings are strictly analogous to those of the βουλή or council of the Greek army. But, like that council, the Olympian court has its silent members: and as Hephaistos prepared for it twenty chairs[1] or thrones, we must suppose this to have been the approximate number of those who were entitled to attend. This is the body, of which the feastings are so gorgeously described; and in it are, probably, included all the deities, who

[1] Il. xviii. 373.

had obtained more than a narrowly local recognition in the Greece of Homer.

But sometimes the gods meet in (ἀγορή) their Assembly.[1] Homer appears to use this phrase on occasions when a great resolution is about to be taken. The Assembly of the Fourth Book defeats the Pact of the Third, and brings the Greeks into the field against the Trojans during the isolation of Achilles. That of the Eighth is designed to insure the absence of their potent patrons from the field of battle. Greatest of all, the Assembly of the Twentieth Book is brought together by a wider summons, including Nymphs and Rivers. This Assembly removes the embargo, and by permitting the battle of the gods, forecasts the corresponding victory of the stronger party upon earth.

In the members of the Olympian Court itself we discern every kind of heterogeneity. There seems to be scarcely a single definite feature that they possess in common: only we may assert that every one of them has a preternatural superiority to man in some one or more particulars, while a few approximate to divine perfections.

They seem, indeed, in no case to be liable to total and final extinction.[2] Yet Arès, having fled from Diomed, declares, not only that he might have remained senseless under the blows of the warrior, but might have suffered (δηρόν) indefinitely long, left among the slain. And the gods may be deposed from Olympos, as Zeus says he would have deposed Arès, if born from any other divine sire than himself.

In the Fifteenth Iliad, Poseidon appears to be

---

[1] Il. iv. 1; viii. 2; xx. 4.   [2] Il. v. 901.

threatened with Tartaros, as the consequence of the formidable conflict between Zeus and himself, which had seemed so imminent. The gods beneath, says Zeus, who form the Court of Kronos, would have become right well acquainted with the battle. As those gods are wholly cut off from Olympian action, this could only have been, as it seems, if Zeus had placed Poseidon where he had already placed Kronos.[1] Even Herè and Athenè may suffer wounds, from which ten whole years will not suffice for their recovery.[2] And if they had persisted in the second descent, then, smitten by the thunderbolt, they would not have been again admitted to Olympos.[3]

The same notion of right which binds men together, prevails among the gods, but may be set at nought by them.[4] The happiness of Olympian Immortals is liable to be impaired and disturbed by quarrels on account of their partialities to men this way or that, as the happiness of men would be disturbed.[5] The community of gods is no less emphatically humanized, than are the individuals. The relations of its members to one another are, however, but partially defined, and are subject to contingency.

Hardly any two deities are of the same dignity; and even when they discharge the same function, they do it under different conditions. Thus Athenè and Arès are the deities of war.[6] Arès fights with his own hand against a mortal: his opponent Athenè does not deign to enter into conflict herself; she incites[7] the

---

[1] Il. xv. 221-228.   [2] Il. viii. 404.   [3] Il. viii. 455.
[4] Il. v. 761.   [5] Il. l. 573-576; v. 883, 884, and 873, 874.
[6] Il. v. 430.   [7] Il. v. 124.

mind, drives¹ the chariot, but only against a god, and impels or diverts the weapon.²

While however Athene thus behaves in relation to Ares, we have no similar example in the action of the Poems, of matters carried to extremity in the upper rank of the Olympian Court. On the contrary, the highest deities of Homer are bound together by a law of mutual respect, even when they take opposite sides of a question or a quarrel, and they show the utmost anxiety to avoid carrying their differences to issue. After all, is it not a folly, they commonly say, to diminish our own happiness on account of beings so inferior to ourselves?

> See the language of Zeus to Athene, Il. viii. 39;
> Of Zeus about Poseidon, Il. xv. 226–228;
> Of Apollo to Poseidon, Il. xxi. 462–467;
> Of Here about Zeus, Il. viii. 427–431;
> Of Athene about Poseidon, Od. xiii. 341–343;
> And, although Hermes is a god of lower stamp, of Hermes to Leto, Il. xxi. 498.

Again, with a great delicacy, Homer never allows any of the higher deities to be named to mortals as being in conflict one with another. Thus when Diomed ascribes to Apollo the escape of Hector, and makes an appeal for himself to divine aid,³ he does not, as on other occasions (e.g. Il. x. 284), name Athene as his protectress, but says,

> 'If perchance I too may have a god for my ally.'

So Poseidon, in the form of Calchas, urging on the two Aiantes, and referring to Hector as claiming to be the

¹ Il. v. 840.   ² Il. v. 290, 856.   ³ Il. xi. 362–366.

son of Zeus, and as perhaps having his aid,[1] suggests that 'some one of the gods' might help one of them to make an effectual resistance. In reply, the Oilean Ajax observes that the pretended Calchas is some one of the gods of Olympos.[2] Thus no deity is placed by name in opposition to Zeus.

And thus it is contrived, that Poseidon shall retire from the field (Il. xv. 218) before Apollo arrives there to renovate Hector (239).

In the Seventeenth Book, when Athene[3] appears, that she may give effect to the altered policy of Zeus, Apollo does not absolutely retire, but the agency of the two is so directed as to avoid collision. For when Athene has incited Menelaos, and Apollo then kindles Hector, the two warriors do not meet in fight. Once more, when Achilles (Il. xx. 450) recognizes the fact that Apollo has carried off Hector, he expresses a hope that τις θεῶν may aid him too. In a word, the greater gods of Homer never are brought into conflict, nor do they exhibit their differences within the human sphere.

In Book xx, Here consults Poseidon and Athene (v. 115) as to the mode of counteracting the agency of Apollo, who is accompanying Æneas against Achilles. 'Let us,' she says, 'force him back: and then some one of us can go to attend Achilles' (119–121). Poseidon, in his reply, is unwilling to bring gods into conflict, 'unless Ares or Apollo should begin, or should hinder Achilles' (132–143) in his work of havoc.

And when, finally, Zeus exhibits the golden scales

[1] Il. xiii. 54–58.   [2] Il. xiii. 68.   [3] Il. xvii. 544.

in the air, that which holds the fate of Hector sinks to Hades, and thereupon Apollo quits him. It is then only that Athene, who was at hand and ready (see v. 187), joins and accompanies Achilles.[1]

But this mutual respect is only one among many notes of difference, which separate the orders of deity in the Olympian Court.

The Olympian personages of Homer may be divided into several classes, in several respects.

Firstly. We may consider them as background and foreground personages. The background personages are little heard of, and scarcely affect the machinery of government for the Homeric world. Such are Demeter, Themis, Leto, Dione, Hebé; such are the Muses, and the Charites or Graces; independently of the Nature-powers, who are summoned to Olympos on great and special occasions, but who take no active part in superintending human affairs at large.

Secondly. The foreground personages may be divided into those of higher and of lower power.

Of higher power we have only Zeus, Heré, Poseidon, Athené, and Apollo.

Thirdly. The Olympian deities may again be divided into two classes, of the higher and the lower ἦθος, or moral tone, respectively. The three first divinities are of the lower, and the two last of the higher, in regard to all those matters which pertain to the morality and to the infirmity, or ἀκρασία, of man.

Zeus, in his Olympian personality, stands with the class to which Heré and Poseidon belong; while, as the traditional representative of providence and the

[1] Il. xxii. 208-214.

Theistic idea, he ranks more justly with Athenè and Apollo.

Of the class lower both in power, and in moral tone, we have Hephaistos, Arès, Hermes, Aphroditè.

All, except the highest gods, in Homer may be said generally to be subject to the following limitations and liabilities:—

1. They do not know what events take place among men, except by the common senses of sound or sight, and when favorably placed; for example, when near at hand, or when sound is loud.

2. They do not know what is in the mind, and must ask to be informed.

3. They shriek or cry aloud from emotion.

4. When they move, it is (*a*) by gradual progression; (*b*) with means of conveyance.

5. They are liable to be hurt and wounded.

6. Human warriors can contend against them.

7. Their worship is peculiar to some races or places.

8. They are even liable to disparagement in communications held by the higher gods with men.

9. They have little or no command over outward nature and the elements.

10. They do not habitually repair to Olympos.[1]

11. Their partialities and propensities are without system, policy, or governing mind.

12. They neither have divine foreknowledge, nor, in many cases, have they prudence or forethought equal to the human.

13. They are not able immediately to influence the human mind.

[1] Where, however, Hephaistos lived (Il. xviii. 146–147); but perhaps for special reasons.

The only deities who may be called absolutely free from all these limitations are Zeus, Athene, and Apollo.

Even Here is subject to some of them: Poseidon to more.

Not even those deities, who are omnipresent upon earth, and take cognizance of all human affairs, are precisely informed as to what takes place in the supernal region; for when Here sent Iris to Achilles, in the Eighteenth Iliad,[1] to urge him to appear before the contending armies, it was done without the knowledge either of Zeus or of any other deity.

Certain special features, as we have seen, and shall further see, are traceable, most of all in the Athene and Apollo of the Homeric Poems, but also in Zeus, and (more forcibly) in Leto and in Iris, as well as in one or two other Olympian personages: and these features, in the case of the two first-named deities particularly, impart to the pictures of them an extraordinary elevation and force, such as to distinguish them broadly from the delineations of other gods, in whom these particular features are wanting. The features themselves are in the most marked correspondence with the Hebraic traditions, as conveyed in the books of Holy Scripture, and also as handed down in the auxiliary sacred learning of the Jews. But while it seems impossible to deny the correspondence without doing violence to facts, on the other hand we are not able to point out historically the channel of communication through which these traditions were conveyed into Greece, and became operative in the formation of the Olympian scheme.

[1] vv. 168–186.

At first sight we should be tempted to suppose that the Phœnician navigators offered the natural and probable explanation of any such phenomena. Because, on the one hand, we know, from the historic books of Scripture, that the Phœnicians were at an early date in habits of intercourse with the Jews; while, on the other hand, they not only were in like habits with the Achaian Greeks of Homer, but also, as far as we can discern, no other nation had a sensible amount of intercourse with Greece; or if there were such, it passed under the Phœnician name.

And again, there is one of the legends of Homer with reference to which the presumption arises with a peculiar force.

Apart from any disposition to premature deduction or imaginative interpretation, it seems obvious to observe upon the striking similarity between the legend of Bellerophon, solicited by the wife of Proitos, and that of Joseph, by the wife of Potiphar.

And the great abundance of tales forming the outer circle of the Odyssey, which (it is hardly too much to say) can only have had a Phœnician origin, and which touch almost every point of the compass except that to the eastward of Phœnicia itself, suggests the likelihood that this enterprising people would not be destitute of reports from that quarter also.

The name of Proitos,[1] appearing on one of the seven gates of Thebes, which mark its Phœnician re-foundation, supplies a positive link between the legend of Bellerophon and the source to which I am ascribing it.

[1] Paus. p. 727.

A second such link is supplied by the written characters, in which Proitos communicated with the King of Lycia respecting Bellerophon. The art of writing, according to the later tradition, was brought by Phœnicians into Greece; and the name of Proitos distinctly connects the text of Homer with that belief.

Our finding the family of Bellerophon in close relations with Proitos tends, of itself, to induce a belief in their ethnical connection. This presumption comes into clearer light when we observe that Bellerophon was an Aiolid.

It must also be admitted that, in supposing any other channels than the Phœnician for the conveyance of those traditions, we should force them up to a very early point of time, namely, that of the separation of the Semitic, and the Japhetic or Aryan, branches of the human family.

It is however admitted that the Olympian scheme has for its distinctive character, or *differentia*, the intense action of the anthropomorphic principle; which pervades and moulds the whole, repelling, and as it were repudiating, on the one hand all abstract speculations about the Deity, on the other the worship of Nature-Powers and of the animal creation. It is also clear, that some of the Hebraic traditions were eminently calculated to develop the anthropomorphic principle. The promise or expectation of a Redeemer, or Deliverer, of man, who should be at once human and divine, laid a basis for the entire system, by annexing the glory of divine attributes to the corporeal form of man. And the seed thus supplied was vivified, so to speak, by the familiar belief in the intercourse of God with the patriarchs, which so readily adapts itself to, if indeed it does not require, the use of a form approaching at least to the human type.

Every race had its own religious traditions. Each modified, or kept, or lost them, in obedience to its ruling tendencies. It does not seem strange that the tribe or tribes, whatever they were, which brought into Greek life and religion what proved to be their central principle, should have clung with a great tenacity to, and preserved far more faithfully than other races of a less fine composition, those traditions which were so well adapted to the effective development of their peculiar genius.

Among the Hebrews, besides what has been enshrined in the Sacred Scriptures, there was a stream of tradition[1] otherwise delivered and relating to the Messiah, which, though it nowhere impugns or even varies, yet vividly illustrates the written record. I subjoin some particulars.

1. The Messiah was to be divine.
2. He was conceived of as 'the Glory of God' in the feminine gender.
3. The relation of His two natures was set forth in the figure of mother and daughter.
4. He was to be the Logos, the Word or Wisdom of God.
5. He was the Lord of Hosts — an idea which would naturally take form in some martial development.
6. He was especially The Light.
7. He was to be the Mediator, through whom the counsels of God take effect upon man.

[1] Studies, vol. II. pp. 48–51.

8. He was to perform miracles.

9. He was to conquer the Evil One, and to liberate the dead from the grave and from the power of hell.

10. And, generally, the divine qualities were all to be reflected in the Messiah (conceived as masculine) or Shechinah (as feminine).[1]

We may probably regard the use of the feminine gender in these traditions as having been either (1) the most convenient mode of impersonating an abstract idea of the Wisdom of God, or (2) as suggested by the arrangements of the Egyptian, or other Eastern religions.

This is not the place to discuss at large the origin of the numerous religions which have existed outside the pale of the Divine revelation. It was a favorite opinion with the Christian apologists, Eusebius and others, that the pagan deities represented deified men.[2] Others consider them to signify the powers of external nature personified. For others they are, in many cases, impersonations of human passions and propensities, reflected back from the mind of man. A fourth mode of interpretation would treat them as copies, distorted and depraved, of a primitive system of religion given by God to man. The Apostle St. Paul speaks of them as devils;[3] by which he may perhaps intend to convey that, under the names and in connection with the worship of those deities, the worst influences of the Evil One were at work. This would rather be

---

[1] Studies, vol. II. pp. 51-53. Taken principally from Schöttgen's Horæ Hebraicæ.
[2] See the Propaideia or Præparatio Evangelica of Eusebius, passim.
[3] 1 Cor. x. 20.

a subjective than an objective description; and would rather convey an account of the practical working of a corrupted religion, than an explanation of its origin or its early course. As between the other four, it seems probable that they all, in various degrees and manners, entered into the composition of the later paganism, and also of the Homeric or Olympian system. That system, however, was profoundly adverse to mere Nature-worship; while the care of departments or provinces of external nature were assigned to its leading personages. Such worship of natural objects or elemental powers, as prevailed in connection with it, was in general local or secondary. And the deification of heroes in the age of Homer was rare and merely titular. We do not find that any cult or system of devotion was attached to it.

The preternatural machinery of the Homeric Poems, besides its other qualities, is singularly complex and comprehensive. Its complexity is doubtless due to the fact, that Homer had to represent and to harmonize the several varieties of religion, which had found their way into the country in company with immigrating races, families, or persons. Its comprehensiveness is owing to that anthropomorphic principle on which it is framed, and which borrowed from earth, and carried up to Olympos, the state, the family, and the individual, as they exist among men.

The bold invention by which the gods take sides in the War of Troy, and decide the controversy by main force in heaven, before it can finally be brought to issue on the plain between the Achaian and Trojan armies, is not a flight of the imagination only. The partisanship of the respective deities, this way and

that, is evidently dictated by sympathies of race.
Neither the blood, nor yet the religion, of the two
countries were wholly separate; but differences of
leaning and of color between them may readily be
discerned upon a close examination. And again,
the mode in which general rules are occasionally
varied in the Poems, irresistibly suggests that there
is a reason both for the rule and for the exceptions;
as, for example, in the care of Poseidon for Æneas
the Trojan, and in his persecution of Odysseus the
Greek. We may also discern the marks of subdivided
attachments. The care of Athenê is exercised chiefly
on behalf first of Odysseus, next to him of Achilles,
and next to him of Diomed. The care of Herê is
for the Pelopid family, and apparently for the Greeks
as the people whom they lead. Irrespectively, then,
of the manifold interest attaching to the Homeric
mythology, both as a religion and as poetry, it is in
truth a main key to the ethnography of the Poems,
and even might on this account be taken as a point of
departure in an investigation, which it influences from
first to last.

The personages of the Homeric Theotechny, under
which name I include the whole of the supernatural
beings, of whatever rank, introduced into the Poems,
are so diversified in character, intellect, and power,
that while they cannot be described under any one
common form, it is difficult to divide them into classes
with anything like precision. Into the following categories, however, we may distribute them with a tolerable approach to accuracy.

1. The Olympian deities; recognized and actual
governors, but with immensely different titles and

prerogatives, either of the inner and Greek world, or of the outer world known more faintly and indirectly to the Greeks.

2. The greater Nature-Powers, with Okeanos at their head, who had apparently been supreme in the prior or Pelasgian Theogony.

3. The lesser Nature-Powers, who continued to hold their ground, at least in local influence.

4. Minor deities of foreign tradition, neither naturalized nor acknowledged in Greece, as not being of sufficient significance to claim admission to Olympos.

5. Rebellious powers.

6. Ministers of Doom and Justice, real or reputed; less than divinities in rank, but more closely associated with the moral order.

7. Impersonated ideas connected with the objects of human desire and aversion, hope and fear.

8. Translated, or deified, heroes.

9. Races intermediate between gods and men.

Again. Many elements of the Hebrew traditions recorded in the Holy Scriptures, or otherwise preserved among the Jews down to later times, appear in the Olympian Court of Homer. But they are not found in all the personages that compose the assemblage; nor even in all those deities whom, from various kinds of evidence in the Poems, we perceive to have been fully recognized as objects of the national worship. Further, in the characters where the features corresponding with Hebrew traditions mainly appear, there is a peculiar elevation of tone, and a remarkable degree of reverence is maintained towards them, so as to separate them, not indeed by an uniform, but commonly by a perceptible and even a broad line, from the remainder of the gods.

Besides the idea of a Deity which in some sense is three in one, the traditions traceable in Homer, which appear to be drawn from the same source as those of Holy Scripture, are chiefly these:— (1) A Deliverer, conceived under the double form, first of the 'seed of the woman'— a being at once Divine and human; secondly of the Logos, the Word or Wisdom of God. (2) Next, the woman whose seed this Redeemer was to be. (3) Next, the rainbow considered as a means, or a sign, of communication between God and man. And finally the tradition of an Evil Being, together with his ministers, working under the double form described by Moloch in his speech, of 'open war,' and of 'wiles;' as a rebel, and as a tempter. This last tradition is indeed shivered into fragments, such as the giants precipitated into Tartaros, and as Atè roaming on the earth; with perhaps a portion of the idea lodged in Kronos, whose common and only description in Homer is 'Kronos of the crooked thought' (ἀγκυλομήτης). The other four traditions appear to be represented in the persons of Apollo, Athenè, Leto, and Iris. Of course it by no means follows that they have no other origin than in these traditions, or that, as they stand in Homer, they represent such traditions and nothing else. Iris, for example, must evidently be considered as an impersonation of a Nature-Power. What seems to me undeniable is that, in the Poems of Homer, the traditions I have named are at the least copiously and richly embroidered upon the tissue, supplied by other accounts of the mythological persons I have named; and that they give to those persons a distinctiveness of character and form, which upon a close and detailed view of the Olympian system, as it is unfolded in the Poems of Homer, cannot well be mistaken by a painstaking and unprejudiced observer. If, in the progress of time, and with the mutations which that system gradually underwent, the marks of correspondence with the Hebrew records became more faint, the fact even raises some presumption that, were we enabled to go yet further back, we should obtain yet fuller and clearer evidence of their identity of origin in certain respects.

Even the highest conception of deity in Homer does not exclude the element of fraud. I will give an example. There can be no question that the prize of the loftiest, most free, and most constant and unvarying intelligence in the whole catalogue of Olympian deities must be given to Athené; who, alone among them, is never ignorant of what it concerns her to know, never exposed to disrespect, never outwitted by an opponent, never disappointed of an end. But, in the great crisis of Hector and Achilles, when the intrinsic superiority of the Greek hero makes him independent of any even more honorable aid, she descends to the mean and shameful artifice of assuming the form of his brother Deiphobos, whom he especially loved and trusted, to induce him to turn and meet his adversary.[1] This arrangement is the more remarkable, because it is somewhat difficult to discern the motive for such an intervention, or to see why Achilles could not, with his extraordinary swiftness of foot, have overtaken Hector apart from any assistance whatever. Perhaps

[1] Il. xxii. 214-247.

it was an artifice of the Poet to uplift the character of Hector, of course in order to glorify yet further the Greek hero, who was to overcome him.

Those pure and lofty traditions, then, which we are justly wont to refer to a primitive revelation as their fountain-head, had already begun to be impaired. And it is only what we ought to expect, if we find that with the lapse of time they suffered further deterioration, and if the persons representing them gradually sunk nearer and nearer to the level of those other Olympian deities who had already in the time of Homer lost, or who perhaps never had possessed, any notes of the sublime conceptions which the Holy Scriptures, and in some degree the auxiliary traditions of the Hebrows, have handed down to us in the greatest purity, and which the peculiar genius that became dominant in the Greek religion had, for a time at least, been able to preserve, if not from all injurious contact, yet from anything like absolute immersion in the mire. The Athené and Apollo of the Olympian system may be compared with the Child in the noble Ode of Wordsworth; about whom, in his infancy, Heaven is lying, who as boy and youth

> Yet by the vision splendid
> Is on his way attended;

but who in process of time parts from it altogether:

> At length the man perceives it die away,
> And fade into the light of common day.[1]

It is no part of the object of this work to institute a detailed comparison between the earliest and the

---

[1] Wordsworth's Ode on the Recollections of Childhood.

later stages of the morality and religion of the heathen world; but I shall now state summarily the results which such a comparison would, I think, reasonably suggest, so far as religion is concerned.

Religion and race have ever run much together. We find in Homer the clear tokens of a composite people, and of a composite belief. With the lapse of time the edges and angles of ethnical differences are worn down. The nation and the creed settle down upon an acknowledged platform; and the distinctive features, though they do not wholly vanish, take a form which it is difficult to trace back to their first origin. All formations, especially if complex, must be examined in their beginnings. The religion of classical and historic Greece is already an old religion. The Poems of Homer enable us to investigate its first inception. We can trace the very finger of the artist on the clay he moulded for his countrymen's behoof. But as the nation was compacted and consolidated, the component parts of the religion also settled down, and their specific differences, like colors running, lost all definite outline.

This loss of distinctive notes in the Greek mythology was a deteriorating and not an improving process. The gods of later times were not relieved from the stains which attach to them in Homer. Some legends, which with him appear in a beautiful and noble shape, became utterly abominable and base. While the level of the higher characters of his Theogony was reduced till it nearly reached that of the lower, the level of the lower was in no way raised. In the processes of change, nothing was given, all was taken away.

But the grand distinction between the Homeric and

the later systems was this: that the earlier scheme was a real, though it was a corrupt, religion. It acted upon life. It menaced the excesses of power. It prescribed the duties of reverence to age and authority, of hospitality to the stranger, and of mercy to the poor. It had one and the same standing with reference to all classes. It did not assign to deity that most ungodlike quality, respect of persons. But in after times, apart from its deeper moral stains, it became wholly severed from the cultured mind; and subsisted mainly as the jest of philosophers and men of the world, the tool of priests and rulers, the bugbear of the vulgar.

Again, it may be noticed that the religion of Homer, subject to varying closeness of relation between different places and particular deities, is, though not an uniform, yet an universal religion.

The Poet evidently supposed that in some manner the Olympian gods governed not the Greeks only, but all mankind. This perhaps is the reason why he has admitted into the Olympian family personages like Arês, Aphroditê, and the Sun, whom we cannot affirm to have been worshipped at the time in Greece; the evidence being, indeed, averse to any such supposition. This element of truth in his conceptions of Deity is clearly exhibited by the banquets provided for his gods among the Aithiopes; by the scene of the Iliad, in which Zeus turns his eyes over the country of the Hippemolgoi and the Abioi;[1] and especially by this, that, in the wide range of the Voyage of Odysseus, though he comes within the special jurisdiction first of Posei-

---

[1] Il. xiii. 6–6.

don, and next of Helios, still there is always a power of supreme control lodged in the Olympian Assembly; a power, by means of which his release from the island of Calypso is finally obtained.

It seems as if his primitive spirit had been unable to embrace the conception, which in later times came into vogue, of different and unconnected deities ruling different portions of mankind; and as if both his own and the prevailing religious sense required that, although the name and worship of many among them had originally come from, or even still belonged to, a foreign shore, yet they should, as far as their importance required him to take notice of them, be bound together into a supreme and organized unity. But, notwithstanding, within the bosom of this unity the character and associations of his own race, which, without doubt, he placed at the head of all mankind, were to be predominant. In this combination of ideas we find the basis, and the warrant, of his Olympian system.

The collective action of the Olympian deities in the government of men is less infirm, more venerable, more divine, than their individual action. When they move together, the more idiosyncrasies, in which they abound, appear to be in a great degree lost and absorbed. The co-operation of the three great Hellenizing deities in the War against Troy is, indeed, the efficient cause of the divine decision in favor of the Greeks. And this again is mythically referred to a vindictive sentiment on the part of each of the men; yet the decision is a righteous decision. And, speaking generally, while the individual members of the Olympian Court are swayed by hate, lust, and greed, they have not any objects which they can pursue in common for the gratification of these appetites or passions; and thus is neutralized the personal bias which so frequently draws them off the line of moral obligation, and more free scope is given, in all their common action, to the exercise of the true governing office.

It is somewhat singular that we have not, in the true Olympian religion, any clear instance of a married deity, except Zeus. Hephaistos is married to Aphroditè only in the Phœnician, or rather perhaps Syrian, mythology of the Eighth Odyssey. In the Iliad he is but wooing Charis.[1] That Amphitritè is the wife of Poseidon is a purely gratuitous assumption, and is in every way improbable, since Amphitritè has no clear or definite impersonation. Helios and Persè had children; but they are wholly within the Eastern mythology. The names of Aïdes and Persephonè are commonly combined in such a way as would be consistent with, and as may even suggest, their being married. But this would scarcely harmonize with his general arrangements, if Demeter was the mother of Persephonè, and if Aïdoneus[2] was an earthy Zeus. And Homer has carefully avoided using any words which would directly place them in this relation. Okeanos and Tethûs, Kronos and Rhea, lie outside the Olympian scheme.

If this observation be correct, the fact is probably to be accounted for in this way: Homer had no idea of a normal marriage without issue. Where there were none, it was a heaven-sent calamity. He could not, then, have divinities distributed in barren pairs. But to have provided them with families would have

[1] Il. xviii. 382.   [2] See infra, Aïdoneus.

placed him in difficulties, such as may sometimes be felt by royalty on earth, with respect to the means of providing for a numerous offspring. It would have been difficult to weave them into the stock of traditions which supplied his raw material. Moreover, as between brothers and sisters, the Greek horror of incest perhaps would ill have allowed the general use of the idea of a matrimonial connection; though Here was the sister as well as the wife of Zeus, and though this double relation was not at all foreign to such Eastern traditions[1] as he had received through the Phœnicians. Thus he was shut up on all sides to arranging his Olympus, as to its younger generation, in the form of the single though manifold family of Zeus.

Again. Within the theological system of Homer, and as a kind of kernel to it, there lies a system which may be called one of deontology, or that which ought to be, and to be done. 'Will' is the supreme element in the mythological action; or, at the least, it is in practice co-ordinate with 'ought,' and it seems to be in conduct the livelier principle of the two. But the idea conveyed in 'ought' has a separate sphere, and ministers of its own, to which even Olympian personages pay regard. Its laws are expressed sometimes in terms relating to destiny: most purely of all in ὅπις and ἐν ῥέζησις; which may truly be said to reflect the moral sense of the gods, and which are never used by Homer to express a mere mental emotion of mankind. They may convey more or less the sense of an emotion, but it is an emotion always springing from and regu-

[1] Od. x. 5–9.

lated by a regard to the essential laws of right, to the themistes of heaven. A third form, in which the dictates of the moral law are expressed and enforced, is in the action of its mute but ever active ministers, the Erinues.

These topics will be opened in their due order. I pass to another head.

Homer informs us in the Eighteenth Iliad that Hephaistos was found by Thetis busy in finishing a set of twenty seats,[1] for the members of the Olympian Court to use in their assemblies. I have observed that, with some allowance for the vagueness common with the Poet in the use of figures, we may take this incident as indicating pretty closely what he meant to be understood as the number of the Di majores, or personages qualified to attend at the Council (boulè) of the gods.

As to nearly the whole of them, there is no difficulty in drawing out the roll:—

I. The children of Kronos:—

    1. Zeus
    2. Poseidon
    3. Aïdoneus
    4. Here 4

II. The secondary wives of Zeus:—

    1. Leto
    2. Demeter
    3. Dionè 3

[1] Il. xviii 872–377.

III. The children of Zeus: —

    1. Athenè
    2. Apollo
    3. Hephaistos
    4. Hermes
    5. Artemis   8
    6. Arês
    7. Persephonè
    8. Aphroditè

IV. Personages not classified, but performing Olympian offices: —

    1. Themis, the Summoner
    2. Iris, the Envoy   3
    3. Hebè, the Cupbearer

                                                    18

Besides these eighteen we have

1. Helios, the Sun, taking part in Olympian proceedings.[1]

2. Paieon, who appears to be ordinarily present there as Healer.[2]

Both these personages came to be absorbed in Apollo: but in Homer they are distinct from him: and, so far as the poet may have had a distinct intention as to number, these two have perhaps the best claim to the Nineteenth and Twentieth places.

3. Another claim, making the Twenty-first, is that of Dionusos; whose position, however, in Homer is faintly marked and somewhat equivocal.[3]

---

[1] Od. viii. 270, 302, and xii. 374–376.   [2] Il. v. 401, 899.
[3] *Infra*, Chap. VIII. sect. Dionusos.

On the whole, we ought perhaps to reject two other names.

1. Eris, or Enuo, the sister and the paramour of Arês.[1] She grows up, and this as it seems habitually, from small to huge dimensions. She remains to witness the battle of the Eleventh Iliad, while the other deities withdraw to their Olympian palaces respectively.[2] She is sent down to the camp at the beginning of the same Book, and shouts from the ship of Odysseus. She is named, too, together with Pallas,[3] in contrast with the effeminate Aphroditê. Yet, on the whole, she is probably no more than a vivid poetical impersonation. In conformity with this supposition, while Arês carries a spear as he leads the Trojans to the fight, she conducts, instead, another form yet more shadowy than her own, that of Kudoimos, or Tumult.

2. Histiê, who is Vesta, and one of the Dî majores, in the Roman mythology, and who is also fully personified in the post-Homeric poetry of the Greeks, can scarcely be considered as a person in the view of Homer. There are indeed invocations to her name,[4] which signifies 'the hearth,' in the Odyssey; but in three cases out of the five it is combined with that of the table for guests.

---

[1] Il. iv. 441.   [2] Il. xi. 3, 4, 73.   [3] Il. v. 333, 592.
[4] Od. xiv. 159; xvii. 156; xix. 304; xx. 231.

CHAPTER VIII.

THE DIVINITIES OF OLYMPOS.

SECTION I. *Zeus.*

ZEUS presents to us a character more heterogeneous and less consistent than that of any other Homeric deity.

He claims a strength superior to the united strength of all the gods;[1] yet he admits that he would have some difficulty[2] in putting down Poseidon singlehanded; and he was actually delivered by a giant[3] from fetters into which he had been, or was about to be, thrown by a combination of that god with Athené and Here.

In many points he inherits the traditions, and is formed upon the conception, of the One and Supreme God. Yet he was one of three brothers, who had parents preceding them: the three were born to equal honor:[4] lot alone decided their several domains. Seniority gives Zeus the first place: yet the filial tie

---

[1] Il. viii. 17-27.
[2] Il. i. 399-406.
[3] Il. xv. 228.
[4] Il. xv. 209.

had not prevented him from imprisoning his own father in perpetuity. He is alike the depository of high moral ideas, and of intense, as well as of debased, human attributes. He bears many different characters; and no one of them is altogether consistent with the rest.

There are five different capacities in which, in order to embrace the entire picture drawn by the Poet, he must be regarded. Four of them are Olympian: one appertains to an earlier theogonic scheme.

1. Zeus is the meeting-point of the Pelasgic with the Olympian or Hellenic system of religion.

2. He is the depository of the principal remnants of monotheistic and providential ideas.

3. He is the sovereign lord of meteorological phenomena.

4. He is the head of the Olympian Court.

5. He is the most marked receptacle of all such earthly, sensual, and appetitive elements as, at the time of Homer, anthropophuism had obtruded into the sphere of deity.

On the epithets and verbal ascriptions of Zeus, we may observe,

1. That they much exceed in number and variety those of any other deity.

2. That with few and special exceptions they are applied to him exclusively.

3. That they divide themselves into classes according as they belong to him,

 a. In respect of national or special worship, as Dodonaios, Idaios, Pelasgicos, Olumpios.

 b. In respect of his chief place in the Hellenic theogony, as air-god: such as ἀστεροπητής, τερπικέραυνος, κελαινεφής, τετρακίκαυνος, ἐριγδουπος, εὐρύοπης.

c. In respect of his character as the Providence and Governor of mankind, and the defender of social and moral laws: such as θεῶν ὕπατος καὶ ἄριστος, πατὴρ ἀνδρῶν τε θεῶν τε, μητιέτης, ξείνιος, ἱκετήσιος: highest and best of gods, father of gods and men, the Zeus of counsel, the Zeus of the guest, the Zeus of the suppliant.

Let us now proceed to this fivefold observation of the Homeric Zeus.

1. *The Pelasgian Zeus.*

At times, the Zeus of Homer appears to border upon the mere Nature-Power: as in the epithet Διιπετής, 'falling from Zeus,' applied to rivers: in Ἔνδιος, meaning ' at noontide,' and recalling the ' sub dio, sub Jove,' of the Latins. Also the expressions, Διὸς ὄμβρος, αἰγαί, ψεκάδες, ὧραι, the rain, rays, snow-flakes, hours or seasons of Zeus, may all be compared with analogous expressions applied to Demeter and to Hephaistos. We may consider all those as being, in their various shades, relics of the Pelasgian worship of Nature-Powers.

We may in fact either consider the Pelasgian Zeus, and the Zeus of the anthropomorphic system, as one or as two. It is probable that two separate clusters of tradition may have belonged to the same name, and that in time they coalesced together, in obedience to the law of public feeling, combined with their respective internal aptitudes. And this condition may have been the solution no less of a great ethnical than a great mythological question.

According to the legend of Thetis, in the First Iliad, there was a time when Herè, Poseidon, and Athenè combined to put him in bonds. He was saved from this peril by Thetis, who fetched Briareus, or Aigaion of the Hundred Hands, to his aid. This giant was stronger than his father Poseidon, and on his arrival the plan was abandoned. Of the three deities named, Heré and Athené are eminently Hellenic, and Poseidon appears to be Phœnician. The meaning of the legend therefore probably is, that the supremacy of the old, and perhaps purely elemental, Zeus of the Pelasgians was endangered by the arrival of the Phœnician and Hellenic immigrants with their respective religious associations: but that an accommodation was afterwards effected, and a Zeus acknowledged, who sufficiently took into himself the Pelasgian element.

The Zeus of Homer is the Pelasgic Zeus, and the Zeus of Dodona; and he is also worshipped by the Helloi.[1] These Helloi appear to represent the Hellenic race in its pre-Hellenic form; and the Pelasgian name, with that of Dodona, places the throne of Zeus within the shadows of the pre-Hellenic period. It is true that, in the Theogony of Homer, this deity has ancestors and antecessors: and he alone, of the family of gods proper to the Pelasgians, is carried over at once into the Hellenic and Olympian system. This may have been both because, as the god of air and light, he answered best among them to that more abstracted and less materialized conception of Deity which the Hellenic mind required; and because there clustered around him whatever traditions of a supreme and single Being the world of human thought had either fashioned or retained. In any case it is plain that the

[1] Il. xvi. 233-235.

Poet, having got rid of all claims of priority by relegating the Nature-Powers to the Underworld, or to the sea-floor, or to the extremities of the earth, is thus enabled to leave his Zeus firmly grounded in authority as the senior god of the Olympian system. And this claim of seniority is the true basis of his supremacy. To this it is, and by no means to mere excess of force, that Poseidon defers in the Fifteenth Iliad, as to a claim profoundly rooted in that moral order, which even gods acknowledge and respect.

It is at the stage where the Past, having been before only cloud and mist, becomes for Homer that shaped tradition which occupied, relatively to his time, the place of History, that Zeus offers to the mind of the Greek hearer the earliest definite point upon which understanding and memory can fix, so that he can be chosen as, for practical purposes, the origin to which all things are to be traced up and referred.

It seems likely that this priority of Zeus may lie at the root of his preference for Troy: a state and people in which we discern the predominance of a mere Pelasgian character, and where the royal family mounts to a greater antiquity than that of any properly Hellenic or Achaian race.

2. *The Divine Zeus.*

To Zeus as Providence belong both a number of separate ascriptions, and a general position, which underlies the whole action of the Iliad. The grandeur of his figure and attributes transcends every other composition. He is identified, in perhaps an hundred places of the Poems, with the word theos, in its more abstracted signification as Providence, or the moral governor of the world. He is the ταμίης πολέμοιο, the arbiter of war: and he exhibits in the sky, on great occasions, the scales in which are weighed contending fates. He is the source of governing authority, and he shows his displeasure when it is abused.[1] He is the distributor in general of good and evil among mortals; for it is on his floor that the two caskets[2] stand, from which are dispensed the mixed and the unmixed lots of men. He has the care of the guest, the suppliant, and the poor; and thus his name becomes the guarantee for three relations, which were and are fundamental to the condition of mankind, considered with reference to social existence. Indeed, in this character he is himself a source of Destiny, as we find from the remarkable phrase Διὸς αἶσα, the fate of, or proceeding from, Zeus.

Zeus approximates to, and perhaps possesses, an ubiquitous or universal supremacy. Hellic and Pelasgian, Idaian and Olympian, he leads the band of the Immortals to feast during an eleven days' absence on the sacrifices offered by the Aithiopes or Ethiopians, who occupied the whole southern line of the world of Homer:[3] and he likewise, in an interval of his cares respecting Troy, casts his eyes in the far north not only over Thracians and Mysians, but over Hippemolgoi and Abioi.[4] His name is likewise acknowledged in the border land of Scherië, and in the outer sphere where Poseidon rules: for, say the brother Cyclops to the brutal Poluphemos, 'Disease comes from the mighty Zeus, and cannot be escaped: pray however to thy father the lord Poseidon.'[5] From this passage we perceive

[1] Il. xvi. 387. [2] Il. xxiv. 527. [3] Od. i. 23.
[4] Il. xiii. 1-6. [5] Od. ix. 411.

that Zeus was not for Homer a mere name for Poseidon in his own kingdom, as Aïdoneus is called 'the Zeus beneath.'[1] The meaning more nearly approaches to a recognition of the Providential character of Zeus, as contradistinguished from his Olympian capacity. In this larger conception his individual existence at times appears almost wholly to merge.

Zeus, however, although no positive limits are affixed to his capacities of perception and knowledge, does not as a matter of course perceive all that is going on among mortals. By an expedient of some *naïveté*, he turns his eyes away from Troy towards Thrace and the righteous nations of the North, when Poseidon is about to come into the field. This god, assuming a disguise, remains there long without being observed, although the sleep of Zeus has not yet come.[2]

And again, to save the body of Patroclos, Here sends Iris on a mission to Achilles, which is concealed from Zeus as well as from the other gods[3] (κρύβδα Διὸς ἄλλων τε θεῶν).

After the Theomachy also, he inquires of Artemis who it was that had maltreated her. Yet he had seen, and had exulted in seeing, the gods as they engaged in conflict.[4]

Besides these physical limitations, Zeus is subject to deceit. He is entrapped by Here through the medium of his passion,[5] and is lulled into a sleep, in order that during his inaction his decree may be disobeyed. In like manner[6] that goddess had completely outwitted him at the time of the birth of Heracles, by obtaining a promise on behalf of a descendant of his who was to

---

[1] Il. ix. 457. [2] Il. xiii. 1–16, 352–356. [3] Il. xviii. 165–109.
[4] Il. xxi. 389, 508. [5] Il. xiv. 352. [6] Il. xix. 97 seqq.

be born on that day, and by then accelerating the birth of Eurustheus in Argos, and stopping that of Heracles in Thebes.

On certain occasions, we find Zeus acting as supreme and single-handed, neither against nor with the Olympian assembly. The grandest of these is at the close of the Odyssey.[1] Athenè, stimulated by her sympathizing keenness, appears to have winked at the natural, but vengeful, disposition of Odysseus towards his ungrateful and rebellious subjects. Zeus, who had previously counselled moderation, launches his thunderbolt; and it falls at the foot of Athenè, who thereupon gives the required caution to the exasperated sovereign. Peace immediately follows.[2]

He has also this marked and paramount distinction, that he never descends to earth to execute his own purposes, but in general sends other deities as his organs, to give effect to his will, or else operates himself from afar, by signs, or by positive exertions of the power which he possesses as god of air.

Zeus, however, is not absolutely omnipresent; for his journey, and his consequent absence from Olympos, are described.[3] But, unlike the case of Poseidon, we have no detail, no succession in his movement. Again, unlike Poseidon, he hears prayer irrespective of the particular place or point from which it is offered.

3, 4. *The Olympian Zeus, and the Lord of Air.*

The chief agency of Zeus in the Poems is as head of the Olympian family and Court.

In this character he is the governor of the air and

---

[1] Od. xxiv. 481, 525–541, 546. [2] Od. xxiv. 546.
[3] Il. i. 420–425.

all its phenomena; the eldest of the trine brotherhood, and the owner of the Aigis, which is the symbol of sovereign power, like the crown, or sword of state, in an European kingdom. To him the gods rise up at their meetings. Though he swears, as other deities do, in confirmation of his word, we have no details as to the form: but we know that the highest mode of conveying his will and word is by the nod peculiar to himself.[1]

Besides those offices in relation to the air, which are more capable of an elemental interpretation, he commands the clouds, the tempests, the winds, the thunder and lightning, the years; he impels the falling star, or launches the thunderbolt.[2] All signs in air belong to him, as does especially the rainbow, which he planted in the clouds.[3] Iris, accordingly, is his personal messenger in the Olympian Court. And when any of the attributes belonging to the region of air are employed by other deities, it is in virtue of a special relation to him. These partners of his power appear to be, exclusively of the rest, Here as his wife; with Athene and Apollo, in virtue of moral and traditional relations with the Supreme Deity, belonging to them respectively.

The arrangement of the trine brotherhood seems to bear peculiar marks of a traditional origin. For, besides the division of power between three, the mode is remarkable. The Greek ideas and practice were founded, more or less, on primogeniture. Yet it is by lot that Zeus receives the air, Poseidon the sea, Aïdoneus the Underworld. This method of division is evi-

---

[1] Il. i. 524–530. Compare Hebrews, vi. 13.
[2] Od. xii. 415–417; xxiv. 549.   [3] Il. xi. 27.

dently meant to save the principle of equality, which the Poet thus curiously interweaves with the superiority of Zeus.

For, as the head of the Olympian Court, it is clear that Zeus is stronger than any single god. It is in doubt whether he is, as he boasts, stronger than the whole. We see that at a former period three were able to coerce him. Perhaps we are to understand this legend as referring to a period of crisis: the conditions of human life may enter into the problem, and his sovereignty may be meant to be understood as one which when once vindicated, became resistless, and was thoroughly consolidated by time. His superiority, however, must in the last resort, like that of other governors, be maintained by main force,[1] when persuasion or verbal command has failed. Nor could it be exercised over the great Poseidon without a struggle.[2] Herè and Athenè, however, single or combined, he threatens freely; and the first of these he had once punished with severity.[3]

Of omnipotence, properly so called, Homer does not seem to have embraced the idea. To this height, indeed, even the philosophy of the ancients never ascended. But none of the epithets of Zeus go so far as to express it, even in forms which might be supposed figurative.

The headship of Zeus, however, is established not only in superior force but, as has been shown, by special marks of respect, and by symbols of sovereignty: it may be added, by the general deference of the gods. Other tokens are observable. There is no

[1] Il. xv. 164–167.   [2] Il. xv. 228.   [3] Il. xv. 18.

patronymic among the gods, except that of Zeus himself. And further, in the Olympian system proper, there is no god born of any divine sire other than Zeus; nor any god born of a goddess, except he be the father; nor any god born of a human mother.

Again, he is undisguisedly the arbiter among the gods. Heré appeals to him on the conduct of Arès, and he permits his Queen to let loose Athené on the Trojans.[1] Arès, when wounded, carries his complaint to Zeus;[2] and Artemis also sits on his knee and makes known to him her woes.[3] This office, as a kind of judgeship in appeal, is a great stay to the power of Zeus.

This headship of Zeus in the Olympian polity is not merely ornamental; it entails the weight of government. The careful reader of the Iliad will be struck by the resemblance between his position among the gods, and that of Agamemnon in the circle of his chieftains. As heralds upon earth are his messengers, so it is at his command that a messenger goes to summon the Olympian assemblies: he commonly,[4] though not universally,[5] introduces the subject of discussion, and, so to speak, manages the debate. He also feels the burden of government over man, when the divine Assemblies are not in session. After the gorgeous scene of the banquet in the First Iliad, the other gods slept, but Zeus slept not; he had in his hands the charge of the Executive, and he summoned Dream to do his bidding.[6]

The idea, to which we give the name of responsi-

[1] Il. v. 765.
[2] Il. xxi. 705.
[3] Il. xx. 13.
[4] Il. v. 872.
[5] Il. iv. 7; viii. 41; Od. i. 32.
[6] Il. ii. 1–7.

bility, is represented in Zeus, and in him only. Other gods appear in the movement of the Iliad with an intermittent agency. But it is Zeus who is charged with the general conduct of affairs, with seeing that the government of the world is carried on. There is no better example of this, than in the Olympian Assembly at the opening of the Odyssey. Odysseus is at the time detained by Calypso in the Island of Ogygiê. The care of Athenê does not reach to him, because he is in the Outer world, under the government, apparently, of Poseidon, his great enemy. Meanwhile, his substance is wasted, and his wife tormented, by the dissolute Suitors. All this exhibits a sad rent in the established terrestrial order. Consequently the gods in general are affected with compassion.[1] But it is the business of Zeus to introduce the subject to them, for their opinion and decree.

At the same time we must observe the skill with which he manages the Assembly. He avoids placing himself in conflict with Poseidon by any hasty assumption of the initiative; and only gives his sanction to the plan of the Return, when Athenê has complained of the detention, and thrown the responsibility of this evil upon Zeus.[2] We may observe a like refinement in the Assembly of the Fourth Iliad. The real object of Zeus in that Assembly is to draw the Greeks into the field, which can only be done by bringing about a breach of the Pact of the Third Book. And this must be done by the Trojans, since the Achaians were keepers of their oaths. But his mode of action is to propose that the accommodation just effected shall

[1] Od. i. 19. [2] Od. i. 62, 76.

be made permanent, and that Troy shall continue to subsist. For he knows very well, that this will put the Hellenizing deities upon proposing a scheme for the renewal of the war, and thus that they will save him from giving offence to those of the Trojan party.

It is not only in the individual characters and the family order, but also in the general form of the polity of Olympos, that we may trace the anthropomorphic spirit of the Homeric religion. That polity is more aristocratic than monarchical. It does not exclude the idea of coercion, even as applied to Zeus himself; for he was put in chains by the united action of Heré, Athené, and Poseidon.[1] Upon the whole, notwithstanding the mutterings of Poseidon in the Fifteenth Iliad, the superiority of Zeus to any single deity is sufficiently established. But although he boasts, that he is able to overcome in mere force the whole Assembly,[2] it is incontestable that the will which ultimately prevails is that of the body, and not of the individual who is its head. His effort[3] to obtain a more favorable solution entirely fails. Homer indeed has balanced the question with his usual adroitness; for, as far as the comparatively narrow plot of the Iliad is concerned, Zeus effects his purpose of glorifying Achilles, by the temporary success of the Trojans whom he loved. But it is the Battle of the gods, and the decisive superiority of the Hellenizing deities, which foreshadows, and makes way for, the victory of Achilles over Hector. And, as regards the general issue of the War, it is evident that the preference of Zeus lies with the Tro-

[1] Il. i. 399–401. [2] Il. viii. 18–27. [3] Il. iv. 14–19.

jans and not with the Greeks. It is then the prevailing sense of the Olympian Court, already represented to us in the Theomachy under the form of physical force, which determines the doom of Troy, and determines it in conformity with justice, but clearly against the bias, if not the outspoken will, of Zeus.

5. *Zeus the type of anthropomorphism.*

The framework of the Olympian system is in itself the most imposing form of development ever given to the principle of anthropomorphism; that principle which, to define it briefly, casts the divine life into human forms. This is effected by Homer with reference to all the main relations of life; the State, the family, and the individual. The State is represented by the Olympian polity as a whole. The relations of the deities among themselves are all thrown into the form of the family. Perhaps it was the sheer necessity of the case, perhaps the fact that the stream of tradition came from the East, which carried with it the consequence that, while the Greek family was thoroughly normal, the family of the Greek gods was based upon polygamy,[1] and upon polygamy attended with what would among men be deemed a license yet more relaxed. In truth, it is the domestic organization of Troy, rather than of Greece, which supplies the earthly original from which the family in Olympos is a copy; although this is a feature accidental in reference to the main design.

For, in Olympos, we have Zeus with Herè as his principal wife; with Leto, Dionè, and perhaps De-

[1] Il. xxi. 499.

meter, as the secondary or subordinate wives. In the rear of these, came all the persons who were the subjects of his adulterous intrigues on earth. Here alone is the Queen, who by reflection attracts, and who exercises, though with a contracted power, the air-governing prerogatives of her husband. The other goddesses I have named are personages, differing in dignity, but agreeing in this, that they are mute and blind in reference to the governing office.

While the Olympian Court, and Zeus as its head, present to our view the weight of political care, and are commonly seen working for good, the individual character of Zeus is of a far lower order than his public capacity would lead us to expect. Into this there enters almost as much of Falstaff, as of Lear into the character of Priam. The basis of it is radically Epicurean. A profound attachment to ease and self-enjoyment is its first governing principle. Except for his pleasures, and indeed with a view to indulging in them, he never disturbs the established order; and he rescuts in a high degree the fiery restlessness, as well as the jealousy,[1] of Heré. The sacrificing man is the pious man: but the love of Zeus for such men appears to be closely associated with the animal enjoyment of the libation and the reek.[2] To avoid trouble, he acquiesces in the death of Sarpedon, whom he singularly loves: he dreads to give offence to the goddess of Night;[3] and he hesitates to grant the request of Thetis, notwithstanding the debt of gratitude he owes her. And generally he hates those gods who trouble him, and in proportion as they trouble him; especially his son Arés.[4]

[1] Il. i. 562. [2] Il. iv. 48, 49; xxiv. 69, 70.
[3] Il. xiv. 261. [4] Il. v. 890.

He is not, indeed, devoid of affections; for he is moved by pity, now for Agamemnon or a Greek chieftain, now for Priam;[1] and he is wrung with genuine grief, as a father, for Sarpedon, over whom he even weeps tears of blood.[2] But he delights to sit on Gargaros, and there to behold the bloody spectacle of the war; he keenly longs to see the ships on fire; he anticipates a lively pleasure from witnessing the very gods in conflict with one another.[3] Not only does he rejoice in the feast, but he glows with sexual passion, and he is subject to the power of Sleep, although that deity can only subdue him by working hard, and moreover somewhat at his peril, so that Herè is obliged to bribe him with a high reward, promised under the sanction of an oath.[4]

In a word, Zeus is the masterpiece of the Homeric mythology, if we consider it with reference to that humanizing or anthropomorphic element, which gave to the religion of Greece its specific national character.

Section II. *Herè*.

The Herè of Homer is a deity of all others the most exclusively and intensely national.

Being such, she is modelled strictly according to that anthropomorphic instinct which governed throughout the formation of the Olympian system. She is proud, passionate, sensual, jealous, vindictive; but all these in strict subordination to the great end, which she pursues with unremitting perseverance, the glorification of the

---

[1] Il. xxiv. 174.
[2] Il. xvi. 459.
[3] Il. viii. 47-52; xv. 600; xx. 23.
[4] Il. xiv. 233, 236, 252, 268, 859.

Greeks. She has no personal or moral preferences, like the regard of Athené for Odysseus, founded upon qualities of character. Zeus is obliged to conceal from her the concession which he has made to Thetis on behalf of her son, the greatest of Greek warriors, but to the detriment of the host at large.[1] She loves Achilles and Agamemnon with an equal love;[2] that is, she loves them, not personally, but for their cause.

Heré is a deity much superior to Poseidon, as exhibiting higher intelligence, with more capacity of far-reaching design, and of the adaptation of means to an end; matters these, in which we have no manifestation of Poseidon's faculties, except in his purely obstinate persecution of Odysseus, for having used with energy the resources of self-defence against a monster.[3] Still there is a total absence of moral elements from the character as it is presented to us. Angered at the lameness of her child Hephaistos, she desires to conceal his birth.[4] Zeus charges her with being ready to eat Priam and his children raw.[5] She borrows the kestos of Aphrodité, and entices Zeus in a scene where sensuality is freely used, though as the instrument of a deeply laid and artful scheme.[6] The motive assigned for her hostility to Troy, is the insult she had suffered by the adverse judgment of Paris.[7]

In the Odyssey, she may be said for practical purposes entirely to disappear. She is mentioned but seven times in the whole poem: thrice, quite incidentally, in a formula where Zeus is called the loud-thundering husband of Heré, and is himself the true subject

[1] Il. i. 545–550. [2] Il. i. 196. [3] Od. i. 20.
[4] Il. xviii. 396. [5] Il. iv. 34–36. [6] Il. xiv. 190.
[7] Il. xxiv. 27.

of the passage; once as the mother of Hebè; and thrice in legend or narrative extraneous to the subject of the poem. Nor is this unnatural. For, in the domestic part of it, there is no question of the Greek nationality: while amidst the Phœnician and Eastern associations of the Outer Geography, a conception so strictly Hellenic could have no part to play.

Though the power of Herè is immense, yet she is not surrounded with that reverence which the Poet always maintains towards Athenè and Apollo. She is not exempted from the touch of defeat and dishonor.

She was subjected to ignominious punishment by Zeus, who suspended her with her hands in chains, and with anvils hanging from her feet.[1] And, in the course of her long feud with Heracles, that hero wounded her with a three-pronged arrow in the right breast, and caused her to suffer intolerable pain.[2]

She alone among the deities is called Argeian Herè, as Helen is called Argeian Helen. In both instances, the epithet appears to be founded on the special relation between the person to whom it is applied, and the head-quarter of Greek power, especially as that power was associated with the Argeian name, and therefore probably with the period of the Perseids. This connection subsisted in Argolis throughout the historic period. In the Iliad, Herè is said to regard the Greeks as her children.[3] She collected the armament against Troy.[4] She carried Agamemnon safely back to Greece.[5] She conducted Jason and the Argo through the terrible rocks,[6] the Planctai, afterwards Symplegades. She hates Heracles, apparently because

[1] Il. xv. 18–21.   [2] Il. v. 392.   [3] Il. xviii. 358.
[4] Il. iv. 24–29.   [5] Od. iv. 513.   [6] Od. xii. 72.

he is in antagonism to the Perseid dynasty.[1] It can hardly be from conjugal jealousy, since Jupiter recounts his conquests in addressing her on mount Ida. In a word, the vigor and activity of her partisanship are such, as to make the more dignified conduct of Athené seem almost tame by comparison.

Her rank in Olympos is among the highest: she must be supposed to sit by Zeus on one side, as we are told Athené did on the other.[2] The gods rise from their seats to her as well as to Zeus, when she comes among them.[3] At times, she acts immediately on the thoughts of man; as when she prompts Achilles to call the Assembly of the First Book, in order to stay the plague;[4] or impels Agamemnon to stay the victorious course of Hector.[5] At other times, Athené is content to be her agent; as when, in the debate with Agamemnon, she stays the wrath of Achilles.[6] But by way of counterpoise, when the two goddesses are about to descend together from heaven, it is Here who harnesses the chariot, and plays in it the inferior part of driver, while Athené bears the Aigis.[7] The promise of her aid against Poseidon greatly relieves the mind of Zeus.[8]

She assumes, like the other higher deities, the human form;[9] and exhibits an extraordinary power over nature, as if entitled, in virtue of her wifehood, to exercise in a manner the attributes of Zeus. Iris is her messenger as well as his.[10] Not only does she order

---

[1] Il. xix. 130-133. [2] Il. xxiv. 100. [3] Il. xv. 85.
[4] Il. i. 55. [5] Il. viii. 218.
[6] Il. i. 194-195; cf. ii. 156; v. 711; viii. 831. [7] Il. v. 745-748.
[8] Il. xv. 49-52. [9] Il. v. 784-792. [10] Il. xviii. 168.

the Winds,[1] but she sends the sun,[2] in spite of his reluctance, to his setting. When, indignant at the boast of Hector, she rocks upon her throne,[3] Olympos shakes beneath her, as it did under the nod of Zeus. She endows the horses of Achilles with a voice.[4] And, conjointly with Athenê, she thunders in honor of the crowning of Agamemnon.[5]

We learn from a speech of Phœnix, that, together with Athenê, she can confer valor. The daughters of Pandareus she endows both with beauty and with sense, while Athenê and Aphroditê provide them with industrial skill and bodily food respectively, and Artemis bestows upon them stature.[6]

Herê takes part, with Athenê and Poseidon, in the great rebellion against Zeus, which all but effected his deposition. She had also been personally favored with a special protection, at the time when Zeus himself deposed his father Kronos, and thrust him into the Underworld.

Of these two myths, the latter seems to suggest its own interpretation. Its scene is fixed in the midst of the great Theogonic crisis, at the point of the transition from the Pelasgian to the Hellenic or Olympian system. That was a moment of danger to her, but we read of no such danger to Poseidon. From this we may naturally infer that Poseidon had no concern at all with the Pelasgian system, and was an importation from a source altogether distinct. Herê, however, had a counterpart below, with which she might readily have been confounded. In that superseded system we

---

[1] This seems the natural construction of Od. iv. 513, and xii. 69–72.
[2] Il. xviij. 239.   [3] Il. viii. 199.   [4] Il. xix. 407.
[5] Il. xi. 45.   [6] Od. xx. 68–72.

find a *Γαῖα*, or Earth, who, with other Nature-Powers, inhabits, and is invoked in, the Underworld. Rescued from that danger, and set high in Olympos, she stands in marked opposition, as an Hellenic goddess, to the older and coarser conception of the same idea, with which she is in direct competition. This will account for the attitude she holds in the Poems. For here she is not only Hellenic, but she is nothing else; and the principle and groundwork of her Hellenism seem to be an intense untiring hatred of what is Pelasgian by race and association, just as if she were the preferred rival of an old Pelasgian deity; as if she had the very root of her being in a strong recoil from the superseded Nature-Power, into which she might relapse, if Hellenism were ever swallowed up by a victorious return of the Pelasgian worship. Born of the Hellenic reaction, its life and hers were bound up together.

Hence too, in all likelihood, we are to account for her place in the legend of the War in heaven. Zeus, like Janus, has two faces. When he deposes Kronos, he shows us his Hellenic, or Hellic, face. But this rebellion is a rebellion of deities, all of them having the most marked Hellenic sympathies, which evidently run against him in this legend, as the head of the old Pelasgian order.

The functional attribute, specially entrusted to Here in her Olympian character, appears to be only that of regulating birth, through the medium of the Eilithuiai. This appears to be an ascription derived from the original character of the all-producing earth. And the anthropomorphic spirit of the Olympian religion is well illustrated by the fact that Homer cuts her off from all other production, both animal and vegetable, but leaves to her only the bringing of man to birth. Human birth bears to Here the same relation as birth generally to Gaia.

Though the Eilithuiai are mentioned as under the control of Here, they were objects of worship; for the pseud-Odysseus mentions the case of Eilithuie at Amnisos in Crete.[1]

On the whole, then, it seems likely that Here, with a name representing Ἔρα, or the earth, is treated by Homer with a transformation suited to the anthropomorphic and personifying spirit of the Olympian religion; divorced, as to her personality, from Gaia, much as Poseidon is held apart from Nereus, and standing towards Gaia as soul to body: the body taking its place with the old elemental deities of the Pelasgians in the Underworld, the soul rising to higher offices. Here, thus detached from gross matter, carries off with her, as to man alone, the great prerogative of earth, that she is the all-feeding and all-bearing: the τροφείη, the πολύφορβος, the φερέσβιος. Accordingly, Here becomes, or remains rather than becomes, the great mother. She is the wife of Zeus, father of gods and men, and she holds among his wives and concubines the queenly prerogative, like Hecuba in Troy; the mother in heaven of some of his children, as Hebe, Ares, and Hephaistos; and, with the Eilithuiai for her ministers, the goddess of all motherhood on earth.[2]

This last, indeed, is her only specialty. Those other and high prerogatives, which invest her with command over Nature, and with the power of direct action on the mind, probably accrue to her as the consort of

[1] Od. xix. 188. [2] Il. xix. 119.

Zeus, and are therefore not her original gifts, but the reflection of his glory.

We have, perhaps, in the Theomachy, at least one vestige of the prerogative of Here as a Nature-Power. It is she who excites Hephaistos against the river Xanthos;[1] and again, the River, parched by fire, makes his appeal to her to relieve him from suffering, with an engagement which he takes to aid Troy no more, not even in its last necessity. Here accedes to his prayer, and checks the action of Hephaistos, who thereupon desists.[2] It seems as if the ground for choosing Here to interpose on this occasion lay in the relation between rivers and the Earth along which they trace their course. This is the only act of a definite nature, with a sensible result, performed by Here within the limits of Troas, a fact which is again in accordance with the construction I have given it, and the apparent bias of the Troic religion towards Nature-worship.

Section III. *Poseidon.*

The most striking feature of the Homeric Poseidon, or rather Poseidaon, is vast force combined with a total absence of the higher elements of deity, whether intellectual or moral. A persistent vindictiveness, indeed, we trace as the groundwork of his entire action in both the Poems: he hates the Trojans, for the offence of Laomedon; he hates Odysseus, because, in the strictest self-defence, he had blinded Poluphemos. By no worthy word or act is he marked in any part either

[1] Il. xxi. 328–330. [2] Ib. 357–381.

of Iliad or Odyssey, unless it be by some natural affection for his descendants, whether they be the youthful warriors of the house of Actor,[1] or the savage, cruel, atheistic Cyclop.

One of the three sons of Kronos and Rhea, he comes next to Zeus in order of birth.[2] He claims an equality[3] of rank; and avers, that the distribution of sovereignties among the three brothers was made only by lot. More than indirectly, he asserts equality, as well as independence. When admonished by Iris that he is junior to Zeus, he acknowledges that there is force in the plea, and he withdraws from the plain of battle as he had been bid; but he reserves a right of resentment, in case Zeus shall not fulfil the decree against Troy. Zeus on his part is delighted at the news; and observes, that it would have cost much labor to coerce him.[4] Again, it is plain that, in the conspiracies against Zeus, he was the acting partner. For it is the superiority of his son to him, that frustrates the design of the whole party;[5] and when Heré attempts to revive the scheme, he pleads in reply, not their collective inferiority, but his own singly,[6] as if he thought that it was, in point of mere force, well-nigh all they would have to rely on.

Apollo is restrained, in the Theomachy, by a sentiment of respect, from coming to blows with Poseidon, as his paternal uncle.[7] And a sentiment precisely similar prevents Athené in the Odyssey from comforting Odysseus by her visible presence, even at her own sanctuary in Scherié.[8]

[1] Il. xi. 749-751. [2] Il. xiv. 174-217. [3] Ib. 186-209.
[4] Il. xiv. 230-235. [5] Il. i. 404. [6] Il. viii. 211.
[7] Il. xxi. 468. [8] Od. vi. 329; xiii. 341.

Though god of the sea, he is not, so to speak, the Sea-god, or the Water-god. He has in him nothing of an elemental deity. He is not placed in as near a relation to water as Zeus is to air, by the epithet Διιπέτης, and the phrase Διὸς ὄμβρος.[1] These very phrases show us that he was not, in Homer's view, the god of moisture, or even of water, generally. The attempts to derive his name from a common root with πόσις, 'drink,' or ποταμός, 'a river,' would therefore be insufficient or inappropriate, even if they were not, as they are, somewhat equivocal. It is remarkable that, while Poseidon supplied a sea-deluge as his contribution towards effacing the Greek trench, it was Apollo who turned upon it the mouths of all the rivers that descend from Ida;[2] which, when Poseidon had accomplished his labor, he in turn sent back again to their proper channels.

Nereus, the true Sea-god of Homer, gave to the element of water that name of nero, in the popular speech of the Greeks, which it still retains.[3] He ever dwells in the depths of the sea, as if he belonged to them, and as if they supplied his atmosphere. But Poseidon has a palace there near Aigai, where his chariot was kept, where the Poet seems to imply that he resided.[4] Yet not exclusively; for he appears at the Olympian Court, on the plain of Troy, on the hill-tops of Samothrace,[5] or on the Solyman[6] mountains; and he singly visits the Ethiopians, to partake

---

[1] Διιπέτης = fallen from Zeus. Διὸς ὄμβρος = Zeus-rain.
[2] Il. xii. 17-35.
[3] Compare the adj. neros, wet, in the late Greek of Phrynichus, the grammarian, A.D. 180.
[4] Il. xiii. 15-22; xv. 219. Od. v. 381.
[5] Il. xiii. 11.
[6] Od. v. 283.

of the sacrifices they offered him.[1] This reference to his being worshipped in a distant quarter is the second sign we have seen of his foreign origin; the first was the want of definiteness in his position of inferiority relatively to Zeus, as though he had been, elsewhere, without a superior.

So again there appears to be in the Outer or Phœnician system an elemental sea-god, Phorcus, who is called ruler of the sea, and after whom a harbor in Ithaca is named.[2]

Prayer appears only to be addressed to him within the Greek world, in the neighborhood of the sea, as by the Envoys in the Ninth Iliad;[3] and by his own descendants, as Nestor in the Third Odyssey, who likewise worships by the shore.[4] He can assume the form of any man; can blunt the point of a spear; can carry off his friends, or envelop his opponents in vapor.[5] He can inspire vigor into heroes; not immediately, however, but by a stroke of his staff.[6] Direct action on the mind appears to be beyond his range. The storms of the Poems, in the Greek or inner world, are not raised by Poseidon. Probably he had not the power to raise a storm, though he can break, as the sea does, fragments from the rocks of the coast.[7] Storms seem to have been regarded as belonging to the province of the air-god. They are imputed to him in a passage of the Twenty-fourth Odyssey;[8] but it would not be altogether safe, perhaps, to rely on that Book, in a case where it seems to vary from the usual order of the Poems.

[1] Od. l. 22, 25.   [2] Od. l. 72; xiii. 96.   [3] Il. ix. 183.
[4] Od. iii. 5. Cf. Il. xi. 728.
[5] Il. xiii. 43, 215; xiv. 135; xiii. 562; xi. 752; xx. 321–329.
[6] Il. xiii. 59.   [7] Od. iv. 506   [8] Od. xxiv. 110.

If, however, Poseidon was less than the absolute lord of water, he was also more.

1. His possession of the Trident (triaina) could hardly be due to a purely maritime sovereignty.

2. His relation to the horse, which is very perceptible, though not of primary rank, in Homer,[1] and which became almost paramount in the later age, cannot be adequately explained by any comparison between that animal and the ship, or the wave.

3. Poseidon is the building-god.

4. Poseidon stands in close relation to the giants and other rebellious personages, who troubled both gods and men.

The existence of these associations for Poseidon, inasmuch as they cannot be explained by virtue of his place in the Olympian system, again urges us to look for the signs of his origin abroad. The key to the inquiry is to be found in the Outer world of the Odyssey. For

1. It is plain that the materials of the narrative, so far as the scene of the poem is laid in that Outer world, must have been derived by the Poet from the Phœnicians, who alone frequented the waters beyond the Ægean and the Greek coasts.

2. In the western portion of the Outer sphere, Zeus practically disappears from the governing office, and Poseidon becomes the supreme ruler.

We have seen that the subordination of Poseidon to Zeus rested on juniority. If Zeus were the chief god of the Pelasgian worship, and Poseidon came in with the Phœnicians, this poetical arrangement is suitably explained; and it exhibits a skilful adaptation to the

[1] Il. xxiii. 277, 306, 584.

conditions under which the Olympian system was constructed. His rebellion against Zeus, in concert with Heré and Athené, appears to show that, as new immigrants arrived in Greece, bearing with them their own religion, the older system was for a time brought into question and endangered as a whole. The delivery of Zeus from this rebellion will be considered in connection with the goddess Thetis.[1]

The Greek legends relating to Poseidon are just such as we might expect with reference to the god of a nautical people, touching at many points about the coast of Greece. He contends with Helios for Corinth, with Athené for Troizen and Athens, with Heré for Argolis, with Zeus for Ægina, with Dionusos for Naxos. Even in the Greece of Homer we find spots specially consecrated to him in Bœotia, in Eubœa, and in Aigialos.

Let us now turn to the Voyage of Odysseus in the Outer world; which begins with the Lotos-eaters, and ends with the Phaiakes of Corfû. Mure[2] suggests that their name is a parody of the name Phoinîkes: Homer paints them as a wealthy, unwarlike people, singularly expert in navigation. This apparent incongruity falls in with the case of Corfû, if it was then inhabited, as it has been in later times, by a stationary, gentle, indolent peasantry, and at the same time held by a dominant settlement or colony of foreigners, ruling it through maritime power. Mure cites Phaïk as a Semitic word for 'magnificent,' and Scher, as meaning 'an emporium.'

In this Phœnician or Outer world, Athené, who had constantly tended Odysseus while in Troas, and who

[1] *Infra*, sect. xxi.   [2] Lit. Hist. of Greece, vol. I. p. 510.

resumes the regular charge of him in Ithaca, systematically abstains from helping him; and wholly disappears until Poseidon has, in the Fifth Odyssey, voluntarily receded from the scene.¹ She declares that respect to her uncle was the motive for her own disappearance.² The presumption then is that this Outer world was a sphere in some way so specially his own, that Athené, whose power and prerogatives in Homer are so extremely lofty, was unwilling to offer him any opposition there.

Accordingly, we have direct evidence that, in relation to the Outer world, Poseidon exercised prerogatives which seem not to have belonged to him within the Greek sphere. He raised the storm which wrecked the raft of Odysseus; gathering the clouds, which was the special function of Zeus, and causing the winds to blow.³

Moreover, in the lay of Arês and Aphrodité, it is evidently Poseidon who presides in the Assembly of the gods, and who consequently negotiates with Hephaistos for the relief of Arês from the net of steel. And just as, at the beginning of the Second Iliad, the other gods were sleeping, but Zeus⁴ (who was responsible) slept not, so here, while the other deities were laughing, Poseidon did not laugh;⁵ as we may suppose, for the same reason. And while, on ordinary occasions, we are always told that the gods assembled in the χαλκοβατὲς δῶ of Zeus, here the words 'of Zeus' are omitted.⁶

Undoubtedly the name of Zeus appears from time to time in those Books of the Odyssey which describe the

¹ Od. v. 380.   ² Od. xiii. 341.   ³ Od. v. 291.
⁴ Il. ii. 1.   ⁵ Od. viii. 344.   ⁶ Od. viii. 321.

wanderings of Odysseus; but his governing office disappears until, in the end of the Twelfth Book, he acts at the instance of Helios (the Sun), and on behalf of the Olympian Court. It is not the abstract, but the working supremacy of Poseidon, which the Poem seems to show. At the same time, the question might be raised whether, as in the later and extraneous tradition the name Zeus was often united with that of Poseidon (as much as to say 'Zeus the supreme deity, in the form and under the name of Poseidon'), so here the word may not improbably have the general force of 'god,' rather than the personal meaning of a particular god. Even in Homer, Aïdoneus is called the Zeus of the Underworld; and so Poseidon may be the Zeus of the sea and the sea-regions. And it is very notable that in Od. v. 303–305, Odysseus ascribes to Zeus that very storm, which we are expressly told that Poseidon had raised.

We have therefore very strong indications from the text of Homer that Poseidon was the god, or the chief-god, of the Phoinikes; and if he was, then, upon their arrival in Greece, he could only be incorporated into the Greek system by some such method as Homer has adopted, in giving him at once a parity and a disparity with Zeus.

Thus the Outer geography affords us the strongest evidence of the Phœnician origin of Poseidon. It shows us more than this, as will be seen when we treat of the position of Helios in Homer.

The view now taken is in harmony with the evidence supplied from other sources respecting Poseidon. Herodotus, deriving the names of the other Greek gods from Egypt, excepts Poseidon. History shows abundantly the prevalence of Poseidonian worship among the Phœnicians and their colonial progeny. Diodorus[1] says an altar to Poseidon was built at the northern extremity of the Red Sea, where was a promontory called Poseideïon, and a grove of palms (Phoinikes). In the war with Gelon, Hamilcar, general of the Carthaginians, offered to Poseidon a magnificent sacrifice, with a view to success in what were mainly land operations. Again, while sacrificing a boy to Kronos, he threw into the sea a crowd of victims in honor of Poseidon.[2] Later in the historic period, when Scipio attacks *Carthago Nova*, he assures his army that he has the favor of Poseidon made known to him in a dream;[3] that is to say, that the foe was deserted by his own national and proper god. Pausanias, again, shows us the worship of Poseidon practised in parts of Greece, whither it never could have come had he been regarded as a mere sea-god; and nowhere more than in Arcadia. Manifestly, if he were the chief and distinctive god of the Phœnician nationality, it is probable that, as that acute race penetrated for traffic into Greece, they would carry with them their worship as they went. And again, in many of the local legends related by that author, which afford evidence of a very trustworthy kind, we find Poseidon possessed of attributes which, in the established religion of Hellas,' belonged properly to Zeus.[4]

Let us now endeavor to examine the special and separate attributes of Poseidon, already enumerated, in the light of his Phœnician associations.

[1] Diod. Sic. III. 41.   [2] Ib. xi. 21; xiii. 86.
[3] Polyb. Bk. x. 11. 7; 14. 12.
[4] See 'Phœnicia and Greece,' in the Quarterly Review of Jan. 1868.

With respect to the Trident, an instrument so unsuited to water, it appears evidently to point to some tradition of a Trinity, such as may still be found in various forms of Eastern religion, other than the Hebrew. It may have proceeded, among the Phœnicians, from the common source of an older tradition; and this seems more probable than its direct derivation from the Hebrews, with whom, however, we know that the Phœnicians had intercourse.

Though the relation of Poseidon to the horse is not explained by his connection with Phœnicia, yet, as this connection points to his supremacy, and thus gives him wider associations than those of a merely maritime deity, it opens a field from which the true explanation may yet be gathered. I have suggested elsewhere a solution of the problem.[1]

Reference to what has been already said of the Phoinikes will show that the relation of Poseidon to them at once explains his character as the building-god.

Lastly, with regard to the giants and monsters. The facts are as follows.

The Cyclops, a godless race, are his children.[2] The impious giants are declared to be of the kindred of the gods:[3] this is probably through Poseidon. By the daughter of their king and arch-tempter Eurumedon, he was the father of the royal house of Scherië.[4] These giants the wicked and cruel Laistrugones are said to resemble.[5] By Iphimedeia, he was the father of Otos and Ephialtes, those monster-youths[6] who

[1] *Supra*, Phœnicians, Chap. V.
[2] Od. vii. 205, 206.
[3] Od. x. 120.
[4] Od. ix. 275, 412.
[5] Od. vii. 56–60.
[6] Od. xi. 305–320.

heaped up the mountains, and perished by the hands of Apollo. He was also the father of Briareus (called likewise Aigaion), who, however, took part against him.[1]

The effort of the two youths recalls the traditions of the Tower of Babel, and of the War in Heaven.

Two considerations may be noticed, which tend to account for the place of Poseidon as the Phœnician god, in relation to many rebellious and unruly spirits.

First, the rough manners of a sea-faring and buccaneering people. Down to the time of Cicero and of the Roman Empire, a rude and ruffian-like character was called Neptuni filius.

Secondly, and in possible connection with what has just been said, Syria was inhabited by Canaanites; and it has been observed that the names given in Scripture to that race indicate great stature and physical force, which became the basis of a tradition that they were a race of giants.[2] To the Greek mind this would very naturally convey that they were children of Poseidon as the Phœnician god. In a word, the Phœnician origin of Poseidon, and that only, appears to supply a key to his position and attributes, such as they are shown in the Olympian system.

Section IV. *Aïdoneus.*

The figure of Aïdoneus, or Aïdes, is one of the most obscure in the whole Homeric mythology. Yet here too there is, as I think, a reward for patient observation; and a clue is to be found which may enable us

---

[1] Il. i. 401–400.   [2] Le Normant, vol. ii. p. 241.

to trace him home to his origin, as a Nature-Power of
an older theogony, rather than what he might at first
sight appear to be, little more than a shadowy creature
of the Poet's imagination.

The particulars respecting him in the Poems are
but few.

He was one of the deities who suffered at the hand
of man: namely, of Heracles.[1] Now the associations
of Heracles in Homer are Hellenic, as we may perceive from the co-operation of Athenè with him; and
therefore this legend, so far as it goes, tends to place
Aïdoneus beyond the line of pure Hellenic tradition.
It is true, that Heracles also assaulted Herè: but the
enmity between them was special, and founded on the
jealousy of the goddess in favor of the ruling house
of the Perseids.

Heracles shot this god in the shoulder with an arrow
at Pulos, not of Messenia but of Elis, according to
Pausanias;[2] and laid him prostrate among the dead,
huge as he was. He rose, went to Olympos, and was
cured by Paieon.[3]

Though a deity of the Underworld,[4] he is the brother
of Zeus, having shared in the partition of the universe
by lot. He is therefore adopted, like Poseidon, into
the Olympian Court, and becomes entitled to appear in
the Hellenic heaven, though supposed usually to abide
in the Shades.

His action in the Poems is singularly faint; an
arrangement of which we shall see the probable reason.
During the battle of the gods, he trembles[5] lest the
earth-shaker Poseidon should split the ground, and ex-

[1] Il. v. 895.   [2] vi. 25. 8.   [3] Il. v. 898–402.
[4] Il. xv. 187, 191.   [5] Il. xx. 61.

hibit the nether region, where he is lord (*anax*), through the chasm. This shuddering may be said to be the single action ascribed to him in the Poems.

We have, however, passages illustrative of his character and functions. Stern and inexorable, he is to men the most hateful of all the gods.[1] This declaration is curiously illustrated by the after history of the Olympian system. In all Greece, says Pausanias,[2] there is no single temple of Aïdes, except at a single spot of Elis, where, according to tradition, he fought on the side of the Pulians against Heracles. And this temple was opened once a year:[3] 'I suppose,' adds Pausanias, 'because men die but once.' This perhaps would have been a more apt reason if men had died once a year.

He is also called the strong,[3] the hateful or loathsome (στυγερός),[4] the gate-closer,[5] and in a recurring formula, the horse-famous (κλιτόπωλος).[6]

Though he is the king of the world below, he seems to exercise no active power there: throughout the Eleventh Odyssey, the duties of government are in the hands of Persephoné, who also has, by the shores of Okeanos, the grove of worship. Odysseus, indeed, offered to him prayer and sacrifice, together with her, in the Underworld:[7] but there is no sign of his having any established worship upon earth.

The helmet of Aïdes was used by Athené[8] to make herself invisible to Arés. We hear of this helmet in Hesiod, as worn by Perseus.[9] It appears to be a symbol of darkness.

[1] Il. ix. 158.
[2] Paus. as already cited.
[3] Od. x. 534; xi. 47, 277.
[4] Il. viii. 368.
[5] Il. viii. 367.
[6] Il. v. 654; xi. 445; xvi. 625.
[7] Od. xi. 44—47.
[8] Il. v. 845.
[9] Scut. Herc. 227.

Twice, however, this deity comes before us in the legend of Phœnix. In the war of Caludon, Althaia, invoking woes on Meleagros, beats the earth with her hands, as she calls on Aïdes and Persephonè; and she is heard and answered from beneath by the Erinūs.[1] In the other passage the process is reversed. The father of Phœnix calls upon the Erinūs, and 'the gods' fulfil his imprecation, 'and Zeus of the Underworld, and Persephonè the awful;'[2] perhaps meaning this, that these are the gods to whom he refers.

Of this dualism in the exercise of the penal office I shall speak elsewhere. But the name here given to Aïdes is very remarkable: he is the Zeus of the Underworld. How comes he by this title? At first sight it indicates some very close relation between him and the traditions of Zeus in some one of their forms; for Poseidon is never called the Zeus of the sea, although, as we have seen, he carries strong marks of supremacy in the Outer world.

The part he takes at Pulos seems to mean that he was the old god of the country, and the patron of the inhabitants in their struggles against the invading Heracles. The epithet 'huge' further tends to associate him with the old Nature-Powers. The continuance of his worship at Pulos in the historic period, when it had disappeared in all other places, is probably to be taken as an indication, that Elis was even in the earliest times a religious centre for Greece, and that Pulos was the head-quarters of the system, so far as Aïdoneus was concerned.

We shall see that, in the worship of Dodona, there

---

[1] Il. ix. 563–572.   [2] id. 453–457.

was a Dioné, associated as queen with the Pelasgian Zeus. This Dioné, to make room for Heré, disappears from active relations to mankind, and becomes a sort of lay-figure in Olympos.

Was there, then, a residuum of the tradition of the Pelasgian Zeus, after the Olympian Zeus had been fully conceived and established? And, as Gaia, or Demeter, or both, represent such a residuum in the case of Heré, does Aïdoneus represent it in the case of Zeus?[1]

This would be an adjustment in full analogy with Homer's general method. And it would at once account for the extremely faint outline which he has given to the figure of his Aïdoneus, and for his giving the executive office in the Underworld to Persephoné. As he keeps back Demeter, that she may not compete with Heré, so he would keep back Aïdoneus, that he might not compete with Zeus.

Plutarch[2] has preserved a tradition, which seems to supply a missing link, respecting an Aïdoneus, who was king of the Molossians; and he thus connects the name with the neighborhood of Dodona. This Aïdoneus releases Theseus, his prisoner, at the request of Heracles: a transaction afterwards transferred to the nether world. Thus one great Hellic personage obtains from him the release of another, which accords with the idea of his priority in time.

Althaius's beating the earth would lead to the conclusion, that Aïdoneus must have sprung from some tradition of an earth-god, and not an air-god. Hesiod, the Pelasgian poet, directs the husbandman to pray to

---

[1] Kreuzer, Symbolik, iv. 477.   [2] Thes. c. 35.

him, as well as to Demeter, to prosper the fruits of the earth.[1]

It is, I suppose, possible that at some period the rude religion of the Pelasgians, not yet having arrived at the Egyptian idea of Air and Earth, as representing respectively the active and the passive principle, may have conceived of Earth as its own supreme deity. At any rate the relation of Aïdoneus to the Zeus of Dodona appears to rest on probable evidence.

And if so, then the argument for considering Aïdoneus as an earth-Zeus, rather than as an air-Zeus, is certainly recommended by various probable suggestions. The general appearance of the aggregate phenomena of Nature or Element worship in Homer, and also in Hesiod, is by no means such as to fall into a single consistent whole, and appears to imply that more than one theogony, or scheme of deity and religion, had preceded the Olympian system. It is almost certain, that a plurality of such schemes must have presented discrepancies one with another.

Moreover, when we regard Zeus as an air-god, he stands in the relation of the active Nature-Power to Earth as the female and passive one. Now this was the notion embodied in the Egyptian system, which may have been carried, in accordance with the report of Herodotus, and either directly or mediately, from Egypt to Dodona. But it is an idea implying a certain refinement, an action of the speculative mind in the discernment of cause and effect. An entirely rude people might perhaps be more likely to associate its idea of a God with the earth, of which the sur-

---

[1] Opp. 436; Döllinger, Heid. und Jud. p. 80.

face constantly tells them a tale of life, while from its bosom spring the stores that sustain their bodily existence.

Section V. *Leto*.

I think that every one who carefully examines the text of Homer with reference to the picture there given of Leto, must be struck alike by the slightness and by the dignity of its outline; and, I may add, by the absence (as far as I know) of any satisfactory attempt to find for her an origin in any pre-existing tradition, either of the Pelasgian Nature-worship, or of the Assyrian or Egyptian systems. Without origin, without function, she seems to be a mother, and nothing more than a mother; yet she is elevated into a commanding position in the Homeric system by the transcendent dignity of her son Apollo.

The only epithets given to Leto in the poems are of a character entirely general: glorious,[1] right-glorious,[2] lovely-cheeked,[3] lovely-haired.[4]

Her action in the poems is extremely circumscribed. She appears in the temple of Apollo, as his minister, with her daughter Artemis, to nurse and tend Æneas.[5] She never performs any governing office of any kind, either upon nature or upon man; though she looks with delight upon Artemis sporting in the wild wood.[6] When she appears in the Theomachy on the Trojan side, and we are in hopes of finding a link to connect her with some definite prerogatives, we find the Poem so contrived, that the door is at once closed

[1] Od. xi. 580. [2] Il. xiv. 327. [3] Il. xxiv. 607.
[4] Il. i. 36.   [5] Il. v. 447.   [6] Od. vi. 106.

upon our curiosity by her release from the necessity of combat.

With this blankness and faintness, let us now compare the high ascriptions of her dignity. It is a great note of honor, that this inactive and hindward deity should find a place in the Theomachy, from which Demeter and Aphroditè are excluded. Hermes is her opponent. But when the time for action comes, he declines the fight: he will not lay hands on the spouse of Zeus: he gives her free leave to proclaim that she has worsted him. She makes no reply.[1] Again, it is the insult to Leto as the mother of only a pair, that is so fearfully avenged on Niobè and her children.[2] And Tituos, the son of Gaia, is tortured in Tartaros, because he sought to offer her violence as she was proceeding to the Pythian temple of her son.[3] In the ascending scale of the mothers of his offspring, she is placed by Zeus after Demeter and next to Herè.[4]

Hesiod marries her to Zeus before Herè; which, considering the supreme rank of Herè in Olympos, appears to be the mark of some very old tradition. She is junior, among the consorts he assigns to Zeus, only to Motis, or the Spirit of Counsel. She is there made the daughter of Titan; and, in the Hymn to Apollo, she appears as a sister of Zeus, and a daughter of Kronos himself. But, colorless as she is in her own being, all this seems to be a marked reflection from the dignity of Apollo.

Some have explained this mute yet lofty personage in conformity, as they think, with the etymology of the

[1] Il. xxi. 497-501. [2] Il. xxiv. 607.
[3] Od. xi. 580. [4] Il. xiv. 327.

name; and they regard Leto as the impersonation of Night, and Night as the mother from whose womb Day, or the Sun, is produced. The etymology appears to be uncertain: yet there may be no great difficulty in supposing an affinity between Leto and latoo, and a derivation from the root lath.[1] Nor is it any conclusive objection to this theory, that we have already a goddess of Night in Homer.[2] For this might be the obsolete Nature-Power, standing in the same relation to an impersonated Leto, as Gaia, or as Demeter, to Here. The idea that the Night is the mother of the Sun, and also is the Moon, does not seem to be an idea much more likely to commend itself to the Greek mind than to represent Chaos as the parent of Cosmos, anarchy of order. At the same time it is conceivable that such an idea might find place in a scheme of Nature-worship. Nor was Apollo united with the Sun in the Olympian scheme of Homer. But, when we perceive the immense reverence accorded to a personage who is without any attribute or office in the poems except motherhood, we cannot but refer to the motherhood the dignity itself.

It is quite possible, though it is not proved, that there may have been in the Pelasgian or in some other mythology, a personage who may be the base of the Homeric Leto, just as there are deities who form the base, or a base, of his Apollo. But as the properties attaching to his Apollo appear to be of an order too high to be justly accounted for by any thing we find in mere mythology, so, and even more, we are driven to seek outside the limits of the system a mode of

[1] Liddell and Scott, in voc. λανθάνω.   [2] Il. xiv. 261.

accounting for the majesty and reverence, with which the Leto of Homer is surrounded.

But if in Apollo there are exhibited, together with other matter, the features of that tradition of a Deliverer, divine, and yet in human form, which was handed down through the line of Patriarchs, and enshrined in the Sacred Scriptures, we have to bear in mind that this Deliverer was emphatically described as the Seed of the Woman. Whether by the woman was meant His mother, or Eve, the general mother of our race, is immaterial to our present purpose. What appears obvious is that, if such a tradition imparted its glory to the character of Apollo, it could hardly fail to shed a portion of collateral lustre upon the person, in whom the human descent was signified and foreshadowed. And it would be no matter of wonder, if the human figure of such a person were elevated to the Olympian Court, whose manifold orders made such admission easy, and whose anthropomorphic principle tended to efface or weaken the lines of separation between its divinities and mortal man.

I conclude, therefore, that in Leto we have a record, and a sufficiently clear indication, whether wrought into the texture of any current mythological legend, or otherwise, of the Hebrew tradition respecting the Woman, of whose seed the Deliverer of mankind was to be.

Section VI. *Demeter.*

The text of Pausanias exhibits by its enumeration of temples and remains, though it does not explain, the widespread prevalence and the great local importance of the worship of Demeter in Greece. And this picture stands in marked contrast with her insignificance in the action of the Homeric Poems, and in the Olympian system.

We may safely assign to her one of the twenty chairs or thrones,[1] wrought for the Assemblies of Immortals in the palace of Zeus. But she nowhere appears as taking part in those Assemblies. She has no place in the Theomachy or in the War. She is never mentioned in the Poems except incidentally.

The actual Homeric evidence concerning Demeter is as follows:—

1. Ground corn, or meal, is called $Δημήτερος ἀκτή$, as fire (or flame) is called $φλὸξ Ἡφαίστοιο$.[2] This is one of the proper associations of a Nature-Power.

2. She is the companion of Zeus in one of the connections, which he relates in Il. xiv. 326. Her child is not named by the Poet either there or elsewhere. But, in the later tradition, we find associated with her, in local worship, under the name of Coré, the Damsel, a great and even awful personage, who thus fills the gap indicated by Homer, and who probably is represented by his Persephoné, queen of the Underworld. Certainly the two have a marked correspondence in character.

3. She has a $τέμενος$ at Purasos in Thessaly,[3] and these land-endowments, as far as we can discern from Homer, were Pelasgian.

4. She is termed $ἐϋπλόκαμος$ and $ξανθή$, fair-haired, and golden-haired, doubtless with reference to the idea beautifully expressed by Tibullus:[4] 'Deponit flavas annua terra comas.'

[1] Il. xviii. 373. [3] Il. xiii. 322; xxi. 70.
[2] Il. ii. 696.   [4] ii. 1. 48.

5. She felt and gave way to a passion for a son or descendant of Iasos; and this took place among the fields.[1] The name of Iasos is obscure, but seems to be certainly older than the Hellenes. Hesiod enlarges the tradition, and says this event came about in Crete, a country at least partially marked with strong Pelasgic features.[2] This powerful element of lust in her character tends further to detach her, as a goddess, from Hellenic associations.

6. She presides over the operation of winnowing; and threshing-floors are consecrated to her.[3]

The later tradition, testifying to an extensively established worship of Demeter, places the most noted seat of it in Attica, which is an eminently Pelasgian district, with Eleusis for its head-quarter.

In the Hymn to Demeter, she herself founds that worship; and reports herself as having come thither, but unwillingly,[4] from Crete. This tradition may point to the epoch when the Phœnicians acquired the dominion of Crete. It certainly points to some decisive change tending to displace her worship.

Pausanias[5] states, that there was in his time a temple of Demeter Pelasgis at Corinth.

Diodorus[6] reports that she merely represents the character of Isis in the Egyptian mythology; that is to say, as earth-goddess and inventress of cultivation.

We have indeed three Homeric personages, all of whom appear to be related to the old tradition of Nature-worship, which made Earth a deity, and a

[1] Od. v. 125.   [2] Theog. 971.   [3] Il. v. 499–502.
[4] v. 123.   [5] II. 22. 2.   [6] i. 13.

female deity.¹ The share of Demeter in that tradition is established by her attributes in connection with food, and by her name of Γῆ μήτηρ, Mother-earth.

Detached as this is from Hellenic associations, we cannot be surprised at our not finding her among the Hellenizing divinities of the War. Nor is it very difficult to conjecture a reason, why she could not conveniently appear among those who were allies of Troy: namely this, that in Greece her personality had been sufficiently severed from that of Gaia, the Earth-goddess proper, by the relegation of Gaia to the Underworld, and probably by the prevalence of her local worship, to allow her a place in Olympos; but in Troas it would seem that this severance may not have been effected, and that the Earth-goddess was worshipped under her own name, like, and together with, the Sun.²

Perhaps the same line of thought may carry us to the reason, why Demeter appears to us without a daughter, and Persephoné, the Awful, without a mother. For Persephoné is the queen of that dark region in which Gaia dwells: but, as being an Hellenic deity, she cannot have a Pelasgian Nature-Power for her mother. Neither can she be made by Homer the daughter of Demeter, because Demeter herself bears many signs of character which associate her with Gaia, but which are wholly absent from the picture of Persephoné.

We find in the Albanian language the same form for the Earth as in Demeter, *deou*:³ though it is

---

¹ See *supra*, p. 241. ² Il. iii. 104.
³ Hahn, Alb. Stud. Lexicon.

combined with a form not found in that tongue, which gives us *memme*, and other like forms, for mother.

The Demeter of Homer, then, seems to be a figure partially Hellenized, principally of Pelasgian conception, and having parts of its material in Eastern tradition.

In Athens, and in Olympia, her statue stood by that of Zeus:[1] and, according to Herodotus, the Scythians treated her as his consort. This is probably no more than the mythological impersonation given to the earth as the female or passive principle, subjected to the action of air, light, and sky.

Section VII. *Dionê*.

We find Dionê present in Olympos, when Aphroditê arrives there after her wound, and is received as her daughter.[2] She was therefore one of the wives of Zeus, who expressly owns Aphroditê as his child:[3] and she, again, expressly names herself as one of the Olympian gods.[4] To console Aphroditê, she relates how Arês had suffered at the hands of Otos and Ephialtes, Herê and Aïdes at the hands of Heracles. But there is nothing in the passage to throw light upon the origin of Dionê herself; and it is the only passage of Homer, in which she appears.

We learn however from Hesiod,[5] that Dionê was one of the daughters of Okeanos and Tethûs. These daughters were sisters to the Rivers. Pherecydes, an Athenian logographer of the fifth century before Christ,

---
[1] Hahn, Alb. Stud. Lexicon, p. 251.   [3] Il. v. 371, 373.
[2] Il. v. 428.   [4] Il. v. 383.   [5] Theog. 353.

represented her as one of the Nymphs of Dodona.[1] The coins of Epiros show the head of a Zeus of Dodona, the Pelasgian Zeus, crowned with oak-leaf,[2] an association sustained by that passage of the Odyssey which refers to the oak, from which the oracles were delivered.[3] Together with the head of Zeus on these coins is a crowned female head, which cannot be the head of Here, as she belongs only to the Hellenic traditions. Strabo[4] says that Dione shared the temple of Zeus at Dodona.

By combining together the fragments of this information, we may come with reasonable evidence to the conclusion, that Dione was of the family of Nature-Powers; and that in this character she was associated with the elder Zeus of the Pelasgians, the air-god, as his wife. Some will have it, that she was the mother of Persephone. In Homer, the line between the deities of the Underworld and of Olympos is broad, and not easily crossed: but Dione is the mother of Aphrodite, and the traditions of Aphrodite, of Persephone, and of Artemis, undoubtedly intermix. Upon the case of Dione, we may make the general observation, that Homer does not pursue an uniform method of dealing with the divinities of all the old Theogonies. The darker and grosser of them, related to the earth, pass into the Underworld. But Okeanos remains, I suppose, in the Ocean-River; and Nereus, we know, inhabits the sea-depth, with his family. The water of rivers is bound by the epithet Diipetes to the realm and to the idea of the air-god: and of the rivers Dione was the reputed sister. Therefore, like the air-god himself, she perhaps

[1] Creuzer, Symbolik, iv. 157.   [2] Ib. iv. 160.
[3] Od. xix. 297.   [4] Strabo, b. vii. p. 329 C.

was sufficiently ethereal in her composition to pass, though but as a dimly-drawn and unimportant personage, into the Olympian court.

Section VIII. *Athene and Apollo.*

These two are by far the most remarkable personages who adorn the Olympos of Homer; and the features, which they possess in common, are so much more numerous and significant than any by which they may be separated, that it will be convenient to treat them together for the purpose of bringing those common features into view. Such differences as subsist between them are much more in function, than in character.

But I speak only of their features as shown in the Homeric text. It is perfectly possible that they may severally represent in singleness groups of traditions which either had been, or which afterwards became, the property of more than one mythological personage. The names of these may be wholly distinct, and their places, outside the Homeric mythology, far apart. But the self-consistency of each of them, upon the page of Homer, is scarcely less remarkable than their mutual relation; a relation which at one and the same time both associates them with one another, and severs them from most of the other members of the Olympian Court.

Their action, however, in the Poems is so extensive and multiform, that it will not be possible to exhibit all its particulars: nor is there the same need for such an operation as in cases where the evidence is scanty.

Still, it is the more needful to make a comprehensive and accurate survey of their attributes and offices, because upon the cases of these two deities will mainly turn the answer to be given to the interesting and important question, whether there is or is not any sensible infusion into the Homeric system of the ideas related to the redemption of mankind, which have been preserved in the Holy Bible and among the Hebrews, and which may be termed for convenience Messianic. To their case, however, that of Leto is an important auxiliary.

1. Unless we explain their position in the Olympian system by the aid of the Hebrew traditions, it offers to our view a hopeless solecism. The Olympian gods are arranged generally in two generations. The really great governing powers are given to the elder of the two, to Zeus, Poseidon, and to Here; with a purity of dignity, though not of influence, to Aïdoneus. All the three first, in one way or other, are representations of some conception of the Supreme Being which had prevailed elsewhere, or at an earlier epoch. But Athene and Apollo present no such character; and, standing as they do in the junior line, we are obliged to ask, why do these two junior deities alone, and in a manner which cannot be mistaken, share and exercise the prerogatives of supreme deity and government? Inferior only in some respects to Zeus, they show no inferiority in any, and in some a marked superiority, to Here or Poseidon.

It is true indeed that both Athene and Apollo recognize the rights of the Uncle, as the Senior, in Poseidon. And, if I am right in considering him as having been the supreme god of a foreign mythology, who was afterwards naturalized in the Hellenic system, we may readily understand why, notwithstanding the coarse material of his being, he, too, is always shielded from palpable dishonor. Yet neither is he suffered to inflict any disgrace or shame on Athene or Apollo. In the case of Apollo, the two part without fighting.¹ In the case of Athenê, Poseidon withdraws when Odysseus is about to pass beyond the special sphere of that god;² and the goddess then resumes the conduct of the affairs of the hero, and guides them to a happy issue. And when, in the disguise of Mentor, she attends the sacrifice of Nestor, and offers prayer to Poseidon, the Poet adds, 'so she prayed; and of herself accomplished all the prayer.'³

Yet more notable is the relation of rank as between Herê and Athenê. Once Athenê appears, namely in the Debate of the First Book, as the messenger of Herê, to prevent the wrath of Achilles from bursting into flagrant violence:⁴ as though Herê had a title to employ her services. Yet, even in this case, Herê, it should be remarked, supplies no instructions; and Athenê frames her discourse after her own will, and with no regard to the special inclination of Herê for Agamemnon. But elsewhere Homer has not scrupled to give to Athenê the first place. Twice the goddesses descend together from Olympos to the field of battle, in the chariot of Herê. It is Herê who yokes the horses, and acts as charioteer. Athenê not only mounts as the warrior beside her, but bears the Aigis of supreme power.⁵

When Thetis arrives at Olympos, in the Twenty-fourth Iliad, she receives the honors of a guest, and is placed by the side of Zeus, Athenê giving way to her. She probably held the second seat of rank on the left side, the first being, as we need not doubt, given to Herê. It is Herê, again, who sends the Sun to his repose.⁶ On the whole, an ingenious division of ascriptions seems

¹ Il. xxi. 468.   ³ Od. v. 380.
² Od. iii. 55–62.   ⁴ Il. i. 195.
⁵ Il. v. 711–752; viii. 381–396.   ⁶ Il. xviii. 239.

to be carried through, by means of which Herè has the higher place in the internal relations of Olympos, but Athenè far excels in all that immediately touches the government of men.

And now as to the dignity of Apollo.

In the ancient Hymn to this god, cited by Thucydides, it is told that the gods rise from their seats as he comes near.[1]

The superiority thus awarded to Apollo cannot be accounted for by anything in the mere order of Olympos, which it seems, indeed, to contravene. The child of Leto the obscure is preferred to the child of great Herè. In a time of wild men and deeds, a god presiding over peaceful functions infinitely outshines the god of war. We must seek for the reason, then, in traditions flowing from another source.

2. In the Fifth Iliad, Homer appears to inform us, that Athenè was born of Zeus without a mother;[2] a statement afterwards developed in the legend, which represents her as having sprung full-grown from his head. Now if the Hellenes had preserved the tradition of the Logos, it was impossible to clothe it, for the purposes of their system, in a more appropriate form. If they had not, how comes it that we have this one only exception made to the accustomed method of parentage? — a method so deeply ingrained in the Greek ideas, that even for Zeus a father must be found.

But Apollo is the child of Leto; and Leto, if we can give the word a meaning, means darkness or oblivion. If Apollo be considered as the Sun, the name of his mother may signify his birth from Night. But the

[1] Hymn, 2–4.   [2] Il. v. 880.

Apollo of Homer's Olympos is not the Sun; and of his functions a very large portion have no relation to the Night whatever. But if Homer saw in his Apollo a son of his Zeus, whose filial relation rested upon traditions anterior to any which the current mythologies supplied, and if the word Leto expressed such an obscurity, this surely appears to supply a rational and consistent explanation.

Thus the differences between the birth of Athené and that of Apollo, according to Homer, correspond with the differences between the two forms of the Messianic tradition represented respectively in the Logos, and the Son of the Woman.

3. But while the rank and the power of these deities were traceable to those of Zeus in the Olympian system, it is plain that their dignity, their sanctitas, was greater than his. They were regarded with a more unmixed reverence, as if the traditions relating to them had been kept more free from earthly elements. These propositions do not rest merely on the general mode of handling them in Homer, but upon distinct and well-defined notes. They are never exhibited in the mood of sensual passion, like Zeus and Heré, to say nothing of lesser deities. This is true, without the least qualification, of Athené. Apollo is stated to have carried off Marpessa the bride of Ideus;[1] and he enters into the ribald jesting of Olympos in the Lay of the Net.[2] But the latter story, as has already been observed, is conceived in the spirit of a foreign mythology; and with respect to Marpessa, it may be remarked, that the numerous intrigues of the mythical

---

[1] Il. iv. 559-564. [2] Od. viii. 334.

gods in Homer are never accompanied with violence, but are invariably made to appear as connections voluntarily accepted; while again they are always attended with the birth of children. In both particulars this story differs from them, and it much more resembles that of Ganymede,[1] who was carried up to be cupbearer in heaven. Perhaps we are to understand that she was taken for the service of the deity at the neighboring shrine of Delphi, where a priestess so long officiated.

But again, these deities, and these alone, are never subjected to disparagement in any other form. Here, as we have seen, had once been wounded, and Zeus had been, or was about to be, enchained; but to these two no violence is ever offered. Further, Zeus is on the very verge of open conflict with Poseidon; but in the Theomachy, the battle between Apollo and his uncle is avoided, while Athene inflicts a terrible reverse on her huge opponent Arès. Again, Zeus himself is, for the time, completely baffled and outwitted by the stratagem of Here; and the Hellenizing Poseidon is enabled to take the field against his orders. But neither Athene nor Apollo are ever deceived or visibly put to shame.

Nor will this appear an easy matter to arrange, when it is borne in mind that these two are the great agents of the two great Olympian deities respectively. It is, however, carefully contrived that they shall never come into actual collision one with the other. Apollo interferes against Patroclos; but Athene is absent. Athene interferes against Hector; but Apollo is absent.

[1] Il. xx. 234.

Again he is absent, in the Doloneia, while she conducts to a prosperous issue the night-expedition of Diomed and Odysseus.[1] In the Chariot-race of the Twenty-third Book, where the contest for the first place is between Eumelos and Diomed, Apollo, the partisan of Eumelos, throws the whip of Diomed out of his hand.[2] Athene restores it, apparently when Apollo has departed, and by breaking the chariot-yoke of Eumelos secures the victory of her favorite. Apollo here, though saved as far as the Poet's art can do it, comes off second best; but only as against Athene. A second instance occurs, where he is brought to suggest, at a time when the Greeks[3] were losing ground, in lieu of the general conflict, a personal challenge from Hector, which was sure to be to their advantage. To appreciate the importance of this consideration, we must observe how other deities are liable to be foiled and worsted: Arès by Athene in the Fifth Iliad, and by Hephaistos in the Eighth Odyssey; Here and Aïdoneus by Herncles; Artemis by Here in the Theomachy; Aphrodite by Diomed; Demeter,[4] and Here too,[5] by Zeus. Zeus himself was delivered from a conspiracy by extraneous aid.

There is a manifest difference to be observed as to the relations of will and affection with Zeus, between these two and the other deities. These alone he calls by the epithet 'dear.'[6] The case of Apollo stands alone as an exhibition of entire unbroken harmony with the will of Zeus, which in all things he regards. When he remonstrates, it is with the body of the gods,

[1] Il. x. 515.   [2] Il. xxiii. 384.   [3] Il. vii. 20.   [4] Od. v.
[5] Il. xv. 18.   [6] Il. viii. 39, xxii. 183; and xv. 221, xvi. 667.

not with Zeus personally;[1] and Herè, rebuking him
for his interference, is at once checked by Zeus.[2]
Though he seems to be the habitual organ for accomplishing his father's designs, he is never so employed
in any purpose which is about to fail; such, for instance, as would have been the defence of Sarpedon.
Zeus himself is by no means so carefully shielded, in
great providential matters, as Apollo.

The necessities of the Poem place Athenè in antagonism to Zeus, and she goes all lengths in the prosecution of her purposes. But, if in opposition to the
chief deity, she is on the side not only of justice, but of
the Olympian decree, to which Zeus himself, his personal partialities leaning one way, and his governing
responsibility another, has felt it right to yield. She
exposes herself, together with Herè, to his threats;
but his anger, in her case, is on account of her threatening him on a special and rare occasion,[3] while Herè
ever leads him an uneasy life;[4] and he seems anxious
to take the first opportunity of reassuring her[5] as his
beloved daughter.

We have, then, in the case of Apollo, an uniform
identity of will with the chief god, and in the case of
Athenè only an exceptional departure from it. This
is a very remarkable feature. In Herè and Poseidon,
it is wholly wanting. In Hermes and Iris we find the
obedience of messengers, but not the unity of counsel
and of mind. In general, such harmony can no more
broadly be asserted of Olympos, than of a kingdom or
court on earth. No traditions known to me appear in
any way to account for it, except those of the Hebrew

[1] Il. xxiv. 33.   [2] Il. xxiv. 65.   [3] Il. viii. 406–408.
[4] Il. i. 561–568.   [5] Il. viii. 39.

race. It is evidently the very picture for which they are calculated to furnish the materials.

The Hellenic religion represents Apollo as the defender of Heaven, and the Deliverer of the Immortals, in some great peril or struggle of contending spirits. He destroyed Otos and Ephialtes, the largest, and after Orion the most beautiful, of all beings reared on earth, at the critical time when they are about to scale heaven by piling the mountains.

This function has no natural connection with the mythological offices of Apollo, great and varied as they are. Neither as physician, harper, poet, prophet, archer, nor angel of death, can he appear entitled to claim the honor thus awarded to him. There is also in Homer a glance at a general rebellion of the Giants and at their fall in consequence of their impiety.[1] The later tradition retains, down to the Augustan age, this account of Apollo with a diversity of accompaniments. In Homer, as the account is by no means to be explained through his Olympian offices, it appears to represent some older tradition, according to which this bright and lofty person, intimately associated with, and specially executing on earth, the divine will, had likewise put down in actual battle a rising of rebellious spirits in the Upper world.

To Athene there is assigned by Homer no function resembling this. But the specialties of a certain divine supremacy are in a manner divided between them. Athene takes a peculiar jurisdiction in the Underworld; and it is the more remarkable because, while she uses it in aid of Zeus, it does not come by

[1] Od. vii. 56–60.

derivation from him. She declares¹ that but for her, Herakles, when he went to fetch Cerberus, never would have escaped the dire streams of Styx. This seems to mean that Zeus could not have delivered him.

Lastly, we cannot fail to observe how the powers and offices of these two deities encroach upon and cut across the provinces of other recognized divinities, with a total absence of any reciprocity in regard to what may be called their special function. Athené, as the goddess of war, not only rivals Arès, but excels him. She is the goddess of art, like Hephaistos, with some distinction, indeed, as he operates upon metals with the aid of fire, and she ordinarily on tissues. Yet not so as to limit her power; for she, together with Hephaistos, instructs the silversmith in all the departments of his art;² and moreover teaches mensuration to the carpenter.³ She presides over industry and over cunning, like Hermes; and she shares with this deity his special function as conductor of the dead.⁴ Again, in parts of her relation to Polity, as Ἀγελείη,⁵ Λαοσσόος,⁶ ἐρυσίπτολις,⁷ she approaches to the office of Themis:⁸ who summons and dissolves assemblies, thus discharging subordinate functions apparently on behalf of the primary political deity.

Apollo, as the healer, discharges the office of Paieon. But while Paieon,⁹ who is somewhat strongly marked as a deity of the Egyptian system, heals with the hand,¹⁰ Apollo has too high a dignity to be thus rep-

---

[1] Il. viii. 362–369; cf. Od. xi. 623–626.   [2] Od. vi. 233, xxiii. 160.
[3] Il. xv. 412.   [4] Od. xi. 626; cf. xxiv. 1.
[5] Ἀγελείη = Spoil-driver, or Folk-leader.
[6] Λαοσσόος = Folk-stirrer.   [7] ἐρυσίπτολις = City-warder.
[8] Od. ii. 69. Il. xx. 4.   [9] Od. iv. 231.   [10] Il. v. 401.

resented. He simply deposits the stunned Æneas in his temple, where Leto and Artemis proceed to treat him:[1] or, in answer to the prayer of Glaucos, heals from afar the wound of that gallant warrior.[2]

Apollo, as the musician, is supreme in the province of the Muses; who are purely poetical and Hellenic impersonations, sometimes one in number, sometimes nine.[3] His concern is with the instrument, theirs with the voice; but they perform together at the Olympian banquet,[4] and have, probably, a community of relation to the Bard.

Apollo, as the agent of Zeus, moves in the same province as Hermes and Iris, especially the latter: but the highest offices are always reserved to him, in which the Divine intention is to take effect. It is left to Hermes to conduct Priam to the presence of Achilles, when the object is only that of a go-between, and the result depends upon the will of the hero.

In the 'Studies on Homer' I called by the name of Secondaries[5] the deities who are thus placed, even in their own departments, below Apollo and Athené. Perhaps the name is not appropriate, since these personages have in general independent traditions of their own. The main point is that we should observe the approach to a divine universality of office and power in Apollo and Athené, which can in no respect be accounted for by the formation of the Olympian family or its laws.

Let us now turn to points connected with the human and terrestrial relations of these great deities.

[1] Il. v. 445–447. [2] Il. xvi. 527–529. [3] Od. xxiv. 60.
[4] Il. l. 603, 604. [5] Vol. ii. p. 69.

They are jointly invoked, together with Zeus, in a solemn but often-repeated formula expressing keen desire; as when Achilles prays, 'Father Zeus! and Athenè! and Apollo! would that every Trojan should perish, and every Greek.'[1]

And they are placed at the climax of honor in another formula:[2]

'Were I honored as are honored Athenè and Apollo.'

This line suggests the question whether, in the time of Homer, some visible form of worship may possibly have been paid to these two deities, as the agents of a Supreme God, presumed to be less accessible than they, and was at the same time not accorded to others. Be this as it may, they are the only deities whose temples are unequivocally named to us in Homer: the temple of Apollo[3] at Chrusè, on Pergamos, and at Putho: the temple of Athenè[4] at Athens, on Pergamos, and in Scherie.

Again, we do not find any local limit to the worship of these deities within the sphere of Greek knowledge and experience. Athenè, the most Hellenic deity, is the patroness of Pelasgian Attica, and is also the object of the supplicatory procession of Trojan women in the Sixth Iliad. She is worshipped at Pulos, in Ithaca, in the Greek camp. Apollo, the great Trojan deity, has his priest among the Kicones, his temple at Putho, his altar in Delos, his grove and festival in Ithaca; and he is the fountain-head of the prophetic gift, which pervades all parts of Greece. He is connected with

---
[1] Il. xvi. 97.   [2] Il. viii. 540; xiii. 827.
[3] Il. i. 39; v. 445; ix. 404.
[4] Il. ii. 549; vi. 88, 297. Od. vi. 320–322.

Killê, with Lycia in the south, and with the Lycian Trojans in the north of Asia Minor. Seers, whom he always endows with vision, are found[1] even among the Cyclops. He feeds the horses of Admetos in Pieriê, claims the daughter of Marpessa in Ætolia, and slays the children of Niobê near Mount Sipulos. In truth, he seems scarcely less universal than that scourge of Death, to which he stands in so near and solemn a relation.

No deity of the Poems, except Zeus, can at all compete with Apollo and Athenê in this respect.

Next, Apollo and Athenê are independent of all the limitations of place: another point in which no other deity, but Zeus, appears to resemble them.

Athens, indeed, appears to be indicated in the Odyssey as the abode of Athenê.[2] Apollo has no abode directly assigned to him. But the sign of omnipresence in both is, that prayer is addressed to them from all places indifferently. Only four times[3] do we find actual petitions to Apollo, and all these in Troas. But we may observe this essential point; that, as in the two last of these for example, he is presumed to be present, and to hear it as a matter of course, without reference to any special residence or function. To Athenê we have no less than twelve prayers given in the Poems, in Ithaca, Scheriê, Pulos, Troy, and the Greek camp; and always to her as an universal not a local power. But even Poseidon, great as he is, never has prayer offered to him, except near the sea, or by his own descendants.

[1] Od. ix. 509. [2] Od. vii. 80, 81.
[3] Il. i. 35-43; 450-457; iv. 100-103, 110-131; xvi. 513-529. Add, however, the references in Il. xi. 363, 364, and l. 65, 478.

In truth, but a small number of deities in Homer are made the subjects of actual invocation. For example, there is no invocation anywhere to Aphroditè, Arès, Hermes, Hephaistos, Demeter, or even Herè. Artemis[1] and Poseidon are invoked: the first in connection with function, the latter with place. We have also addresses from mortals to the deities presiding over the Oath, or ruling in the Underworld. But general prayer is addressed only to Zeus, Pallas, and Apollo.

Again, these favored deities are exempt from physical or other infirmity or need in general. They are never excited by mere personal passion. Neither of them individually eats or drinks; as Hermes, for example, does, at the dwelling of Calypso,[2] or as Iris fears lest she should lose her share of the Ethiopian hecatomb.[3] Neither of them sleeps, or is weary, or is wounded, or suffers pain. They are never introduced as delighting in sacrifice apart from obedience. Artemis sends the boar to Caludon because she had been forgotten in the offerings:[4] but Apollo's wrath, in the First Iliad, is not for the want of prayer or hecatomb, it is on account of the shame and wrong done by Agamemnon to Chruses his priest.[5] Diomed and Odysseus are dear to Pallas: but she never asks or commends their bounty at the altar, as Zeus commends that of Hector, and of Odysseus himself.[6] When sacrifice is offered to Apollo, in the First Iliad,[7] after the restitution, his pleasure is not stated to have been in the savor of it, but in the hymn of praise which was addressed to him. Zeus can accept the victims

[1] Od. xx. 61.   [2] Od. v. 94.   [3] Il. xxiii. 207.
[4] Il. ix. 530.   [5] Il. i. 65, 93.   [6] Il. xxiv. 68. Od. i. 66.
[7] Il. i. 473.

even while he frustrates the petition:[1] but when Athenè in like manner declines a prayer of the Trojans, she is not stated to accept the offering;[2] and the idea that when offended she can be appeased by mere offerings is thus practically repudiated.[3]

Again, attributes of bulk stand at the bottom of the scale of excellence. They are indirectly assigned to Pallas by the weight of the Aigis which she carries.[4] This is possibly on account of the direct competition which subsists between the huge Arès, as a god of war, and herself, presiding over the same province.[5] Bulk is never ascribed to Apollo.

Again, as to locomotion. Apollo and Athenè move without the use of any instruments, such as wings, chariots, or otherwise. Their journeys are usually undistributed and instantaneous. They set out, and they arrive.[6] On one occasion only, Athenè employs the foot-wings[7] which were used by Hermes. But there are details and steps in the movements of Hermes, Poseidon, and Herè.[8]

The ordinary Olympian deity, when offended by mortals, most commonly makes his appeal to Zeus for redress. Thus Poseidon acts with respect to the Greek rampart; Aphroditè, tacitly, after her wound by Diomed; Arès, in the same condition; and Helios, after his oxen have been devoured by the crew of Odysseus.[9]

But the retributive action of Apollo, in the Plague of

---

[1] Il. ii. 420. [2] Il. vi. 311. [3] Od. iii. 143–147.
[4] Il. ii. 448. [5] See Il. xviii. 516.
[6] Od. i. 102–103. Il. xv. 150. [7] Od. i. 96.
[8] Od. v. 50–58. Il. xiii. 17–31; xiv. 225–230.
[9] Il. v. 869, 426; vii. 445. Od. xii. 377–388.

the First Iliad, is wholly independent, and is the more remarkable since he wastes the army of the Greeks to the great peril of an enterprise promoted by such powerful divinities. In the Third Odyssey,[1] on the return of the Greeks, we are told that Zeus designed evil for them by reason of their crimes, wherefore many perished by the wrath of Pallas; that she could not be appeased, and that Zeus suspended calamity over them. There is no sign here of an appeal to Zeus, but rather of an identification of the two agencies in the providential government of the world.

Again, Apollo and Athene administer powers which are otherwise the special or exclusive property of Zeus.

The air-functions of that deity are sometimes, indeed, exercised by Here. This may reasonably be accounted for by her relation to him as wife. No kindred reason is available for the selection of these two among his children for an office so elevated. Athene, with Here, thunders in honor of Agamemnon:[2] and she can cause the winds to cease, or to blow.[3] So he too sends for the Greek ship a toward breeze.[4] But the most significant of all the participations of the supreme power is confined to Athene with Apollo. Both of them in turn carry the Aigis in the Fifth and Fifteenth Iliads respectively.[5] And, in truth, these two deities seem throughout the Iliad to share with Zeus the function of Providence; the one as towards the Trojans, the other as towards the Greeks.[6] Indeed, in the Odyssey more especially, they fill the very highest offices of divine government over the minds of men; which appear to be conducted by Pallas, much more than by Zeus himself.

[1] Od. iii. 132 seqq.
[2] Od. v. 109, 382-385, et alibi.
[3] Il. v. 735-742; xv. 229.
[4] See Studies on Homer, Olympos, pp. 115-122.
[5] Il. xi. 45.
[6] Il. l. 479.

There is a very peculiar function attaching to the divine supremacy, in the signification of coming events to men by the flight of birds, and by atmospheric signs. This power, being connected with the future, is distinguished from the general power over external nature. It is shared with Zeus principally by Apollo, but also by Athené. He sends the Kirkos, or wheeling falcon, to Thrace, as an omen of success to Telemachos:[1] she, a heron to cheer Odysseus and Diomed in the Night-excursion of the Tenth Iliad.[2] She stupefies and bewilders the Suitors as their ruin approaches: but his agent, Theoclumenos,[3] announces, and he therefore may be considered as supplying, the portents which beset the Hall of the Palace before the final catastrophe.

Nägelsbach observes, that the power of signs is confined to Zeus, Heré, Apollo, and Pallas.[4] But the signs exhibited by Heré, the thunder of the Eleventh Iliad, and the gift of speech to the horses of Achilles, involve no knowledge or signification of the future. The prediction delivered by the horse Xanthos appears to be his own, and not the gift of the goddess.

It may be affirmed generally, that both these deities, but especially Athené, exercise a power over external nature almost without limit. Assuming the human form, they can make themselves visible to one person only among many.[5] They, and none but they, frame images of human beings which can speak or fight:[6] Pallas alters at will the figures and features of Odysseus, Penelopé, and Laertes; having command, ap-

[1] Od. xv. 526. [2] Il. x. 274.
[3] Od. xx. 345–371. [4] Hom. Theol. iv. 16; p. 147.
[5] Il. i. 198, and (apparently), xvii. 321–324.
[6] Il. v. 449. Od. iv. 796, 825.

parently, of some organic power over matter and vital force. While Athenê's jurisdiction as to storms is unlimited, Apollo diverts rivers from their beds, and makes them converge upon a point.[1]

In like manner they act upon the mind of man by infusing fear, courage, counsel, as the case may be. These operations are never assigned to any deity except those of the first order in Olympos.

But when Poseidon breathes valor into the two Ajaxes, he does it by striking them; just as when he has to convert the ship of the Phaiakes into a rock, he drives it downward with a blow of his hand.[2] On the other hand, Apollo infuses courage into Hector and Glaucos, and heals also the wounds of the latter chieftain,[3] without any outward act. Most of the corporal changes effected by Athenê in the Odyssey are similarly brought about. Only in the case where she effects a total transformation of Odysseus, she touches him with her wand.[4]

This exception, as a rule, from the use of instruments in giving effect to their will, is a sign of a high conception, on the part of the Poet, with respect to their divine power. In the Kestos of Aphroditê, in the wand of Hermes, an intrinsic virtue resides, apart from the will of those personages respectively. These are not mere symbols: they are causative seats of power. That Apollo and Athenê do not use any such vehicle, is a sign of force, essential, independent, and supreme, over matter.

Yet once more, as to the common features of these extraordinary personages.

[1] Il. xii. 24.
[2] Il. xvi. 528.
[3] Il. xiii. 59. Od. xlii. 164.
[4] Od. xiii. 429; xvi. 172, 456.

Their moral standard is conspicuously raised above that of the Olympian family in general.

Athenê has the purity of Artemis, whom in all other points she eclipses. This prerogative is expressly acknowledged in the ancient Hymn to Aphroditê.[1] No such statement can be made of any other among the active goddesses: not of Herê, Thetis, or Demeter; much less of Aphroditê herself.

So we have in the Poems sons of Zeus, of Poseidon, of Arês, of Hermes; all of them the fruit of their intrigues with women; but no son of Apollo. Hephaistos, indeed, is exempt from the charge, probably on account of his personal deformity. Down to the time of Æschylus,[2] Apollo retained the epithet of 'the pure.' Later still, it had been lost;[3] and the legend of Marpessa, which by no means requires such a construction in Homer, had been read in the light of the later tradition, and had descended to the common level. His share in the scene described by the Lay of Demodocos may perhaps be accounted for by the fact that the subject belonged to a foreign theology, though it may have been one which was already beginning to act upon Greece.

I do not however attach to the term 'purity,' in an inquiry of this nature, its full Christian sense; in which it appears as one portion of the panoply of a complete and almost seraphic virtue, and is elevated as well as sustained by the spirit of the marvellous religion to which it belongs. The moral characters of Apollo and Athenê are lofty, if measured by the Olympian standard, although they will not bear the tests

---

[1] vv. 8, 10.   [2] Suppl. 222.   [3] S. Clem. Alex. p. 20, B.

which the Christian system would apply. Apollo descends from his height, in the scene where he strikes Patroclos from behind, and knocks his armor off, so as to bring the Greek hero into that unequal position in which even the keen national feeling of the Poet would allow him to be conquered by a Trojan. And Pallas undertakes a mean office when she incites Pandaros to a breach of the Pact. Counsel, with her, certainly degenerates at times into craft and fraud.[1] But these drawbacks are in both cases exceptional. Speaking generally, the two are beautiful and majestic delineations; and Athené in particular has many of the characteristics of the Eternal Wisdom, which came forth from the bosom of God.

The distinctive functions of Apollo, which sever him from Athené, are many. The highest are these four: that he is familiarly employed by Zeus, with whom he has a perfect conformity of will, as his agent in the government of human affairs; that he is the champion of Zeus and of Heaven against the rebellious powers; that he is the minister of death; and, finally, that to him alone there seems to be committed an absolute knowledge of the future, and the administration of that prophetic gift which Calchas, though acting in and for the Greek army, held from him.[2] Athené, on the other hand, is occasionally the agent of Zeus, with whose will, however, she is less uniformly associated.[3] Apollo has also, besides the gifts of the bow, of healing, and of song, a special association with the light.

The ministry of death, exercised by Apollo for men as by Artemis for women, is most of all remarkable

[1] Il. iv. 86–92. Od. xiii. 299.   [2] Il. i. 72.
[3] Il. iv. 70. Od. xxiv. 539–545.

on account of its twofold aspect. It is sometimes penal, as with Ariadne;[1] or even a terrible vengeance, as with the children of Niobè.[2] It is sometimes a tranquil and painless deliverance from the burden of the flesh, as in the island of Suriè.[3] Another peculiarity of this prerogative is, that it refers to death produced without second causes. All other deaths whatever in the Poems, natural or violent, appear to be referred to second causes. There is a mythological impersonation of Death (Thanatos) provided by the Poet, to which to refer them. The death brought about by Apollo and Artemis is an exceptional death, in the point of being directly due to their supreme will and special ministry.

And this is at least a wonderful phenomenon in the Olympian system, especially when we consider how gloomy and repulsive, in the view of Homer and his age, was the extinction of our mortal life, and the prospect of the region that lay beyond it. Here is, as matter of fact, a tradition of a Power that was to take away the sting from Death, preserved for the time, but for the time only, among a people who surrounded death in general with associations of a wholly different character. Even if it stood alone, we should be driven surely to treat it as derived, through whatever channel, from some ancient and signal promise of a Deliverer for the human race. It does not however stand alone, but forms part of a multitude of varied testimonies, all converging upon the same point.

Athené, besides her great special prerogatives of War, Policy, and Industrial Art, is invested generally with yet greater power than Apollo, and rises to a still

---

[1] Od. xi. 324.   [2] Il. xxiv. 606; cf. vi. 205.   [3] Od. xv. 407.

higher grade of moral majesty. She seems also, by virtue of a latent partnership in the divine supremacy, to partake of or represent something analogous to several of his peculiar gifts. She enters into his knowledge of the future; for in the Ithacan cave she foretells to Odysseus all that he has yet to suffer.[1] And if he is the champion of the gods in Olympos (an office which she shared with him in the later tradition), she, as I have above observed, possesses a jurisdiction in the Underworld,[2] which appears to cross and over-ride that of its appointed rulers. Though she cannot avert death from a mortal, she can afterwards extricate him from its grasp.[3]

The limits of this work forbid me to pursue the mythological history of Athene and Apollo through the later literature of the Greeks and Romans. They continue, it may be said generally, to hold positions of great splendor, but the distinctive character of their features as a whole is gradually enfeebled and effaced.

Even the hasty reader of Homer cannot fail to be struck with it; but it is only by a minute and careful observation of particulars that the whole case can be brought out. It then becomes fully manifest that, by not one, but a crowd of attributes and incidents, they are severed from the general body of the Olympian deities of Homer, and closely associated together, though very far from being even substantially identified, far less confused. These attributes are partly intellectual, partly moral. The general result is to render their position grossly anomalous and wholly inexplicable, if the explanation of it is only to be sought in

[1] Od. xiii. 306. [2] Il. viii. 362–369. Od. iv. 750–753.
[3] Od. iv. 752, 753.

the laws of the Olympian system, or in such traditions as the older nature-worship, or the Egyptian, or Syrian, or Phœnician mythologies could supply.

But when we turn to the Hebrew annals, we find there a group of traditions, belonging to what may be termed the Messianic order, which appear to supply us with a key to the double enigma. The general characteristics of the Messianic anticipations are in marked conformity with the common prerogatives of Pallas and Apollo. And the distinctions of the two deities fall in, not less clearly, with the twofold form in which those anticipations are presented to us; the one, which pointed to a conception more abstract, and less capable of being confounded with mere humanity; the other, to a form strictly personal, and intimately associated with our nature.

In these resemblances, there appears to be found a very strong presumption, that the Hellenic portion of the Aryan family had for a time preserved to itself, in broad outline, no small share of those treasures, of which the Semitic family of Abraham were to be the appointed guardians, on behalf of all mankind, until the fulness of time should come.

It is obvious that such traditions, when cut off from their fountain-head, supplied a material basis for that anthropomorphic character which distinguished the Greek religion from first to last, and associated it so closely with the whole detail of life. For, according to their tenor, the conception and representation of deity in human form were no idle fancy, but were the great design of the Almighty God for the recovery of an erring, suffering, and distracted race.

On the importance of these propositions I need not

dwell. The more they are important, the more it is to be desired that they should be strictly noted. The intention of these pages is both to invite, and somewhat to assist, all such as shall be disposed to undertake the pains of such an investigation.

Section IX. *Hephaistos.*

Hephaistos bears in Homer the double stamp of a Nature-Power, representing the element of fire, and of an anthropomorphic deity, who is the god of Art, at a period when the only fine art known was in works of metal produced by the aid of fire.

As Homer gives us faint traces of the elemental god of air in en dios, and as his Nereus is still represented in the n e r o of modern Greek for 'water,' so he actually employs the name Hephaistos in one passage undeniably for fire,[1] if he does not also mean the flame of fire in other passages where he mentions 'the flame of Hephaistos.' This deity is worshipped in Troas, where he has a wealthy priest.[2]

Hahn finds in the fou k i-a of the Albanian tongue, signifying force, the root of the word Vulcanus;[3] and quotes Varro, 'ab ignis vi et violentiâ Vulcanus est dictus.' Schmidt connects the name with fulgere and fulmen.[4]

Hephaistos is not one of the seven astral deities of the East, who stood in relation to seven metals.

It is doubtless in a double or plural tradition that we are to seek the explanation of our finding Hephaistos, on the one hand, bearing the marks of antiquity

---

[1] Il. ii. 426.   [2] Il. v. 9.   [3] Alban. Studien, p. 252.
[4] Deckmann, Inventions, Art. Metals.

which belong to a Nature-Power, and, on the other hand, made known to us as an infant, the offspring of Zeus and Here, whose mother sought to hide him, that is to put him out of the way, on account of his lameness: a sure sign that, in the view of Homer, he was, so far as regards his higher character of Art-master, a deity of more recent introduction. This part of the traditions can relate to no mere fire-god. He is saved by Thetis, the grand mediatress of the Theogonies, and Eurunome, the daughter of Okeanos; and hid by them in a submarine cavern, where, with the tidal flood of ocean ever gurgling in his ears, he spends his time for nine years in working clasps, and necklaces, and other trinkets.[1] Such an assemblage of images is highly Phœnician, that is to say Eastern, in its color.

The combination in this place of Thetis, a sea-goddess, and the ocean-deity, is remarkable; and stands, I think, alone in Homer. I understand it to betoken the dual course of tradition relating to Hephaistos. The Okeanos of Homer is the sire of gods, or their source.[2] This may indeed relate to the Nature-Powers, rather than to the Olympian gods, from whom Okeanos stands somewhat widely apart. If so, Eurunome has her share in the transaction as a representative of the older dynasty of gods, and Thetis as a personage who has the *entrée* to the newer circle. But it seems more probable that as Okeanos, the father of Persê, and father-in-law of Helios, has strong Eastern associations, Eurunome represents the newer and higher character of Hephaistos imported from the East, and that Thetis, according to her own stock, befriends him as a Nature-Power.

[1] Il. xviii. 394–405.   [2] Il. xiv. 201.

Both the water of Ocean, and the connection of fire with fine art in metals, probably attach Hephaistos to the channels of Phœnician, in its widest sense of Eastern, tradition: while he may have represented the simple element of fire in the Pelasgian systems of religion.

The latter relation accounts for his being worshipped in Troas, even while he is one of the deities who, following his chief bent, takes decidedly, though not passionately, the Greek part in the quarrel. And, accordingly, it is under the rude conception of mere fire that he is matched, in the Theomachy, with the river Xanthos, whom he exhausts by drying up the stream, and thus sorely afflicts, until Here intercedes.

Through all his other marked operations in the Poems, Hephaistos, instead of resolving himself into the element, remains entirely anthropomorphic, although he is so far from satisfying the Greek ideal of a god in respect of form. He is such in the Olympian banquet at the close of the first Book, at the smithy or forge in his own palace, and again in the lay of Demodocos.

Married to Aphrodite in the Odyssey, he appears in the Iliad as the husband of Charis.[1] Now Aphrodite is a real member of the mythological system, whereas Charis is loosely and faintly delineated, and seems almost to hover between an idea and a person. Some have treated these two representations as discrepant, and have used them in support of the theory, which separates the authorship of the two Poems. Others (myself included) may have suggested modes of re-

[1] Od. viii. 269; Il. xviii. 382.

conciliation between them, which are insufficient.[1] Having now arrived, I think, at adequate proof of the Eastern or Phœnician character of the mythology, as well as the scenery, of the whole sphere of the Voyages, I find in this fact the simplest explanation of a difference, which, instead of any longer impeaching, rather tends to sustain the unity of authorship. Hephaistos and Aphroditê, as husband and wife, owe that relation probably to a Syrian or Syro-Phœnician source. Hephaistos and Charis, in the sense of the Hellenic mythology, together represent, with a perfect propriety, the strength and the grace, the beauty or charm, which require to be combined in works of Art. Nägelsbach, accordingly, treats this marriage as allegorical.[2]

The Poems, however, establish a relation, be it allegorical or not, between the Charites and Aphroditê; for the Charites receive her on her return from the scene of the Net to Cyprus, where they bathe, anoint, and vest her. One junior of their band, promised by Herê as a wife to Hupnos, or the god of sleep, in Lemnos, is named Pasitheê. Two handmaids of Nausicaa in Scheriê draw their beauty from the Charites. There is therefore some evidence to give them a personality beyond that which the single mind of the Poet can confer. Their relation to Eastern personages suggests that they may have had a place in Eastern tradition; while it seems that they acquired with time a recognized character and worship in Greece.[3] Professor Max Müller derives their name, as well as that of

[1] Studies, vol. ii. p. 257.   [2] Hom. Theol. p. 114.
[3] Welcker, vol. i. p. 696. Dr. Schmidt in Smith's Dict. sub. voc.

the Harits or Horses of the Sun, from the Sanscrit root gh a r, to glitter, to render brilliant by oil.[1]

The deity of Hephaistos is matchless within the sphere of his own art. It is in concert with Athené, that he grants to mortals the gift of manual skill;[2] but his own works are the most wonderful recorded of any god. In addition to every charm of grace and splendor, they have the actual gift of life. In Olympos, the metal handmaids of the limping god both think and speak;[3] and in Scherié, the porter-dogs of Alkinoos[4] have perpetual existence, and perpetual youth. Even in the inanimate Shield there are varied signs of life.[5] A certain kindliness of nature marks the intervention of Hephaistos, in the first Book, to stop a quarrel[6] between his parents; and that he was endowed with warm affections is evident from the recital he there gives of a former effort made by him to save Heré from the wrath of Zeus, which entailed on him a fall from heaven to earth,[7] as well as from the warm gratitude[8] he displays towards Thetis for the benefit she had conferred on him. His conduct respecting Heré is the more praiseworthy, in proportion as her attempt upon his deformed infancy had been unnatural.[9] In the lay of the Net, under the heaviest provocation his conduct is not vindictive.

Hephaistos is the architect of the palaces of the gods,[10] as well as the artificer of the most conspicuous works of Art mentioned in the Poems.[11] He made a lock for

---

[1] Lectures on Language, II. 373, 375.
[2] Od. vi. 233; xxiii. 160.
[3] Il. xviii. 417.
[4] Od. vii. 91–94. [5] Infra, Chap. XIII. [6] Il. i. 571–589.
[7] Il. i. 590–594. [8] Il. xviii. 395. [9] Il. xviii. 395–397.
[10] Il. i. 607; xiv. 167, 338. [11] Il. viii. 195; Od. iv. 617.

Herè which not only no man, but no god could open.[1] Lemnos appears to be his chosen abode, as a volcanic isle: of other similar islands or spots, in the later mythology, we find the like recorded.

Out of his own art, he carries no signs of divinity in Homer; he does not act on general nature, or on the human mind, unless in a case where the sons of his own Priest are concerned; and these he merely conceals in a cloud of vapor, a power which even Aphroditè seems to exercise on behalf of the body of Hector. His powers of perception are so limited, that, in the lay of Demodocos, he is ignorant of what takes place, during his absence, in his own house, until the Sun informs him, whom he again employs as a spy; nor, in the Twenty-first Book of the Iliad, is he aware of the danger in which Achilles stands from the united Rivers, until Herè informs him, and bids him act.[2]

Section X. Arès.

The Arès of Homer, like his Poseidon, exhibits that idea of deity which both rises above man, and sinks much below him: in point of strength divine, in point of mind and heart simply animal. He is a compound of deity and brute.

But Arès is greatly inferior to Poseidon in that class of conceptions, to which both, in a marked manner belong. Glory and awe surround the one, from his unfailing might, and his high origin. Arès represents a huge mass of animal force; but he is so exhibited in the action of the Iliad, as to fall into much of the contempt

---

[1] Il. xiv. 167, 8.   [2] Il. xxi. 329 333

(in a certain sense) which is evidently meant to attach to Aphrodite.

It seems safe to assume that a god, and more especially a god of war, whom Homer represents as wounded and disabled by a Greek warrior, could not, in the time of Homer, have been a deity of acknowledged worship and renown in Greece. Nor is there found in the Poems any trace of such worship. No prayer or sacrifice is offered to him: he has no general command over the mind of man, or over external nature. It is said, indeed, that he entered into Hector while that chieftain was engaged in putting on the armor of Achilles;[1] but this appears to treat him simply as a passion, just as in other places his name becomes a synonym for war, or for a spear. None of the five great gods of the Poems are ever said thus to enter into (as if it were to be contained in and circumscribed by) the spirit of a man; the highest divine agents effuse, so to speak, and inspire a temper, but do not impart themselves. He has, however, a special relation to the martial spirit, which he stirs in Menelaos,[2] and which he confers as a gift in the Odyssey upon the Pseudodysseus; but only in conjunction with Athene.[3] This may be taken, however, as a sign that he was known to some extent within Greece; in Crete, for example. In Greece, too, he is the father of Ascalaphos and Ialmenos;[4] and the wall of Thebes is the teichos Areion.[5] Lünemann[6] observes, that Arès represents the idea of raw courage. He does not represent courage as Homer conceived it. He has no skill, resource, or even perseverance in war, whether against Athene or against Diomed; but rather a stupid

[1] Il. xvii. 210.   [2] Il. v. 563.   [3] Od. xiv. 199, 216.
[4] Il. ii. 512.   [5] Il. iv. 407.   [6] Wörterbuch in voc.

insensibility, which rushes on the spear's point.¹ And, when he has felt it, he flies off, and howls under the pain: two operations never (I think) permitted by Homer to a wounded Greek; perhaps not even to a wounded Trojan. He groans again after his discomfiture by Athenê in the Theomachy.²

In battle with the Solumoi, Arês is said to slay Isandros, the son of Bellerophon. This may mean no more than that Isandros fell in the war.³

Represented as dwelling in Olympos, he is unaware of what has taken place on the battle-fields of Troas; he learns by accident the death of his son Ascalaphos; and when rushing forth to avenge it, he is arrested by Pallas, who strips off his armor, scolds him sharply, and replaces him in his seat.⁴ She habitually, indeed, to use our homely phrase, bullies him.⁵

Thus inferior in action to Athenê, he only divides with her the prerogative of presiding over war. On the Shield of Achilles, the two are represented⁶ as the patrons respectively of the two opposing hosts; and in a variety of passages⁷ besides that already referred to, their common, or rather rival, possession of this field of action is exhibited. For example, in the Twentieth Iliad,⁸ while Athenê shouts to urge on the Greeks, Arês does the like for the Trojans.

In the Fifth Iliad,⁹ he envelops the fight in darkness: but, as if to account for so powerful an operation by a deity of his secondary rank, the Poet goes on to say that he was fulfilling the orders of Apollo, who had bid him incite the Trojans.

¹ Il. v. 849-863.　² Il. xxi. 417.　³ Il. vi. 203.
⁴ Il. xv. 110-142.　⁵ Il. v. 760.　⁶ Il. xviii. 516.
⁷ Il. v. 430, xvii. 398, xx. 358.　⁸ 48-53.
⁹ 505-511.

THE DIVINITIES OF OLYMPOS.

He was overcome and bound by the youths Otos and Ephialtes (whom Apollo conquered); and he would have perished in his bonds, had not Hermes released him, after an imprisonment of thirteen months.[1] Immortal he is;[2] but, it appears, only just immortal.

He is thirsty, not of sacrifices in the ordinary way, but of human blood.[3] According to Ammianus,[4] the Thracians of history propitiated him by sacrificing the lives of prisoners.

So limited are his perceptions, that Pallas, by putting on a particular helmet, can prevent his recognizing her.[5]

His flesh is tender, like that of all the gods: but he is described principally by bulk and mass.[6] When Athené smites him to the ground, he extends over nine pelethra, or about seven hundred feet,[7] in length.

On escaping from the net, in the Eighth Odyssey, he repairs to Thrace. From thence, with his ideal son Terror, he comes forth to make war upon the Ephuroi (a race whom their name appears to associate with the Greeks), or with the Phlegyai. In Thrace clearly was his home. Thrace appears to have been known by the name of Aria.[8] Berkel connects the two names together.

If, on the one hand, Arès was not fully established as an Hellenic deity, still he is a son of Herè, in the Olympian family, and there is a lack of special links between him and the Trojans. It appears that he wavered between the two parties: nay, even that he

---

[1] Il. v. 385–391. [2] Ib. 901. [3] Ib. 280.
[4] xxvii. 4. [5] Il. v. 845.
[6] Il. ii. 479; vii. 208; viii. 349. [7] Il. xxi. 407.
[8] Steph. Byzant. in voc. Thrakè.

had promised to take part with the Greeks, and had then changed his mind. He is accordingly called turncoat (alloprosallos),[1] and is a special object of the wrath of Here, who makes known in Olympos the death of his son Ascalaphos,[2] with the hope that he may avenge it on the Trojans, and so change sides again. This he is evidently about to do, in despite of the prohibition of Zeus, when Pallas stops him, lest more trouble should arise from the wrath of the Sire. When he suffers defeat in the Theomachy, Pallas tells him it is because the Erinues of his mother Here pursue him.[3] The whole nation of the Thrakes, however (as we now understand Thrace), with whom he is specially associated, are among the allies of Troy in the War.[4]

It is difficult, from the materials afforded by Homer, to trace the god Arès up to his origin. But his prominent place in the Italian mythology renders it probable, that his worship may have prevailed among the Pelasgian forerunners of the Hellenic race. Welcker thinks that he had had a divine cultus at an early date among some race alien to the Greek, from which the Hellenic gods proper displaced him, and that there are traces of him as a Nature-Power.[5] Both ideas would be verified if he could be tracked to a Pelasgian or quasi-Pelasgian source; and this too would give a propriety to his siding with Troy; which, however, poetical necessity went far towards exacting, in order to give even the faintest show of equality to the Trojan party in Olympos.

[1] Il. v. 831. [2] Il. xv. 100-112. [3] Il. xxi. 412.
[4] Il. ii. 844-846. [5] Gr. Götterlehre, i. 414.

Section XI. *Hermes.*

The part played by Hermes in the Iliad is secondary. His only important manifestation is when, in the Twenty-fourth Book, he appears by order of Zeus to Priam, under the semblance of a young prince; and attends him, with amiable care, on his way to and from the scene of his arduous errand. But this mission is neither political nor military. It is only social and domestic. It is eminently illustrative of the peculiar function of Hermes, which is, to be the god of expedients, resource, and help; the accommodating and genial god.[1] This character is expressed alike in his epithets, such as criounios[2] and akaketa,[3] and in his conduct. His agency is, as a rule, beneficial to those with whom he deals: hence he is chosen to be the guide of Priam: hence he assures Calypso that he has come to her unwillingly at the command of Zeus, cautiously alleging, however, the length of way and want of provision on the journey, as his reasons.[4] He is the person employed to admonish Aigisthos[5] not to commit the meditated crimes: a warning, which aimed at saving him from vengeance.

Hermes is the son of Zeus and Maias.[6] He is the giver of increase, dōtor eaōn:[7] and it is perhaps in this capacity that Eumaios, the swineherd, consecrates to him a seventh portion, at the meal-sacrifice in his hut, on the arrival of Odysseus.[8] Like the majority of the other gods, he has one or more human children

[1] Il. xxiv. 334.
[2] Never harmful.
[3] Od. I. 88.
[7] Od. viii. 335.
[5] Rare helper.
[4] Od. v. 99–102.
[6] Od. viii. 335; xiv. 435.
[8] Od. xiv. 435.

born clandestinely:[1] but, whenever we hear of him, it is as the giver of some gift, or renderer of some service. Yet the idea of concealment inheres in his functions. When the question is raised in Olympos as to delivering the body of Hector, the first expedient is, that Hermes should steal it.[2] Again he steals Arès out of his confinement.[3] His prerogatives however embrace not only thievery, but also perjury, as it was he who conferred both these gifts on Autolucos.[4] Yet perhaps, considering his general character of usefulness without hurt, we may possibly presume that these objectionable faculties were only given for some defensive or beneficial end. In Homer, he has no relation to industry, or skill in manufacture: these belong to Athené and Hephaistos. But he seems to be the agent or envoy of the Olympian assembly: and his office as the god of increase, together with his relation to pilfering, place him in connection with the business of exchange, at a period when commerce, so beneficial in itself, is notwithstanding a near neighbor not only to fraud on the one hand, but to violence on the other.

He never hates, or punishes, or quarrels, or is incensed with any one. Nor is he troubled with self-love. Though ranged on the Greek side in the poem, and in the Theomachy, he declines the contest with Leto, his appointed antagonist, as a wife of Zeus, too great for him to cope with: and tells her she may give out that she has worsted him.[5]

In the Fourth Iliad, Zeus chooses Athené for the mission to Pandaros, to persuade him to break the

[1] Il. xvi. 181. [2] Il. xxiv. 24. [3] Il. v. 390.
[4] Od. xix. 396. [5] Il. xxi. 497–501.

covenanted truce.[1] This office would have seemed every way more suitable to Hermes. The reason that it is not committed to him may probably be, that he was unknown in Troy. In the Twenty-fourth Book, he describes himself to Priam as a Myrmidon and an esquire of Achilles, nor does he announce himself as a god until it becomes necessary that he should depart, and leave the old King alone within the cantonment of the formidable hero. Priam does not then in any manner recognize him personally, or address him in his divine capacity.

The functions discharged by Hermes appear to point to a connection with the Phœnicians, as the great merchants of the time. The name of his mother Maia is not connected by Homer with Phœnicia, except by the negative evidence that, like Dionè the mother of Aphroditè, she does not appear in the list of the attachments of Zeus given in the Fourteenth Iliad, where all the intimacies have their scene laid or supposed in Greece, Greek traditions alone appearing to be admitted. In the Hymn to Hermes the gap is supplied, and Maia is declared to be the daughter of Atlas, who is with Homer a personage entirely Phœnician.

Again, Hermes manifestly has a personal relation with Calypso,[2] who welcomes him as αἰδοῖός τε φίλος τε;[3] terms, which are much beyond the limit of ordinary courtesy; which are employed in the very special case of Zeus and Thetis;[4] and which Herè flatters herself she shall deserve at the hands of Okeanos and Tethûs, provided she shall succeed in bringing them together again.[5] Calypso was the daughter of Atlas: and it

[1] Il. iv. 69. [2] Od. v. 88. [3] Revered and loved.
[4] Il. xxiv. 111. Cf. Il. xviii. 394. [5] Il. xiv. 210.

is probable that Maias was her mythological sister, and Hermes her nephew. We have another sign of the ties between him and Calypso in this, that Odysseus obtained from her the account of the proceedings in Olympos about the oxen of the Sun, and that she had had it from Hermes.[1] This could hardly be on any other footing than that of a mythological relationship, really indicating an ethnical affinity. He was systematically worshipped by the people of Scheriè before retiring to rest.[2]

We find him yet again employed, within the circle of the Phœnician traditions,[3] to instruct Odysseus as to the means, by which he may safely encounter Kirkè and her enchantments. I again use the word Phœnician as including, for Homer, what was Egyptian or Eastern.

Other remarkable incidents are recorded of him. It was he who, together with Athenè, conducted Heracles in safety, with the formidable dog, out of Hades;[4] and he likewise escorts the souls of the Suitors from Ithaca to the Underworld.[5] He, moreover, carried to Pelops, from Zeus, the sceptre which Hephaistos had wrought.[6]

Hermes is an agent rather than a mere messenger: and, as a messenger, he is pretty clearly distinguished in this vital respect, that he goes not, like Iris, upon the personal errand of Zeus or Here, but he carries the collective resolution of the Olympian Court.[7] His general office is best represented by the word d i a c t o r o s or agent, hers by a n g e l o s or messenger. He may be called the god of intercourse.

[1] Od. xiii. 390. [2] Od. vii. 137. [3] Od. x. 275–307.
[4] Od. xi. 623–626. [5] Od. xxiv. 1–14. [6] Il. ii. 104.
[7] Od. i. 38, 84. Cf. Il. xxiv. 24.

His very marked name, Argeiphontes, is nowhere explained in Homer; or in Hesiod; or in the Homeric Hymn. It is discussed fully by Welcker:[1] and the constructions put upon it tend to connect him with the East, and with the astronomic worship. In the system of the Persians, as stated by Origen, the seventh or mixed metal is assigned to him.[2] The first verse of the Twenty-fourth Odyssey connects him with Arcadia through Cyllene. Hahn finds in the Albanian language words capable (chermes, tourme,) of relation to his name. It is quite possible that two or more streams of mythological traditions may meet in him; but his dominant relations are evidently Eastern.

But as this deity, of great importance and highly diversified attributes in the later mythology, is of secondary consequence in Homer, I pass on.

Section XII. *Artemis.*

We must not be discouraged if, especially in the case of a deity of the second order like Artemis, we find much difficulty in discerning the precise channel through which she reached her actual place in the Hellenic mythology, as daughter of Leto, and sister of Apollo, with the other attributes attaching to her.

On the whole, however, it seems that there is much truth in the observation of Müller, who says she was worshipped 'as it were a part of the same deity'[3] with Apollo. She is in the main a reflection of her

---

[1] Gr. Götterlehre, vol. i. pp. 336 seqq.
[2] Beckmann, Hist. of Inventions, Art. 'Metals.'
[3] Müller's Dorians, vol. ii. ch. 9. The chapter contains much information on the worship of Artemis.

brother, much in the same manner as, saving the substitution (as it may be called) of the sisterly for the conjugal relation, Herè is a reflection of Zeus. The relation of atmosphere to earth, which had been recognized outside of the Olympian scheme, became, under the anthropomorphic law of that scheme, the relation of King and Father Zeus, to Queen and Mother Herè. The affinity of Sun to Moon, acknowledged already as divinities in eastern, and probably also in Pelasgian, systems of religion, undergoing a like transmutation, appears in the Olympian scheme as the relation of the brother Apollo to the sister Artemis. For we have already seen the reasons for supposing that in Troy itself the Sun was worshipped as the far-darting Apollo. If there was a Sun-worship there, so in all likelihood there was a worship of the Moon. But Olympian laws seem not to allow an acknowledgment in the action of the Iliad of the relation between Apollo and the Sun; nor, by parity of reasoning, can they recognize any relation of Artemis to the Moon.

That such a relation subsisted out of Greece, we may readily suppose. The traditions, on which Homer had to employ his plastic power, varied and heterogeneous, were on that very ground the more elastic and flexible, partly in things, but especially in names. Identity is as hard to follow in them, as it is easy in human life. They seem to form, disform, and re-form before us, like the squares of colored glass in the kaleidoscope as it is turned about by the hand. One group of these traditions, which when associated compose a *nebula*, appears before us in severalty, divided between the three individualities of Artemis, Persephonè, and Aphroditè. Another form of the severance, wholly Greek in spirit, comes before us in the double tradition of the celestial and the earthly or sensual Aphroditè; and to the celestial Aphroditè the Artemis of Homer bears no small resemblance. Indeed it seems likely that, as Homer found or shaped the old Earth-tradition in several forms, of which the portion least earthly, and most sublimed, became his Herè, so probably there may have lain before him a variety of forms of the tradition of the Moon-goddess, in association with highly varied ascriptions, the most ethereal and purest part of which took, we may suppose, its place in the Olympian system as his Artemis.

But the relations of wife and sister respectively, in which Herè and Artemis are placed, are probable due to the anthropomorphic principle, and to that method of copying for heaven the things seen and known on earth, according to which the Theo-mythology of Homer is constructed. And the remarkable participation of Artemis in the high prerogatives of Apollo is notably like the participation of Herè in the prerogatives of Zeus. In this participation, this greatness by reflection, consists principally the dignity of each goddess. The rude material, which as Nature-Powers they respectively offered to the hand, is thus lighted up with an extraordinary splendor.

The Homeric signs of relation between Artemis and the Moon are of the same kind with those of Apollo to the Sun; but fainter in proportion to smaller energies, and a more confined activity. The terrible clang of the arrows of Apollo is reflected in the rattle of those of Artemis.[1] His golden sword is represented in her

[1] Il. l. 46; xvi. 183.

golden distaff.[1] She is also golden-throned, and uses golden reins.[2] These are epithets suitable to the moon.

Hahn finds no root for the name Artemis in the Albanian tongue; and we cannot in this way trace it to the Pelasgian religion. But in 'Charnea,' meaning the moon, he detects the Anna Perenna of the Latins, of whom Ovid[3] says, 'Sunt quibus haec luna est;' and likewise the Anaïth or Tanath of Egypt, who is taken by some to be the analogue of Artemis.[4] On the whole we seem to have a groundwork in the scheme of Nature-worship, on which the Homeric tradition of Artemis is built, and which places her on the Trojan side.

The great function which in Homer she shares with Apollo, is that of being the minister of Death, in the double sense of a deliverance or translation, and of an infliction penal in its nature. In the first capacity, Penelope asks her aid, that she may be set free from the persecutions of the Suitors:[5] and in like manner she dismisses from life the women, and Apollo the men, of the happy island of Syriè, where want and sickness are unknown.[6] But she likewise slays Ariadnè, for her lapse from chastity in Diè;[7] and avenges on the daughters of Niobè (as Apollo does on the sons) the offence of their mother.[8] As the Huntress-queen, she is the destroyer of life in animals, and perhaps this office was committed to her as an inferior portion of the ministry of death, more suitably placed in her

[1] Il. xx. 70.   [2] Il. vi. 205; ix. 538.   [3] Fast. iii. 657.
[4] Hahn. Alban. Stud. pp. 250, 277.   [5] Od. xx. 61.
[6] Od. xv. 407.   [7] Od. xi. 324.   [8] Il. xxiv. 604-609.

hands than in those of her brother Apollo; as if she had, so to speak, the leavings of his great offices.

The inferiority, indeed, of Artemis to Apollo is very strongly marked in Homer, although the relation of Moon to Sun was most suitably represented in an anthropomorphic religion by placing them as brother and sister. In the Fifth Iliad, when Apollo carries Æneas to Pergamos, and places the disabled chief in his own temple, Leto and Artemis are found there,[1] to nurse and restore him; not in any shrine of their own, nor in one common to the family. And again in the Theomachy, Artemis, contending with Here, is subjected to sad indignity, and actually whipped with her own bow and arrows.[2] She is here treated with none of the special respect that is given, not only to Apollo and Athené, but to Leto. This convinces me on further reflection[3] that her Olympian relation to Apollo is more probably based upon physical facts, than upon participation in the higher traditions.

Her agency, however, is ubiquitous; perhaps in virtue of facts belonging to the same order; yet it would be singular, if her worship obtained among Hellenes earlier than that of the Sun. So, however, it seems to have been. A generation at least before the War, Artemis is worshipped in Calydon, and she sends the Boar thither to avenge the lack of sacrifice.[4] We are thus enabled to conjecture that in this instance, even before the hand of Homer was applied to mythologic manipulation, the Hellenic mind had done its work, and she was fairly impersonated in the capacity which we find that she fills in the Poems. We meet her in

[1] Il. v. 445.
[2] Il. xxi. 489–496.
[3] Studies on Homer, vol. II. pp. 110, 144.
[4] Il. ix. 538–542.

Troas, where she taught Scamandrios[1] to hunt; she is invoked in Ithaca by Penelopê;[2] her part in the legend of the daughters of Pandareos belongs probably to Crete; and we have seen her agency in Suriê, and in Diê.[3] Again, in Ortugiê she took the life of Orion. And the Artemis of Homer has no relation to any one or more places in particular.

Apart from the ministry of death, and from this apparent attribute of omnipresence, her powers, in regard both to Nature and to the mind, are those of the lower or secondary order of the Olympian Court. But, in the matter of personal beauty, she is the rival of Aphroditê; and here she appears to absorb that part of the tradition which afterwards went by the name of the heavenly Aphroditê. One most frequent illustration of great beauty is a comparison with Aphroditê the golden; and it is to her that Achilles refers[4] as the model of loveliness. But the incomparable Nausicaa, who appears to be the poet's ideal of youthful beauty combined with purity and excellence,[5] is likened by Odysseus to Artemis in countenance, bearing, and stature. And again, in the case of the daughters of Pandareos, while it is Here who confers upon them beauty of feature, and Aphroditê simply purveys food for them, it is Artemis who gives them stature, which I suppose to include all that relates to beauty of figure. It is noteworthy that stature is never mentioned (I think) in connection with Aphroditê, and I suppose it therefore to be in the province of Artemis.

While this attribute marks the point at which the traditions appropriated to her touch upon those of

[1] Il. v. 49–52. [2] Od. xx. 61, 71. [3] Od. v. 123.
[4] Il. ix. 389. [5] Od. vi. 150.

Aphrodité, on the other hand the epithet ἁγνή, the severely pure,[1] seems to indicate her point of contact with Persephoné, the Queen of Hades. The two forms were, as we know, afterwards fused into one.

Section XIII. *Persephoné*.

Persephoné the Queen of Hades is called by Homer the 'severely pure' (ἁγνή), the 'majestic' (ἀγαυή), and the 'terrible' (ἐπαινή). And she represents what we might reasonably expect from her position as Queen in the Underworld: a mixture of Pelasgic and of Eastern traditions. Of the former, because all the Pelasgic Nature-Powers had been disposed of by carrying them into that nether sphere; of the latter, because the site of the Underworld of Homer was in the East, the entrance to it by the point of the rising of the Sun.[2]

She is represented as ruling together with Aïdoneus, and by no means as merely his wife. Introduced together with him into the Legend of Phœnix by his father, and also by Althaia,[3] she seems even to be charged in chief with the sovereignty. She gathers the Women-shades for Odysseus, and she disperses them. It is she who, as he fears, may send forth the head of Gorgo should he tarry over long; who may have deluded him with an Eidolon or shadow in lieu of a substance; who endows Teiresias with the functions of a Seer.[4] On the shores of Ocean, just before the point of descent in the far East, are the groves of

---

[1] Od. v. 123; xviii. 202; xx. 71.   [2] Od. xii. 1–4.
[3] Il. ix. 457–569.   [4] Od. xi. 226, 385, 634, 213; and x. 494.

Persephonè. Aïdoneus does no personal act in the Poems, except that with her he executes the imprecatory vow of the father of Phœnix;[1] and that he trembles lest the crust of earth should be riven by earthquake, during the battle of the gods.[2] Notwithstanding his high rank as the brother of Zeus, she is the principal, and he is the secondary figure in the weird scenery of the Eleventh Odyssey.

It seems very probable that she represents that old Pelasgian tradition of the awful Damsel, which had, as we know especially from the mythological itinerary of Pausanias, such extraordinary longevity and power in the Greek religion. Together with this, we have to consider 1. her Eastern site, 2. her gift to Teiresias, alone among the dead; connecting her on the one hand with Apollo, the God of foreknowledge, but on the other with the Phœnicians, and with the Eastern associations of which they were the channels.

The name Persephonè appears to attach itself by etymology to other names in the Homeric Poems; all of which are Eastern in their associations. Persè, the daughter of Okeanos, is also the wife of Helios, and the mother of Kirkè, who dwells in Aiaiè. Each of the three points of contact thus established is a link to the East. Perseus, the founder of the dynasty which precedes the Pelopids, is the son of Zeus and Danaè, a parentage which, as we have already found, we may properly consider as implying a foreign, and an Eastern, origin. In the person of Perseus, the son of Nestor,[3] the name is continued in the Neleid House,

[1] Il. ix. 456, 457. [2] Il. xx. 61-65. [3] Od. iii. 414.

which appears to have been of Phœnician extraction. The national designation of Achaians appears also not improbably to connect itself with the Persian race through the name Archaimenidai and otherwise,[1] which may not improbably have contributed an element to the formation of the Greek nation.

Our first historical notice of that race is about the middle of the ninth century before Christ,[2] when Shalmaneser II found them in South-western Armenia. This point approximates to the region, in which the imagination of Homer placed the shadowy dwelling of Persephonè.

In the later tradition, she becomes united with Artemis, and so related to Apollo; a relationship of which perhaps we have a single Homeric trace in her command over the knowledge of the future.

SECTION XIV. *Aphroditè*.

The Aphroditè of Homer was a goddess, for she is the daughter of Zeus, and of Dionè, whose residence is in Olympos, and who belongs to the divine order.[3] She is also herself expressly stated to belong to it.[4] But it does not appear that she had as yet come to be a goddess of the Hellenic religion properly so called.

In order to estimate her position in the scheme of Homer, the following circumstances should be considered:—

1. There is no trace of her worship, or of any influ-

---

[1] See Studies on Homer, vol. I. p. 557.
[2] Rawlinson's Ancient Monarchies, ii. 874; iii. 849.
[3] Il. v. 370, 881, 883.   [4] Il. v. 337–342; xx. 105.

ence exercised by her over mortals, either in Greece, or among the Greeks.

2. She is never once exhibited by Homer in a favorable light; sometimes in a neutral one; more commonly in an odious or contemptible point of view.

3. Though herself a model of personal beauty,[1] she was not the goddess of beauty, inasmuch as she had not the power to confer the gift. Beauty is not included in the properties[2] conveyed by the Kestos; and it is Heré who endows the orphan daughters of Pandareos with beauty, while Aphrodité has no other office assigned to her in their rearing, than supplying them with food, and preferring to Zeus, when they are grown up, the prayer that they may marry.[3]

4. She is wounded by Diomed, and is apparently destitute alike of the powers of resistance, of vengeance, and of endurance. We can hardly suppose that a deity exhibited in a light so contemptible, as is Aphrodité in the Battle of the Fifth Iliad, was as yet an object of Hellenic worship.[4]

5. Her helplessness after receiving her wound from Diomed is remarkable. While Arés rides spontaneously to heaven,[5] Aphrodité is led out of the battle by Iris,[6] and makes a petition to her brother Arés for the loan of his chariot and horses, that she may by their means be carried to Olympos.

In the Lay of the Net, she is reported as going from Olympos to Paphos without aid:[7] possibly because this is a descent, not an ascent; or more probably because in a Syrian episode her rank would be more fully recognized than in an Hellenic poem.

[1] Il. ix. 389.
[2] Il. xiv. 198, 215.
[3] Od. xx. 66-75. Cf. Il. v. 429.
[4] Il. v. 311-380.
[5] Il. v. 864-870.
[6] Il. v. 353.
[7] Od. viii. 362.

6. No place is assigned to her, even on the losing side, in the Theomachy, which determines or ushers in the issue of the Iliad. And this is the more remarkable, because a fifth deity is wanting to make up a number equal to the five deities of the Greeks; and Leto, who is elsewhere in the Poems a perfectly mute personage, is introduced in order to fill it.

7. The only place where she is named among the Olympian family, is in the Lay of the Net, a tale apparently of Phœnician importation, and of Syrian origin. She bears the name of Cypris; and her place of abode is Cyprus, where were her altars, and her glebe or domain.[1] She was therefore worshipped in that island; and we may trace her worship as far westward as Cythera, from the following circumstances: first, she is twice called Κυθέρεια;[2] and secondly, Κυθήρα are called ζάθεα, an epithet which always indicates the special relation of the place to some deity. Her relation to Paris[3] proves that she was in some manner acknowledged in Troas; and the taunt of Helen respecting her supposed favorites in Meonia and Phrygia is to be taken as showing that she was also recognized as a deity in those regions. In effect she was an Asiatic deity; and her name and worship were crossing the sea by steps towards the Greek Peninsula. But she must have been of small account in Asia Minor, or she could hardly have failed to find a place in the Theomachy.

8. The power of this goddess over external nature is extremely limited. The greatest manifestation of it is where she 'with ease' draws Paris out of the fight,

---

[1] Od. viii. 362. [2] Od. viii. 288; xviii. 193. [3] Il. iii 380–382.

wrapping him in vapor.[1] In the Fifth Book, it is when she is slyly dragging off Æneas, covered with her robe, that Diomed pursues and wounds her, 'knowing that she was an effeminate or strengthless deity.'[2]

She is however invested with a certain superintendence of marriage in its physical aspect; and in this capacity she sends to Andromache the nuptial gift of her hood or head-band.[3]

Athene, taunting her upon her wound, makes the supposition[4] that she got it in undressing some Greek woman that she had persuaded to elope with one of her beloved Trojans. Nay, Helen also bitterly reproaches her, advising her to cease altogether from pretending to divinity; and Aphrodite, in the Third Iliad, only overcomes her by the violence of her threats.[5] From these it appears, if indeed proof were wanting, that this character, odious on the side of lawless indulgence, has its base in simple appetite, and in no degree carries the softening accompaniments of gentleness or compassion.

In the Odyssey it is contrived that the Suitors, before they are put to death, shall offer gifts to Penelope; perhaps by way of partial requital for the waste of the substance of Odysseus. With this view, the Queen[6] issues from her chamber, like to Artemis or golden Aphrodite. Aphrodite is introduced here, because passion was the motive of the Suitors. But the deity, at whose suggestion Penelope thus adorned herself, was Pallas. Had Aphrodite been worshipped in Greece, this office surely would have fallen to her. It is yet

[1] Il. iii. 380.
[2] Il. v. 429; xxii. 470.
[3] Il. iii. 416–417.
[4] Il. v. 831.
[5] Il. v. 422–425.
[6] Od. xvii. 37.

more noteworthy, that the whole design is executed by Pallas. Penelope is lulled to sleep; and then Pallas applies ambrosion to her face, 'such as Aphrodité uses when she goes among the Graces.' But Aphrodité herself is excluded from the entire process.

Even in the Lay of the Net, apparently a legend of the Eastern mythology, the Poet seems to intend to make the guilty pair ridiculous by sending them off, when released, so rapidly and in silence.[1]

9. She is never invested with any of the higher attributes, such as foreknowledge, omnipresence, or command over the mind of man. Her only power seems to be that of stimulating passion.[2]

10. We now know that the planetary worship of the Assyrians was brought by the Phœnicians into Greece, and that each deity was associated with a particular metal. We find in Cyprus, the land of copper, with a Phœnician colony, the worship of Aphrodité. We may safely then refer the origin of this Olympian personage to the Assyrian mythology.

The local indications of her worship, as proceeding from the East, are in accordance with the traditions which under the names of Astarté, Ashtoreth, Mylitta, Mitra, exhibit to us a similar character as held in honor there. The marriage with Hephaistos bears a similar witness; the more remarkable, because it is only recognized in the mythology of the Outer world, drawn from the Phœnicians, while in the Iliad he is the suitor of Charis. Aphrodité, however, is placed by Homer in relation with the Charites, Eastern personages, whose name corresponds with the Sanscrit Harits,

[1] Od. viii. 360.   [2] Il. xiv. 215-217; xxiv. 30.

meaning originally 'bright,' and afterwards the horses of the dawn.¹ In very late mythology, Aphroditè appears as the daughter of Poseidon,² and thus acquires a new note of Eastern origin.

In historic Greece, we find the double tradition of the heavenly and the promiscuous Aphroditè. It would seem as though any elements of the former character, known to Homer, were assigned by him to his chaste Artemis, the rival in beauty of his Aphroditè. The pure tradition was, according to the view of Max Müller, the original basis of the character of Aphroditè; and he thinks that it was 'afterwards debased by an admixture of Syrian mythology.'³ He gives to this word his favorite meaning of the 'dawn.' Some old traditions however connect Aphroditè as Astartè with the Moon.⁴ There has been therefore an intermixture of the traditions, which ultimately distributed themselves between Artemis, Aphroditè, and Persephonè; and there is a certain correspondence of the two first, as we find them in Homer, with the vulgar and the heavenly Aphroditè of later times respectively.

Of the name there seems to be no sign in the Albanian tongue, which brings down to us so much of the old speech of the Pelasgoi. But the root of the name Venus is found in the Gegian branch of the language.⁵

¹ Max Müller, Lect. on Language, Second Series, p. 370.
² Pausanias, Corinthiaca.
³ Lectures, Second Series, p. 373.
⁴ Hahn, Albanesische Studien, p. 250. 'Wir glauben diese Verbindung mit dem in so vielen Sprachen dem Hahnrei zukommenden Hörnern zusammen stellen zu dürfen.' p. 251. See Smith, Dict. Bibl., Art. Ashtoreth.
⁵ Hahn, ibid.

Dioné, the mother of Aphrodité, resides in Olympos. Homer affords us no means of tracing her origin or functions; but from other evidence we have been enabled to interpret her as a Nature-Power of the Pelasgian worship. If this is so, then probably we are to consider her motherhood to be assigned to her, not in virtue of that Syrian character of Aphrodité, which we trace in the South, but of the place which Aphrodité (or Venus) appears to have held in the Trojan system, and therefore in the Pelasgian cultus of the Nature-Powers.

SECTION XV. *Dionusos.*

The traditions of Dionusos in Homer are as dark as they are slight. On the one hand he is the son of Semelé; and we have no case in the Homeric Theogony where a deity is born of a woman: but Semelé is mentioned in the list given by Zeus among the mortal mothers of his children, who stand separate from the goddess mothers. She comes between the unnamed mother of Minos, and Alcmené;[1] and the birth of Dionusos thus appears to be parallel with that of Heracles. Dionusos is, however, called in this passage 'a joy to mortals;' which may of itself faintly seem to sever him from the race. Neither is there in the Poems any clearly divine act assigned to him. The Homeric Hymn to Hermes treats Semelé as the daughter or descendant of Kadmos.[2]

But on the other hand there is a great resemblance between the good offices of Metis to him and to Hephaistos.[3] When the terrible Lucourgos attacks

[1] Il. xiv. 323–325. [2] v. 57.
[3] See *supra*, Sect. Hephaistos.

and scourges his nurses, he trembling takes refuge in the sea; and Thetis receives him in her bosom.[1] This is confirmed indirectly by the Odyssey,[2] which represents him as the giver to that goddess of the golden urn which she used for the ashes of Achilles; doubtless in requital for her services, which are thoroughly in keeping with her character as the great mediatress in matters respecting contrasted or competing worships.

The conclusive test, however, is found in this, that the recital concerning Lucourgos is offered to illustrate a class of cases where outrage is offered by mortals to deities; and the scourging of his nurses is treated as an offence to himself, for which, accordingly, not however by him, but by Zeus, Lucourgos was smitten with blindness, and then cut off prematurely.[3] Homer must therefore be understood to include him in the phrase 'gods of heaven.'

In the Odyssey we have a probable sign of his worship. Ariadnê is put to death in Diê, supposed to be Naxos, by Artemis, when Theseus is carrying her to Athens. Artemis does this 'upon the testimony of Dionusos.'[4] The only probable construction of these words which offers itself is, that Theseus landed with Ariadnê in Naxos, as Paris had landed with Helen in Cranaê, and that Dionusos procured the intervention of Artemis to avenge a meditated profanation; which presumes that the island, or some place in it, was sacred to him. It is also likely, that the epithet ἠγάθεον applied to the Nuseïan mount, means that it was sacred to him as a god.

[1] Il. vi. 136.   [2] Od. xxiv. 74.
[3] Il. vi. 129-140.   [4] Od. xi. 321-325.

Nägelsbach observes,[1] that Homer places neither him nor Demeter in Olympos by any distinct recital or declaration. But in both cases the recognition of deity, coupled with the personal relation to Zeus, appears to make good the title.

At the same time, I have pointed out an inconsistency which I do not know how to rectify. The traditions are not closely pieced together.

What is most clear about Dionusos in Homer is, first, that his worship was extremely recent; secondly, that it made its appearance in Thrace,[2] to which belongs the Nuseïan mountain; thirdly, that it was violently opposed on its introduction, a fact of which we have other records, as for example, in the Bacchæ of Euripides.

Lucourgos, who resisted and punished it, was the son of Druas; and Druas was alive and a warrior in the youth of Nestor. Consequently, Dionusos was an infant, that is, his worship was in its infancy, not more than two generations before the War of Troy. The Hymn addressed to Dionusos describes how Tursenians found him on the shore, and brought him over sea. The coloring of this legend is Phœnician; as is that of the legend, if such there were, that gave him the isle of Naxos as the seat of his worship. It is also on the sea shore that he appears, according to Homer; and it is in Thrace, where there would seem to have been Phœnician manufactures of metal. Again, he obtains a work of art, probably Phœnician, from Hephaistos,[3] just as does Phaidimos, the king of the Sidonians.[4]

[1] Hom. Theol. p. 115. [2] Nägelsbach, p. 9.
[3] Od. xxiv. 74. [4] Od. iv. 615–619.

And the name of Semele[1] itself, according to general traditions, supports the Phœnician association thus established at a variety of points.

We cannot perhaps treat the Dionusos of Homer as the discoverer of wine, and father of its use, in Greece; for it is universal and familiar, while he appears to be but local and as yet strange. The novel feature, which connects itself with his name, seems to be the use of wine by women; and the effect produced, in an extraordinary and furious excitement, which might well justify not only jealousy, but even forcible resistance to demoralizing orgies. It seems then, as if this usage was introduced by immigrants of a race comparatively wealthy and luxurious, and was resisted by, or on behalf of, the older and simpler population.

The later account of Hesiod makes Dionusos the husband of Ariadne, who was the daughter of Minos. The poet of Ascra thus places him within the circle of Phœnician traditions.

Though Homer has represented this personage as a god, and though, as we see, traces of his worship are not wanting, yet the human maternity might possibly indicate that we should do best to regard him as a deified mortal, rather than as a god from the beginning of his existence. In this case, we are to suppose that the fascination of the usage he introduced not only proved so powerful as to overrule all opposition, but likewise generated a halo which was reflected on his birth, and caused his deification by a process more rapid than that which took effect upon Heracles or the Tyndarids. In the later time, greater consistency was given to the legend by a parallel deification of Semele, his mother.

[1] Hymn to Dionusos, v. 57.

Homer has attached no ennobling epithet or circumstance of dignity to the name of Dionusos, unless we so regard the eulogy of Zeus[1] under an excess of excitement. The Poet acts in this case as in the cases of Arès and Aphroditè; since he has no reverence for either drunkenness, or violence, or lust.

Section XVI. *Helios, or the Sun.*

It is sometimes stated, that Helios, or the Sun, does not appear as a god in the Iliad, but only in the Odyssey. This is not so. As far as the Odyssey is concerned, he appears only in the Outer, not in the Inner, world. In the Iliad his personality is undeniable, though very faint. The Sun hearing all, as well as seeing all, is certainly a person.[2]

Again, all will remember the long day of the Iliad, with the close of which the successes of the Trojans were to end. When the appointed moment came, at the command of Herè the Sun went, unwillingly,[3] to his rest beside the Ocean stream.

Here then he is a person, though in the background. In the Odyssey, he reappears with more marked effect. In the Lay of Demodocos, it is he who first makes known to Hephaistos the intimacy of Arès with Aphroditè,[4] and then undertakes to act as spy upon the guilty couple. The Island of Thrinakiè, placed by Homer not far from the entrance to the Euxine, is his island.[5] Here are his oxen, and his sheep, tended by the care of his daughters, whose mother was

[1] Il. xiv. 825.   [2] Il. iii. 277.   [3] Il. xviii. 239.
[4] Od. viii. 270, 302.   [5] Od. xii. 127, 261, 274.

Neaira, and who were called Phaëthusa and Lampetië.[1] These animals the crew of Odysseus had been warned on no account to molest. Under the direst pressure of famine,[2] however, they at length slew certain of the oxen; having first vowed that on their return to Ithaca[3] they would build a temple to the Sun and store it richly; a sign, it may be remembered, that such an edifice would be a novelty in the island. Portents, such as we nowhere else encounter in the Poems, wait upon the deed; the hides of the animals creep about, and the flesh, even when roasted, lows upon the spits.[4] Notwithstanding the Sun's all-seeing function, it is Lampetië who carries him the news. It seems possible, however, as Odysseus was asleep, that we are to understand the deed to have been done by night. The god makes his complaint in the court of the Immortals, to which he is thus proved to belong;[5] and he demands reparation for the loss of his oxen, with whom ' he disported himself night and morning.' Failing it, he declares that he will thenceforward shine in Hades. Zeus at once promises to destroy the crew at sea, which is done accordingly.[6]

The extraordinary sanctity ascribed to these oxen is wholly alien to the genius of the Greek mythology. But when we turn to the East, and observe that Phœnicia was impregnated with Egyptian traditions, we find the sacredness of the ox, and its relation to the Sun, indicated in the consecration of Apis to Osiris; while the function of the ox in agriculture also falls in with the earlier form of the religion, which appears to have

---

[1] Od. xii. 132. [2] Od. xii. 330, 353. [3] Od. xii. 345.
[4] Od. xii. 394. [5] Od. xii. 377. [6] Od. xii. 403–419.

regarded Isis as the land, or passive principle, and Osiris as the Nile-god, who taught to the Egyptians the use of the plough.

And again, we find in the temple of Jerusalem, for the erection of which Solomon called in the aid of Phœnician workmen, the forms of twelve oxen,[1] supporting a brazen sea.[2] These were made by King Hiram of Tyre; and they symbolize at once the Egyptian religion, with other Oriental forms of fable, and the maritime pursuits of the Phœnicians.

It is also remarkable, that the use of the ox for meat appears to cease in the Outer world of the Odyssey. In the land of the Cyclops, we find only sheep and goats. And it is with mutton only that Kirkè stocks the vessel of Odysseus.

All these indications agree together. In other respects, too, Helios is marked as an Eastern god. He is the father of Aietes, and of Kirkè, dwelling near the Eastern Okeanos;[3] and the island of Aiaiè is indicated as the place of his rising.[4] The fact of his sporting with the oxen night and morning goes far to show that Homer did not think the earth a plane, but round, perhaps as upon a cylinder, and believed that the West and East were in contact. But only in the East does he give the Sun a dwelling. Aietes, the son of Helios, carries the exclusively Phœnician epithet of ὀλοόφρων.

Further, we may notice that, as long as the Voyage of Odysseus is in the West and North, we hear nothing of the Sun. Poseidon rules in the land of the

---

[1] 1 Kings vii. 24, 25, 44. [2] 1 Kings vii. 13.
[3] Od. x. 188. [4] Od. xii. 4.

Cyclops, stirs the northern sea into a tempest, and is supreme in Scherié. It is in Aiaié, and Thrinakië, that we are brought into contact with this deity, and both these islands appear to lie in Homer's East.

Thus the Sun, by many concurrent signs, is marked out to us as an Eastern deity. There is not in the Odyssey the faintest trace of his identification with Apollo. The traditions respecting him were doubtless conveyed by the Phœnicians; but we cannot say that they were Phœnician in themselves. The division of regions to which I have adverted, seems to point to Poseidon as the god of Phoinikes proper, and to Helios as the god of the Canaanitish population of Syria to the Eastward. Among them it is not improbable that, at the period represented by Homer, the Egyptian belief extensively prevailed, but Assyrian elements may also enter into this conception.

In the Iliad, though not in the Odyssey, we have a sign of the process which finally incorporated the traditions of Apollo with the Sun; while the humanitarian spirit of the Olympian system of Homer seems to have resisted the operation. The plague of the First Book can hardly represent any thing else than the miasma rising from the marshes of the Troad, and the arrows of Apollo are the rays of the sun causing the moisture to evaporate. We find a family of epithets applied to Apollo, which evidently glance at the solar properties: Hekaergos, Hekatebolos, Hekobolos. It is somewhat remarkable that these epithets, which are only used twenty-five times in the other forty-seven books of the Poems, are met twelve times in the First Iliad alone. It is also likely that the epithet Phoibos may glance at the relation between Apollo and the Sun, already recognized beyond the borders of Greece, and possibly also in the old Pelasgian religion of the Peninsula. Again we have the term Lukabas applied to the year. It is probable that in the religion of Troy, where Nature-worship seems to have prevailed more largely, Apollo and the Sun were identified, and that this union made it convenient for the Poet to place Apollo on the Trojan side in the war. Whilst Poseidon built the walls of Troy for King Laomedon, Apollo fed his oxen; and we have seen the close relation between these animals and the worship of the Sun. And this interpretation accounts for what otherwise would be most difficult to explain: I mean the fact that Helios does not appear in the Theomachy, nor does he under that name take part in the war, though his inclination towards the Trojans is plainly declared. Troy was probably a sort of meeting-point for Greek and Asiatic systems. But in the Phœnician or Syrian mythology of the Outer world, Apollo and Helios can appear together, because the Eastern conception of the latter ran no risk of being confounded in the Greek mind with the purely anthropomorphic idea of the true Homeric Apollo.

SECTION XVII. *Hebè.*

Hebè is a deity, whose offices are very clearly set forth, but whom we can scarcely consider as having a perceptible root in any tradition beyond the circle of the Greek mythology.

She is the Cup-bearer, who pours out nectar for the gods.[1] She puts together the parts of the chariot of

[1] Il. iv. 2.

Here, though Here herself yokes the horses to it, before her descent to the field of battle.¹ She performs the offices of the bath for Arès, after he has been healed by Paieon.² Again, we find her in the Eleventh Odyssey, as the celestial bride of Heracles, and in an obelized verse, as the daughter of Zeus and Here.³

Her offices are exclusively Olympian; and she is nowhere brought into relations with our mortal state; one sign among many that she is probably to be regarded as a purely ideal conception.

Her name in Greek expresses youth adult, or full age just attained. Her marriage with Heracles appears to signify that the divine gift of an unending youth is imparted to him when he reaches Olympos.⁴ Homer assigns to her the epithet callisphuros, prettily ankled, which he only gives to those who are to be understood as youthful persons; Danaë, Ino, and Marpessa.⁵

She may well be conceived as the daughter of Zeus in that general sense, according to which he is the father of divinities in general; and thus it must be, in all likelihood, that the Muses, the Hours, and the Nymphs in general are his daughters. But these personages are not daughters of Here, who has but few children, and those due apparently to special traditions. In truth she expresses the idea of youth,⁶ and is perhaps but a thought seized and personified. There is no note in Homer of her worship on earth, which however is mentioned by Strabo and Pausanias:

¹ Il. v. 722, 731.   ² Il. v. 905.   ³ Od. xi. 602–604.
⁴ Hes. Theog. 944–955. Ov. Met. ix. 400.
⁵ Il. xiv. 319; ix. 557. Od. v. 333.
⁶ Nägelsbach, Hom. Theol. p. 41.

and Hahn finds no trace of her in the Albanian language.

It is the distinct and clear, though simple, account given by Homer of her functions, which seems to give her a place in the Olympian court upon one of the twenty thrones of Hephaistos.

Section XVIII. *Themis.*

Slightly as her outline is drawn, we cannot refuse to reckon Themis among the ordinary members of the Olympian Court, for the simple reason that we find her actually installed there. When, in the absence of Zeus, Herè enters the company of the Immortals, and they rise in honor of her,[1] it is from Themis, who came first to meet her, that she accepts the cup of greeting. This is evidently because she had been presiding: for Herè, who is troubled at the view, invites her to continue to preside.[2]

Again, in the Twentieth Iliad, all the deities, including the minor Nature-Powers (whom Homer probably recognizes as divine because they continued to hold their ground in local worship), are invited to the Great Assembly which is to decide finally the fate of Troy: and it is Themis who summons them.[3]

In the Second Odyssey, Telemachos describes himself as making his prayer to Zeus, and to Themis,[4] who collects and dissolves public assemblies generally.

Nevertheless, I apprehend we are not to look for her origin in any foreign traditions, but simply to regard her as a creation of the Hellenic mind, and probably

---

[1] Il. xv. 85.   [2] Il. xv. 95.
[3] Il. xx. 4.   [4] Od. ii. 68, 69.

of the mind of our Poet himself. Like Hebé she represents, in the main, the deification of an impersonated idea.[1]

In reference to terrestrial affairs, the name Themis signifies civil right, and is the basis on which are founded the relations of the whole political and social order. If Olympos was to be fashioned into a quasi-commonwealth, such a personage could hardly be dispensed with in its formation, among a race with whom the political spirit was so strong as among the Greeks of the heroic age.

Even Hestié, who represents the principle of the family order, in the same way as Themis represents the groundwork of the State, though she is not impersonated by Homer, yet is at the least on her way to impersonation, and attains fully to it after his time. She was less necessary to the theogonic scheme of the Poet; for, though the family is involved in the Olympian arrangements, it does not embrace the whole of them, whereas Olympos gives the complete picture of a Court and a Polity.

Hahn[2] derives the name of Themis from θεμ, 'I speak,' and observes that the statue of this deity was placed over against the bema of the orators in Athens.

Section XIX. *Paieon.*

In the Fifth Iliad, Dioné recites that when Aïdes, wounded by Heracles, repaired to Olympos, Paieon (or Paian) applied anodyne drugs to his shoulder, and healed him.[3] It is evident that the presence of

[1] Welcker, Gr. Götterlehre, I. 700.
[2] Alban. Studien, p. 258. [3] Il. v. 395-402.

this deity there, as the healer, was regarded by the
Poet as habitual; for when Ares has been wounded
by Diomed, and appears in the palace of Zeus, his
father, after rebuking him, commands Paieon[1] to heal
him, which accordingly is done forthwith, as by one at
hand.

In the Fourth Odyssey, Helen, after using the drug,
which produces the effect of opium, and may indeed
be opium, states that she obtained it from the Egyptian Poludamna, wife of Thon;[2] and adds that every
Egyptian is eminently a physician, since they are of
the race of Paieon.

Apollo is a healer as well as Paieon: but while
Paieon heals by instrumental causes after the manner
of a man, Apollo heals Glaucos immediately, as by a
divine action.[3]

The Phaiakes are called angchitheoi, near to divine, because the royal house of Alkinoos is descended
from Poseidon. Something like this may be meant
with respect to the Egyptians and Paieon: or just
possibly they may be called children of Paieon for no
other reason than their medical skill, without actually
implying that the traditions relating to the person of
Paieon were Egyptian.

But the word Paieon, which is the name of this
deity, is also twice used in the Iliad for a hymn: first
for the hymn of purgation, addressed to Apollo, after
the offence of the First Book has been expiated; secondly for the hymn of triumph sung by the Greek
soldiers over the lifeless body of Hector.[4]

---

[1] Il. v. 899.   [2] Od. iv. 227 seqq.
[3] See *supra*, sect. viii.   [4] Il. i. 473; xxii. 391.

A singular relation is thus established between Paieon and Apollo, somewhat like that between the Sun and the same deity; as though Homer had not been willing to treat as amalgamated, or even had actually severed into two personages traditions which had already, and elsewhere, been combined; for the reason that parts of them did not seem to be of sufficient elevation to suit the rest, and to be proper for the equipment of so gorgeous a figure as his Apollo.

The name paian became subsequently the established name of those Hymns to Apollo, which were sung in connection with victory and deliverance, especially, as it seems, upon a completed act of purification.[1]

Welcker observes that, even down to a late epoch, the separate personality of Paieon had not altogether been submerged, as Cicero mentions a statue to him.[2]

It is however possible that he may be, like Hebè, a purely ideal personage, not rooted in former or in foreign tradition, and representing in a physical way the office of healing in Olympos itself, as Hebè represents the faculty of youth among the divine race.

Section XX. *Iris.*

Iris, constantly introduced in the Iliad as the ordinary messenger between Olympos and mankind, and likewise among the gods themselves, is nowhere mentioned in the Odyssey. Yet the name of Iros is given

[1] Müller's Dorians, vol. i. pp. 819, 820. (Transl.)
[2] Welcker, Gr. Götterlehre, vol. i. p. 695.

to Arunios the vagrant, because it naturally fell to him to circulate messages and news; and it is evidently derived from, or from the same source with, the name of this deity.[1]

Her office in the Iliad is not exclusive. Themis is the pursuivant who summons the gods to the great assembly;[2] and Hermes is the envoy or agent who, in consequence of the general resolution of the gods respecting the body of Hector, is employed to conduct Priam to and from the presence of Achilles.[3]

In the Odyssey, Zeus does not act in his individual capacity, but only as head of the Olympian Court; and Iris is his personal messenger rather than the agent or envoy of the Olympian Court. There is therefore no obvious place for her in a poem where the conduct of affairs rests, in the Greek sphere, with Athéné, and beyond that sphere either with Poseidon, or with the collective body of the gods.

The name of Iris is also the Greek name for the rainbow; and the correspondence is very remarkable between her office of messenger from heaven to man, and the traditional function of the rainbow as a sign that the great covenants of Nature remain undisturbed.[4] As it is only by the tradition recorded in Scripture that the rainbow has this meaning, and not by any obvious natural significance, it appears hard to explain how Homer came to combine the two ideas, except by supposing that his race drew the association from the same early source from which Moses and the earlier descendants of Abraham obtained it.

It is true that Homer nowhere recognizes the relation

[1] Od. xviii. 7.
[2] Il. xxiv. 333 seqq.
[3] Il. xx. 4.
[4] Genesis ix. 12–15.

of the Messenger-Goddess to the rainbow. He does not, even on any high occasion, assign to her an epithet of color. But this is precisely of a piece with his manner of separating the deities of his anthropomorphic system from the mere Nature-Powers of other theogonies: his Zeus from the Air, his Apollo from the Sun, his Artemis from the Moon. Iris as the Rainbow would have been wholly out of place in Olympos.

This separation from the older deities he has marked, in the case of Iris, after a most curious fashion. In the Twenty-third Iliad,[1] she carries to the palace of Zephuros the prayer of Achilles for a Wind to consume the pyre of Patroclos. She finds the Winds at table, and they eagerly solicit her to sit and feast with them. She answers that she has not time: if she tarries, she will lose her share of a banquet which the Ethiopians are just about to provide in their country for the Immortals. This want of time is evidently an excuse devised by good manners: in truth, the higher deity of the Olympian order will not stoop to keep company with the mere agents of Nature. And this, although Homer has given them animation, for Boreas is the Sire of the Trojan mares.[2] His impersonation, then, was not a human one, like that of the Olympian system.

In the case just mentioned, the prayer of Achilles is addressed to the Winds. But apparently the Poet does not allow them the faculty of hearing when they are invoked; for it is Iris who, spontaneously it appears, charges herself with the supplication, and in the character of metanggelos, inter-messenger, carries it to them.

[1] 198-212.   [2] Il. xx. 223.

In one¹ other case, when she appears to Helen, and exhorts her to repair to the Wall of Troy, no one is named as sending her; but as she has here the title of messenger expressly attached to her name, it is probable that we are to understand she is despatched by Zeus.

When, however, Aphroditè is wounded by Diomed, in the Fifth Iliad, Iris comes to her assistance,² and here, without doubt because her action is spontaneous, she is not called messenger. She drives the chariot of Arès, which carries the wounded goddess to Olympos.

Though Iris hears prayer, she does not appear to be an object of worship, and her spontaneous action is confined to the business of the gods. It serves perhaps additionally to mark her Hellenic character that, when she appears to Achilles, she is without disguise, and is addressed by him in her proper character;³ but when she addresses⁴ Priam it is with the voice of Polites, and she comes⁵ before Helen in the character of her sister-in-law Laodikè. When she carries the order of Zeus to Priam, in the Twenty-fourth Book, she announces herself as the messenger of Zeus, but there is no proof or even sign of his being acquainted with her personally.⁶

Her mission to Achilles is remarkable, because she is sent by Herè. In this instance alone, she obeys the order of a deity other than Zeus.⁷ It is one of the instances in which Herè exhibits a command over aerial phenomena, apparently in virtue of her wifehood;

¹ Il. iii. 121.   ² 853, 365.   ³ Il. xviii. 182.
⁴ Il. ii. 791.   ⁵ Il. iii. 121.   ⁶ Il. xxiv. 173.
⁷ Il. xviii. 168.

and it bears an independent witness to the connection between Iris and the rainbow.

In every other case (I think) Iris is sent personally by Zeus, from the message for Priam in the Second Book of the Iliad, to those for Thetis [1] and Priam in the Twenty-fourth.

By much the most important errand with which she is intrusted is the mission to Poseidon in the Fifteenth Iliad, where she carries the order for his withdrawal from the field of battle. Supporting it with skill and persuasiveness, she by these means induces him to obey.[2]

Section XXI. *Thetis.*

Thetis is not to be regarded as properly an Olympian deity in the restricted sense of the phrase; yet by reason of her great influence in the Iliad, she is entitled to a marked position of her own.

The origin of Thetis in Homer is elemental only, and her attributes as a goddess are feeble. She does not act upon the course of Nature; she does not influence the mind: her powers of knowledge and vision are limited; she deplores her own lot among the Immortals; she is subject to weeping; she was married to Peleus much against her will. In no single instance throughout the Iliad does she exercise any divine power: nor is there in the Poem the faintest sign of worship as paid to her in any place.

But while her power, strictly so called, is thus bounded, her influence and consequence are immense. She is the pet deity of the Poet; or rather the engine

[1] Il. xxiv. 77, 143.   [2] Il. xv. 157-210.

he has chosen to carry through his theurgic process. It is her request to Hephaistos, that in a moment sets him to work upon the arms for Achilles; and when, in answer to the summons of Zeus, she repairs to Olympos, she is received with an extraordinary respect. But the chief act performed by her is the exercise of influence over Zeus in the First Book, where she overcomes his undisguised reluctance to act, growing out of his fears of a conjugal quarrel; and obtains his assent to her petition or demand, that the Trojans may prevail in the war, until the Greeks shall have made full reparation to her son Achilles.[1]

This is termed ἐξαίσιος ἀρή;[2] a prayer lying outside the provisions of destiny and the moral order, or one which caused them to vary from their course. The meaning of the phrase is not hard to discover. The cause of the Trojans in the war was radically unjust. The moral law required their discomfiture. In this channel ran the main stream of justice and of Providence. The request of Thetis was not in itself unjust, for her son, who had so powerfully fought for the just cause, had been deeply wronged by Agamemnon, the head of the Greeks. But it tended to delay the consummation of a greater justice in a world-wide quarrel; and for a time it set aside the moral purpose of divine government. Interposing a secondary obstacle, it deflected the current from its course; and an immense influence must be supposed to have been possessed by Thetis, who, and who alone, by her personal intervention, produced this extraordinary effect.

While she is thus a deity of far greater importance

[1] Il. i. 505–510. [2] Il. xv. 598.

than her rank in the preternatural order would lead us
to suppose; there is no personage, either sublunary or
celestial, that appears to bear more or deeper marks of
the moulding hand of the Poet. Some find in her only
a transposition of the primitive but obsolete deity
Tethūs, the wife of old Okeanos. Her name Thetis
also appears to be found in the dēti of the Albanian
tongue, meaning the sea.[1] On the other hand, as one
of some thirty or forty daughters of Nereus, himself an
elemental god, though practically superseded by Poseidon,
there is really no regular place for her in Olympos.
She has all the appearance of a character shaped and
turned to account for the purposes of the Poem: while,
at the same time, there are functions ascribed to her
which seem to imply a higher parentage than that
assigned to her, and to support the hypothesis which
makes her a reflection, as it were, of an older deity.
For though, of the regular Olympian divinities, Aphroditè
is among the lowest, she is expressly declared to be
of a higher order than Thetis.[2]

In her marriage to Peleus, there is nothing that resembles
the clandestine or lawless and transitory connections
with mortals, that are ascribed to Demeter, to
Aphroditè, and to the Nymphs. It is the result of
solemn divine Counsel,[3] and it is celebrated by the
whole Olympian Court. She had habitually sat[4] as
Queen in the palace of Phthiè, and in the discharge of
her motherly cares she had supplied Achilles with a
chest of garments for the war.[5] Though at first sight
the birth of Achilles may seem to be the counterpart

[1] Hahn, Alban. Studien. p. 252.   [2] Il. xx. 105.
[3] Il. xviii. 85; xxiv. 60.   [4] Il. i. 396; xvi. 574.
[5] Il. xvi. 221-224.

of that of Æneas, they are really opposed in every feature: the one is lawful, solemn, permanent wedlock, the other occasional and secret lust. Thetis herself, indeed, appears to have been reluctant at the time to marry Peleus; and she rendered obedience only to an order of the gods in general.

The purpose of the Poet in giving this high and unexampled sanction to the union, is not difficult to trace. For her agency is the hinge on which turns, in the first place, the reconciliation of the old and the new Theogonies; in the second, of the Pelasgic and the Hellenic nationalities; in the third, of the rival purposes of the gods (so far as the general scheme of Homer admitted them) with regard to Troy. I think we may find, that the marriage of Peleus to Thetis signifies and records the union, both on earth and in Olympos, of the Pelasgian and Hellenic systems.

The worship of Zeus, as we know, was Pelasgian, and therefore pre-Hellenic. The revolt of the three great deities of the new scheme, Here, Athene, and Poseidon, against him, seems to signify the tendency of the new worship, with its anthropomorphic or humanizing forces, to effect the overthrow of the former creed, cherished by the older but less intelligent and less powerful population. And the pure Nature-Powers indeed disappear; but Zeus, whose relation with Nature is in its most refined region, that of air, and who represents, too, the central principle of Theism, survives the change. The agency employed for his relief is that of the hundred-handed giant, called Briareus by the gods, that is, in relation to the old religion, but Aigaion by men, that is, under the new.[1] It seems to be in virtue

[1] Il. i. 403.

of his being a giant that he is the son of Poseidon; but his having a place both in the old and the new Theogonies evidently fits him to be the reconciler, and his being under the influence of Thetis, which is shown by his obeying her call, harmonizes with her double relation.

That relation is again indicated by her good offices to the child Hephaistos, whose adoption into the Hellenic Theogony, notwithstanding his Pelasgian associations and his leaning to an elemental character, she seems to have procured.[1]

And in yet a third instance do we find her discharging a like office. Such were the troubles excited by the introduction of the worship of Dionusos, that it seems to have been all but cast out of the country; but, as we have already seen, she gave him a refuge, which he appears to have requited with the gift of a golden (or gilded) amphora, the work of Hephaistos.[2]

For this office of reconciler between the creeds and ideas of the two nationalities, she has been carefully prepared by the fancy and skill of the Poet. Independently of the apparent association with Tethus, she is rooted in the Pelasgian system by her owning Nereus for a father. An ample counterpoise, however, has been provided, and in part by a most curious contrivance. She is the mother of Achilles, who is himself the highest specimen of the pure Hellenic type, and whose Phthian country is, in a pre-eminent sense, already the land of Hellenes and Achaians.

Something, however, is added, that the transition may not be too abrupt, and that an Hellenic color may

[1] Il. xviii. 394–407. See sect. ix. Hephaistos.
[2] Il. vi. 136. Od. xxiv. 73.

be made to attach even to the extraction of the great hero.

In the Eighteenth Iliad,[1] when his mother issues from the depths, she is followed by a long train of sisters; and the names of no less than thirty-three of them are given in a string. No catalogue of names approaching to this length is to be found anywhere in Homer. The nearest to it is in the Eighth Odyssey, where he describes his Phaiakes repairing to their Games.[2] Here he gives in rapid succession the proper names of sixteen youths of Scherié. On examination, we find that every one of them has relation to ships and navigation. It is therefore evident that the long list has a meaning. He desires to illustrate the especial, if not exclusive, devotion of the people to nautical pursuits. Now, on examining in a similar manner the catalogue of Nereids, we find that their names, instead of being, as is often the case with his Immortals, of an etymology that cannot be ascertained, are in nearly every instance pure Hellenic appellations, and that they even include the name Doris.[3] It is extremely difficult to suppose that Homer should have deviated so widely from his usual practice as to these lists, without a reason. And the reason seems to be obvious; namely, his desire to give a sort of Hellenic character to the family of Nereus, (whose name he never introduces except once in the patronymic,) as the maternal ancestry of Achilles.

From the obligations thus conferred, Thetis is in a condition to use urgency, though not authority, with Zeus; and honor is done to her son at the expense of

---

[1] Il. xviii. 39–49.   [2] Od. viii. 111–116.   [3] Il. xviii. 45.

the Greek army, notwithstanding the murmurs and devices of the Hellenizing deities. In like manner, she has no difficulty in obtaining from Hephaistos, on a similar ground, the gift of the Arms. In each case it is not a mere act of grace and favor, but the requital of a benefit received. In the case of Zeus, it is the more noteworthy, because the prayer of Thetis is declared to be in the nature of a deviation from the appointed course of destiny,[1] which had long ago fixed the downfall of Troy.[2] And again he signifies his attachment to her, when, though most of the gods recommended that the body of Hector should be removed by stealth, he arranges that she shall have an opportunity of giving glory anew to her son, by advising him to accept the ransom[3] which is to be offered by Priam.

The other principal particulars given us respecting Thetis are as follows.

During the action of the Poem she habitually resides with 'the old man her father,' in the depths. We may suppose that this was because she was now released from any direct maternal duties in the house of Peleus.

Here was her nurse; and was the special designer of the marriage.[4] Here again we observe the meeting of Hellenic and Pelasgic elements. The undisguised reluctance of the bride[5] may have been due to her prevision of the time when Peleus her husband would be overtaken by old age; but I rather think it may have been inserted by Homer in order to separate the case of Thetis broadly from those of Demeter and Aphroditê.

She has an union of strong human affections with

[1] Il. xv. 598. [2] Il. 3. 305-330. [3] Il. xxiv. 107-111.
[4] Il. xxiv. 60. [5] Il. xviii. 434.

THE DIVINITIES OF OLYMPOS.

the fainter attributes of deity. Besides what we have already seen, she hears from beneath the prayer of Achilles, but then he offers it from the shore, and looking seawards.[1] She also hears his wail over Patroclos; but it was an awfully loud one.[2] She herself joined in the audible lament.[3] She was aware of his appointed destiny,[4] but was under the necessity of applying to him to know the cause of his grief. So at least she asserts, though her own son seems to contradict her.[5] She suggests to him to seek comfort in sensual indulgence.[6] In his sorrow, however, she watches over him night and day, besides inspiring him with courage for the field.[7] And when summoned to Olympos in the matter of Hector's ransom, she appears there in deep mourning.[8]

Upon entering the divine Assembly, she is received with the utmost deference, Athené yielding her place by Zeus, which Thetis takes.[9] This may be a proceeding of delicate courtesy, having reference either to her sorrowing state, or more probably to the honorable customs of hospitality.

On repairing to Hephaistos to obtain the Arms, she dispatches her sisters to inform old Nereus of what had happened.[10] When the gift is ready, she herself, descending like a falcon from Olympos, carries the Arms to the tent of Achilles.[11]

The point of the sea, at which she dwells with her father, is between Samothrace and Imbros.[12]

---

[1] Il. i. 348–85 f. [2] Il. xviii. 85. [3] Il. xviii. 37, 71, et alibi.
[4] Il. i. 416–418; xviii. 95. [5] Il. i. 363, 365; xviii. 63.
[6] Il. xxiv. 130. [7] Il. xxiv. 72; xix. 37.
[8] Il. xxiv. 93. [9] Il. xxiv. 100. [10] Il. xviii. 139–147.
[11] Il. xviii. 616; xix. 3. [12] Il. xxiv. 78.

She came once more to the camp on the yet more sorrowful occasion of the death of Achilles.[1] She then appointed the great contest between Ajax and Odysseus for the arms of the departed hero.[2] She supplied the famous urn, to receive his ashes; which was the work of Hephaistos, and the gift of Dionusos. She also supplied the prizes for the funeral games,[3] which she obtained from the other gods, more richly endowed, as is probable according to the idea of the Poems, than herself.

The epithets applied to Thetis are generally connected with her marine extraction, and of these Arguropeza, the silver-footed, is the most characteristic; or else they relate to her good disposition.

She is plainly not an Olympian deity in the sense of belonging to the ordinary Assembly. Of this her reception as a guest in the Twenty-fourth Book appears to be a positive sign; and it is in harmony with all that we can see of her origin.

Most of the later tradition respecting Thetis appears to be but arbitrary comment and embellishment. The authentic *data* are few. She had a temple, according to Strabo, between Old and New Pharsalos, in Thessaly; doubtless owing to traditions of local worship, which had grown out of the distinguished honors assigned her in the Poems.[4] Pausanias mentions a case in which, during the Messenian wars, a priestess of Thetis, named Cleo, was taken and found to have in her possession an ancient wooden statue of the deity. This appears to have been the only temple to her which existed south of Thessaly;[5] but there was

[1] Od. xxiv. 47, 55. [2] Od. xi. 546. [3] Od. xxiv. 85.
[4] Strabo, ix. p. 431. [5] Paus. iii. 14, 4.

a tale of a statue of her, planted by Menelaos over against Cranaē,[1] on his return from his wanderings. It is not improbable that, after the Troica, there may have been tendencies to establish this worship, and that they were afterwards effaced from the want of a sufficient basis for such a divinity. Hesiod adds nothing to the Homeric account.[2]

I cannot help leaning to the belief that, whether she is or is not a transformation of Tethūs, she is, in most of what we hear of her, a creation of Homer for the purposes of his work; and that, as the Poet of Greece, engaged in building up her nationality and religion, he has employed her as a most effective instrument for signifying that union of ethnical and theogonic elements, which he in part commemorated, and in part brought about.

With reference to the etymology of her name, it is perhaps worthy of remark that the only office of mediation at all resembling hers is ascribed to Tethūs, who, with her husband Okeanos, gives shelter and nurture to Herè,[3] at the great crisis when Zeus was thrusting his father Kronos down to the Underworld.[4]

---

[1] Paus. xx. 2. [2] Theog. 244, 1006. [3] Il. xiv. 201-204.

[4] It would be matter of great interest to know how far, apart from any theory, the names of the Hellenic divinities are really derivable from the Sanscrit: and in the recent work of M. Jacolliot, *La Bible dans l'Inde*, a list of many of them is given with Sanscrit roots, in many cases seemingly appropriate. But for one ignorant, like myself, of that language, this etymology must rest upon authority: and the general propositions of M. Jacolliot's work are not sufficiently restrained and circumspect at once to inspire confidence in his judgments.

CHAPTER IX.

FURTHER SKETCH AND MORAL ASPECTS OF THE OLYMPIAN SYSTEM.

I. *Various Orders of Preternatural Beings.*

I HAVE dwelt largely on the Olympian Deities. The goddess Thetis has received a separate supplemental notice, on account, not of her mythological rank, but of her essential share in the machinery, both human and theogonic, of the Iliad. Also it is essential to give some attention to the deities or impersonations connected with Duty, Doom, and Justice. With respect to all other preternatural figures appearing in the Poems, it will nearly suffice to present their names according to the classification which has been already stated.

1. The Nature-Powers:—

> Okeanos: the source of deities (θεῶν γένεσις).
> Il. xiv. 201.
> Tethûs: the mother of deities. Il. xiv. 201.

These two were married, but estranged. Il. xiv. 206. It is probable that Homer intends by these expressions to represent Okeanos and Tethūs as the general parents of the various dynasties of gods; and it can only be from a supreme respect to Okeanos that, when all other Rivers are summoned to the Great Olympian Assembly, he alone is not called,[1] because he could not appear there in his proper place, as head and Sire of all.

> Gaia. In the Underworld. The word means Land, rather than Earth.
>
> Nereus. In the sea. Never expressly named; but only called 'the aged father of Thetis,' and signified in the Patronymic of Nereides.
>
> Kronos and Rhea. In Tartaros. Welcker thinks that Kronos (Time) is a mythical reflection from the conception of Zeus, who alone has in Homer the title of Kronides. Rhea he takes, as kindred to Ern,[2] to be an Earth-goddess of one of the old associated races of the Greek Peninsula. Rhea is clearly placed in association with Okeanos and Tethūs, by her delivering over Here to their care.
>
> Amphitritē, the moaning sea (ἀγάστονος), is mentioned in the Odyssey; in a very faint personification. In later mythology, she becomes a wife of Poseidon. The passages where she is named, as well as the fact that she is only named in this poem, will admit of our referring her to the circle of Phœnician traditions.[3]

2. The Minor Nature-Powers: —

> The Rivers: of whom are specially named —
>   Xanthos or Scamandros. Il. xx. 71.

---

[1] Il. xx. 7.   [2] Welcker, I. 143; II. 216.
[3] Od. III. 91; v. 422; xii. 60, 97.

Asopos. Od. xi. 260.
Spercheios. Il. xxiii. 144.
Alpheios. Il. xi. 728.
Enipeus. Od. xi. 238.
Axios. Il. xxi. 141, 157.

The Nymphs —
    Daughters of Zeus. Il. vi. 420. Od. vi. 105.
    The Mountain Nymphs. Il. vi. 420.
    The Grove Nymphs. Il. xx. 8.
    The Fountain Nymphs. Il. xiv. 444; xl. 381; xx. 9. Od. xiii. 356.
    The Meadow Nymphs. Il. xx. 9.
    The Nymph Abarbareè. Il. vi. 22.
    Worship of Nymphs. Od. xiv. 435.
    Their Altar. Od. xvii. 211.

The Nymphs mentioned thus far are named as having been summoned to the Great Olympian Assembly.
    The Nymphs of the Sun, Lampetiè and Phaëthousa. Od. xii. 132. Their mother is Neaira. Od. xii. 133.
    The Nereids, sisters of Thetis, dwelling in the sea. Il. xviii. 38.

The Winds: never admitted to Olympos; but worshipped; viz.
    Zephuros. Il. xxiii. 195, 200, 208.
    Boreas. Il. xx. 223; xxiii. 195, 208.
    (Notos and Euros are not mentioned as separate impersonations.)

3. Mythological Personages of the Outer, or Phœnician Sphere.

    Helios, father of Aietes and Kirkè. Od. x. 138.
    Kirkè. Od. x. 136.

Calypso, daughter of Atlas. Od. i. 52.
Ino Leucotheë. Od. v. 333. A deified mortal. Proteus. Od. iv. 385. Declared to belong to Egypt.
Atlas, the Pillar-bearer, and sea explorer. Od. i. 52.
Maias, mother of Hermes. Od. xiv. 435.
Thoosa. Od. i. 71.
Phorcûs. Od. i. 72. 'Ruler of the sea:' in relations with Poseidon through his daughter Thoosa.
Aietes, brother of Kirkë. Od. x. 137.
Persë, mother of Kirkë and Aietes. Od. x. 139.
Aiolos. Od. x. 2. A semi-deified mortal.
The Sirens: two in number. Od. xii. 52.

4. The Rebellious Powers are —

Kronos (probably). Il. xiv. 203.
Titans (perhaps). Il. xiv. 279.
The Giants. Od. vii. 59, 60.
Tituos. Od. xi. 576.
Otos and Ephialtes. Od. xi. 305 seqq.

But it is not easy to distinguish in all cases between powers rebellious, and powers simply deposed or superseded.

Passages relating to the punishment of rebellious powers, according to the Sacred or Hebrew tradition, are to be found in Job xxvi. 5; Prov. ii. 18, xxi. 16; cf. Gen. vi. 4, 5; in 2 Pet. ii. 4, 5; Wisd. xiv. 6; Ecclus. xvi. 7; Baruch iii. 26, 28.

5. Ministers of Doom.

Atë.
Erinues.
Moira, Moirai, Aisa, Kataclothes.

These will be mentioned severally.

C. Poetical Impersonations.

    The Muses, daughters of Zeus: their number is only mentioned by Homer in Od. xxiv. 60. The invocation is most commonly in the singular. They are, however, nine in all.
    The Fates (Kēres, Cataclothes).
    The Prayers (with Atè).
    Ossa, Rumor. Il. ii. 93; Od. xxiv. 413.
    Deimos, Terror. Il. iv. 440, xxi. 37, xv. 119. Probably son of Arēs.
    Phobos, Panic. Ibid. A son of Arēs. Il. xiii. 299.
    Kudoimos, Tumult. Attends upon Enuo. Il. v. 593.
    Eris, Discord. Il. v. 740. See *supra*, Chap. VIII.
    Oneiros, Dream. Il. ii. 6–54.
    Hupnos, Sleep. Il. xiv. 231.
    Thanatos, Death. Il. xiv. 231, xvi. 454, 682.
    Alkè, Might. Il. v. 740.
    Iokè, Rout. Il. v. 740.
    Arpuiai: the Storm-winds. Od. i. 241; repeated xiv. 371, xx. 77; cf. 63. Of these Podargè is named as the mother; who bears to Zephuros the two immortal horses of Achilles, Xanthos and Balios.

II. *The Erinues.*

There are three chief descriptions of preternatural force recognized in the Homeric Poems.

1. The will and power of the Olympian deities.
2. The binding efficacy of Destiny.
3. The obligations of the moral order.

The first of them may be described, from its mixed character of truth and fable, as the Theomythology of the Poet.

The second is his Necessitarianism.

The third is his Deontology.

But none of these are scientifically set forth or viewed; and no one of them has an exclusive sway.

In the first, a personal will is everywhere apparent; and though this will is largely used in sustaining moral ideas, yet with them are mixed mere propensities and partialities, and even passions and vices.

In the second and third, personality and will are thrown into the background. As his first rests on 'shall,' so the second is based on the idea we convey by 'must;' but the third is founded on 'ought.'

The second, if absolute, is perhaps among the most immoral and degrading of all philosophical systems; but those, who have given it a logical assent, have seldom adopted it as the rule of life; and in Homer it has only a very limited range. It is rarely held up to us apart from some reference either to the personal will of the gods, or to the moral order; and it never appears as the single, ultimate, overruling force.

The third corresponds with the second in its generally, though not invariably, impersonal character; and the ideas belonging to the two respectively are sometimes mixed in the words μοῖρα, which leans however to the idea of force, and αἶσα and δαίμων, which contain more of the moral element. There is also a relation between the idea of Zeus, and that of Fate, exhibited in the remarkable phrase Διὸς αἶσα, the fate of, that is, proceeding from, Zeus.

But in the rear of this law of the great Ought, or the moral order of the Universe, there is a personal agency, which in Homer is principally charged with enforcing its observance; that namely of the Ἐρινύες. With the progress of time, and the growth of moral corruption, the function of these venerable ministers of Right comes more and more to be, not enforcing the observance, or repairing the breach, but simply punishing the offender; and they themselves gradually assume the power of Furies, dressed in every imaginable horror. The later pictures of them are coarse and vulgar, compared with the awful yet noble figures of the Erinues of Homer, in whom is really represented, more than in Zeus himself, the idea of an ultimate Divine Judgment, together with compensating and rectifying powers.

The action of the Erinues is to a certain extent mixed with that of the subterranean or avenging gods. When the father of Phœnix prays the Erinues to make him childless, the imprecation is fulfilled by 'the gods, and (or namely) the nether Zeus and the awful Persephonē:' and again, when Althaia invokes these two deities for the punishment of Meleagros, it is the Erinūs who from Erebos hears, and accomplishes, the prayer.[1] The Erinues are invoked by Agamemnon to witness to his asseverated oath concerning Briseis, as punishers of the perjured; together with Zeus, Gaia, and the Sun.[2] The Erinues of Epicastē haunt her son Œdipus.[3] In his father's house, Telemachos apprehends that, should he dismiss his mother, her Erinues will come upon him:[4] and Odysseus, when the Suitor Antinoos has hurled the stool at him, invokes upon him 'if,' or, 'for surely,' 'there are such,' the gods and Erinues of the poor.[5]

The functions of the Erinues are not confined to mortals. They affect also the gods. When Arēs is

[1] Il. ix. 440–457 and 565–608.   [2] Il. xix. 258–260.
[3] Od. xi. 279.   [4] Od. ii. 135.   [5] Od. xvii. 475, 476.

laid prostrate in the Theomachy, Athené tells him his fall is due to the Erinues of his mother Heré, whose side he had abandoned.[1] And, when Iris finds it difficult to induce Poseidon to obey the behest of Zeus by withdrawing from the field of battle, she reminds him that the Erinues are with the elder.[2]

The horse Xanthos receives a voice from Heré, to warn Achilles of his fate: when he has done it, the Erinues arrest his speech.[3]

When Agamemnon has to confess his ἄτη or sin in the matter of Briseis, he says, 'I however am not to blame, but Zeus, and Fate, and the Erinūs that stalks in cloud.'[4]

When the daughters of Pandareos have received all manner of gifts by the agency of the gods, and Zeus is being asked to find them husbands, instead of this, the Harpuiai or Hurricanes, who are either storm-blasts or subordinate ministers of vengeance, carry them off, and deliver them to the Erinues to deal with.[5]

Thus far, in eleven cases out of the twelve in which Homer introduces these remarkable personages, they evidently appear as the champions and avengers of the moral order, in all forms, and against all persons whatever.

They are never subject to the order of any Deity. The gods indeed are subject to control, or even punishment, by them. Zeus is never mentioned in this relation: but their office expressly reaches to Poseidon. Their agency is wholly anterior to, and independent of, all volition whatever. They represent Law in

[1] Il. xxi. 410–414.   [2] Il. xv. 204.   [3] Il. xix. 418.
[4] Il. xix. 87.   [5] Od. xx. 66–78.

action. But, besides punishing offenders, they actually stop and repair infractions of the moral or settled constitution of the world, as in the case of the horse Xanthos. They therefore represent not only right as opposed to wrong, but order as opposed to disorder: and, in this respect, they supply a very characteristic product of the symmetrical mind of the Greeks.

The Erinues of parents, of elders, of the poor, and the like, are the sanctions of those great relations, in which moral obligation has its roots for the mass of men.

In the case of the offence of Œdipus, will was not concerned: yet it is enough for them that law was violated; and they appear in order to avenge it.

In the case of the orphan daughters of Pandareos, it is simply excess which they appear to resent. All personal gifts, even their food, were conveyed to these maidens by the direct agency of deities. This abnormal provision, lying far beyond, was therefore in derogation of the established laws for the government of the world: it left no space for human volition, effort, or discipline. This is the probable ground for the remarkable intervention of the Erinues against the damsels.

The twelfth and remaining case represents the close-sticking, or tenacious, Erinūs[1] ($\delta\alpha\sigma\pi\lambda\tilde{\eta}\tau\iota\varsigma$) as insinuating an Atè or offence into the mind of Melampous. Neleus had made it a condition of obtaining the hand of his daughter Pero, that the Suitor should bring him certain oxen of Iphiclos. This Melampous undertook to do, on behalf not of himself but of a brother; though it entailed a year's imprisonment, which as a Seer he must be supposed to have known beforehand. We

[1] Od. xv. 225-231. Compare 'Post equitem sedet atra cura.' Hor. Od. 8. 1, 40.

have to ask, in what did the offence consist? Was it an imprudence or folly thus to expose himself? or was the theft an offence against the laws of good neighborhood or guestship? In either case we do not escape this difficulty, that it was suggested by the Erinūs. This is a representation not easily brought into accordance with any of the other Homeric references to the Erinues: which, though severe beyond the limits of justice, nowhere else appear as the instigators of evil. It seems to be peculiarly strange, because of the habitual care of the Erinūs to maintain the established order, and not merely to punish the breach of it.

It is true that, in the Odyssey, Athenè is said to restrain the Suitors from discontinuing their evil deeds. But these are men who had long persisted in a profligate and cruel disregard of all the laws of duty.[1] No such consideration will apply to the case of Melampous. Agamemnon, indeed, blames the Erinūs for his own fault: but this is a mere excuse. The whole legend of Melampous is given in a form somewhat cramped; and, like other passages in the later books of the Odyssey, suggests that it had not been fully wrought out by the Poet. Possibly, but I cannot say more than possibly, this may account for the mode in which the Erinūs is introduced. We may also remark that here only she is called by the name of goddess; which appears rather inconsistent with her position.

Whether we are to regard the Erinūs as really capable of being a tempter or not, the conception

[1] Od. xviii. 155, 346.

deviates from the highest form of rectitude by administering punishment, in the case of Œdipus, to an involuntary offence. But here the elements of good greatly preponderate; and there is something noble as well as awful in these beings, watching with so much care over constituted laws, and maintaining or restoring the equilibrium of the moral world. It is by an immense declension that these sublime Erinues become the savage Furies of the Latin Hades.[1]

The name of Erinûs is traced etymologically by Professor Max Müller to the Sanscrit Saranyû, a name of the Dawn:[2] which, as importing discovery by means of light, would connect it with the office we have been considering.

III. *Atè, the Temptress.*

The Atè of Homer, as a person, represents a Temptress, who insinuates into the mind error or crime, begun in folly, and ending in calamity. Among the later Greeks it is Calamity simply, with a shadow of Destiny hanging in the distance.

The Homeric Atè means and wishes ill to mortals; but seems to have no power to hurt them, except it be through channels wholly or partially opened to her by their own erring or bewildered volition. Even Deity is not exempt from her illusions: for, before the birth of Heracles,[3] she it is who leads Zeus to promise what will, through Herè's craft, overturn his own most dearly cherished plans. For this excess of daring,

[1] Æn. vi. 556, 571.   [2] Lectures on Language, ii. 484, 516, 562.
[3] Il. xix. 96 seqq.

Zeus seizes her by the hair, and hurls her from Olympos to Earth,[1] apparently taken to be her native seat.

For she[2] is his eldest daughter; his daughters too are the Litai, or prayers, that lag behind her. She is vigorous and nimble, prowling about for mischief. They are limping and decrepit: they cannot see straight before them.[3] In this allegory, we have man ready and quick to err, slow to repent. We have also a living power of Evil extraneous to him, and ever soliciting him to his own loss and ruin. Here is a picture in substance much resembling the Serpent of the Book of Genesis, the Satan of Scripture, and the punishment he has undergone.

The temptations of Atè are to acts, also called atai, variously shaded between folly and sheer crime. The most innocent atè of Homer is perhaps the sleep of Odysseus in Thrinakiè, during which his crew consume the oxen of the Sun.[4] He may, indeed, be regarded as in some sort responsible for his comrades: yet he had bound them by oath[5] not to commit the acts.

We cannot be surprised if occasionally we find moral government in Homer out of joint, as in the case lately observed, where the Erinūs is said to send an Atè.[6] Agamemnon complains that his Atè was sent to him by Zeus, together with Destiny and Erinūs;[7] but this is an exhibition of a weak and self-excusing character, rather than a normal example of the thought current in that age.

[1] Il. xix. 126–133.   [2] Il. xix. 91.   [3] Il. ix. 499–514.
[4] Od. xii. 372.   [5] Od. xii. 303.   [6] Od. xv. 234.
[7] Il. xix. 87.

Besides the Atè of Zeus, of Agamemnon, and of Odysseus, we have in Homer the following chief examples:

Of Dolon, Il. x. 391.
Of Melampous, Od. xv. 233.
   These are offences against prudence.
Of Paris, Il. vi. 356; xxiv. 28.
Of Helen, Od. iv. 261; xxiii. 223.
Of the Manslayer, Il. xxiv. 480.
Of the drunken Centaur Eurution, Od. xxi. 295–302.
   These are moral transgressions.

The higher form of human wickedness, deliberate and self-conscious, is, as we shall see, not atè but atasthaliè.

IV. *Fate or Doom.*

The words used in Homer to signify Fate, Doom, and Destiny, are Kēr, also in the plural Kēres; Kataclothés; Moira; Aisa; and Moros.

Of these, Kēr approaches most frequently to a distinct impersonation; has the faintest trace of any moral element, distinct from the mere machinery of an iron system of decrees; and is of the darkest color, as it always implies doom or death, never a fated blessing. Kēr again is the destiny of an individual; not of law governing the world. It is, however, on no occasion eluded or contravened.

The Kataclothés or Spinners are only mentioned in Od. vii. 197. They are personal: and the epithet 'weighty' or 'oppressive' is attached to them. They partake of the character of the Kēres.

Neither of these touch the great questions, how far

destiny overrules the human will, and how far it is separate from, or even superior to, the divine will.

The word Aisa means the destiny of a particular person:[1] or the moral law for the government of conduct;[2] or that moral law as proceeding from Zeus or Providence personally, as the Dios aisa,[3] daimonos aisa: or lastly a separate power moving and ruling affairs.[4] In this last and gravest sense, Aisa is not very prominently used. Again, it is but rarely and faintly personified; it contains more of the moral element, more of *ought* than of *must*: though, when used to mean Death it is irresistible, because the law of death cannot be directly cancelled. Otherwise, it may be overcome. In Il. xvi. 780, the Achaians gain the upperhand against the Trojans, in spite of Aisa. But this particular Aisa was no more than the decree of Zeus, which gave that one day of success to the fortunes of Troy. The dominant idea of Aisa generally is not blind command, but an ordained law of right: a law without doubt very liable to be broken.

Moira, like Aisa, means an allotted share: but it is less ethical, more contracted, and more sovereign and resistless. Moira deals with each man: but we scarcely hear of the Moira of a man. It may mean good fortune, and has this sense in opposition to ammorié:[5] it requires a darkening epithet to give it the adverse sense.[6] It is however often used for death. It may be the divine will embodied, as we have the Moira of the god, or the gods;[7] but never of any named god, which seems to place it somewhat higher

[1] Il. i. 416.   [2] Il. iii. 60.   [3] Il. xvii. 321.
[4] Il. xx. 127; xvi. 441.   [5] Od. xx. 76.   [6] Il. xii. 116.
[7] Od. iii. 269; xxii. 413.

than Aisa. Nothing in Homer is actually done contrary to Moira: but such things seem to be regarded as not beyond the bounds of possibility.[1]

It is not however incapable of receiving the moral element. To speak generally, morsimos is destined, aisimos is right. But when Antinoos is killed, he is killed according to Moira,[2] that is rightly: and the term catamoiran connects it with the moral order, in the sense of propriety.[3]

In the order of action, then, Moira is above Aisa; in the order of law, below it.

Moros in Homer is never personified. Referred to an individual it seems to mean his death: and etymologically it corresponds with the Latin *mors*. It is never associated with the deity. But it is like Aisa in receiving the sense of the moral law. And here it corresponds with the Latin *mos, moris*. For mortals bring calamity on themselves in defiance of moros, and in similar defiance Aigisthos commits his crimes.[4] This can hardly mean that he was too strong for Destiny; but he was too strong for Right.

In none of these forms does Destiny ever fight with the gods; or, unless it be in the shape of Death, defy them. The later Greek mind elaborated the idea of a Fate apart from, and higher than, the gods.[5] But, in Homer, not even the human will is controlled in such a manner as to suggest or sustain the Necessitarian theory. Indeed we find the gods helping Destiny against man: as when, in the Second Iliad,[6] the Greeks would,

[1] Il. xx. 336.   [2] Od. xxii. 54.   [3] Il. x. 169.
[4] Od. l. 34, 35.
[5] Æsch. Ag. 993; Herod. l. 91; Philem. Fragm. 86.
[6] Il. ii. 155.

against Moros, have returned to their country after the rush from the Assembly, had not Here urged Athene to stay the torrent of home-sick emotion: and Apollo entered Troy, lest the Greeks should take it, against Moros, on the day of the fall of Hector.[1] Nor is the Fate of Homer absolutely blind: on the contrary it shows rather a tendency at times to grow into a sort of rival Providence, as in 'The Fates have ordained for man a hardy mind.'[2]

And when, in order to obtain a comprehensive view of the field of human action, we turn to the general plan of the two Poems, we find that in each case they work, not according to the impulsion of a blind and occult force, but rationally, towards the fulfilment of a divine or Olympian decree, announced at the outset, and steadily pursued to the end.[3]

V. *Animal Worship.*

Although Animal worship has played so considerable a part in the religions of the East, the traces of it in Homer are few, and, with one exception, they are also faint.

That exception is the extraordinary sanctity attaching, in the Twelfth Odyssey, to the Oxen of the Sun, which I have treated as belonging to the Phœnician system, and as foreign to the Olympian religion.[4]

Other traces seem to be rather dubiously discoverable, as follows:

(*a*) The introduction of the immortal horses, Xanthos

---

[1] Il. xxi. 517. [2] Il. xxiv. 49.
[3] Il. 1. 5; iv. 62–64. Od. i. 76–79.
[4] See *supra*, Helios, Chap. VIII.

and Balios; the gift of speech, conferred for the moment by Heré on Xanthos; and, what is of more weight, the gift of prevision, which enabled him to foretell his master's death. That gift he did not derive from the goddess. But, when he had thus spoken, the Erinûs interfered to arrest this violation of the natural order.[1]

(*b*) The assumption by deities of the forms of birds: viz.:—

By Athené, Il. vii. 59; Od. i. 320, iii. 372, xxii. 240.
Apollo, Il. vii. 59.
Hupnos, Il. xiv. 290.
Ino Leucotheé (Phœnician), Od. v. 337.

(*c*) The horse in Homer generally has not only a poetical grandeur, but a near relation to deity, which I am unable sufficiently to explain: but which, it seems possible, may be the reflection or analogue of the place assigned to the ox in the East. Several circumstances, and among them the practice of describing a champaign country as one suited to feeding the horse,[2] combine to show how completely, for the Greek, this noble creature stood at the head of the animal creation.

Some have pointed to qualities belonging to the brute creation as the possible groundwork of the extraordinary system of religion, which regarded animals as fit objects of worship: the unity and tranquillity of animal life, which makes it, as it were, a colorless medium for an inward spirit to inhabit: and the sin-

---

[1] Il. xix. 404-418.
[2] Il. ii. 287, and in fourteen other places.

gular instincts by which it appears in a manner to apprehend the future.[1]

For my own part, I am not able, even after reading the argument of the learned and able Mr. Davison,[2] to escape from the belief that the hypothesis of a divine command, given before the races recorded in Scripture were multiplied and dispersed, affords by far the most rational and satisfactory explanation of the wide extension of the practice of animal sacrifice, and of its remarkable uniformity as between races such as the Hebrews and the Hellenes, who had no communication together, and little indeed of anything in common. At the same time, it is an hypothesis only, and has not been demonstrated.

But if mankind thus offered certain animals to their gods, under what they esteemed a divine authority, it is not difficult to perceive the chain of association by which those animals might themselves, in process of time, very easily be taken for symbols of the godhead, and might again, from being mere symbols, grow to be esteemed the real shrines of its glory, and thus to attract the worship which is its due.

VI. *On the Modes of Approximation between the Divine and the Human Nature.*

The anthropomorphic principle of the Greek religion found for itself, in a spontaneous manner, several distinct forms or channels of development, for the closer association of the races of gods and men.

---

[1] Döllinger, Heid. u. Jud. vi. 130, p. 424.
[2] Inquiry into the Origin and Intent of Primitive Sacrifice. London, 1825.

The deification of heroes and benefactors after death appears before us in Homer as begun, yet, at least in the Olympian mythology, as incomplete. No person, avowedly of human origin, has yet been advanced to the rank of deity with the full consequences both of an abode in heaven, and a worship on earth.

Yet the consummation of the process is imminent. All the materials are prepared; and all the steps taken, except the final one which combines them into a consistent whole.

The elements of what was soon to be a system are found in Homer principally as follows: —

1. The ascription of human forms, manners, affections, passions, and other qualities, to the gods in general, lying at the root of the Homeric mythology as an anthropomorphic system, firmly lays the ground for further assimilation and intercommunion of the two orders of being.

2. Divine beauty, strength, influence, and intellect, are ascribed freely in a long list of epithets and phrases, to the mortals most eminent for these properties: and even the epithet θεῖος, meaning simply 'divine,' is attached, in the two grand cases of the Protagonists Achilles and Odysseus, to the living personages of the Poems, and to a larger number of the most eminent among the dead. This second head of preparation is as it were the counterpart of the first.

3. Birth from a divine progenitor, and even from a divine father, is ascribed to many personages who are active in the Poems, as well as to many who were dead.

4. Passion for beautiful or distinguished men is freely ascribed to goddesses, in a number of instances.

Among these were some, especially Aphroditè and Demeter, who were already in part, and whom at a later date we find fully and unequivocally, adopted into the Hellenic religion. But it is remarkable that such passion is in no case throughout the Poems ascribed to any of those goddesses who were either the most elevated or else the most national: Herè, Athenè, Leto, Artemis. A higher and purer idea of woman was entertained among the Achaians, and reflected in their religion, than in the elemental or the oriental systems.

5. More closely to the purpose than anything that has yet been stated, are the instances of Ganymede and Cleitos, translated to heaven and the society of the Immortals for their beauty:[1] of Tithonos, taken up to be the husband of Eos or the morning; possibly of Marpessa, whom Apollo 'snatched up:'[2] and of Ino Leucotheè,[3] who locally, that is, in the great sea region, has from being a mortal risen to the honors and character of deity. Aiolos, too, may be considered as nearly approaching to the character of a deified Personage.[4]

These, indeed, are all foreign, or extra-Hellenic, traditions. But of Hellenes, we have Castor, and Poludeukes or Pollux, who, even while on alternate days alive though not among men, and still in the lower regions, yet have by gift of Zeus had divine honors allotted to them:[5] and more still, we have Herakles,[6] who, while his Wraith is in the Shades, himself dwells among the gods, and has Hebè, who

---

[1] Il. xx. 233. Od. xv. 250. [2] Il. ix. 564.
[3] Od. v. 333-335.   [4] Od. x. 1.
[5] Od. xi. 298-304.   [6] Od. xi. 601.

is apparently a goddess proper, assigned to him for his mate.

6. We have also the case of Dionusos, whom, as having been born of a woman, we must apparently take to have been at the outset a mortal, but who had, as is pretty clear, in the time of Homer already become an Olympian god.

7. Asclepios underwent a subsequent deification; but in Homer he is a mortal only, for his sons, Podalirios and Machaon, bear the title of Asclepiad,[1] and no mortal in Homer ever derives a patronymic from a god.

8. To whatever inferences the case of Dionusos may lead, there is no other in which we find a trace or suggestion of worship in its proper sense, as paid to any deceased or translated hero. Yet there are two instances of what may be called initial worship, which must not be overlooked. Achilles, besides the fat of oxen and sheep, casts four horses, two dogs, and twelve Trojan youths, upon the funeral pyre of Patroclos.[2] This is, however, I think, to be interpreted purely as a gratification to the departed spirit. In the Eleventh Odyssey we advance a step further, though some may think the Oriental character of the scenery of the Poem in this part ought to be taken into account. Odysseus, by express order from Kirkè, besides making a libation, sacrifices a ram and a sheep on the spot, with invocation to the gods, of whom Aïdes and Persephone are named; and permits the dead successively to drink the blood, that they may tell him what he wants to know.[3] Here we see, dominant and un-

---

[1] Il. ii 731; iv. 204. [2] Il. xxiii. 171-176. [3] Od. xi. 35, 44-47.

mixed, that idea of actual enjoyment by the objects of the sacrifice, which in the case of ordinary offerings to the gods is combined with other ideas more proper to the notion of worship. But besides this, Odysseus is also enjoined to promise, and he promises accordingly, that, on his return to Ithaca, he will offer (and here the sacrificial words ῥέζω and ἱερεύω are employed) a black sheep to Teiresias, and a cow that has never calved to the dead in general.[1] This vow seems to come within a step, at least, of the full idea of worship. We do not hear of its fulfilment on his return home: but this may be because we are not carried by the Poem to a perfect settlement of the difficulties which he finds awaiting him. Prayers (εὐχαί and λιταί) are here expressly mentioned as used in the propitiation of the dead. But these are the entire mass of dead, not selected spirits of the great or brave.

One marked, and yet rather obscure, form of the connection between the gods and the human race in Homer is that of divine filiation. It is with much diffidence that I offer any explanation of this subject. A very large number of cases are recorded by the Poet, in which the parentage of a god is expressly assigned to some human house or hero. In some instances it arises by inference; as when he calls Bellerophon, the son of Sisuphos, descended from the god (θεοῦ γόνος,[2]), which can only mean, as Sisuphos was descended from Aiolos, that Aiolos was the offspring of a god. So, again, in the Legend of Nestor,[3] we are told that the young heroes of the line of Actor were saved from death by their ancestor Poseidon. The Iliad enables

[1] Od. xi. 29–33.   [2] Il. vi. 191.   [3] Il. xi. 751.

us to trace this line up to Azeus,[1] who must either have been a reputed son of the god, or may more probably have been an Aiolid, and thus descended from him, like the heads of so many other great houses. Amphimachos, another Actorid, is slain in the Thirteenth Iliad: whereupon Poseidon is exceedingly vexed at heart for his τιωνή, or descendant.[2]

To examine more thoroughly into this matter, let us take first for consideration the case of the great Ancient Houses, represented by their chiefs in and before the Trojan war. We find expressly assigned to Zeus the stocks of

    1. Perseus,   4. Heracles.
    2. Minos,   5. Minos,
    3. Aiacos,   6. Dardanos.

And to Poseidon those of

    1. Actor (probably through Aiolos),
    2. Pelias,
    3. Neleus,
    4. Bellerophon, through Aiolos,
    5. Cretheus, (and Eumelos,) through Aiolos.

Again it appears, upon examination, that Homer very commonly characterizes by the epithet ἀνώγων persons of recognized divine descent. This epithet he gives to members of the families of

    1. The Pelopids,
    2. Odysseus,
    3. Telamon.
    4. Portheus (ancestor of Meleager and of Tudeus),
    5. Salmoneus and Augeias (through Aiolos,) with a very few others of less distinction.

[1] Il. II. 513, 621.   [2] Il. xiii. 206.

But the question arises, why is Homer so reserved, in many of these cases, with respect to the immediate connection between the first ancestor and the divine stock? The case where we should have expected it to be most clearly declared, is that of the great sovereign house of Agamemnon. But not a word is said by him expressly on the subject of the birth of the Pelopids; and the sceptre comes first into the hands of Pelops,[1] whereas tradition names Tantalos as the first ancestor, and this Homer in no way contradicts. In the case of Dardanos, on the contrary, which is the counterpart to that of the Pelopids, the line is traced straight up to Zeus.[2]

The natural explanation seems to be that, here as in so many other cases, Homer's functions as Chronicler were circumscribed by his feelings of nationality; and that he acted on his usual rule of never knowingly referring, or providing means to refer, anything Hellenic to a source admittedly foreign. Therefore, where the oldest recognized ancestor is an undoubted Greek, as in the case of Aiacos or Heracles, he gives the divine parentage; but where the line ran up to some one, who had not been completely or adequately Hellenized, there no distinct declaration is given, and we are left to form a judgment for ourselves, from slighter indications, or from the fact that there is a general representation of the Kings and Chiefs of the heroic age as heaven-descended. In the case of Dardanos, there could be no corresponding motive for reticence.

It will be observed, that all the very ancient houses in Homer, say those of from four to seven generations

[1] Il. ii. 104. [2] Il. xx. 215.

back, as well as the most distinguished modern ones, like those of Aiacos and Heracles, are referred either to Zeus, the supreme god of the Pelasgians and Hellenes; or to Poseidon, who appears to have been the supreme god according to the conception of the Phœnician immigrants. So far, then, as these cases are concerned, it seems needless to travel far in search of an explanatory hypothesis. In fact if there was a tradition, such as we find from the Scriptures to have prevailed among the Hebrews, and by which man in his first inception was viewed as standing in the relation of sonship to the Almighty, it is in accordance with all likelihood that, in process of time, this illustrious extraction should come in popular estimation to be confined to chiefs or ruling men.

This explanation is however principally available for the class of Kings and Princes, who are called Zeusborn and Zeus-nurtured; and for those individual cases, which are of the greatest antiquity, and where no name of a mother is preserved. When we find a maternal name, a new element of difficulty is introduced. This difficulty may be deemed secondary in cases like those of Minos and Perseus; because there the mother may be nothing more than an indication, supplied by tradition, of the national extraction of the son. The mother of Minos is simply 'the daughter of an illustrious Phœnician,' and Danaë has her counterpart in a local Phœnician name. But what are we to say of Alcmenê, the mother of Heracles?[1] of Laodamia, the mother of Sarpedon?[2] of Astuochê, the mother of Ascalaphos and Ialmenos?[3] of Polumelê,[4]

[1] Il. xix. 98.
[2] Il. ii. 513.
[3] Il. vi. 198.
[4] Il. xvi. 180.

the mother of Eudoros? perhaps also, of Turo, the mother of Pelias and Neleus?[1] All these are women, having a place and an individuality as well defined as any other pre-Homeric women of the Poems.

The explanation commonly given of these cases has been that they were cases of mere bastardy, covered with the illustrious names of deity. May it not however be said that, if this be true, then nowhere did those connected with the birth of illegitimate children take so amazingly high a flight as among the Greeks; since, not content with equality, they gave them a higher title, by extraction, than the lawful offspring of the family themselves enjoyed? Of bastardy, as commonly understood, we have plenty of examples in the Homeric poems. Sometimes, as in the case of Eudoros, a person born out of wedlock was reared upon the same footing as a legitimate child. But when this is done, it is always mentioned as a thing worthy of note, evidently because more or less exceptional.

I cannot help thinking that these singular cases of persons who had a known mother, and who supplied the want of a known father by claiming the parentage of a god, were not cases of common bastardy, but that they are rather to be explained by reference to the ancient customs of what may be called marriage by violent abduction, or violation without dishonor, practised in ancient times by the men of one tribe upon the daughters of another.[2] Of the traces of this custom, ancient history is full; and even modern manners, in certain cases, aye at our very doors, visibly retain

[1] Od. xi. 235, 254.
[2] See MacLellan on Primitive Marriage, Edinb. 1865.

them. It seems to me that where, in the incidents of a tribal raid, some noble maid or even some matron of high birth fell a victim to the lust of an invader, it was agreeable to likelihood, as well as to social justice, that a clear line should be drawn between such cases and cases of dishonor willingly or corruptly incurred; and that either the involuntary mother at the time of the birth, or her offspring as he grew up, and went among his fellows without having like them a father to point to and to lean on, might exceptionally, and under favoring circumstances, have contrived to imitate for themselves the old tradition of the descent of kings from gods. The choice of the deity might in such cases be influenced by the particular worship in vogue among the aggressive tribe.

The correlative cases, of legendary births due to the passion of goddesses for men, may perhaps admit of a similar explanation. The probable difference in the facts being, that these would be instances where the mother disappeared, and the child remained in the possession of the father. This remark may possibly apply to Æneas, son of Aphrodite; to Aisepos and Pedasos, sons of the Naiad Nymph Abarbarce; to Satnios, the son of another Naiad; and to Iphition, the son of a third.[1]

The birth of Achilles from Thetis will not fall into either of these categories; since it is represented as having taken place in regular wedlock. My conjecture respecting this birth is, that it may possibly be a pure invention, due to Homer himself, though perhaps suggested by the legends current in his day, respecting the

---

[1] Il. ii. 821; vi. 21; xiv. 444; xx. 384.

attachments contracted by goddesses to mortal men. Such a fiction would be comparatively easy in the case of one who, like Peleus, was a reputed immigrant into the country which he ruled.

I sum up then by observing that we find, over and above the use of language properly figurative, four main channels of approach for the human nature to the divine,

1. Translation.
2. Mixed Composition.
3. Affiliation.
4. Deification.

And affiliation again, if I am right, appears in at least four shapes,

(a) The ascription of a Divine birth or nurture to Kings and Princes as a class.
(b) The ascription of a particular god as ancestor to a sovereign house. This god is always either Zeus or Poseidon.
(c) More recent births from a divine father.
(d) Births of men from a goddess; few, and all recent.

VII. *The Homeric View of the Future State.*

The picture of the future state of man in Homer is eminently truthful as a representation of a creed which had probably fallen into dilapidation, and of the feelings which clustered about it; and it is perhaps unrivalled in the perfectly natural, but penetrating force, with which it conveys the effect of dreariness and gloom. It does not appear to be in all respects coherent and symmetrical; and, while nothing betokens that this defect is owing to the diversity of the sources from which the traditions are drawn, it is such as might be due to the waste wrought by time and change on a belief which had at an earlier date been self-consistent.

The future life, however, is in Homer used with solemnity and force as a sanction of the moral laws, especially in so far as the crime of perjury is concerned.[1] The Erinues dwell in the Underworld, and punish perjurors. As the Erinues are invoked with reference to other offences,[2] we may therefore presume them also to have been punishable in the Underworld.

The world to come is exhibited to us by Homer in three divisions.

First, there is the Elysian plain, apparently under the government of Rhadamanthûs, to which Menelaos will be conducted, or rather perhaps translated, in order to die there; not for his virtues, however, but because he is the husband of Helen, and so the son-in-law of Zeus. The main characteristic of this abode seems to be easy and abundant subsistence with an atmosphere free from the violence of winter, and from rain and snow. Okeanos freshens it with Zephyrs; it is therefore apparently on the western border of the world.[3] Mr. Max Müller conjectures that Elysium (ἤλυθον) may be a name simply expressing the future.[4] The whole conception, however, may be deemed more or less ambiguous, inasmuch as the Elysian state is antecedent to death.

2. Next comes the Underworld proper, the general receptacle of human spirits. It nowhere receives a

---

[1] Il. iii. 297; xix. 259. [2] See Erinues, sect. III. supra.
[3] Od. iv. 561–569. [4] Lectures on Language, ii. 562, n.

territorial name in Homer, but is called the abode of Aïdes, or of Aïdes and Persephonē. Its character is chill, drear, and dark; the very gods abhor it.[1] Better to serve for hire even a needy master, says the Shade of Achilles, than to be lord over all the dead.[2] It reaches, however, under the crust of the earth; for, in the Theomachy, Aïdoneus dreads lest the earthquake of Poseidon should lay open his domain to gods and men.[3]

Minos administers justice among the dead, as a king would on earth. But they are in general under no penal infliction. Three cases only are mentioned as cases of suffering: those of Tituos, Tantalos, and Sisuphos.[4] The offence is only named in the case of Tituos; it was violence offered to the goddess Lōtō. Heracles suffers a strange discerption of individuality; for his cidolon or Shade moves and speaks here, while 'he himself is at the banquets of the immortals.'[5] Again, Castor and Pollux are here, and are alive on alternate days, while they enjoy on earth the honors of deities.[6] Here, then, somewhat conflicting conditions appear to be combined.

Within the dreary region seems to be a palace, which is in a more special sense the residence of its rulers.[7]

The access to the Underworld is in the far East, by the Ocean River, at a full day's sail from the Euxine, in the country of the cloud-wrapt Kimmerioi.[8] From this point the way lies, for an indefinite distance, up the Stream; to a point where the beach is narrow, and

[1] Il. xx. 65.
[2] Il. xx. 61. Comp. Od. xi. 302.
[5] Od. xi. 601–627.
[7] Od. xi. 627, 635.
[3] Od. xi. 489.
[4] Od. xi. 576, 582, 593.
[6] Od. xi. 300–304.
[8] Od. xi. 9–14. See Chap. XIII. sect. 3.

where Persephoné is worshipped in her groves of poplar and of willow.[1]

3. There is also the region of Tartaros, as far below that of Aïdes, as Aïdes is below the earth. Here dwell Iapetos and Kronos, far from the solar ray.[2] Kronos has a band of gods around him, who have in another place the epithet of sub-Tartarean; and the name of Titans.[3] It does not appear whether these are at all identified with the deposed dynasty of the Nature Powers, whose dwelling is in the Underworld;[4] and with whom the human Dead had communication, for Achilles charges the Shade of Patroclos with a commission to the River Spercheios.[5]

The line, therefore, between the realm of Aïdes and the dark Tartaros is obscurely drawn; but in general we may say that, while the former was for men, the latter was for deposed or condemned Immortals. We hear of the offences of Eurumedon and the Giants with their ruler;[6] and, though their place is not named, we may presume them, as well as Otos and Ephialtes, to be in Tartaros, in addition to the deities already named.[7] Hither it is that Zeus threatens to hurl down refractory divinities of the Olympian Court.[8]

This threefold division of the unseen world is in some kind of correspondence with the Christian, and with what may have been the patriarchal tradition; as is the retributive character of the future state, however imperfectly developed, and the continuance there of the habits and propensities acquired on earth.

[1] Od. x. 509–512.   [2] Il. viii. 16, 479.   [3] Il. xiv. 274, 279.
[4] Il. iii. 278.   [5] Il. xxiii. 144–153.   [6] Od. vii. 58–60.
[7] Od. xi. 318. Il. v. 385, 407.
[8] Il. v. 897, 898; viii. 10–17; 401–406.

VIII. *The Olympian System in its Results.*

The history of the race of Adam before the Advent is the history of a long and varied but incessant preparation for the Advent. It is commonly perceived that Greece contributed a language and an intellectual discipline, Rome a political organization, to the apparatus which was put in readiness to assist the propagation of the Gospel; and that each of these, in its kind, was the most perfect that the world had produced. I have endeavored elsewhere to show with some fulness what was the place of Greece in the Providential order of the world;[1] and likewise what was the relation of Homer to the Greeks, and to their part of the Divine plan, as compared with the relation of the Sacred Scriptures to the chosen people of God.[2] I cannot now enter on that field at large; yet neither can I part without a word from the subject of the Olympian religion.

In the works of Homer, this design is projected with such extraordinary grandeur, that the representation of it, altogether apart from the general merits of the Poems, deserves to be considered as one of the topmost achievements of the human mind. Yet its character, as it was first and best set forth in its entirety from the brain of the finisher and the maker, is not more wonderful than its subsequent influence and duration in actual life. For, during twelve or fourteen hundred years, it was the religion of the most thoughtful, the most fruitful, the most energetic portions of the human

[1] Address to the University of Edinburgh, 1865.
[2] Studies on Homer, vol. II. Olympos, sect. x.

family. It yielded to Christianity alone; and to the Church it yielded with reluctance, summoning up strength in its extreme old age, and only giving way after an intellectual as well as a civil battle, obstinately fought, and lasting for generations. For the greater part of a century after the fall of Constantinople, in the chief centres of a Christian civilization in many respects degenerated, and an ecclesiastical power too little faithful to its trust, Greek letters and Greek thought once again asserted their strength over the most cultivated minds of Italy, in a manner which testified to the force, and to the magic charm, with which they were imperishably endowed. Even within what may be called our own time, the Olympian religion has exercised a fascination altogether extraordinary over the mind of Goethe, who must be regarded as standing in the very first rank of the great minds of the latest centuries.

The Olympian religion, however, owes perhaps as large a share of its triumphs to its depraved accommodations, as to its excellencies. Yet an instrument so durable, potent, and elastic, must certainly have had a purpose to serve. Let us consider for a moment what it may have been.

We have seen how closely, and in how many ways, it bound humanity and deity together. As regarded matter of duty and virtue, not to speak of that highest form of virtue which is called holiness; this union was effected mainly by lowering the divine element. But as regarded all other functions of our nature, outside the domain of the life to god-ward, all those functions which are summed up in what Saint Paul calls the flesh and the mind, the psychic and the bodily life, the tendency of the system was to exalt the human element, by proposing a model of beauty, strength, and wisdom, in all their combinations, so elevated, that the effort to attain them required a continual upward strain. It made divinity attainable; and thus it effectually directed the thought and aim of man

'Along the line of limitless desires.'

Such a scheme of religion, though failing grossly in the government of the passions, and in upholding the standard of moral duties, tended powerfully to produce a lofty self-respect, and a large, free, and varied conception of humanity. It incorporated itself in schemes of notable discipline for mind and body, indeed of a lifelong education; and these habits of mind and action had their marked results (to omit many other greatnesses) in a philosophy, literature, and art, which remain to this day unrivalled or unsurpassed.

The sacred fire, indeed, that was to touch the mind and heart of man from above, was in preparation elsewhere. Within the shelter of the hills that stand about Jerusalem, the great Archetype of the spiritual excellence and purification of man was to be produced and matured. But a body, as it were, was to be made ready for this angelic soul. And as when some splendid edifice is to be reared, its diversified materials are brought from this quarter and from that, according as nature and man favor their production, so did the wisdom of God, with slow but ever sure device, cause to ripen amidst the several races best adapted for the work, the several component parts of the noble fabric of a Christian manhood and a Christian civilization. 'The kings of Tharsis and of the isles shall give presents: the kings of Arabia and Saba shall bring gifts.'[1] Every worker was, with or without his knowledge and his will, to contribute to the work. And among them an appropriate part was thus assigned both to the Greek people, and to what I have termed the Olympian religion.

[1] Ps. lxxii. 10.

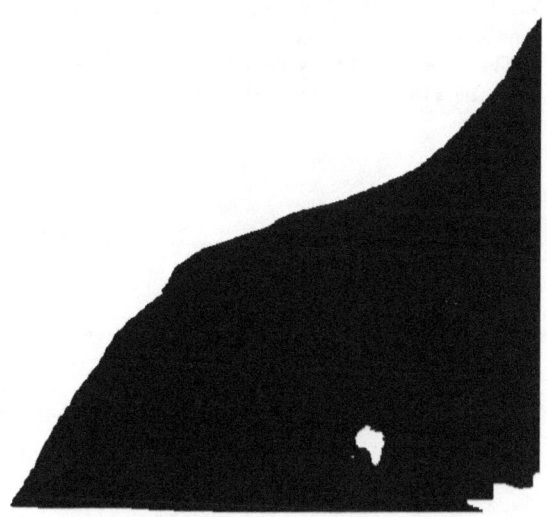

CHAPTER X.

Ethics of the Heroic Age.

Section I.

In general outline, we may thus sum up the moral character of the Homeric Greeks, favorably regarded.

A high-spirited, energetic, adventurous, and daring people, they show themselves prone to acts of hasty violence; and their splendid courage occasionally even degenerates, under the influence of strong passion, into ferocity, while their acuteness and sagacity sometimes, though more rarely, take a decided tinge of cunning. Yet they are neither selfish, cruel, nor implacable. At the same time, self-command is scarcely less conspicuous among them than strong, and deep, and quick emotion. They are, in the main, a people of warm affections and high honor, commonly tender, never morbid: they respect the weak and the helpless; they hold authority in reverence. Domestic purity, too, is cherished and esteemed among them more than elsewhere; and they have not yet fallen into the lower depths of sensual excess.

The Greek thanks the gods in his prosperity; witness the case of Laertes. It is perhaps less remark-

able that in his adversity he appeals to them for aid.
If, again, he is discontented, he complains of them;
for he harbors no concealed dissatisfaction. Ready
enough to take from those who have, he is at least as
ready to give to those who need. He represents to the
life the sentiment which another great master of manners has given to his Duke of Argyle, in the 'Heart of
Mid Lothian:' 'It is our Highland privilege to take
from all what *we* want, and to give to all what *they*
want.'[1] Distinctions of class are recognized, but they
are mild and genial; there is no arrogance on the one
side, nor any servility on the other. Reverence is paid
to those in authority; and yet the Greek thinks in the
spirit, and moves in the sphere, of habitual freedom.
Over and above his warmth and tenacity in domestic
affections, he prizes highly those other special relations
between man and man, which mitigate and restrain
the law of force in societies as yet imperfectly organized. He thoroughly admires the intelligence displayed in stratagem, whether among the resources
of self-defence, or by way of jest upon a friend, or
for the hurt or ruin of an enemy; but life in disguise
he cannot away with, and holds it a prime article in
his creed that the tongue should habitually represent
the man.[2]

From these facts, if taken alone, we might be tempted
to suppose, that the Greeks of the Homeric age were
an inhuman and savage race, who did not appreciate
the value of human life. But this is not so. They
are not a cruel people. There is no wanton infliction
of pain throughout the whole operations of the Iliad;

---

[1] Scott's Novels and Tales, 8vo. ed., x. 288. [2] Il. ix. 312.

no delight in the sufferings of others, no aggravation of them through vindictive passion. The only needless wounds given, are wounds inflicted on the dead body of Hector.[1] It seems to be not a disregard of human life, but an excess of regard for courage, which led them to undervalue the miseries incident to violence.

The character of Heracles, or Hercules, is one of which we hear much more evil than good in the Poems, if indeed we hear any good at all. The climax of his misdeeds is in the case of Iphitos, the possessor of certain fine mares. Heracles became his guest, slew him, and carried off the animals.[2] Yet, he is nowhere held up to reprobation. Indeed he seems to be a sharer of the banquets of the gods, and has Hebé for his wife; his Shade, or Eidolon, however, dwelling in the Underworld.[3] If this passage be genuine, we can only suppose his crimes to be redeemed, in the public judgment, by his courage, together with his divine extraction. And the passage is supported by the application to him of the epithet theios, which is given in the Poems only to the two Protagonists, Achilles and Odysseus, among the living, and to the most distinguished among the dead. Certainly, the indignation of the Greeks is against Paris the effeminate coward, much more than Paris the ravisher. The shame of the abduction lay in the fact that he was the guest of Menelaos.[4] And the guilt of Aigisthos finds its climax in this, that he slew Agamemnon by stealth, at a banquet, like a stalled ox.[5] Piracy, again, was

[1] Il. xxii. 371. [2] Od. xxi. 21–30.
[3] Od. xi. 601–604. [4] Il. iii. 351–354.
[5] Od. i. 35–37; iv. 524–535; xi. 409–420.

regarded, at the very least, with a moral indifference,[1] which continued down to the time of Thucydides in many parts of Greece.[2] Even Odysseus, the model-prince, when he has destroyed the Suitors, and is considering how he can repair his wasted substance, calculates upon effecting it in part by occasional free-booting.[3] To the principle, then, he freely gives his sanction; although he probably attacked the Kicones as allies of Troy;[4] and he disapproved, as it appears, of the raid upon the Egyptians, which in one of his fables he imputes to his ship's company.[5] This act is denominated an outrage;[6] and some disapproval of pirates is implied in another passage.[7] But it is faint. Piracy was a practice connected on one side with trade, and on the other with fighting; and it seems to have been acquitted of guilt for the reason that the gains of the pirate's life were the fruit of bravery combined with skill, and were not unequally balanced by its dangers. And piracy seems to have been practised only upon foreigners; of course such foreigners only as did not come within the range of any bond of guestship.

Religion, however, had a considerable moral force.

The connection in the age of Homer between duty on the one side, and religious belief and reverence on the other, is well seen

(a) Negatively, by the faithlessness and ferocity of the Cyclops towards men, while he avows his contempt for Zeus and the gods.[8]

(b) By the fact that the persons addicted to sacrifice

---

[1] Od. iii. 72.   [2] Thuc. I. 5.   [3] Od. xxiii. 357.
[4] Od. ix. 40.   [5] Od. xiv. 259 seqq.   [6] Od. xiv. 262.
[7] Od. xxiv. 111.   [8] Od. ix. 273-280, 350, 368-370.

and religious observances are with Homer the upright and good men: such as Hector in the Iliad, and Eumaios in the Odyssey.[1]

(c) As our word 'righteous,' founded on right, and embracing morality, extends also to piety, so in Homer the corresponding word dicaios clearly embraces duty towards the gods.[2] The Abioi,[3] an uncivilized nation, are with him 'the most righteous of men.'

(d) Conversely, the character of the theoudēs, or god-revering man, is identified with that of the stranger-loving, and opposed to that of the insolent, the savage, and the unrighteous.[4]

(e) The wicked man cannot by sacrifices secure the fruits of his crime. Aigisthos offers them in abundance: but the gods destroy him by the hand of Orestes.[5]

(f) Though the outward act of sacrifice did not of necessity imply a corresponding frame of mind, yet it was of religious tendency. The ordinary offering, at the common meal, of a portion to the deity as the giver, may be compared with the 'grace' among Christians. In solemn celebrations, and sometimes indeed at the private meal,[6] prayer and thanksgiving were commonly combined with the rite.

(g) The gods, as we have already seen, were thought, in a real though incomplete measure, to be rewarders of the good, and punishers of the bad.

(h) There was a strong general belief in the efficacy of prayer, testified by its practice.

[1] Il. xxiv. 68. Od. xiv. 420.
[2] Il. xlii. 0.
[3] Od. III. 272-275; l. 85-43.
[4] Od. iii. 132-138.
[5] Od. vi. 120.
[6] Od. xiv. 423.

We must not deny the reality of moral distinctions in Homer upon any such ground as that he sometimes describes greatness and strength by names rather denoting virtue, and mentions, for example, the services 'which the inferior render to the good.'[1] The language even of our own day has not yet escaped from this very improper confusion. We still speak of the 'better classes,' and of 'good society.' By him, as by us, the error is escaped in other cases: for he calls the Suitor-Princes 'very inferior men.'[2] And the word agathos, or good, has unquestionably in some passages a solely moral meaning:[3] while it is never applied to any bad man or action, however energetic or successful.

There was a voice of conscience, and a sentiment ranging between reverence and fear, within the breast. Sometimes this ascended to a point far higher than the mere avoidance of crime. After his conquest of the Hupoplakian Thebes, Achilles would not despoil the body of the slain king Eetion, and burned it with the precious armor on. He was restrained, not by general opinion, but by the inward sentiment called sebas.[4] To strip the corpse would have been the usual course. Telemachos endeavors, of course in vain, to arouse in the minds of the Suitors a nemesis[5] of self-judgment, or sense of the moral law. To this nemesis (often inaccurately rendered as revenge) Menelaos appeals, when exciting the Greeks to defend the body of Patroclos[6] from insult. But the whole matter is best learned from an address of Telemachos to the Suitors, where he says (a) 'rouse within you of yourselves a nemesis (or moral sense); and (b) an

[1] Od. xv. 324. [2] Od. xxi. 325. [3] Il. vi. 162; ix. 341.
[4] Il. vi. 417. [5] Od. i. 138.   [6] Il. xvii. 254.

αἰδώς (a sense of honor, or regard to opinion of your fellow-citizens); and (c) fear the wrath of the gods.'[1] These three principles were the three great pillars of morality. The motive of αἰδώς may be stirred by the δήμου φάτις, or public sentiment, which we find to have been an engine of great power with Phœnix,[2] and even with Penelope and Nausicaa. This αἰδώς is a sentiment which has ultimate reference to the standard of opinion; but it does not require that opinion to be in present and immediate action. It it self-judgment, according to the standard supplied by the ideas of others; as nemesis is self-judgment by the inward law. This αἰδώς ranges through a great variety of sub-meanings,— deference, tenderness, scrupulosity, compassion, self-respect, piety, bashfulness, honor, and every form of shame, excepting false shame. Hesiod says in his iron, or post-Homeric age, that αἰδώς, along with νέμεσις, had vanished from the earth.

With respect to blood-shedding, the morality of the Greeks of Homer was extremely loose. To have killed a man was considered a misfortune, or at most an error in point of prudence.[3] It was punished by a fine payable to relatives, which it was usual to accept in full satisfaction. But fugitives from their vengeance were everywhere received without displeasure or surprise. Priam, appearing unexpectedly before Achilles, is compared to a man who, having had the misfortune to slay somebody, appears on a sudden in a strange place.[4]

The cases of such homicides are numerous in the Poems. It may be enough to observe that Patroclos,

[1] Od. ii. 64–67.   [2] Il. ix. 460.
[3] Il. ix. 632.   [4] Il. xxiv. 480–482.

whose character is one of great gentleness, committed one in his youth without premeditation,[1] and was therefore given over by his father Menoitios into the honorable charge of Peleus: that Ajax had received Lycophron after homicide, and 'honored him as if a beloved parent:'[2] and that Telemachos receives Theoclumenos, and gives him the place of honor, when he had simply announced himself as a fugitive from the vengeance of the powerful kindred of a man whom he had killed,[3] without stating anything about the cause.

It is difficult, however, to trace in Homer the existence of an universal law of relative duty, between man and man as such. The chief restraints upon misdeeds were to be found in laws, understood but not written, and which were binding as between certain men, not between all men. These were

1. Members of a family.
2. Members of a State or nation.
3. Persons bound by the law of guestship.
4. Suppliants and those whom they addressed.

The weakest point of the Homeric system of ethics is its tenderness (to say the least) for fraud under certain conditions. This has ever been indeed a difficult chapter in the science of Ethics: it is probably one, in which the human faculties will ever, or very long, remain unequal to the task of drawing at once clearly and firmly, in abstract statement, the lines of discrimination between right and wrong. In Homer, however, we seem to find the balance not doubtfully determined, but manifestly inclining the wrong way. Into

---

[1] Il. xxiii. 86.   [2] Il. xv. 429-440.   [3] Od. xv. 260 seqq.

the mouth of Achilles, indeed, he has put the most
powerful denunciation of falsehood ever uttered by
man.[1] Pope's rendering is not quite unworthy —

> 'Who dares think one thing, and another tell,
> My heart detests him as the gates of hell.

This, however, we may consider as in great part belonging to the single character of Achilles. It is a principle worked out in his entire conduct, without a single flaw. His soul and actions are sky-clear. Among the Homeric deities, there is nothing that approaches him in this respect. Indeed it is especially in the region of the Immortals that we find the plague-spot planted. In Athenè, by far the loftiest of his Olympian conceptions, we find a distinct condescension not simply to stratagem, but to fraud: and she, with Odysseus, finds a satisfaction, when they respectively allow to one another the praise of excelling all others within this department, she among the gods, he among mortal men.[2]

At this we may not be greatly surprised; for force and energy already outweigh the moral element in the whole conception of the supernatural: and the character of Odysseus, with its many and great virtues, has a bias in this direction. But we may be much more surprised to find what we may fairly call a glorification of cunning, if not of fraud, exhibited in the character of that Greek chieftain, who, next to Achilles, may be thought most to approximate to the ideal of Homeric chivalry. Diomed meets the noble Glaucos on the field: they explain, and recognize as subsisting

---

[1] Il. ix. 312 (Pope, v. 412).   [2] Od. xiii. 294 seqq.

between them, the laws of hereditary guestship. The Greek then proposes the exchange of arms, which Glaucos accepts: and Diomed obtains the value of a hundred oxen in return for the value of nine.

We may, however, observe, that Achilles, in whom comes out the bright blaze of perfect openness and truth, is not only the Coryphœus of the Greek band of heroes, but he is above all things the type of Hellenism; the model of that character, which Homer considered to belong to his race. And, as far as we can perceive, though there is a delight in the use of deceit as stratagem for a particular end, the general course of thought is unreserved and open: the Poems show us nothing like life in a mask.

The idea of sin, considered as an offence against the divine order, has by no means been effaced from the circle of moral ideas in Homer. It seems to be strongly implied in the word ἀτασθαλίη, which is applied to deep, deliberate wickedness; to sinning against light; to doing what, but for a guilty ignorance, we must know to be wrong. For, when it is intended to let in any allowance for mere weakness, or for solicitation from without, or for a simply foolish blindness, then the word ἄτη is used. And I doubt whether, in any one instance throughout the Poems, these two designations are ever applied to one and the same misconduct. It is certainly contrary to the general, and almost universal, rule. The atasthalíē is something done with clear sight and knowledge, with the full and conscious action of the will: it is something regarded as wholly without excuse, as tending to an entire moral deadness, and as entailing final punishment alike without warning and without mercy. Nothing can account

for the introduction into a moral code of a form of
offence conceived with such intensity, and ranked so
high, except the belief that the man committing it had
deliberately set aside that inward witness to truth and
righteousness which is supplied by the law of our
nature, and in the repudiation of which the universal
and consentient voice of mankind has always placed
the most awful responsibility, the extremest degree of
guilt, that the human being can incur.

The wicked man, thus hardened in his deliberate
wickedness (ἀτασθαλίη), is then driven on by the deity,
that is, as we should say, by a divine order and dis-
pensation, in his mad career. Of this penal mechanism Athené is, in the Odyssey, the instrument. When
the stool has been hurled at Odysseus disguised in his
own house, and the insolence of the Suitors has reached
its height, Telemachos tells them 'ye are mad with excess of food and wine: some deity now drives you.'[1]
Before this we are told 'Athené would not let the
haughty Suitors stop in their biting insolence.'[2] And
when Amphinomos has received the friendly but very
solemn warning of Odysseus,[3] he is shaken inwardly,
and a presentiment of calamity presses on him. Here
the Poet goes beyond that 'hardening of Pharaoh's
heart,' with which a comparison is naturally suggested,
and indicates that, even while he was suffering this
pain, which may almost be construed into a state of
indecision, Athené held him entangled inwardly in the
meshes of his guilt, that he might be conquered by
Telemachos.[4] The subsequent attempt of Amphinomos to restrain outrageous excess appears to show,

[1] Od. xviii. 406.   [2] Od. xviii. 346.
[3] Od. xviii. 125-150.   [4] Od. xviii. 155.

that he was still at this time halting between two opinions. The sentiment of the Poet, usually so just, appears here even to tremble on the verge of a dark fatalism. But this belongs to ulterior and later processes of thought. What we have here to notice is, how very deeply the idea of moral guilt was engraven in the mind of the Poet, and therefore probably of his age.

The peculiar word atasthalié is chiefly used by Homer to describe the prolonged and hardened wickedness of the Suitors. The weakest case of its application is to the obstinate folly of Hector in refusing the counsel of Poludamas, and thus ruining the Trojan cause:[1] but here it is applied by the hero himself, not by any one else to him.

The view of patience in the Ethics of Homer is a very noble one. It is with him a prime virtue. Indeed, the characteristic merit of one of the Protagonists, Odysseus, is to be patient (πολύτλας), as his distinguishing intellectual endowment is to be πολύμητις; resourceful, elastic, versatile. This patience of the Homeric hero is as far as possible from being a mere acquiescence in fatality, or a cowardly retirement from the battle of life in order to put the soul to sleep. It is full of reason and feeling; it involves and largely partakes of self-restraint; it might almost be defined as moral courage. It is an active, not a passive function of the mind. Its action, indeed, is generally confined to the inward sphere. Yet it is not always so confined.[2] And it is always on the verge of, and ever capable of being developed into, the most heroic energy.

[1] Il. xxii. 104. [2] Il. xxiv. 505.

The sense of justice is also very strong in the poems. Agamemnon indeed is unjust, as well as rapacious; but, notwithstanding his sense of responsibility, and his fraternal affection, Agamemnon is not a character towards whom Homer intends to attract our sympathies. The Greek chieftains seem never among themselves to deviate from fairness, except in the case of the chariot-race. It is singular that three thousand years ago, as now, horse-racing should have been found to offer the subtlest temptations to the inward integrity of man. The winning positions of Diomed[1] and Eumelos in the race are reversed by a divine intervention, which throws Eumelos into the very last place. And it seems to be from a sense of substantial justice that Achilles proposes to commit what would have been a technical breach of it by giving him the second honor. But Antilochos, who has gained the third place against Menelaos by a sheer trick, remonstrates; and Achilles, with his supreme courtesy, introduces for Eumelos an additional prize to avoid even the semblance of wrong. Then comes the turn of Menelaos, who vehemently protests against the proceeding of Antilochos. The young warrior, who had been greatly excited against Eumelos, at once acknowledges the justice of the complaint, and offers to give Menelaos not only the prize in question, but anything else that he possesses, rather than offend him. Upon this Menelaos, not to be outdone in the contest of high manners, and without doubt recollecting that all his competitors are suffering in the war on his behalf, at once surrenders the second prize and takes the third. Thus, notwithstanding the device

[1] Il. xxiii. 373–402.

effected in the race itself, a strong sense of right predominates in the whole scene of the distribution, and governs the final adjustment.

The high estimate of the virtue of justice, thus observable, perhaps connects itself with that strong political genius which had already found development among the Greeks, inasmuch as justice is to political society as its vital spark. But again, justice is moral symmetry; and in it the exact spirit of the Greek would, on this ground, find at least a strong speculative satisfaction, which would help to determine the habits of the mind and life.

The idea of self-restraint, which seems to admit only of a limited application to the order of deities, is exceeding strong in the Homeric man, where he at all approaches excellence. Hence we find, in various forms, excess among the Immortals, such as would not have been tolerated in the Achaian circle. The howling of Arês[1] in pain when wounded, his loss of all power of reflection on learning the death of his son,[2] and the license which prevailed among the gods, with only few exceptions, in matters relating to sexual passion, are striking examples. But the same observation may be made in lesser matters. Inextinguishable laughter is excited in the Olympian Court, when the gods see Hephaistos limp about to minister the wine. But the Achaians never laugh with violence. If there could be a case warranting it at all, it would be one like that of Oilean Ajax, when he slipped and fell amidst the ordure.[3] Even here, however, self-control is not lost. They only smiled, or laughed mildly or gently (ἡδὺ γελάσσας), at the strange predicament.[4]

[1] Il. v. 860.   [2] Il. xv. 115.   [3] Il. xxiii. 777.   [4] Il. xxiii. 784.

The self-command of heroes, which is thus observable in minor matters, extends also to the greatest. When we find any virtue prominently exhibited in the two Protagonists, we may without more ado be certain that Homer intends to give it a very high place. And by far the greatest instances of self-command are given us in these two characters. On this basis is founded the singular courtesy of Achilles, in the midst of his resentment, to the heralds who came by order of Agamemnon to remove Briseis.[1] When he was in danger of losing himself for the moment, on the occasion of the First Assembly, a divine interposition took place to enable him to hold his equilibrium. And many times, when he feels the tide of wrath rising within him, he seems to eye his own passion as the tiger is eyed by its keeper, and puts a spell upon it so that it dare not spring. When, for example, he is sensible that the incautious words of Priam[2] are kindling within him a fire that might blast the aged suppliant, he seizes the moment, and, ere it is yet too late, bids him to desist. Whenever, after the death of Patroclos, his mind goes back upon the thought of Agamemnon and the wrong, he breaks sharply away from the subject.[3] So it is with this tempestuous character. But not less remarkable is the self-command of Odysseus. This extends to all circumstances: it suffices alike for the cave of Poluphemos; for enforcing silence in the body of the wooden horse; for bearing in his disguise the insults of the Suitors. But most of all in point is that wonderful speech in answer to the insolence of Eurualos,[4] the

[1] Il. i. 329–336.   [3] Il. xxiv. 560.
[2] Il. xvi. 60; xviii. 112; xix. 65.   [4] Od. viii. 165–185.

Phaiakian prince, which teaches us more than any composition with which I am acquainted, up to what a point emotion, sarcasm, and indignation can be carried without any loss of self-command.

The fiery Diomed also offers us, in his submission to the reproof of Agamemnon, a fine example of this great quality.[1] But in truth it extends to the army, that is, the nation. We see it in their stern silence on the march, and in the battle-field. And their manner of applause in the Assembly is always described by a term different from that which the Poet uses to describe the corresponding indication of feeling among the Trojans. The Greeks usually shouted (ἐπίαχον) their applause; the Trojans rattled or clattered it (ἐπικελάδησαν).

In truth, there lies at the root of the Homeric model of the good or the great man, in a practical form, that which Aristotle has expressed scientifically as a condition of moral virtue; a spirit of moderation, a love of τὸ μέσον, or the mean. There should be moderation in sorrow,[2] moderation in wrath, moderation in pleasure. Not a mean between extremes of mere quantity; but a true mean, an inward equipoise of the mind, and in the composition of mental qualities, abhorring excess in any one of them, because it mars the combination as a whole, and throws the rest into deficiency. This sentiment is conveyed by Homer in a multitude of slight and fine shadings of expression, like that insensible action of the hand in driving which keeps a straight instead of a fluctuating line. We trace it in the frequent expression οὐδὲ ἔοικεν: in ἐπαίσιμος: in the

[1] Il. iv. 411–418.   [2] Il. xxiv. 418.

πιστὸν ἔπος: in the φρὴν ἐμπεδος: in the censure implied by μέγα ἔργον, and in a multitude of other expressions.

This being so, it follows that one of the qualities most unequivocally vicious in Homer is an absolute implacability; that state of mind towards which Achilles for a time appears to lean; first, with regard to the Greeks, secondly, with regard to Hector; to both the living and the dead. It is a sin against Nature, rather than one of mere infirmity; because the very first requisite of such a feeling, to give it even colorable justice, is that the person entertaining it should himself be without fault, or weakness, or shortcoming of whatever kind.

This law, of moderation in quantity, was bodily as well as mental. Homer sings the praises of wine; but he reprehends even that mild form of excess which does no more than promote garrulity.[1] When the Greeks are about to suffer calamity in the Return, he lets them go in a state of drunkenness to their Assembly.[2] Elpenor dies by an accidental fall from drunkenness, and his character is accordingly described in terms of disparagement.[3] A legend is introduced to show the mischief of this vice, which even the Suitor Antinoos condemns.[4] No character esteemed by the Poet ever acts in any matter under the influence of liquor. It was for him the dew, not the deluge, of the soul; and it was nothing more. The gods indeed sit by the bowl the livelong day;[5] but for men it is not seemly to tarry for hours at the sacred (that is regular and public) feast. And this, not only in cases like

---

[1] Od. xiv. 463-466.
[2] Od. x. 552-560; xi. 61.
[3] Od. iii. 139.
[4] Od. xxi. 293-304.
[5] Il. i. 601.

that of wine, where the truth is obvious, and the excess repulsive; but in instances where it would less be expected. 'Do not go to bed too soon: excess of sleep is itself ἄτη, a trouble.'[1] 'Do not admire,' says Odysseus, 'or wonder at your father to excess.'[2] 'I disapprove,' says Menelaos,[3] 'of excess, either in attachments or in aversions: better to have all things in moderation.' The exact word is αἴσιμα, according to αἶσα, which may be said to signify the moral element of measure, order, just proportion, in fate.

This general disinclination to excess is happily exemplified in relation to excess of wickedness.

The extremest forms of human depravity are unknown to the practice of the Greeks in the Homeric age. We find among them no infanticide; no cannibalism; no practice, or mention, of unnatural lusts: incest is profoundly abhorred, and even its unintentioned commission in the case of Oidipous and Epicaste was visited with the heaviest calamities. The old age of parents is treated with respect and affection. Slavery itself is mild; and predial slavery apparently rare. There is no polygamy; no domestic concubinage; no torture. There are no human sacrifices; and even down to the time of Euripides the tradition subsisted that they were not a Greek but a foreign usage.[4] The legend of the seizure of Ganymedes, which was afterwards deeply tainted with shame, is in Homer perfectly beautiful and pure. Adultery is detested. The lifelong bond of man and wife does not wholly yield even to violence: absence the most prolonged does not shake it off: and there is no escape

---

[1] Od. xv. 394. [2] Od. xvi. 202, 203. [3] Od. xv. 70.
[4] Eurip. Iphig. in Aul. ἔθος μὴ πάτριον.

from it by the at best poor and doubtful invention of divorce.

There is undoubtedly something savage in the wrath of Odysseus against the Suitors, as there is in the wrath of Achilles against Agamemnon and the Greeks. Neither of these two is represented to us as a faultless personage. But when they err, it is in measure and degree; in the exaggeration of what, as to its essence, virtue justifies, and even requires. But an exceeding nobleness marks the rebuke of Odysseus to the Nurse Euruclcia, when she is about to shout in exultation over the fallen Suitors. 'It is wrong,' he says,[1] 'to exult over the slain, who have been overthrown by divine providence, and by their own perverse deeds.'

So again, while Hecuba wishes she could find it in her heart to eat Achilles, Achilles[2] utters a similar wish with regard to Hector. But the wish is that he could prevail upon himself to perform the act; which accordingly he cannot do. From these passages, as well as from the case of the Cyclops, we may learn that cannibalism was within the knowledge, though not the experience, of the nation; that it might even come before them as an image in the hideous dreams of passion at seasons of extreme excitement, but never could enter the circle of their actual life.

Indeed, the manifestations of mere personal revenge in the Poems are almost wholly among the divinities, not the mortals. The vengeance of Achilles has reference not to an arbitrary or imaginary code, but to a gross breach by Agamemnon of the laws of honor and justice. The vengeance of Odysseus vindicates not

[1] Od. xxii. 412.   [2] Il. xxii. 846.

merely the duty of political obedience, but the violated order of society, against depraved and lawless men.

The point, however, in which the ethical tone of the heroic age stands highest of all is, perhaps, the strength of the domestic affections.

They are prevalent in Olympos; and they constitute an amiable feature in the portraiture even of deities who have nothing else to recommend them. Not only does Poseidon care for the brutal Poliphemos, and Zeus for the noble and gallant Sarpedon, but Arès for Ascalaphos, and Aphroditè for Æneas. In the Trojan royal family, there is little of the higher morality; but parental affection is vehement in the characters, somewhat relaxed as they are in fibre, both of Priam and of Hecuba. Odysseus chooses for the title, by which he would be known, that of the Father of Telemachos.[1] The single portraiture of Penelopè, ever yearning through twenty years for her absent husband, and then praying to be removed from life, that she may never gladden the spirit of a meaner man, could not have been designed or drawn, except in a country where the standard, in this great branch of morality, was a high one. This is the palmary and all-sufficient instance. Others might be mentioned to follow, though none can equal it.

Perhaps even beyond other cases of domestic relation, the natural sentiment, as between parents and children, was profoundly ingrained in the morality of the heroic age. The feeling of Achilles for Peleus, of Odysseus for his father Laertes and his mother Anticleia, exhibits an affection alike deep and tender.

[1] Il. ii. 260.

Those who die young, like Simoeisios[1] by the hand of Ajax, die before they have had time to repay to their parents their threptra, the pains and care of rearing them. Phœnix, in the height of wrath with his father, and in a country where homicide was thought a calamity far more than a crime, is restrained from offering him any violence, lest he should be branded, among the Achaians, with the stamp of parricide.[2] All this was reciprocated on the side of parents: even in Troy, as we may judge from the conduct and words of Hector,[3] of Andromache,[4] of Priam.[5] While the father of Odysseus pined on earth for his return, his mother died of a broken heart for his absence.[6] And the Shade of Achilles in the Underworld only craves to know whether Peleus is still held in honor; and a momentary streak of light and joy gilds his dreary and gloomy existence, when he learns that his son Neoptolemos has proved himself worthy of his sire, and has attained to fame in war. The very selfish nature of Agamemnon does not prevent his feeling a watchful anxiety for his brother Menelaos.[7] Where human interests spread and ramify by this tenacity of domestic affections, there the generations of men are firmly knit together; concern for the future becomes a spring of noble action; affection for the past engenders an emulation of its greatness; and as it is in history that these sentiments find their means of subsistence, the primitive poet of such a country scarcely can but be an historian.

---

[1] Il. iv. 473–479. [2] Il. ix. 459–461. [3] Il. vi. 476.
[4] Il. xxii. 438–507. [5] Il. xxii. 424. [6] Od. xi. 196, 202.
[7] Il. x. 234–240.

We do not find, indeed, that relationships are traced in Homer by name beyond the degree of first cousins.[1] But that the tie of blood was much more widely recognized, we may judge from the passage in the Second Iliad, which shows that the divisions of the army were subdivided into tribes (φῦλα) and clans (φρήτραι).[2] Guestship likewise descended through generations: Diomed and Glaucos exchange arms, and agree to avoid one another in fight, because their grandfathers had been xenoi.[3]

The intensity of the Poet's admiration for beautiful form is exhibited alike with reference to men, women, and animals. Achilles, his greatest warrior, is also his most beautiful man: Ajax, the second soldier, has also the second place in beauty according to Odysseus.[4] Nireus, his rival for that place, is commemorated for his beauty, though in other respects he is declared to have been an insignificant personage.[5] Odysseus, elderly, if not old, is carried into rapture by the beauty of Nausicaa.[6] Not Helen alone, but his principal women in general, short of positive old age (for Penelope is included), are beautiful. He felt intensely, as appears from many passages, the beauty of the horse. But this admiring sentiment towards all beauty of form appears to have been an entirely pure one. His only licentious episode, that of the Net of Hephaistos, he draws from an Eastern mythology. He recounts it as sung before men only, not women; and not in Greece, but in Scherié, to an audience of Phœnician extraction and associations. It is in Troy that the gloating eyes of

[1] Il. xv. 419-422, 525, 554.
[2] Il. vi. 215, 224—231.
[3] Il. ii. 671-675.
[4] Il. ii. 862.
[5] Od. xi. 550.
[6] Od. vi. 151-169.

the old men follow Helen as she walks.[1] The only Greeks, to whom the like is imputed, are the dissolute and hateful Suitors of the Odyssey. The proceedings of Heré in the Fourteenth Iliad are strictly subordinated to policy. They are scarcely decent; and a single sentiment of Thetis may be criticised.[2] But the observations I would offer are, first that all the questionable incidents or sentiments are in the sphere of the mythology, which in several important respects tended to corrupt, and not to elevate, mankind. Secondly, how trifling an item do they contribute to the great Encyclopædia of human life, which is presented to us in the Poems. Thirdly, even among the great writers of the Christian ages, how few will abide the application of a rigid test in this respect so well as Homer. And lastly, let us observe the thorough rectitude of purpose which governs the Poems: where Artemis, the severely pure, is commonly represented as an object of veneration, but Aphrodité is as commonly represented in such a manner as to attract aversion or contempt: and when, among human characters, no licentious act is ever so exhibited, as to confuse or pervert the sense of right and wrong. The Poet's treatment of Paris on earth, whom he has made his only contemptible prince or warrior, is in strict keeping with his treatment of Aphrodité among Immortals.

With regard to anything which is unbecoming in the human person, the delicacy of Homer is uniform and perhaps unrivalled. In the case of women, there is not a single allusion to it. In the case of men, the only allusions we find are grave, and admirably handled.

[1] Il. iii. 156-158.   [2] Il. xxiv. 130.

When Odysseus threatens to strip Thersites, it is only to make him an object of general and unmitigated disgust.[1] When Priam foretells the mangling of his own naked corpse by animals,[2] the insult to natural decency thus anticipated serves only to express the intense agony of his mind. The scene in which Odysseus emerges from the sea on the coast of Scherié, is perhaps among the most careful, and yet the most simple and unaffected, exhibitions of true modesty in all literature. And the mode, in which all this is presented to us, suggests that it forms a true picture of the general manners of the nation at the time. That this delicacy long subsisted in Greece, we learn from Thucydides.[3] The morality of the Homeric period is that of the childhood of a race: the morality of the classic times belongs to its manhood. On the side of the latter, it may be urged that two causes in particular tend to raise its level. With regular forms of political and civil organization, there grows up in written law a public testimonial on behalf, in the main, of truth, honesty, and justice. For, while private conduct represents the human mind under the bias of every temptation, the law, as a general rule, speaks that which our perceptions would affirm were there no such bias. But further, with law and order comes the clearer idea and fuller enjoyment of the fruits of labor; and for the sake of security each man adopts, and in general acts upon, a recognition of the rights of property These are powerful agencies for good in a great department of morals. Besides these, with a more imposing beauty, but probably with less of practical efficacy,

---

[1] Il. ii. 262.   [2] Il. xxii. 74–76.   [3] i. 6.

the speculative intellect of man goes to work, and establishes abstract theories of virtue, vice, and their consequences, which by their comprehensiveness and method put out of countenance the indeterminate ethics of remote antiquity. All this is to be laid in one scale. But the other would, I think, preponderate, if it were only from the single consideration, that the creed of the Homeric age brought both the sense and the dread of the divine justice to bear in restraint of vice and passion. And upon the whole, after the survey which has been taken, it would in my opinion be somewhat rash to assert, that either the duties of men to the deity, or the larger claims of man upon man, were better understood in the age of Pericles or Alexander, of Sylla or Augustus, than in the age of Homer.

Perhaps the following sketch of Greek life in the heroic age may not be far wide of the truth.

The youth of high birth, not then so widely as now separated from the low, is educated under tutors in reverence for his parents, and in desire to emulate their fame; he shares in manly and in graceful sports; acquires the use of arms; hardens himself in the pursuit, then of all others the most indispensable, the hunting down of wild beasts; gains the knowledge of medicine, probable also of the lyre. Sometimes, with many-sided intelligence, he even sets himself to learn how to build his own house or ship, or how to drive the plough firm and straight down the furrow, as well as to reap the standing corn.[1]

And, when scarcely a man, he bears arms for his country or his tribe, takes part in its government,

---

[1] Od. xviii. 366–375.

learns by direct instruction, and by practice, how to rule mankind through the use of reasoning and persuasive power in political assemblies, attends and assists in sacrifices to the gods. For, all this time, he has been in kindly and free relations, not only with his parents, his family, his equals of his own age, but with the attendants, although they are but serfs, who have known him from infancy on his father's domain.

He is indeed mistaught with reference to the use of the strong hand. Human life is cheap; so cheap that even a mild and gentle youth may be betrayed, upon a casual quarrel over some childish game with his friend, into taking it away. And even so throughout his life, should some occasion come that stirs up his passions from their depths, a wild beast, as it were, awakes within him, and he loses his humanity for the time, until reason has re-established her control. Short, however, of such a desperate crisis, though he could not for the world rob his friend or his neighbor, yet he might be not unwilling to triumph over him to his cost, for the sake of some exercise of signal ingenuity; while, from a hostile tribe or a foreign shore, or from the individual who has become his enemy, he will acquire by main force what he can, nor will he scruple to inflict on him by stratagem even deadly injury.[1] He must, however, give liberally to those who are in need; to the wayfarer, to the poor, to the suppliant who begs from him shelter and protection. On the other hand; should his own goods be wasted, the liberal and open-handed contributions of his neighbors will not be wanting to replace them.

[1] Od. xiii. 252-270.

His early youth is not solicited into vice by finding sensual excess in vogue, or the opportunities of it glaring in his eye, and sounding in his ear. Gluttony is hardly known; drunkenness is marked only by its degrading character, and by the evil consequences that flow so straight from it; and it is abhorred. But he loves the genial use of meals, and rejoices in the hour when the guests, gathered in his father's hall, enjoy a liberal hospitality, and the wine mantles in the cup.[1] For then they listen to the strains of the minstrel, who celebrates before them the newest and the dearest of the heroic tales that stir their blood, and rouse their manly resolution to be worthy, in their turn, of their country and their country's heroes. He joins the dance in the festivals of religion; the maiden's hand upon his wrist, and the gilded knife gleaming from his belt, as they course from point to point, or wheel in round on round.[2] That maiden, some Nausicaa, or some Hermione of a neighboring district, in due time he weds, amidst the rejoicings of their families, and brings her home to cherish her, 'from the flower to the ripeness of the grape,' with respect, fidelity, and love.

Whether as a governor or as governed, politics bring him, in ordinary circumstances, no great share of trouble. Government is a machine, of which the wheels move easily enough; for they are well oiled by simplicity of usages, ideas, and desires; by unity of interest; by respect for authority, and for those in whose hands it is reposed; by love of the common country, the common altar, the common Festivals and Games, to which already there is large resort. In peace he

[1] Od. ix. 5–11; xiv. 193–198.   [2] Il. xviii. 504–602.

settles the disputes of his people, in war he leads them the precious example of heroic daring. He consults them, and advises with them, on all grave affairs; and his wakeful care for their interests is rewarded by the ample domains which are set apart for the prince by the people.[1] Finally, he closes his eyes, delivering over the sceptre to his son, and leaving much peace and happiness around him.[2]

Such was, probably, the state of society amidst the concluding phase of which Homer's youth, at least, was passed. But a dark and deep social revolution seems to have followed the Trojan war; we have its workings already become visible in the Odyssey. Scarcely could even Odysseus cope with it, contracted though it was for him within the narrow bounds of Ithaca. On the mainland, the bands of the elder society are soon wholly broken. The Pelopid, Neleid, Œnid houses, are a wreck: disorganization invites the entry of new forces to control it; the Dorian lances bristle on the Ætolian beach, and the primitive Greece, the patriarchal Greece, the Greece of Homer, is no more.

Section II.

We must not dismiss the subject of Ethics or morals without considering what is both a criterion and an essential part of it, namely, the position held by Woman in the heroic age.[3]

Within the pale of that civilization, which has grown

---

[1] Il. ix. 580; xii 313.   [2] Od. xxiii. 281-284.
[3] For a fuller exposition, see Studies on Homer, Olympos, sect. 9. See also Mr. Buckle's Lecture on Woman, in Frazer's Magazine.

up under the combined influence of the Christian religion as paramount, and what may be called the Teutonic manners as secondary, we find the idea of Woman and her social position raised to a point higher than in the Poems of Homer. But it would be hard to discover any period of history, or country of the world, not being Christian, in which women stood so high as with the Greeks of the heroic age.

I will here very briefly illustrate this proposition under several heads; and first, that of marriage with its accessories.

The essence of Homeric marriage seems to have lain in cohabitation, together with a solemn public acknowledgment of the relation of the parties as man and wife, and with an attendant ceremonial such as is represented on the Shield of Achilles. This might apparently be preceded by cohabitation with the intention of marriage. Hence Briseis is called by Achilles his wife;[1] yet in the very same speech he speaks of himself as open to marriage with another woman; and Briseis, in her lament over Patroclos, says,[2] 'Thou wouldst not let me weep, but saidst thou wouldst make me the wife of Achilles, and take me by ship to Phthiè, and feast (i.e. celebrate) my marriage among the Myrmidons.' So that the full accomplishment of the union was apparently to follow the expected return; and she was in the meantime a wife-designate.

It is in the interest of the woman that the law of marriage should be strict, and that marriage should be

---

[1] Il. ix. 335, 340 seqq.

[2] Il. xix. 295 seqq. I omit the word κουριδίην, which would require a discussion.

single. Among the Homeric Greeks we have not the slightest trace of polygamy; or of a woman taken from her husband, and made the wife of another man during his lifetime. The Suitors always urge Penelope to re-marry, on the ground that Odysseus must be dead, and that there is no hope of his return. A shorter period of absence, than that assigned to him, is recognized by the law of England as making re-marriage legal. A presumption of death brought near to certainty must, under the conditions of human affairs, be taken to suffice; for, says Butler, with a sweep of comprehensive wisdom, 'Probability is the very guide of life.'[1] But in the case of Agamemnon, there was no presumption of death; and, accordingly, the act of Aigisthos is described by Zeus as a double outrage, made up of two crimes; the last part of it being the murder, but the first the simple fact of the marriage.[2]

Even the violent bodily abstraction of the wife, as in the case of Helen, does no more than destroy the marriage for the time. When she is recovered, she resumes her domestic place. There is no such thing as a formal and final dissolution of a marriage, except by death. In the narrative, and by the Trojans, as well as by herself, Helen is called the wife of Paris; yet we never find this acknowledgment in the mouth of a Greek. Nay, Hector even calls Helen the wife of Menelaos:[3] but this may mean the past wife. Menelaos never treats what had occurred as setting him free from his obligations to Helen. And the long resistance of Penelope, presented to us in the Odyssey as a central

[1] Introduction to the Analogy.   [2] Od. i. 36.
[3] Il. iii. 53.

object of our interest and admiration, could not have been chosen for this purpose by the poet, unless it had been in conformity with the actual Greek idea of a genuine and lofty virtue.

Concubinage is practised by some few, and as far as we are informed only by few, of the Greek chieftains before Troy: yet this also is single. Of actual domestic concubinage we have no example. But Agamemnon threatens to take Briseis home with him.[1] This, however, is done under angry excitement. In the Assembly, he thinks it necessary to give the reason of a proceeding, which he apparently perceived would require a justification; and it is, that he prefers her in all respects to Clutaimnestra. But we have no trace, in the Return, of any chief's carrying a concubine home with him. The wife of Amuntor adopted an extreme measure to prevent her husband from falling into a lawless connection;[2] and Laertes, from an apprehension of conjugal trouble, respected the maidenhood of his young bondwoman.[3] These instances, if they show that the man was not exempt from passion, bear very emphatic testimony to the position of the wife.

The relations of youth and maiden generally are indicated with extreme beauty and tenderness in the Iliad;[4] and those of the unmarried woman to a suitor, or probable spouse, are so portrayed, in the case of the incomparable Nausicaa, as to show a delicacy and freedom that no period of history or state of manners can surpass.[5] On her return home, Alkinoos, far from re-

[1] Il. i. 29, 118. [2] Il. ix. 451. [3] Od. i. 433.
[4] Il. xviii. 567, 593; xxii. 127, 128. [5] Od. vi. 275-288.

proving her, thinks she should have shown more forwardness to entertain the shipwrecked stranger. We often hear of a parent, who gives or promises a daughter in marriage: but like expressions[1] are applied to sons. The very fact that the profligate and violent Suitors always confine themselves to a moral pressure, and profess to submit to the choice of Penelopè, is of itself a probable witness to the recognized free-agency of the woman of the period.

In that early state of society we hear of no such personage as an elderly bachelor or spinster. Nor, within due limits of age, could there, I presume, be a prolonged widowhood. The apparent connection of Helen with Deiphobos,[2] after the death of Paris, should probably be read in the light of Trojan usage. But whenever Penelopè, or others in her name, contemplate the death of Odysseus, and her consequent release, that change is always treated as the immediate preface to another crisis, in the choice of a second husband.

Marriage, in Homer, is the very pivot of life. War is the deadly enemy of woman. On the capture of a city, her lot is exile, and the conqueror's bed. The familiarity of this idea renders it remarkable that we should not hear much more than we do hear of concubinage among the Greeks of Homer. Of professional prostitution, we have no trace at all.

As the restraints imposed upon marriage are in general among the proofs of its high estimation, I proceed to observe that the Greeks regarded incest with horror, even when, as in the instance of Oidipous and Epicastè, it was involuntary. Passing on from ex-

[1] Il. ix. 394. Od. iv. 10.   [2] Od. iv. 276.

treme cases, we may observe, that the connection of Phœnix with a woman at once presented an insurmountable bar to the unlawful passion of his father for the same person. It appears however probable, though not certain, that Diomed was married to his mother's sister.[1] In Scheriè, the king Alkinoos had his niece for his wife:[2] but this is in the Phœnician circle. In Troy, Iphidamas marries the sister of his mother.[3]

It is observed that, in the classical period, the law of incest in Greece, instead of being tightened, was relaxed.[4] The older sentiment about it is the more remarkable, because of the extreme looseness of the code applied to supernatural beings.[5]

A series of words for the different relationships by affinity, includes the word einater for the husband's brother's wife, to which we have no correlative in English; and the terms, in which these relationships are spoken of, testify to the definiteness and solidity of the marriage bond.

We have a single case of a woman who attempts the breach of her own marriage-vow. It is Anteia, the wife of Proitos; but the family was Phœnician.

Thus, then, we have in the Poems a picture of Greek marriage as to its unity, freedom, perpetuity; as to the restraints upon it, and as to the manner in which breaches of it, and substitutes for it, were regarded. This picture, so striking in itself, becomes yet more so by comparison with Eastern manners, even as they were exhibited in the Hebrew race. It is also in glar-

---

[1] Il. v. 412; xiv. 121. [2] Od. vii. 65, 66.
[3] Il. xi. 220-226.   [4] Friedreich's Realien, iii. 2.
[5] Il. iv. 441; xvi. 432. Od. x. 7.

ing and painful contrast with the lowered estimate of woman among the Greeks of the classical period, and with their loathsome immorality.

More important, however, than any particulars is the general tone of the intercourse between husband and wife. It is thoroughly natural: full of warmth, dignity, reciprocal deference, and substantial, if not conventional, delicacy. The fulness of moral and intelligent being is alike complete, and alike acknowledged, on the one side and on the other. Nor is this description confined to the scenes properly Hellenic. It embraces the conversation of Hector with Andromachê, and is nowhere more applicable than to the whole character and demeanor of Nausicaa—delineations probably due rather to the Hellenic experience of the Poet, than to any minute observation either of Phœnician or of Trojan manners. Of rude manners to a woman there is not a real instance in the Poems. And to this circumstance we may add its true correlative, that the women of Homer are truly and profoundly feminine. As to the intensity of conjugal love, it has never passed the climax which it reaches in Odysseus and Penelopê.

Presents were usually brought by the bridegroom; dowries sometimes given with the bride. With a wife returning in widowhood to the parental home, the dowry returned also.[1] On the other hand it would appear, from the Lay of the Net, that a fine was imposed upon the detected adulterer,[2] as well as on the manslayer. In some instances, personal and mental gifts serve in lieu of possessions, as recommendations in suing for a wife.

[1] Od. ii. 132. [2] Od. viii. 348.

Lastly, with respect to the employments of women.

It appears to be at least open to question whether they were not capable of political sovereignty.[1] The suggestion of the text seems to be that Chloris was queen in Pulos when Neleus married her; and the mention of Hûpsipulé with Jason is best accounted for by supposing, conformably to tradition, that she reigned in Lemnos.[2] On the departure of Agamemnon Clutaimnestra was left in charge, with the Bard as an adviser;[3] and in Ithaca Penelopê had a similar regency, apparently with the aid of Mentor.[4]

Priesthood appears not to have existed among the Hellenes of the Homeric age; but in Troas, where we find it, a woman was priestess of Athené. This was Theano, the wife of Antenor; and she is said to have been appointed to her office by the Trojans. The seizure of Marpessa, or Alcuoné, by Apollo, may have had reference to some religious ministry at Delphi.

The domestic employments of women are pretty clearly indicated in the descriptions of the Palaces of Kirkè and of Odysseus. The outdoor offices were performed in Ithaca by men, who likewise prepared the firewood, killed, cut up, and carved the animals, and carried to the farm the manure that accumulated about the house. The Suitors also had male personal attendants. The women performed the indoor operations generally, including the fetching of water and the grinding of flour.

Another employment discharged by women has given rise to misunderstanding; namely, their waiting on

[1] Il. vii. 468, 469. Od. xi. 281-285.
[2] Il. vii. 469.   [3] Od. iii. 263-268.
[4] Od. ii. 225-227; xix. 322; xx. 129-133. Il. vi. 297-300.

men for purposes connected with the bath. Damsels of the highest rank performed this duty for strangers. But the delicacy of the early Greeks, with regard to any undue exposure of the person,[1] was extreme; and, though they may have differed from our merely conventional usages, it cannot be imagined that they departed from propriety in a point where a people far less scrupulous would have respected it. The error has lain principally in failure to observe that in the words used for washing, bathing, and anointing, the actual operation is described by the middle voice,[2] and the words louō, chriō, niptō, in the active, in general signify supplying another person with the means of performing these offices for himself.[3] The same rule I believe to hold good with respect to the word which describes dressing after the bath (ballō).

[1] Il. ii. 260-264.
[2] So Wakefield. See Il. x. 572-577; Od. vi. 96, 219, 220, et alibi.
[3] Od. vi. 210, 218, 222; vii. 296. Even Od. x. 361 need not be an exception.

CHAPTER XI.

POLITY OF THE HEROIC AGE.

The Poems of Homer are the seed-plot of what is best and soundest in the Greek politics of the historic period. Nor are we, the moderns, and, as I think, the British in particular, without a special relation to the subject. In part we owe to these ancient societies a debt. In part we may trace with reasonable pleasure an original similitude between the Homeric picture and the best ideas of our European and our British ancestry. What are those ideas? Among the soundest of them we reckon the power of opinion and persuasion as opposed to force; the sense of responsibility in governing men; the hatred, not only of tyranny, but of all unlimited power; the love and the habit of public in preference to secret action; the reconciliation and harmony between the spirit of freedom on the one hand, the spirit of order and reverence on the other; and a practical belief in right as relative, and in duty as reciprocal. Out of these elements, whether in ancient or in modern times, great governments have been made. The Homeric Poems exhibit them all, if not in methodical development, yet in vigorous life.

Even war required a basis of right, perhaps rudely defined; and retribution a *corpus delicti*. Hence the readiness with which the offer of Paris[1] to decide the war by single combat is accepted; and hence it may be that when Agamemnon anticipates the death of Menelaos from his wound, he judges also that, on that event, the army will return home.

Personal reverence for sovereigns is undoubtedly a powerful principle in the governments of the heroic age. There is for them a kind of divinity that doth 'hedge a king.' Odysseus, wishing to arrest the sudden impulse of the army to return, furnishes himself with the famed Sceptre of Agamemnon, as a token of his title to be heard. This principle, which has survived almost every modification of political forms, could not but be lively at a period when probably no great number of generations had passed since the exchange of nomad for settled life. For society, in the nomad stage, has something of the organization of the army; and it is still either in view or in actual experience of the time when the family, forming itself around its head, had not yet grown into the tribe; much less the tribe into the people.

But, while this reverence existed under all social forms, the characteristic difference of the Homeric states is to be found in the qualifications by which on every side it was hindered from passing into excess. The monarch was controlled by the princes or chiefs assembled in the council ($\beta o u \lambda \acute{\eta}$); an institution which the Odyssey mentions in Scheriè, and the Iliad (informally) in Troy; so that we must presume it to have

---

[1] Il. iii. 96–112.

been in the view of the Greeks not a merely local institution, but a prime element of human society. The mass, however, of the free citizens were also called together in the Agorè, or Assembly, to consider any matter of cardinal importance; and appeal was made to their reason in speeches which, for aptitude and force, to this day extort the admiration, and perhaps defy the rivalry, of the moderns.

It is upon a just balance of forces that good government now mainly depends. In the Homeric age, there were no detailed or even defined provisions to secure this balance. Even the name of law (nomos) is unknown, though the name of public right (themis) is familiar and revered. Into the Greek Constitutions, described by Aristotle, a multitude of expedients for that purpose had been introduced by human ingenuity. Yet those constitutions were subject to frequent and most violent changes, usually attended by the absolute ejectment of the defeated party from house and field. And even when not under disturbance they commonly exhibited a strong bias towards excess in one quarter or another. To the Troic period, too, revolutions were not unknown. But the idea of government, which then prevailed, was perhaps both more strongly fortified by religious reverence, and likewise better founded in reciprocal duty, than that of later times. The separation and conflict of interests between the different parts of the community had not become a familiar idea; particular classes did not plot against the whole; we hear little of the tyranny of kings, or the insubordination of subjects. A worse era was about to follow. As in the case of the Crusades, so during the War of Troy, the absence of the rulers prepared the way for social convulsion. And Hesiod, living at a time later probably by some generations, looks back from his iron age with an admiring envy on the heroic period.

'The early monarchies,' says Thucydides, 'enjoyed specified[1] prerogatives;' and Aristotle assures us that they were monarchies[2] upon terms, and depended on a voluntary allegiance. The threefold function of the King among the Hellenes was (a) chiefly perhaps, though not exclusively, to administer justice[3] between man and man; (b) to command the army, and (c) to conduct the rites of religion. Sometimes the sovereignty was local, or subaltern; sometimes, as perhaps in the case of Minos[4] and of Priam, and even of Peleus, but clearly and broadly in that of Agamemnon,[5] it was a suzerainty over other Kings and princes, as well as a direct dominion over territory specially appropriated, and perhaps also over an unclaimed residue of minor settlements and communities. Besides the towns, which supplied Agamemnon with his division of the army, he claimed to dispose of the sovereignty of other towns, which lay in the south-west of the Peloponnesos.[6]

The Homeric Kings, however, constitute in the Iliad a class by themselves. The greater part of the chiefs do not bear the title of Basileus, but had probably that of anax, prince, or lord. Some of these were like Phoinix under Peleus; but most of them in no other subordination than to Agamemnon. The only duty to the suzerain of which we hear is that of military

[1] i. 13. [2] Arist. Pol. iii. 14, 15, ver. 10. [3] Il. ii. 204–206.
[4] Thucydides, l. 4, says that Minos appointed his sons to be local or deputed Governors.
[5] Il. ii. 108, 483; xxiii. 890. [6] Il. ix. 149–153.

service. His superior rank¹ is acknowledged; so that both he, and apparently Menelaos, on account of his relationship, are termed 'more kingly'² than the other Kings. These gradations in the order may perhaps be compared to those of a modern Peerage or Noblesse.

The King, as such, stands in a special relation to deity. The epithet theios, divine, is only applied to such among the living as have this relation. The King is also Diotrephes, or reared by Zeus, and Diogenes, or born of Zeus; and these titles are given rarely below the kingly order even to a prince or ruler, if of inferior degree or eminence. It is expressly declared that Kings derive the right to rule³ from Zeus, from whom descended, by successive deliveries, the sceptre of Agamemnon. In the Greek army the Kings alone seem to constitute the council of the Generalissimo. Scarcely on any occasion does a ruler of the second order appear there. The kings are called Basilées, or Gerontes (elders), or perhaps Koiranoi; but the leaders at large are Archoi, or Hegemones, or (ἀριστῆες) the aristocracy.

In the Catalogue, the command of some of the divisions is held as it were in commission; or, in other words, rests with two or more persons jointly and severally, on a footing of parity between themselves. But wherever there is a King, he either appears alone, in his capacity of General, as Agamemnon, Menelaos, Odysseus, Nestor, Achilles, the greater and the lesser Ajax; or with other leaders who are distinctly under him, as Diomed⁴ and Idomeneus.⁵ These nine persons

---
[1] Il. 1. 186. [2] Il. ix. 160; x. 239.
[3] Il. ii. 101, 205. [4] Il. ii. 563–566.
[5] The Catalogue, Il. ii. 645–652, might leave doubtful the position

are the only undeniable Kings of the Iliad, as may appear from comparing together Il. ii. 404–409, Il. xix. 309–311, and from the transactions of Il. x. 84–197. Particular phrases or passages might raise the question whether four others, Meges, Eurupulos, Patroclos, and Phoinix, were not viewed by Homer as being also Kings. Probably his idea of the class was not so definite as ours; but on the whole the line, which excludes these and all the other chiefs from the kingly rank, is drawn with considerable clearness. The King, as viewed in the Iliad, must be a person combining three conditions: first, he is subordinate to none but Agamemnon; secondly, he has in all cases marked personal vigor and prowess; thirdly, if his dominions are small, he must either be of surpassing strength of body at least, like the Telamonian Ajax, or of vast powers of mind as well as limb, like Odysseus.

Among the bodily qualities of the Kings, one is personal beauty. This attaches peculiarly to the Trojan royal family, and it is recorded even of the aged Priam in his grief.[1] At the head of all stands Achilles. Odysseus has this endowment, though in a less marked degree. Ajax, in the Odyssey, appears to compete with Nireus, in the Iliad, for the second place. It is never predicated individually, I think, of any single man below the princely station, although when the crew of Odysseus were re-transformed at Ainiê into human shape, they are collectively said to have been by far larger and more beautiful than before.[2]

of Meriones; but it is fixed by the terms θεράπων and ὀπάων, applied to him in Il. x. 58, xxiii. 113, et alibi; which, though perhaps more than Squire, means less than Colleague.

[1] Il. xxiv. 631.   [2] Od. x. 396.

Personal vigor is also a condition, not only of assuming, but almost of continuing in, the exercise of sovereignty.[1] Laertes quitted his throne at a time anterior to the departure of Odysseus for the war, long before the period of decrepitude,[2] and probably when his activity had but begun to diminish. Achilles, in the Shades,[3] inquires whether Peleus still occupies the throne, or has retired from it on account of his years. Nestor, indeed, yet occupies the royal seat; but perhaps it is on account of his notable talents, combined with the greenness of his old age. The word αἰζεὸς, which signifies a man in his full strength, when joined with Diotrephes, or royal, is applied to princes as a class, and thus testifies to the custom I have described.[4] Telemachos was the proper heir to his father's throne;[5] but he was only coming to, though close upon, full age, and he had not yet assumed its privileges at the point where the action of the Poem begins.

Over and above the work of battle, the Prince is peerless in the Games. Of the eight contests of the Twenty-third Iliad, seven are conducted entirely by the Kings and chiefs. The exception is the boxing-match. And Epeios, the winner in this match, himself declares[6] that he does not possess the gifts necessary for distinction in battle; an indication by the way, among many, of the immense value set by Homer upon skill as compared with mere strength.[7] The prizes, too, which are given in the boxing-match appear, when compared with the other rewards, to show the reputed inferiority of this accomplishment.

[1] Grote, Hist. Greece, vol. ii. p. 87.   [2] Od. xi. 174, 184.
[3] Od. xi. 495.   [4] Il. ii. 660. Comp. Il. xvi. 716.
[5] Od. i. 386.   [6] Il. xxiii. 670.   [7] Comp. Il. xxiii. 315–318.

So likewise with the gifts of music and song. Usually, of course, we look for them to the Bards. Upon the Shield, in the procession of youths and maidens who bear the grapes from the vineyard, a boy attends them to play and sing, probably because it did not comport with the dignity of the Bard to exercise his art while in bodily motion; for presently we come to another scene, where he plays, without moving, to the dancers.[1] There are but two certain indications of (so to speak) amateur song and playing. The lyre which Achilles used was among the spoils of the city of Eetion, and may possibly have belonged to that King himself.[2] On this lyre Achilles himself played during his retirement. And our other musician is Paris.[3]

But the kingly character in Homer is also all-comprehensive; and it sometimes embraces even the manual employments of honorable industry. Odysseus, in the Island of Calypso,[4] is a wood-cutter and ship-builder: Odysseus on his throne was the carpenter and artisan of his own bed,[5] so elaborately wrought: Odysseus, in disguise, challenges Eurumachos the Suitor to try which of them would soonest mow a meadow,[6] and which drive the straightest furrow down a four-acre field.

Such were the corporal accomplishments of the Homeric King. He was also, in the exercise of higher faculties, Judge, General, and Priest. In addition to all these, and as binding them all together, he was emphatically a gentleman. In Agamemnon, indeed, there is a half-sordid vein, which mars the higher type;

[1] Il. xviii. 509, 604.
[2] Il. ix. 186-188.
[3] Il. iii. 54.
[4] Od. v. 243, 261.
[5] Od. xxiii. 195-201.
[6] Od. xviii. 366-375.

though he corresponds in general to the eulogy of Helen,[1] as a good King and a valiant soldier. Nestor, Diomed, Menelaos, are markedly gentlemen in their demeanor. The character of Odysseus, caricatured and debased by the later tradition, abounds in Homer with similar notes. Quick in the sense of undeserved reproof from his chief, he appeals only to the confutation which his conduct in the field will supply.[2] When grossly insulted by Eurualos, his stern and masterful rebuke is so justly measured as to excite the sympathy of strangers.[3] But the best exhibition of the profound refinement inhering in the character of Odysseus is, perhaps, afforded by the scene in which he first appears before Nausicaa,[4] after his escape from the devouring waters.

It is, however, in Achilles that courtesy reaches to its acme. In the First Iliad, he hails with a genial kindness the heralds who came on the odious errand of enforcing the removal of Briseis, and he at once reassures them by acquitting them of blame;[5] though as we know

> 'The messenger of evil tidings
> Hath but a losing office.'

In the Ninth Book, while still in the Wrath, we find him bidding the envoys of Agamemnon a hearty welcome.[6] In both cases he anticipates the new comers with a speech, of which the promptitude is itself a delicate stroke of the best manners. The most refined, however, of his attentions is perhaps that shown to Agamemnon, after the reconciliation, on the occasion

[1] Il. iii. 179. [2] Il. iv. 349-355. [3] Od. viii. 165, 896.
[4] Od. vi. 115 seqq. [5] Il. i. 334. [6] Il. ix. 187.

of the Games. It was difficult to exclude the chief King from the sport of Kings; inadmissible to let him be worsted; impossible either to make him conquer those who were his superiors in strength, or to place him in competition with secondary persons. Achilles avoids all these difficulties by proposing a ninth, or supernumerary match, with the sling; and then at once presenting the prize to Agamemnon with the observation that, as his excellence is known to be paramount, there need be no actual trial.[1]

Yet these great chiefs, so strong in every form of power, bravery, and skill, can upon occasion weep like a woman or a child. A list of the passages, in which the tears of heroes flow, would probably by its length cause astonishment even to those who are aware that a susceptible temperament prompted them, and that a false shame did not forbid them, thus to give vent to their emotions.[2] Every one of them, unless it be the aged Nestor, would be included: we should find there even Agamemnon, whom we may probably consider as the prince least richly furnished in this department of our nature.

Thus far we have spoken mainly of the persons. The office, which these persons bore, was hereditary, in the line of the eldest son. Yet though the practice prevailed, the definition was, in this and in other cases, not so sharp as ours. Menelaos, the brother of Agamemnon, partakes in a certain limited degree of his dignity: is specially solicited, with him, by the priest Chruses;[3] receives, jointly with him, the presents offered by Euneos[4] for leave to trade with the army;

[1] Il. xxiii. 884-897. [2] Comp. Juv. Sat. xv. 131-132.
[3] Il. i. 16. [4] Il. vii. 470.

and is held more royal than the other chieftains.[1] Probably when Thuestes succeeded Atreus, it was on account of the childhood of Agamemnon, which prevented his fulfilling the conditions of strength and vigor necessary for holding the monarchy.

The case of Telemachos supplies us with an express declaration of the title of the son to succeed his father.[2] But Antinoos the Suitor, at a time when Odysseus was supposed to be dead, states his hope that Zeus will never make the youth king of Ithaca. The answer is far from claiming that unconditional right to the throne of the islands, which it asserts to the estates of Odysseus;[3] and leaves room for the supposition, that the succession was liable to be more or less affected by personal qualifications, and by the assent or dissent of the nobles, or even of the community. Even at this time, however, Telemachos assumed in the Assembly the seat of his father.

Telemachos, indeed, is an only son. But, in the case of the Pelopids, Agamemnon appears to succeed to the paternal throne, and Menelaos to govern Sparta in right of his wife. Of the two brothers, Protesilaos and Podarkes, in the Catalogue, the former, who is the elder, commands the force from Phulakè and its sister towns.[4] He was, however, we are expressly told, braver, as well as older. The position of Antilochos in the Iliad as the elder son of Nestor, and of Thrasumedes, after his death, in the Odyssey, appear to be sufficiently marked.[5] In four cases of the Catalogue, pairs of brothers are named as in command, without any distinction formally drawn between them.

[1] Il. x. 32 and 239. [2] Od. i. 387. [3] Od. i. 396.
[4] Il. ii. 695-708. [5] Od. iii. 412, 439-446.

The Olympian arrangements bear, perhaps, the most emphatic testimony to the higher dignity and authority of the elder brother. For it is only in that capacity, that the superiority of Zeus is confessed by his juniors.[1] They are not, however, excluded from inheritance; and the respective provinces are taken by lot.

On the whole, we seem to have the custom or law of primogeniture sufficiently, but not over-sharply, defined.

The Homeric King, decked out with attributes almost ideal, appears before us, so far as Greece is concerned, in not a threefold only, but a fourfold, character; besides being Priest, Judge, and General, he is also, as King, a great Proprietor.

Priesthood is a function touching the daily course of life. Besides the solemn and public sacrifices, the meat of each meal is an offering; the word 'to sacrifice,' hiereuein is used as meaning 'to kill;' the animal ready to be killed is hiereion, a sacrifice. Yet there appears to be no professional priest among the Hellenes. We hear of many priests in the Poems: but of none of them can we positively assert that they were Greek. The priest is referred to, together with the prophet and dream-teller, in the first Assembly of the Iliad: but the Greeks are there[2] in a land of priests; and as Achilles plainly points to the prophet Calchas, who immediately afterwards rises to speak, so it is probable that he may point to the priest Chryses, who had already visited the camp. Among the chief professions of a Greek community, enumerated in the Odyssey,[3] the priest does not appear. Though priests are wanting, prophets are not;

[1] Il. xv. 204-207. Od. xlii. 142.
[2] Il. l. 62. [3] Od. xvii. 883-885.

POLITY OF THE HEROIC AGE.

and in this important passage, the class of prophets is the first named. One passage only speaks of priests within the local limits of Greece:[1] it refers to a generation before the War; and it is quite possible that, both then and subsequently, there may have been priests in Greece of Pelasgian institution. Wherever there was a τεμενος, or glebe, probably there was a priest to live upon the proceeds. But the only sacred glebes of which we hear in Greece are (I think) the glebes of Sperchcios and of Demeter,[2] both of them old Pelasgian deities.

In conformity with this view, we find that among the Hellenes, in the public and solemn sacrifices, the priestly office is performed by the King. Moreover, the assistants are termed νέοι,[3] young men. This supports a conjecture suggested to me by the resemblance of the words, that hieros and gerōn have been originally identical in root. In Greece down to the present day the monk is called calo-gero (the French *caloyer*). It was to the Father, as such, that in the origin of society the offices both of King and Priest generally accrued. To the Father, in the time of Homer, the ordinary consecration or offering of the meal appertains, as he presides at the domestic board.

The office of the Judge seems to be, more than any other, proper to the King. It probably constituted his only official employment which was at once permanent (that of war being occasional), and of a nature[4] to weigh upon the mind. But it should be understood as including all deliberative work. On the Shield,[5] the trial of a cause is conducted by the Elders; perhaps

---

[1] Il. ix. 575.
[2] Il. xxiii. 148; Il. 696.
[3] Il. i. 463. Od. iii. 460.
[4] Il. i. 238; Il. 204; ix. 98; xvi. 386.
[5] Il. xviii. 506

in the character of delegates. Causes must have been
conducted by natural equity, or by what in Ireland was
called Brehon, that is judge-made, law. Probably
custom had already established some rules with respect
to fines for homicide and adultery, if not for other
offences.

The duty of the King as General is best exhibited
by the whole plan of the Iliad. Here the King, if in
full vigor, assumes the captain's office as a matter of
course, and quits his house and throne to discharge it.
Peleus,[1] the father of Achilles, remains at home, because
he is disabled by old age. Nestor, retaining more of his
bodily vigor, goes to war, but acts in the camp chiefly as
a counsellor, and at no time actually handles arms.

Never has the idea of regal duty and responsibility,
both in general, and with respect to war in particular,
been more nobly set forth than in the speech of Sarpedon to Glaucos,[2] in the Twelfth Iliad; before the high-
souled speaker proceeded to execute what was, on the
Trojan side, by far the greatest exploit of the War.

Lastly. In consideration of the duties and burdens
of his office, the King was a great Proprietor. A
domain[3] (temenos) was set apart for him out of
the common stock of territory (from temnein, to
cut, to carve out). The class had apparently two other
sources of revenue. They received presents from
merchants, for leave to trade; of which we find an
example also in the Book of Genesis.[4] The practice
of offering such gifts is probably to be regarded as the

---

[1] Il. xxiv. 487. Od. xi. 497. [2] Il. xii. 310–328.
[3] Il. xii. 313; vi. 194; ix. 578; xx. 184. Od. vi. 293; xi. 185; xvii. 299.
[4] xliii. 11. Il. vii. 467–475. Od. vii. 8–11.

germ of Customs-duties, or taxes on the import and export of goods. The other was from fees on the administration of justice.[1] Of these, we have the earliest rudiment represented on the Shield; where lay two talents of gold, to be awarded to the judge whose sentence in the cause should be most approved.[2] In time of war, too, Agamemnon was charged with appropriating a very large share of the prizes to himself.[3]

But the King was expected to be liberal in his official entertainments, so to call them, to his chiefs and nobles, over and above the general duty of hospitality.[4] This, probably, was the excuse of the Suitors for devouring the substance of Odysseus. It appears, at any rate, that friends of the royal house frequented the table at the palace, as well as its enemies, though perhaps not so constantly.[5]

The King might also obtain private property. Laertes lived, in his old age, on an estate thus acquired.[6] And, in the First Odyssey, we find a distinction between the house of Odysseus with the lands about it, to which Telemachos was to succeed as of right, and the kingly dignity with whatever might attach to it.[7]

Such was the position of the King. Agamemnon, however, was a King of Kings: more or less resembling what we now call a Suzerain, or the highest feudal superior of the middle age. Thucydides is of opinion that the fear of him[8] had more to do than good will, or than the oath of Tundareus, in the formation of the

[1] Il. ix. 155. [2] Il. xviii. 508. [3] Il. ix. 333.
[4] Il. ix. 70. Od. vii. 49, 98. [5] Od. xvii. 68.
[6] Od. xxiv. 206. [7] Od. i. 397, 402. [8] i. 9.

confederacy which undertook the war of Troy. National sentiment, and the hope of booty, might also contribute powerfully to this extraordinary effort. We have, however, no means of tracing in the Poems any interference of the Suzerain, beyond his own proper dominions, in the ordinary government of the country; or any duty owed to him, except in war.

The general reverence for rank and station, the safeguard of publicity, and the influence of persuasion, are the usual and sufficient instruments for governing the army, even as they governed the civil societies, of Greece. The few words quoted by Aristotle[1] from some text of the Iliad which was current in his day and place, signifying that Agamemnon had a right of life and death, cannot reasonably, without a context, be made to convey a theory of military discipline out of harmony with the tone and analogies of the poem, and belonging to the definite ideas of the present rather than to the free life of the older time. Moreover, as these words (πὰρ γὰρ ἐμοὶ θάνατος;) afterwards disappeared from the text of the Poem, the most natural inference seems to be that they were not finally approved as genuine.

It is in the Assemblies, that the great transactions of the army are decided. There, arises the quarrel with Achilles; there, the tumultuary impulse homewards; there, that impulse having been checked, it is deliberately resolved to see what can be done by the strong hand against Troy. There it is settled to ask a truce for burials, and to erect the rampart. There the second proposition of Agamemnon to return to Greece is made, and is summarily overruled.[2] There the

---

[1] Aristot. Pol. iii. 14, 15. [2] Il. ix. 26-28, 50.

Council is appointed to sit, which despatches the abortive mission to Achilles. There Agamemnon confesses and laments his fault, and the reconciliation with the great chief is sealed. There, finally, arises the dissension of the two sons of Atreus, after the fall of Troy.[1]

The ranks traceable in the army are:
1. The Kings: Basileis or Koiranoi.
2. The Leaders under the rank of King.
3. The officers of minor command.

Both these last come under the name of hegemones. The ships had each her kubernētēs or pilot, who probably commanded as well as steered: and there were a number of tamiai, or stewards, whom we may regard as the commissariat of that day.[2]

The privates of the army are called by the names of laos, the people; demos, the community; and plethūs, the multitude. But no notice is taken, throughout the Poem, of the exploits of any soldier below the rank of a high officer. Still, all attend the Assemblies. On the whole, the Greek host is not so much an army, as a community in arms.

On the nature of the arms employed by the bulk of the force, it is not easy to pronounce with confidence. There were heavy-armed, who fought with spear, sword, axe, and stone; javelin-men, who used a lighter dart; archers; and hippeis, those who fought from the chariot. Though the art of riding, in our sense of it, was known, it was not used in battle. One passage appears to speak of the Trojans as attacking with javelins and arrows, and of the Greeks as resist-

[1] Od. iii. 139.   [2] Il. xix. 42–45.

ing with the weapons proper to the heavy-armed;[1] another distinctly describes the first in the same manner:[2] and on the whole I judge that the Greek soldiery, with its solid march, were combatants, in the main, using weapons of weight; the Trojans somewhat less so. Only the Trojans distinguish themselves as archers, in the persons of Pandaros and Paris: but there were bowmen in the Greek army also.[3]

Two modes of fighting were in use: the open battle of main force, without strategy or tactics, and liable to panic. The other was the lochos, or ambuscade. As a severer trial of nerve and moral fortitude, this latter was held in higher estimation, and was reserved to the chiefs.[4] We must not say that Achilles would have been inferior to any man in any act of martial skill or daring: but in the Poems, as they stand, Odysseus has been chosen as the prince of ambush.[5]

The Council was composed of chief persons, who bore the name of gerontes,[6] or elders: a name which was probably in its origin personal, and had by degrees become, like that of Senator in later times, official. In the Council of the Army, Nestor is old, Idomeneus near upon old age: Odysseus might be called elderly, though still in the perfection of strength.[7]

In the Second Book, the Boulé or Council is summoned by Agamemnon, to prepare for the Assembly.[8] The same persons meet before the solemn sacrifice,[9] without being called a Council. They meet again, as a

---

[1] Il. xv. 707-712.
[2] Il. ii. 720; iii. 79.
[3] Od. xviii. 261-264.
[4] Il. xviii. 509-520; xiii. 276-286; l. 227.
[5] Od. iv. 277-288.
[6] Il. ii. 53.
[7] Il. xxiii. 791.
[8] Il. ii. 53.
[9] Il. ii. 404-409.

Council, by appointment of the Assembly, in the Ninth Book;[1] and send the Envoys to supplicate Achilles. In the Seventh Book, this body plans the truce and the rampart.[2] It is spoken of as an institution evidently familiar.[3] The disorganized society of Ithaca does not afford scope for a regular Council; but a place is set apart for the elders in the Agorè,[4] and Odysseus in his youth had been sent on a mission by Laertes and his Council.[5] In Scherié, Nausicaa meets her father[6] on his way to the Boulé. The members of the Army-council contend freely in argument with Agamemnon; and Nestor takes the lead in that body, and observes to Agamemnon that it is his duty to listen as well as to speak, and to adopt the plans of others when they are good.[7] This institution was one utterly at variance with anything like absolutism in the command.

In the Homeric ideas upon Polity, perhaps the most remarkable of all is the distinction accorded to the power of speech. The voice and the sword are the twin powers, by which the Greek world is governed; and there is no precedency of rank between them. The power of public speech is essentially a power over large numbers; and, wherever it prevails, it is the surest test of the presence of the spirit and practice of freedom. The world has repeatedly seen absolutism deck itself with the titles and mere forms of liberty, or seek shelter under its naked abstractions; but from the use of free speech as the instrument of governing the people, it has always shrunk with an instinctive horror. The epithets and incidental passages with

[1] Il. ix. 10, 89. [2] Il. vii. 344, 382. [3] Od. iii. 127.
[4] Od. ii. 14.   [5] Od. xxi. 21.   [6] Od. vi. 53-55.
[7] Il. ix. 100-102.

which Homer honors it, show much of his mind.[1] But the most emphatic testimony to its importance, and to the state of things which it betokens, is the free, signal, and varied excellence of the Homeric Speeches.

In the case of speakers, Homer is less chary of description than his wont: and he has exhibited to us in action too a great variety of manners. There is Thersites, glib, vain, and saucy.[2] There is Telemachos, full of the gracious diffidence of youth, but commended by Nestor for a power and a tact of expression beyond his years.[3] Menelaos harangues with a laconic case.[4] We have the Trojan elders, whose volubility, and their shrill thread of voice, Homer compares to the chirp of grasshoppers.[5] Nestor's tones of happy and benevolent egotism flow sweeter than a stream of honey.[6] Phoinix would, in unskilful hands, have been a pale reflex of Nestor's garrulity without his sagacity; but his speaking is redeemed by his profound and absorbing affection for Achilles, which gives him as it were a different centre of gravity. Far above all these soars Odysseus, who when he first rises, with all his energies concentrated within him, seems to give no promise of display; but when his deep voice issues from his chest, and his words drive like the flakes of winter snow, then, says the Poet, for mortal to compete with him is hopeless.[7]

But yet there is another speaker who, when he rises to his noblest, seems as though he were scarcely mortal. Homer leaves the eloquence of Achilles to stand self-

---

[1] Il. i. 490; ix. 438–443. Od. xi. 510–516; ii. 150; viii. 170–173.
[2] Il. ii. 212.   [3] Od. iii. 23, 124.   [4] Il. iii. 213.
[5] Il. iii. 150.   [6] Il. i. 249.   [7] Il. iii. 216–223.

described. That chief modestly pronounces himself to be below Odysseus in the use of oratory. It seems to me that his speeches may challenge comparison with all that we find in Homer; and with all that the ebb and flow of three thousand years have added to our records of true human eloquence. Even here, Homer's resources are not exhausted. The decision of Diomed, the irresolution of Agamemnon, the bluntness of Ajax, are all admirably marked in the series of speeches allotted to each respectively. Scarcely anywhere is mediocrity to be found; and perhaps the greatest example on record of a perfectly simple nobleness is to be found in the speech of Sarpedon to Glaucos on the duties of kings.[1]

With respect to the power of speech, and the capacity of being moved by it, the performances of the Poet are truly the best picture of the age itself. Unlike great poems, great speeches cannot be made, except in an age and place where they are understood and felt. The work of the orator is cast in the mould offered him by the mind of his hearers. He cannot follow nor frame ideals at his own will; his choice is to be what his time will have him, what it requires in order to be moved by him, or not to be at all.

If the power of oratory proper is remarkable in Homer, so likewise, and perhaps yet more, is the faculty of what in England is called 'debate.' In Homer's discussions, every speech after the first is commonly a reply. It belongs not only to the subject, but to the speech that went before; it exhibits, given the question and the aims of the speaker, the exact degree of as-

[1] Il. xii. 310–328.

cent and descent, of expansion or contraction, which
the circumstances of the case, in the state up to which
they were brought by the preceding address, may
require. The debate in the Assembly of the First
Book, and that in the Encampment of Achilles,[1]
are, as oratorical structures, complete and consummate.

A people cannot act in its corporate capacity without
intermission; and the King is the standing representative of the community. But though he be the pivot of
its functional and administrative activity, the Agorè,
or Assembly, is the centre of its life and vital motion.
The greatest ultimate power possessed by the King is
that of exercising an influence upon his subjects, there
gathered into one focus, through the combined medium
of their reverence for his person, and of his powers of
persuasion. There is no decision by numbers; the
doctrine of majorities is an invention, an expedient, of
a more advanced social development. In Olympos, a
minority of influential gods carry the day against the
majority, and against their head, in the great matter
of the Trojan war.

The interference of Thersites in the Debate of the
Second Iliad, and his attempt to bring the Assembly
back to the impulse of returning home, were followed
by sharp corporal chastisement, and by the menace of
the last degree of personal disgrace. But the very
attempt to interfere by suggesting such audacious proposals, and those from a person so contemptible, may
perhaps be taken as an indication that freedom of
debate generally prevailed.

Il. ix. 225–655.

In one of the scenes represented on the Shield of Achilles, new evidence is afforded us, that the people took a real part in the conduct of affairs. An Assembly is sitting. A criminal suit is in progress. The parties plead on either side, and challenge a decision; and the people, taking part some one way and some the other, encourage them by cheering. The heralds keep order, and stay the interruptions when the time arrives for the judges to speak.[1] This applause of itself asserts the recognized interest and participation of the people; for it contributes both to the decision, and to the spirit and efficacy of the means of persuasion, by which that decision is to be influenced. Not only so; but it seems to have been by popular vote that the two talents were to be awarded, which lay on the floor, and were to be given to the Elder who might pronounce the soundest judgment.[2] Finally, in the Assembly of the Seventh Iliad, Idaios arrives from Troy with an offer to restore the stolen property, but not Helen herself. Diomed repudiates it, and his opinion is echoed back in the cheers of the army. Agamemnon then addresses himself to the herald, 'Idaios, you hear the sense of the Achaians, how they answer you; and I think with them.' Thus the acclamation was also the vote.[3]

That which we do not find in Homer is the submission of the minority to the majority in any public or deliberative meeting. This without doubt is an expedient of much later date. But where difference of opinion prevails, the Assembly breaks into opposing factions. So it was in the drunken Assembly men-

[1] Il. xviii. 502. Cf. ii. 211. [2] Il. xviii. 508. [3] Il. vii. 381.

tioned in the Odyssey;[1] and the minority which then
set sail was afterwards again divided.[2] In like manner,
of the Ithacan Assembly in the Twenty-fourth Odyssey,
the majority determined on neutrality, but the minority
took arms. And, throughout the Voyages, we see how
freely the crews of Odysseus both spoke and acted,
when they thought fit, in opposition to his views.
These illustrations might be yet further extended.

The truth is, that everywhere among the Greeks of
Homer we find the signs of an intense corporate or
public life, subsisting, and working side by side, with
that of the individual. Of this corporate life, the
Agorè is the proper organ. If a man is to be described
as great, he is always great, in debate and on the field:
if as insignificant, then he is of no account either in
battle or in council. The two grand forms of common
and public action are taken for the tests of the individual man.

When Homer wishes to describe the Kuklopes as
living in a state of barbarism, he says, not that they
have no kings, or no towns, or no army, but that they
have no Assemblies, and no administration of justice.[3]
The source of life lay in the community, and the community met in the Agorè. So deeply imbedded is this
sentiment in the mind of the Poet, that it seems as if
he could not conceive an assemblage of persons having
any kind of common function, without their having, so
to speak, a common soul too in respect of it.

Of this common soul, the organ, in Homer, is the
Tis or 'Somebody:' by no means one of the least
remarkable, though he has been perhaps the least re-

[1] Od. iii. 189.   [2] Od. iii. 162.   [3] Od. ix. 112.

garded, among the personages of the Poems. The Tis of Homer seems to be what in England we now call Public Opinion: the immediate impression created in the general mind by public affairs, or by the conduct of the chiefs. We constantly come upon occasions, when the Poet has to tell us what was the prevailing sentiment of the Greek army. He might have done this didactically, or by way of narrative. He has adopted a method more poetical and less obtrusive. He proceeds dramatically, through the medium of a person and of a formula, 'Hereupon, thus spoke somebody:'

ὧδε δέ τις εἴπεσκεν.

This would be sufficiently noteworthy if we found it only among the Greeks in war, and again in peace: for, when Odysseus causes music and dancing in his palace, with a view to producing an impression on the people of the town of Ithaca, it is Tis who tells what it was.[1] But it is not only in a normal state of things among his own people, that Tis is found. When Greeks and Trojans meet for the purpose of the Pact, there is a Tis for the Trojans also.[2] The Suitors, again, are a body of dissolute and selfish youths, and are competitors with each other for a prize which but one among them can enjoy. Yet in some sense they are bound together by a common interest of iniquity; and, although we are introduced to many of them individually by their speeches, yet they too have a Tis[3] who expresses their general sentiment on occurrences as they pass. Too broad to be confined to Greece, this

[1] Od. xxiii. 148–152. [2] Il. iii. 319. [3] Od. ii. 324.

conception is not even restricted to mankind: and Tis appears in Olympos, expressing the common or average sentiment of the assembled gods.[1]

This remarkable and characteristic creation remains, I believe, the exclusive property of Homer. But perhaps we may discern in the Homeric Tis the primary ancestor of the famous Greek Chorus. Like Tis, the Greek Chorus is severed from all mere individuality, and expresses the generalized sentiment of the body or people to which it belongs, in the highest and best sense which their prevailing standard will allow.

Except in the mouth of the scoundrel Thersites, nothing like political discontent appears in any part of the Poems of Homer. The popular sentiment adverse to Odysseus on his return to Ithaca is probably a personal resentment, not only for the death of the Suitors, but for all the crews of his good ships lost in the War and on the Voyage. There is no invidious distinction between class and class, nor any of the social feuds which might be its result. No recognized portion of the community is imagined to require repression or restraint from the government. The King, or Chief, is uplifted to set a high example, to lead the common councils to common ends, to conduct the public and common intercourse with heaven, to decide the strifes of private persons, which might bring danger to the common weal, and to defend the borders of the common territory from invasion.

For the chief component parts of Greek society, we have first the King and his family. Round him are his Korukes, serjeants or heralds, his only executive

[1] Od. viii. 823.

government: his Bard, ever giving delight and receiving respect: his Seniors, who assist in council, and in judgment: his Nobles, the only wealthy of the period. From them the Prince or King seems to be in general pretty broadly distinguished; for the rule is that the legitimate son, the heir-apparent, contracts marriage beyond his own borders. But Megapenthes, the serf-born son of Menelaos, marries in Sparta itself.[1]

Under the name of demioergoi,[2] which includes both the professional men and the skilled laborers of the community, Homer includes the prophet, the physician or wound-healer, the carpenter or wright, and the Bard.[3] The fact that the worker in metals is not included, tends to show, in accordance with all the other evidence of the Homeric text, that this kind of labor had not attained to any great degree of development in Greece.

That the pursuits of manual labor were not below the notice even of princes, we find from the case not only of Odysseus, but of Paris,[4] who joined in the building of his own palace; and of Lucaon, who was cutting young wood for his chariot, when, for the first time, he fell into the hands of Achilles.[5] Bards, heralds, and seers, are all persons of general influence and importance.[6] We hear of merchants only within the Phœnician circle: as Mentes of the Taphians, and again from the mouth of Eurualos in Scherié.[7] We have also

---

[1] Od. iv. 5, 10, 797; xl. 65; *et alibi*.   [2] Od. xvii. 383.
[3] In another place he adds the herald, Od. xix. 135.
[4] Il. vi. 314.   [5] Il. xxi. 35.
[6] Od. iii. 267; xvii. 263; xxiv. 439.   [7] Od. i. 183; viii. 161.

in Scherié αἰσυμνεται, or masters of the ceremonies, who make the arrangements needful for the dance.[1]

There are inferior professions of partially skilled hand-laborers; among whom it is interesting to notice the drain-digger; the fisherman, named only in Ithaca;[2] the charioteer, and the woodman, for both of whom, says the Poet, as well as for the pilot, skill avails far more than force.[3]

But the persons named in connection with special employments are rather classes, distinguished from the general body of the community, than the parts which make up the aggregate. They seem all to be picked men. Considering on the one hand the position of the masses in the Assemblies, and the appeals there made to them, on the other, the absence, in both the Poems, of anything like an extended personal following attached to the kings or chiefs, I come slowly to the conclusion, as most agreeable to the evidence, which is far from demonstrative, that the bulk of the community were probably small or peasant proprietors, tilling their own lands. The mode of their equipment as heavy, not light, armed soldiers, tends to sustain this conclusion. Even the sons of the slave Dolios appear to put on the ordinary armor.[4] We have then probably before us, in the composition of early Greek society, that mixture and gradation of fortunes, which so much contribute to the unity and strength of a community: the eminent men leading because they were the best, and the mass content to follow them for the same good reason.

The representation of the state of society and of

[1] Od. viii. 258.
[2] Il. xxiii. 315–318.
[3] Od. xxiv. 419.
[4] Od. xxiv. 496.

opinion in Ithaca, contained in the Odyssey, is extremely curious. The term *Βασιλεύς*, so carefully limited in the Iliad, is here extended to the chief nobles; as it is in Scherié to the twelve principal persons who were counsellors of Alkinoos: and, along with it the epithet *διοτρεφής* undergoes a similar enlargement. Since Homer drew from hearsay his materials for treating of Scherié, we cannot reason confidently upon its institutions in their minute detail. But, when he speaks of Greek society, the case is different. And, in effect, what the Poet shows us in the dominions of Odysseus is a great political change, brought about by the absence, through a prolonged period, of a powerful influence much more personal than traditional. Kingship subsisted at that period in virtue of the strong mind and strong hand of the King. Only the αἰζῆος, the man within the flower of his manhood, was equal to it. Laertes from his age, Telemachos from his youth, Penelope as a woman, and thus open to the access of suitors, were unequal to the charge. In the absence, then, of the true King, each minor personage of the order of nobles apparently set up as king. Moreover local attachment prevailed over central influences; and the people, at least of the town, were with the opponents of Odysseus. Except on his own estate, the influence of his family, after a course of years, was gone. Telemachos can only say that by no means are the whole of the damos[1] or people averse to him. The Suitors, shut within the palace for the terrible assault of Odysseus, feel that, if they could but get out into the town, so as to give the alarm, they should be safe.

---

[1] Od. xvi. 114.

After the fact, Odysseus proposes by a stratagem to arrest any rumor of the slaughter.[1] On finding Laertes, he declares, 'we have no time to lose.'[2] He had quitted the town at once, evidently as having no hope there. A civil war is the sequel to the return of the legitimate Sovereign, who has only to rely, after the favor of the gods and his own powerful mind, upon a mere handful of dependants. Odysseus calls the Suitors, whom he had destroyed, the stay or strength[3] of the community; and the Shade of Agamemnon recognizes them as the flower of men.[4] Doubtless their party was strengthened by their King's having lost all his comrades, and by the biting appeal[5] they were thus enabled to make to the relatives of the dead. His sources of aid seem to have lain in Pulos and in Elis.[6] Of the Ithacan Assembly, near half[7] went to take arms against Odysseus; while the others stood neuter. The great Chief had on the moment but twelve men in all to resist them: three of his family, nine serfs.

A flood of light is thrown, from this picture in miniature, upon the structure of society, and the nature of political power among the Hellenes of the heroic, or the immediately post-heroic, age.

Laws can hardly exist without writing; and, in the age of Homer, writing, or what stood in its place, was at most no more than the secret of a few families of Phœnician extraction. It was certainly unavailable for any purpose of general interest. A Greek word for 'law' is not to be found in Homer. With him, νομός means a tract of pasture.[8] We find however (a) δίκη

---

[1] Od. xxiii. 137-140.   [2] Od. xxiv. 324.   [3] Od. xxiii. 121.
[4] Od. xxiv. 106-108; cf. 429.   [5] Od. xxiv. 428.
[6] Od. xxiv. 430, 436.   [7] Od. xxiv. 463.   [8] Od. ix. 217.

and δίκαι, (b) θέμιστες. The latter appear to be the principles of right; the former, those principles of right put into action by judicial proceedings, when they have become matter of contention; the two[1] are clearly enough to be distinguished.

In the absence of law, strictly so called, the Oath was of peculiar importance. It was so solemn, that the only special offence, expressly marked out for punishment in the other world, is the offence of perjury.[2] And it was so effectual, as not only to bind man to man, but deity to deity.[3] The river Styx was the great Oath of the gods,[4] evidently implying their liability, not indeed to death, but to deposition; and the possibility that they might exchange bright Olympos, as the older dynasties of Nature-Powers had exchanged it, for the dreary Underworld. The Trojans break faith and oath in the Fourth Iliad: the Greeks never. Yet Autolucos, the father of Penelope, had received from Hermes[5] the gifts of pilfering and perjury; and thus moral corruption had begun to distil from depraved belief.

The xeinos or xenos, in the largest sense, comprehends and brings together three very different classes.

1. The itinerating beggar,[6] ptochos pandemios, who, in days when money did not exist as a circulating medium, sought relief in the form of hospitality, relief in kind; and in some sense paid for it by carrying news.[7]

2. The Suppliant (hiketēs), who may be of station high or low, but who appears with a suit for shelter,

[1] Od. ix. 215.
[2] Il. xiv. 278; xv. 36–40.
[3] Od. xix. 390.
[4] Od. xviii. 1.
[5] Il. iii. 279.
[6] Il. xv. 37.
[7] Od. xviii. 7.

subsistence, or other aid, under the pressure of some peculiar necessity or calamity.

3. The xeinos proper; the guest, whose need arises simply out of the fact that, being away from home, he has not his resources at hand, and therefore seeks to have them supplied in the home of another.

Slavery is not a prominent feature of Greek society in the Homeric age. It would appear to have been nearly or perhaps wholly confined to the establishments, in-door and out-door, of the chiefs. The language of Achilles in the Underworld, 'rather would I serve for hire even with a poor employer,' seems to imply that hire was the ordinary basis of service. If Odysseus had had very numerous slaves, without doubt he and Telemachos would have been represented in the Odyssey as having raised and armed them against the party of the Suitors; which they did with the mere handful at their command. The slaves appear to have been few, in comparison with the number of the community. The demos or free people, who constituted the Assemblies, seem also to have composed the mass of the population of cultivators.

The two sources named for supplying slaves are
1. War;
2. Kidnapping.

In all cases this kidnapping is of single individuals. We hear of it as practised by the Phœnicians, the Taphians (a branch of the Phœnicians), and the Thesprotians. Not by the Greeks; though Melanthios, the goatherd in the Odyssey, without doubt a serf, as he was the son of a serf,[1] among his other insolences, threatens to carry away Eumaios, and sell him.[2]

[1] Od. xvii. 212; iv. 736.   [2] Od. xvii. 249.

We do not hear of any physical want or suffering in connection with the condition of slaves; nor ought we to interpret too rigidly the prophecy of Hector concerning Andromache, as proving that they were treated with rudeness.[1] But Homer saw both the enfeebling and the depressing effect, the moral blight, of even a mild slavery, and has recorded it in golden words. With Homer, a slave is but one half of a man.[2]

Slaves, from the circumstances of the case, were often of birth and manners not unequal to those of their masters. Eumaios was the son of the ruler of his country; and was brought up together with Ctimene, the daughter of Laertes.[3]

The slavery of Homer's time is a mitigated slavery. It nowhere appears in association with wanton cruelty or oppression. The slave may be familiar with his master: Odysseus, on the Return, is kissed by his slaves. The slave may acquire property, may be the master of other slaves, as Eumaios was of Mesaulios;[4] finally, he is trusted with arms. A good master is expected to supply his slave with a wife.

The absence of the chiefs and army from Greece for a lengthened period, without any danger arising from this source, of itself appears to prove, that slaves must have constituted an element numerically insignificant in that country. Another reason for this belief is to be found in the fact, that no distinction appears to have been drawn, as in after times, of a nature to make laborious manual employments dishonorable. As it was part of the prized accomplishments of a King like

---

[1] Il. vi. 454–463. Comp. Il. xxii. 484–507; where not slavery, but orphanhood, is supposed.   [2] Od. xvii. 323.
[3] Od. xv. 413, 363.   [4] Od. xiv. 449.

Odysseus to be able to drive the plough, we may be almost sure that field-labor could not have been, either universally or generally, intrusted to the hands of slaves.

The general picture presented to us is, that of free self-governing agricultural societies under mild aristocratic rule, the mass living in a self-sufficing independence; and only a comparative handful, it is probable, dependent in any degree, however small, on the assistance of slaves for the management of their households and estates. At the same time, as between the serf and the thēs or laborer for hire, it is material to remember that, in the Homeric period, wages could only be paid in kind, as there was no currency available. This being so, the hired freeman, if without other resource, might perhaps, as to material comforts, be in no better position than the bondman.

We have no trace of slavery in the Greek army, nor of any large or numerous class of slaves anywhere. The probable inference again, is, that slaves constituted but a limited proportion of the community.

It is possible that gold and silver may to a very trifling extent have been used as a common measure of commodities, or medium of exchange. For gold is frequently mentioned as a constituent part of stored wealth; and we can hardly suppose that it was so stored simply for use in the manufacture of commodities for the owners by gilt plating or otherwise. But, on the other hand, other commodities are not valued in gold or in silver. Only the payment of the Judge's fee, or prize, in gold, on the Shield of Achilles, approaches to a case of the use of gold money. It is like the semata or signs on the tablets of Proitos, the germ of a practice rather than the practice itself.

The arms of Glaucos and of Diomed, the tripod which is the first prize for wrestlers in the Games, and the skilled captive woman who was the second, are all valued or priced in oxen;[1] and the ox is the commodity which represents in Homer what we now term the measure of value, as far as it can be said to be represented at all. The captive Lucaon fetches for Achilles the value of a hundred oxen:[2] Eurucleia is sold to Laertes for the value of twenty.[3] The Suitors promise to Odysseus the value of a hundred oxen each, as ransom.[4] The most detailed account in the Poems of a commercial transaction is in the Seventh Iliad, where Euneos gives wine in exchange for slaves, hides, copper, iron, and oxen. The four first-named commodities he might well carry away from a camp for sale elsewhere. As to slaves, for example, the skilled woman of the Iliad is worth only four oxen: Eurucleia in Ithaca worth twenty. They represent respectively the prices of an exporting market with a glut, and of a market of import with a demand from over sea scantily supplied. The oxen which Euneos took, he possibly took from those who were overstocked, and sold again on the spot to such as chanced to want them.[5]

Thus we can understand why Æschylus represents the ox as the earliest sign impressed on money.[6]

Among the leading political ideas exhibited in the Homeric Poems will be found the following:—

Authority to rule is derived from heaven, and the

[1] Il. xxiii. 702–705.   [2] Il. xxi. 79.   [3] Od. I. 431.
[4] Od. xxii. 57–59.   [5] Il. vii. 467–475.   [6] Agam. 37.

abuse of this authority, the corruption and the crimes of rulers, are marked by divine judgments on a land.

Equality is not dreamt of; but liberty is highly prized.

A strong sense of responsibility weighs upon the mind of any ruler not utterly corrupt.

The possessions and honors of kings are not unconditional, but are held by them in trust for the performance of public duties; among these, in order that they may set an example to the people in time of danger.

The gravest matters affecting the public interest are debated and decided in the Assemblies of the people.

Discussion is conducted in general by persons enjoying weight from their age, station, birth, or ability; in a word, by the class possessed of leisure and social influence; but the deliberation and assent of the Assemblies are free.

A public opinion readily forms and freely circulates among the people, approving or condemning the acts of those in authority.

Publicity attends all judicial and deliberative proceedings; but a council of chiefs often privately prepares matter for the Assembly.

The will of the Assembly takes effect in the Act of the Executive.[1]

Speech is the great accomplishment of man; and is the main instrument of government in peace, as the sword is in war. These two powers, representing moral and martial force respectively, stand in a position of honor peculiar to themselves.

[1] Od. iii. 99.

These political ideas are traceable in the Olympian, as well as in the human, society; but their application and development are less satisfactory in that upper region.

The bond that held Greek society together in the Homeric time, and that secured the basis on which it was to be organized and developed, was fivefold; and the strands of this well-knit rope are represented respectively by single words.

1. Θεός, the Deity, and the worship of Immortal and unseen Beings in all its various forms.
2. Θέμις, the principle of social right and duty, chiefly as between neighbors and fellow-citizens.
3. Ὅρκος, the ultimate sanction of good faith.
4. Ξεῖνος, representing the basis of kindly and friendly relation, and of good offices among men, beyond the limits of polity and of class.
5. Γάμος, the great institution of marriage, determining the relation between the two varieties of human kind; constituting the family, and providing for the continuance of the species.

The one great creative and formative idea which runs through the whole of these is Reverence, that powerful principle, the counter-agent to all meanness and selfishness, which obliges a man to have regard to some law or standard above that of force, and extrinsic to his own will, his own passions, or his own propensities.

The five given above are the main channels into which the stream is distributed. But they have many subdivisions or specific forms, such as —

Reverence for Parents;
Reverence for Kings;

Reverence for the old;
Reverence for beauty; of which perhaps the very noblest example ever given is the manner in which Odysseus is struck by Nausicaa. One much lower, and more Asiatic, is that of the Trojan δημογέροντες, or Elders, when Helen goes forth to the Wall;[1]
Reverence for the opinion of fellow-men;[2]
Reverence for the dead;
Reverence for the weak and poor.

These emotions and habits of reverence were to the Greek mind and life what the dykes in Holland are to the surface of the country; shutting off passions as the angry sea, and securing a broad open surface for the growth of every tender and genial product of the soil.

[1] Od. vi. 149 seqq. Il. iii. 154–158.   [2] Il. ix. 459–461

CHAPTER XII.

RESEMBLANCES AND DIFFERENCES BETWEEN THE GREEKS AND THE TROJANS.

This subject, which has been treated with some detail in the 'Studies on Homer,'[1] will now be touched on only so far as to present its main heads.

Sufficient reason has perhaps been given for the belief that there is a double ethnical relation between the inhabitants of Troas and of Greece. The common soldiery appear to correspond, without any sensible inferiority of the Trojans, who, however, appear to have been in greater proportion lightly armed; and all that we learn of the people tends to associate them, in blood and language, with what we may largely call the Pelasgian and more archaic element in Greece. The ruling houses, again, are connected in the bonds of hospitality, as appears from the visit of Paris to Menelaos. The son of Anchises resided in Greece.[2] Diomed has the xenial relation with the Lycian Glaucos. Relations to the line of the personage termed Aiolos, so powerful in Greece, are visible in the Dardanian royal family.

---

[1] Vol. III. Dios, pp. 145-247.   [2] Il. xxiii. 296.

When we turn to language, a near relation, perhaps that of substantial identity, seems probable. A Greek name, Astuanax, lord of the city, is expressly stated to have been given by the Trojans to the son of Hector. The Trojan army, indeed, is stated to have spoken various tongues; but this is placed in immediate connection with the presence of the Epicouroi or allies,[1] one race of whom, the Carians, are called speakers of a barbarous, meaning probably a wholly foreign, language.

In the matter of religion there is little, if any, difference between the mere names of such gods as are brought prominently forward. As the great controversy was to be fought out in Olympos, no less than on earth, Homer was in a manner compelled to find a meeting-point for the mythologies of the respective parties. We find mentioned expressly the worship in Troas of Zeus, Athené, Apollo, and Hephaistos. Leto and Artemis attend in the temple of Apollo on Pergamos. Arès must have been known as a god to those, for whom he fights. Aphrodité was eminently Trojan, as we see from her favor for Paris; her passion for Anchises; her marriage-gift to Andromache; her ministerial charge over the body of Hector;[2] and from the biting taunts of Pallas, of Helen, and of Diomed.[3] Hermes is said to give increase to the flocks of Phorbas;[4] yet does not appear to be recognized as a known Trojan deity by Priam, when he gives his name, and specifies in addition that he is an immortal god.[5] Poseidon had a deadly quarrel with Troy, but

---

[1] Il. ii. 803–806.   [2] Il. xxiii. 184–187.
[3] Il. iii. 400–402; v. 348–351, 420–425.   [4] Il. xiv. 490.
[5] Il. xxiv. 461.

was in close and friendly relations with the Dardanian branch.[1] Here is named as the wife of Zeus, and as slighted in the Judgment of Paris.[2]

Now, a great River — not the humanized spirit of a River, but the River itself — the Scamandros, or Xanthos, of the Ilian plain, appears in the Theomachy, and fights on the side of Troy against Hephaistos. Here is an indication, which cannot be mistaken, that a Nature-worship, alien to the Olympian system, prevailed in Troas. We have other signs of this great and, probably, fundamental distinction of the two religions. While Here is so faintly sketched, her Pelasgian prototype, Gaia, is an object of ordinary worship in Troas, although in Greece she is banished to the Underworld. And the Sun (Helios) of the Iliad sympathizes with the Trojans, while the Apollo of the First Book shows signs of affinity with that luminary, that are rooted perhaps in his name Phoibos, but that are not allowed any place or recognition in the Olympian scheme. Of all single passages, that which most gives the key to the distinction is the speech of Menelaos before the Pact,[3] where he proposes a joint act of religion to be performed on behalf of both parties. The Greeks are to offer a single lamb to Zeus; and the Trojans two, one of them to the Earth, the other to the Sun. Eös, the morning, another Nature-Power, is made known to us as the bride of Tithonos, and may therefore be set down among the deities of Troy. It does not seem clear that she was in any way impersonated in Greece.

It is very probable, that Hephaistos and other dei-

[1] Il. xx. 290-292.   [2] Il. x. 329; xiii. 826; xxiv. 29.
[3] Il. iii. 103.

tics may have been known under forms of tradition
variously modified, in Troas and in Greece respectively; and, indeed, in different portions of one and
the same country. These forms, however distinct or
discordant, the plan of Homer required him in some
manner to amalgamate.

So much for abstract belief. As to the modes of its
development, they would appear to have been on the
Trojan side sacerdotal, on the Greek imaginative. In
the Greek system, besides the great Olympian deities,
we have the gods of the older dynasty, and of the
Underworld; the Giants; the Nymphs, and other personages, anthropomorphically conceived, and presiding
over groves, rivers, meadows; the great ethical figures of the Destinies and the Erinues, of Atè and
the Prayers; and a multitude of purely poetical impersonations, such as Terror, Rumor, and the like.
In Troas, we seem to find none of this large and
varied apparatus, except the names of certain Nymphs,
who are mentioned as mothers of human children. Indeed, even the future state seems to have been feebly conceived in Troy;[1] and the oath of Hector to Dolon[2]
makes no allusion to the penalty of perjury, which,
as we see, was incurred by Pandaros without shame
or hesitation. Not only do we still hear of the illustrious Shade of Patroclos after death, but the passage
of the souls of the Suitors from Ithaca is vividly described in the Odyssey;[3] but of the Trojans nothing
is ever told us beyond the grave, except one or two
repetitions of the mere formula that they went to
Hades. A materializing religion is not favorable to

[1] Il. vi. 422; xxii. 482.   [2] Il. x. 329.   [3] xxiv. 1-10.

the retention of the belief in a future state; and human experience seems to have established widely, up to the present point of the history of the race, the connection between such a belief and the repression of perjury.

But when we turn to sacerdotal institutions and ritual forms, again the contrast is a striking one.

The three subjects of priesthood, temples, and glebes, seem to be closely connected; especially the first and third: for where there was an estate, we may be pretty sure that there was some official person, namely, the priest, to live upon the proceeds.

Now we never hear of a temenos, or consecrated glebe-land, for any deity, except four times. There is the temenos of Zeus in Gargaros;[1] of Demeter in Thessaly;[2] of Aphroditê at Paphos;[3] and of the River Spercheios in Thessaly.[4] The first is in Troas; the third in Cyprus; the other two stand in evident connection with the old or Pelasgian worship.

Let us next look to the Priests of the Poems. We have Chruses, the Priest of Apollo in Troas; Maron, a priest of the same deity at Ismaros, among the Kikones, allies of Troy; and again in Troas, Dares, priest of Hephaistos; Dolopion (arētēr, literally pray-er) of Scamandros; Theano, priestess of Athenê; Onetor, priest of the Zeus of Ida. But neither in the Greek army, nor in Greece itself, have we any mention of a priest contemporary with the Poems. Especially in the case of Ithaca this negative evidence is strong. I refer back to what has been already said on this subject in the description of the kingly office.

[1] Il. viii. 48.
[2] Od. viii. 362.
[3] Il. ii. 696.
[4] Il. xxiii. 148.

Besides the Priests, there is the separate order of Prophets. These are fully known in Greece under different names, and are recognized as one of the regular standing professions in a community at peace, while Calchas is the mantis or prophet of the army. These organs of the deity interpret sometimes from signs and omens, sometimes without them. There was some degree of approximation between the two characters. A prophet, or seer, might be an inspector of sacrifices, though he did not offer them.[1] On the other hand, a priest was supposed to be capable of interpreting the divine will.[2] But distinctions of the social state serve sufficiently to manifest the separation of the two characters, even independently of the fact that the seer or prophet never offers sacrifice. For the last-named personage is distinguished from the rest of the community only by the possession of his gift; whereas the priest appears to be wholly exempted from military service, and a kind of sanctity attaches to his character, as is most of all clearly shown by the fact that the offence of Agamemnon, which brought the Pest upon the Greek army, consisted only in his refusal to take ransom for the captive daughter of a priest, an act which he probably might have ventured with impunity in the case of the child even of a prince. Yet the teaching office, as far as we can trace it at all, seems to lie less with the priest, than with the prophet.[3]

With respect to temples, it is plain that Apollo had a temple at Putho, and probable that Pallas also had one at Athens. No temple is named in Ithaca. They

---

[1] Il. xxiv. 221. Od. xxii. 318.   [2] Il. i. 62.
[3] Od. xxii. 310–315.

seem to have abounded in Troas: and, in the Sixth
Odyssey, the building of temples[1] is named as one of
the elements of the construction of a city. It does not
follow that these temples were in all cases roofed
buildings: they may have been in some instances no
more than consecrated inclosures. Even in the Greek
camp, there was a central place for Assemblies, and for
Suits: and here were the altars of the gods.[2] We are
not entitled to infer from the existence of a temple in
any particular place, the existence of a priesthood.

The grove (ἄλσος) appears to have been a common
form for the site of religious worship, both in and out
of Greece.

In Troy, we hear of a statue or image of Athené,[3]
to which was offered the Robe, presented by the Trojan
women in their solemn procession. And on the Shield
of Achilles there are delineated figures[4] of that goddess
and of Arès respectively, together with those of the
armed bands under their several patronage. But no
sanctity attends these figures; they are simple representations of Art. We have no trustworthy trace of
a statue used in worship, except the solitary case just
named in Troy. And the common expression of Homer, that the disposition of events lies in the lap of
the gods, is perhaps sufficiently explained by the anthropomorphic character of the Olympic scheme, if
indeed it requires even that explanation.

Lastly, the Trojans appear to be distinguished[5] for
punctuality and liberality in sacrifice. But we hear of
much neglect of this matter on the part of the Greeks.

[1] Od. vi. 10. [2] Il. xi. 806–808. [3] Il. vi. 303.
[4] Il. xviii. 516–519. [5] Il. iv. 48.

Menelaos, one of the best and purest characters among the Greek chieftains, was punished for his omission to offer up the proper hecatombs, by a long and trying detention in Egypt.[1] A like neglect was the cause of difficulties in the general Return of the Greek army.[2] And before Troy, in the hasty construction of the trench and rampart, the whole of the army forgot the proper hecatombs.[3] The Trojans, then, much excelled their enemies in religious observance. It seems also true that, as between Greek and Greek, the pious observers of the law of sacrifice were the better men. But we can in no manner claim for the Trojans a morality superior to that of their opponents.

Rather, indeed, the reverse. In the War of Troy, justice is plainly with the Greeks. Of course I speak of the delineation of the case such as we have it in Homer, and do not inquire how far the Poet may have caused the scale to incline on behalf of his country by the weight of his own thoughts and wishes. The crime of Paris would have been gross, had it been merely an elopement. But it was an abduction; and an abduction, too, attended with mere thievery of goods. These features in our eyes are aggravations; probably, in those of Homer and his contemporaries, they may have tended to mitigate the offence, by imparting to it some of the features of war.[4] And, in those days, abduction was probably not regarded as criminal in itself. But there always remains the grave offence of violated hospitality. And accordingly, while Helen shows marks of aversion for Paris, the Trojan people hate

---

[1] Od. iv. 351–353.   [2] Od. iii. 141–146.   [3] Il. vii. 450.
[4] Compare the case of Heracles and Iphitos, Od. xxi. 22–30.

him like black death.[1] He contrives to hold his place by effrontery, and by bribes;[2] and he is the object of sharp rebuke from Hector.[3] With the exception of Menelaos, we find much less indignation among the Greek chiefs, than we might have expected. Perhaps we may reasonably consider that in this, as in many later cases, the original causes of the quarrel were to a great extent lost and absorbed in its following incidents. Christian ideas, again, would fix a deeper guilt on Paris, especially under the actual circumstances, according as his adulterous connection was more prolonged. But the offence of Paris is regarded in Homer as arising from want of self-control, rather than from hardened wickedness. It is always treated as an atè, into which weakness enters, and not, like the conduct of the Suitors, as an atasthalìè, which is purely deliberate and hardened. The evil act once perpetrated, Paris had a marriage of fact with Helen, who was installed into the family of Priam: and of this marriage, odious as his character must be held, he is in some sort the defender. It was not wholly unlike the stealing of a birthright; which, once acquired, was valid. So the offence of Helen did not lie in living with a man who was not her husband, so much as having taken one husband in exchange for another.

It is not unlikely that a more base and less manly morality among the Trojans may help to account for the patient endurance of so much privation and calamity for the sake of a man, who did not even redeem his vices (so to speak) by personal courage, or by refinement of manners.[4] This conjecture is certainly

---

[1] Il. iii. 428–430; vi. 352. [2] Il. vii. 354–364; xi. 123.
[3] Il. iii. 46–53. [4] See the whole of Il. iii.

sustained[1] by the remark of the Senators on the wall.
In Ithaca the same idea is ascribed to the dissolute
Suitors.[2] But much of the cause must, I think, have
lain in a difference of institutions. The outward forms
of polity were not, indeed, broadly different. We have
on both sides a King; a Council, or Councillors at the
least; and an Assembly. But we have no indications
of that spirit of freedom in the Trojan community,
which found such noble scope in masculine debate,
and even in positive action, among the Greeks. On
both sides we find the germ of after-history: the
Trojans bearing in many points the more Asiatic, the
Greeks the more European stamp. The one type leans
to fraud, where the other inclines to force. King Laomedon defrauds Poseidon and Apollo; Anchises steals
from Laomedon, Paris from Menelaos: when Pandaros
most grossly breaks the public faith, there is no
reproach: Euphorbos wounds Patroclos in the back.
The mild Menelaos declares, that the sons of Priam
cannot be trusted.[3] Though a single passage in the
Odyssey places flat perjury, as well as theft, under the
patronage of Hermes,[4] the Greeks appear, throughout
the Iliad, to pursue an honorable course of conduct.

A tendency, again, to sensual excess appears to run
in the royal line of Troy, under much less of restraint
than we find in the Greek houses. This is especially
remarkable in the mythology. Aphrodite and Eōs,
goddesses markedly Trojan, and Demeter, who is at
least Pelasgian, condescended to irregular relations
with men.[5] So it is with the Naiad nymphs of

[1] Il. iii. 156.   [2] Od. xviii. 160-212.   [3] Il. iii. 105.
[4] Od. xix. 396.   [5] Od. v. 121-127.

Troas.¹ But about the goddesses recognized by the Homeric Greeks, Pallas, Artemis, Persephonê, and even Here, we hear nothing of the kind.

The polygamy of Priam is wholly without counterpart in Greece. It seems, however, to be not that of a dissolute man, but of the head of a family regularly organized: not personal, but traditional. He had fifty sons, nineteen of them from the single womb of Hecuba;² and twelve daughters. Besides Hecuba, who was the principal queen, there were other recognized wives; and behind them again were concubines, or else, which seems less probable, women in no permanent relation whatever to the King. As ten sons of Antenor (besides one spurious son) are mentioned in the Iliad, all within the fighting age, and as his wife Theano is still blooming (*calliparëos*), it seems highly probable that he, too, may have had more wives than one.

Again, while the guilty act of Paris appears to have been regarded without moral disapproval in Troy, the first act of Aigisthos, the corruption of Clutaimnestra, was regarded by the gods as a crime,³ even apart from the murder of Agamemnon: and their sentiment probably expresses the average moral judgment of the country. Again, it was the main part of the guilt of the Suitors, which drew down so terrible a retribution, that they sought to wed Penelopê while her husband might still be supposed to be alive.⁴

The prevalence of polygamy, even in the highest families, is obviously adverse to the rule of an hered-

---

¹ Il. vi. 21; xiv. 444; xx. 384.   ² Il. xxiv. 496; vi. 244, 248.
³ Od. i. 35.   ⁴ Od. xxii. 38.

itary succession to the crown. And it seems more than doubtful, from the Poems, whether this rule was observed on the Trojan side as fully as in Greece. Sarpedon and Glaucos are both called Kings: yet they belonged to the same kingdom, and they were cousins. Again, Sarpedon evidently had the chief place: yet Glaucos was the representative of the royal house in the male line, Sarpedon only in the female. Among the Greeks the title of King is only given to one person in one country, who must be either in possession, or heir-apparent.

In the recital of the genealogy from Dardanos, Æneas does not give a precedence of superiority to either branch; and he leaves[1] us to doubt, or to inquire from some other sources, which line was the senior, the Trojan or the Dardanian. Again, Achilles expressly taunts that chieftain as a candidate for the succession in Troy after the death of Priam.[2]

Further, it appears open to much question, which of the sons of Priam himself we are to understand to have been the eldest. The whole responsibility of command evidently lay upon Hector; and there can be no doubt, even if it were only from the name given to his infant son by the people, that he was already the king-designate in the public view. But that name would have had little special significance, had Hector been sure of the succession by mere seniority. While the ability and value of Hector are of themselves sufficient to account for his prominent place, it is very difficult, except upon the supposition that seniority was more or

[1] Il. xx. 231-240.   [2] Il. xx. 178-183.

less the competing element with merit, to account for various features in the position of Paris. Alone among the children of Priam, he enjoys the title of Basileus or King, which is never given to Hector. Although utterly insignificant as a warrior, he is the chief in command of the second among the five divisions of Trojans in the great battle of the Twelfth Book, as Hector is of the first.[1] Except Hector, Paris is the only prince who has a separate dwelling of his own on the hill of Pergamos. The other princes all, married as well as unmarried, sleep in the palace of their father. His expedition to Greece does not absolutely imply his being the eldest son; but perhaps best accords with that otherwise far from improbable supposition.

Again; Paris, according to the representation of the Iliad, had been in manhood for at least twenty years. But Hector had one child only, a babe in arms. The word hebè, which expresses a full-grown, but still a blooming, manhood, is applied to Hector,[2] but not to Paris. It is applied indeed to Odysseus in Scherié; but this is when he had been preternaturally beautified under the restoring hand of Athené; and also in the complimentary speech of a host.[3] We cannot suppose Hector to have been very different in age from Andromaché: but she must still have been young, for her own grandfather had been alive during the War.[4] And finally, in her lament over her husband, she distinctly calls him young.[5] So much as to the apparent seniority of Paris; and, with this,

[1] Il. xii. 93. [2] Il. xxii. 363. [3] Od. viii. 136.
[4] Il. vi. 426–428. [5] Il. xxiv. 725.

for the less defined and more lax law of succession in Troy.

The relation of Priam to the districts or countries, which supplied the several contingents of his force, is but indistinctly conveyed to us. Yet it is probable from the arrangement and expressions of the Trojan Catalogue, and from minor circumstances, that, besides his kingdom of Ilion, he exercised over Dardania, and at least three other districts, an authority more or less like to that of Agamemnon over the Greek chieftains. However this may be, even the ancients justly described the Trojan war as the conflict of the Eastern with the Western world. And it foreshadowed other yet greater conflicts, down to our own day.

Within the kingdom of Troy, we can more clearly discern the inferior compactness of political society, and its lower spirit of intelligence and freedom. We have every sign that the Trojan Elders did not act collectively as a Council.[1] This is an important defect in such a body with reference to the means of moral influence. But Assemblies met. There Antenor proposed, and Paris refused, the surrender of Helen: popular discontent was expressed; and we are expressly told, that he was able to procure the defeat of other such proposals only by corruption.[2] An Assembly agreed to ask a truce for the burial of the dead. In an Assembly, Hector somewhat curtly put down the opposition of Poludamas as a stranger.[3]

But we have to remark, in the Trojan Assembly, as follows:—

[1] Il. ii. 788, 789.   [2] Il. vii. 869.   [3] Il. xii. 211-214.

1. That there is no sign of its having been guided by men of wisdom and valor, but only by age and rank.

2. That oratory does not seem to have been employed in it as an instrument of persuasion.

3. That the Elders, who assist Priam in public affairs, are simply the old men, and not, as with the Greeks, the chief and able men, belonging to the high families of the State.

4. The Trojan Assembly does not clearly appear to have been convened on special occasions: but perhaps rather to have sat in permanence, in the sense of having only consisted of such persons as might chance to be present, at any given moment, in the places of public resort.[1]

There seems in Troy — as in the institutions we now term Asiatic — to be nothing to stand between royalty and the people. There was thus less balance of forces, less security against precipitate action; a state of facts in all likelihood accompanied by less respect for public morality, less security for private rights.

The Poet has given us, evidently of set purpose, a minor indication of Trojan inferiority, in the contrasts he presents of the silence and self-possession of the Greeks, with the din and buzz of the Trojans, as they marched to battle. At the burying of the dead, both armies wept and were silent: but the silence of the Trojans was because great Priam forbade a noise.[2] A Trojan Assembly is uneasy and excitable:[3] never a Greek one. Even for the expressions of approval,

---

[1] Il. ii. 788; vii. 414. Studies, pp. 237 seqq.
[2] Il. vii. 420–432.   [3] Il. vii. 346; iii. 2, 8; iv. 429, 436.

different words are used: the Greeks were eager and vehement, the noise of the Trojans was promiscuous and tumultuous. In a word, all through the Poems, the Greek mind is evidently endowed with a finer sense, and a higher intelligence.

CHAPTER XIII.

THE GEOGRAPHY OF HOMER.

SECTION I. *The Catalogue.*

THE Catalogue of Homer is a great attempt to construct what may, for those times, be justly called a cadastral account of Greece; together with an outline of the Trojan force, sufficient for the purposes of the Poem.

In 348 lines, it contains 501 proper names, spread over diverse and very irregular tracts of country, and including many which belonged to personal history and genealogy. To recite this part of the Poem with accuracy evidently required a great effort of memory. To write it, would have required no more effort, perhaps indeed less, than the average tenor of the Iliad. Now the Invocation to the Muses at the commencement, the most formal and elaborate which the Poems contain, clearly shows that the Bard was about to undertake a weighty task. Thus the Catalogue, together with its introduction, becomes a powerful piece of evidence to show that the Iliad was not written but recited.

Next; the Genealogies of the Greek Catalogue,

eleven in number, testify in a remarkable manner to
the historic aims of the Poet, which led him to connect
all his leading personages with the past, at the very
time when he was securing to them a deathless heri-
tage in the future. Again, the Poet has avoided the
error of confounding his primary with his secondary
leaders. The greater chiefs have their descents traced
singly, in various parts of the Iliad, so as to give them
due prominence. But in the Catalogue a number of
secondary genealogies are massed together.

In his performance of this operation, where a re-
citing Bard was to lose the aid commonly afforded him
by the natural continuity of his subject-matter, Homer
has sought for a substitute in a kind of mental figure-
drawing. He divides the whole territory of Greece
and the Islands into three circles, more or less regular
and perfect; with a fourth figure of the nature of a
zigzag.

The first circle begins with the Bœotians and ends
with Mycenæ; containing nine contingents.[1]

The second is a zigzag, beginning with Lacedæmon,
and ending with the Aitoloi; and comprises seven
contingents.[2]

The third is part of a circle of islands, beginning
with Crete, and ending with Carpathos and other small
islands. This portion gives four contingents.[3]

In the fourth, or Thessalian portion,[4] it is more
difficult, and in some cases hardly feasible, to identify
the sites; but, as far as may be, the Poet appears to
adhere to the same circular arrangement. Here also
we have nine contingents.

[1] Il. ii. 494–680. [2] 581–644. [3] 645–680. [4] 681–759.

In each, then, of these four divisions of the territory, the Poet makes his figure his guide, and proceeds from each district to the one lying next to it on the proper line, until the figure is completed. Water sometimes intervenes; but no territory seems to be skipped over.

Thus there is a clue all along, except indeed at the points of transition from one division to another. For these, also, he seems to have provided. In each case he ends with a district, the neighbor to which, according to the line of his figure, has already been disposed of. Thus in the first, were he to go beyond Mycenae, he would find himself among the Bœotians again. So that he is as it were reminded, by this contrivance, to recommence.

In the Trojan Catalogue, I find but two genealogies; and one of them is that of the Pelasgian leader. Now the Pelasgian blood, it will be remembered, seems to be the common bond between the masses on each side.

In the Greek Catalogue, Homer specifies the respective amounts of the contingents of force supplied from the different portions of the country. This is evidently meant to give to each chief and district his due position, relatively to the rest. In Troas he pursues no such arrangement; for he had no such object. And among the Epicouroi, or Allies,[1] there was another difficulty; as they came and went in successive reliefs, whereas the Achaians were a permanent force.

Generally, I cannot but think that the comparison of the two Catalogues is highly unfavorable to the

[1] Il. ii. 816–889.

theory which regards Homer as an Asiatic Greek: a
theory which, in my opinion, should also be repudiated
upon more comprehensive grounds. The Greek Catalogue is charged throughout with what I may call local
color and with visual epithets: epithets which imply
some personal familiarity, and raise up a prospect or
scene before the mental eye of a reader or a hearer.
In the fifty-two lines of the Trojan Catalogue, it would
be difficult to point out more than eight of these:
the precipitous tops of Tereiè and Mucalè; the fertile
Larissa; the wide-flowing of the limpid Axios; the
eddying Xanthos; the dark water of Aisepos; the
lofty Erythinoi; the wooded hill of Phtheiroi.[1] Four
only of these come from Asia Minor to the south of
Troas, with which Homer is supposed to be so familiar.
On the other side of the Ægean, ten at least of such
epithets are found within the thirteen lines that describe the places, which supplied the Bœotian contingent.

SECTION II. *The Plain of Troy.*[2]

The leading topical points in the plain of Troy are
as follows:—

1. The Scamandrian plain,[3] near the river Scamandros, forming the northern and western part of the
Trojan plain, and reaching up to or near the Encampment.

2. The Ileïan plain,[4] near the city, lying south and
perhaps east from it.

[1] Il. II. 825, 829, 841, 849, 855, 868, 869, 877.
[2] Of this subject, no notice was taken in the ' Studies on Homer.'
[3] Il. II. 465. [4] Il. xxi. 558.

3. The Scaian Gates,[1] north of the city, the ordinary way of exit to the plain. Near them is the phēgos.[2]

4. The Dardanian Gates, south of the city, communicating with Dardania on the hill. Il. xx. 216–218.

5. The junction of the rivers. Il. v. 774.

6. The ford of Xanthos, and the monument of Ilos near it. Il. xxiv. 349.

7. The ἐρινεός, or wild fig-tree, near this ford (346–353 and 692–694), and the tomb of Ilos. Here was a σκοπιή or place convenient for observation, and a wagon road. All these are near the city. Il. vi. 433; xi. 166, 167; xxii. 145.

8. The θρωσμός, or roll, of the plain near the northern extremity, and the Encampment of the Greeks. Il. x. 160; xi. 56; xx. 3.

9. The Mound of Aisuetes, near enough to the Encampment for observations. Il. ii. 793.

10. The hillock Baticia, in the southern part of the plain, at some distance from the city. Il. ii. 813.

11. The two fountains of Scamandros. Il. xxii. 147.

12. The mouths of the two rivers, distinct one from another. See Il. xii. 21.

13. The quarters of Achilles and of Telamonian Ajax respectively, marking the extremes east and west of the Greek Encampment by the shore. Il. xi. 5–9.

The chief questions which arise are two.

1. In what manner can the description given by Homer of the several parts be combined into a self-consistent whole?

2. In what manner can that description be reconciled with the actual geography of the plain of Troy understood, as it best may, from its present condition?

---

[1] Il. iii. 145, et alibi.   [2] Il. vi. 237.

The first of these two questions presents no insurmountable difficulty.

We have to imagine an irregular oblong lying north and south; the north end formed by the coast and the Greek line of ships and cantonments, from that of Achilles on the west to that of Ajax on the east, running along it; the eastern side, by Simoeis; the western by Scamandros, with rough and steep banks above, and with marshy lands near the mouth. The southern part of the plain is closed by the roots of Ida; and in the south-western corner lies the city with a gate southwards towards the hill, and towards Dardania which lay within its recesses; also a gate (the Scaian Gate), with the ground descending towards the plain northwards.

Passing from the north towards this gate, and having on the right hand the river, we come along a waggon-road to the wild fig-tree, where is the mound or tomb of Ilos, used apparently as a place of observation, like Batieia and the tomb of Aisuetes,[1] at the other end of the plain. This is hard by the river. We then have the Scaian Gate on the left; and farther on are the two fountains of the Scamandros, near to which Hector passes, in making the circuit of the city.

It is plain, that there was a communication between the rivers; but probably one dry in summer; and we may take notice that it was not in the fierce Scamandros, but in Simoeis, that there lay both heroes and their spoils; and this in the dust, not in the waters, as Virgil has vividly, but carelessly, represented.[2]

The ford of Xanthos we must understand to be a ford leading to the westward, not one crossed between

[1] Il. ii. 793. [2] Æn. i. 100.

the city and the camp. With these suppositions, the topography of the plain appears to be self-consistent.

The best examination I have been able to make of the second question leads me to the conclusion that the description of Homer cannot be accurately fitted to the natural features of the plain, as they now are, or even as we can probably suppose them to have been some three thousand years ago.

There is no site near the two fountains, on which the city can have been placed, of such a nature as to allow of the threefold circuit ascribed to Hector flying, and to Achilles pursuing him.

The general idea conveyed by the Iliad of the distance between the city and the encampment is, that it was short. After the second Battle, in Book viii. Hector holds an Assembly. The Trojans had pressed upon the Greek entrenchment, and their gathering is away from the ships, τόσσι νεῶν (v. 490); but this seems to be explained by what follows as meaning simply clear of the field of battle, whereon lay the dead bodies. And it is expressly called 'near' (ἐγγὺς) that is, near the ships, in Il. ix. 232. But Hector proceeds to give directions for fetching oxen and sheep, with wine and corn, from Ilion for the immediate repast; and herewith the wood for cooking and for watchfires (505-507).

Again, in Il. viii. 532, Hector says, 'to-morrow we shall see whether Diomed will drive me from the ships to the wall (evidently of the city), or whether I shall slay and spoil him.' Now the idea of the pursuit from the ships to the wall and the corresponding movement of the armies, are wholly inapplicable to a distance of five or six or more miles.

On the whole, the length of the plain, and the dis-

tance of the two fountains from the shore, are not
in harmony with the descriptions of the forward and
retrograde operations of the armies which took place
on the great day of battles, ending with the unwilling
retirement of the Sun in Il. xviii. 239. Other incon-
sistencies of a like nature might be pointed out.

On the other hand, the number of the natural features portrayed, and the actual correspondence of most
of them, when taken individually, with those we now
discern, establish the general authenticity of the scene.
They also lead to the conclusion that Homer may have
seen it in person; or may, by the power of a vigorous
imagination, have conceived its general character, and
the relative position of the points, from the narratives
of eye-witnesses.

But it seems plain, that he did not sing either on the
spot, or to persons minutely acquainted with the topography; and not unlikely, that he generalized his materials, and used them with a certain license, as a poet,
for the purposes of his art.

Lastly: I cannot but observe the analogy between
this loose placement of objects, each of which singly
had been vividly conceived, and the indefinite method
of handling geographical points on a large scale, in the
Outer Voyage of the Odyssey. In the latter case we
are morally certain that he spoke at secondhand; and
this tends to diminish the unlikelihood that the Song
of Troy was composed without personal experience of
the spot to aid the work.

SECTION III. *The Outer Geography.*

The geography of Greek experience, as exhibited by Homer, is limited, speaking generally, to the Ægean and its coasts, with the Propontis as its limit in the North-east, with Crete for a southern boundary, and with the addition of the western coast of the peninsula and its islands, as far northward as the Leucadian rock. Respecting that rock, and respecting the conformation of Corfù (Scherié) and the shape of Ithaca, Homer had some accurate information. But a visit to that region in 1858-9 convinced me that the Poet, who described the view of Corfu[1] from the north as lying on the sea like a shield, never could have seen it; that he was not personally acquainted with the topography of Ithaca; that he guessed at, and over-estimated, its size; and, as is demonstrable from several passages in the Odyssey,[2] that he has given it a wrong relative position.

Beyond the limits I have named, all ordinary navigation was conducted by the Phœnicians; and upon these mariners, possibly in a few cases on their settlers or colonists in Greece, Homer must have depended for his information. At any period, such information could only give rise to very inaccurate geographical results. But we cannot even expect a resemblance to the actual face of earth, in a case where not only are the points described by those who would naturally seek both to excite and to deter, but where they could be nowhere arranged and digested, except only in the brain of the

[1] Od. v. 281.
[2] Especially Od. iv. 844–847, and Od. ix. 25–26; lines which it has in vain been attempted to force into conformity with actual geography.

Poet, ideally compounding in the mind what fell upon the ear.

It appears to me, that interpreters have been wholly wrong, when they have laboriously strained their endeavors to fit the Outer Geography of Homer to the actual surface of the globe. Unwilling to recognize error in his descriptions, they have closed their eyes to much really indisputable evidence of it that the text supplies; and have, after a sort, assigned to him geographical knowledge which he did not possess, at the expense of that mental self-consistency, and that plastic power, with both of which he was endowed in a degree never surpassed among the sons of men. It was no reproach to him, if he believed in a great sea, connecting the Adriatic and the Euxine; but it would have been at variance with all the rules of his mental action, if he had spoken without any definite meaning, when he treats of sailing and floating distances, of the direction of the wind, or of the position of the stars: if he had forgotten his distinction between land of the continent and island, or if he had placed the sunrise in the West.

No doubt his descriptions are very vague in some cases, and especially as to the Island of Calypso. The fact seems to be, that he was misled not only by falsehood, but by truth. When informants, speaking of the same region, described it as one of all but perpetual day, and also as one of night all but perpetual, although both those statements were true, he had not the key to their truth in the annual revolution of the earth combined with the declension of its axis from the perpendicular; and thus he could only seek refuge in vagueness from contradiction. Again, when he heard of great sea-currents, which set through the Bosphorus, the

Straits of Messina, the Straits of Yenikalé, and the Straits of Gibraltar respectively, what means could he possess, considering the palpable points of resemblance, of effectually separating each one of these from the others? Hence it is, as we shall find, that he carries his Thrinakiè (or Sicily) to the immediate vicinity of the Bosphorus, consecrates it to the Sun, and places there the Oxen and the Nymphs belonging to that deity.

The proper object of our search is, not a forced accommodation of Homer's conceptions to a basis of fact with which he was unacquainted, but simply a copy, if we can get it, of the map, which he constructed in his brain from the materials supplied by Phœnician discourse or legend. And the proper mode of search must be, to take for our primary authority his own statements of distance, direction, and physical features; and then, but only in subordination to this rule, to see where and how far they fit any portion of what actually exists; moreover, whether they so correspond with it as it is situate in its proper place, or as he has arbitrarily transplanted it to some other.

There are fractions of border-land, between the Inner or home, and the outer or wholly foreign sphere, which receive somewhat of a mixed treatment. To this group Scheriè belongs: and the land of the Lotos-eaters possibly may be but another phase of Egypt. Epirus again, and the country of the Glactophagoi and other nations, over whom Zeus directs his view at the outset of the Thirteenth Iliad,[1] belong to this zone, as does Phœnicia, if not Cyprus.

[1] Il. xiii. 3–6.

Our data for constructing an Homeric map of the Outer Geography seems to be chiefly as follows:—

1. The points of the horizon marked for morning and evening respectively, connect themselves with two of Homer's winds. His Zephuros is akin to zophos, and knephas, the darkness:[1] his Euros to ēōs,[2] the morning, and perhaps to his euroeis, an epithet used by him four times only, and in each case to describe the Underworld. Sunrise and sunset, with him, verge, though not perhaps with uniform precision, to the south of East, and to the north of West respectively.

2. And such are the directions, from which Zephuros and Euros blow. But it is plain, as Zephuros blows from Thrace upon the Ægean,[3] that his range also approximates to the north pole on the western side: and further, that, as Boreas blows from the same quarter, he takes up the next arc of the horizon, and may be defined as a north-north-east wind; a title which the same wind, as far as my memory serves me, still bears in the Adriatic. Again, Euros and Notos, the third and fourth of Homer's winds, are associated together as a pair, raising the Ægean from the South nearly as Boreas and Zephuros catch it from the North. The greater portion, however, of the arc covered by the southern pair is to the east of the Pole, by the northern pair to the west. It is not probable that Homer had names for winds from all points of the compass, or that he did more than mark inartificially the directions from which the winds of his actual experience principally blew. Notos may probably be a South

---

[1] Buttmann, Lexil. in voc. κλαυτς.
[2] Liddell and Scott, in voc.
[3] Il. ix. 4.

wind, blowing from near that pole on either side: Euros is between Notos and the east.

8. Next to these, we have to mark Homer's measures of sea distances. Of extended land distances he has no measures at all; a separate proof of the very limited range of the land experience of the Greeks.

(*a*) Homer measures the time of a voyage from Troas to Phthia; and from Crete to Egypt.[1] The result of these measurements is, to give some ninety miles as a good average day's journey of a ship using sails or oars, under favorable circumstances. With peculiar good fortune, that distance might be exceeded.

(*b*) In a floating or drift passage on the waves, we can trace Homer's idea of what was possible by the supposed transit of Odysseus from a point near Crete to the Thesprotoi. It appears to be about half the rate of a ship's motion, or two miles an hour.

(*c*) The floating of a raft may probably be taken at a little more, or two and a half.

Thus we should have ninety-six miles, forty-eight miles, and sixty miles a day as our results respectively.

These are, of course, but rude measures, yet they are not unimportant aids in our inquiry.

(*d*) The rate of a Scherian ship is described by comparison with a bird's flight, or a four-horse chariot scouring the plain. 'It would go,' says Alkinoos, 'to Euboea (or perhaps to Euboea and back) in a day.' We cannot, I think, put it at less than thrice the speed of the ordinary ship.

The key to the great contrast between the Outer Geography and the facts of nature lies in the belief

[1] Il. ix. 362. Od. xiv. 257.

of Homer, that a great sea occupied the space, where we know the heart of the European Continent to lie. Proofs and indications of this belief are to be found, such as to place it beyond denial or even doubt.

(a) For example, we find one of these in the voyage of the Phaiakes to Euboea, which was certainly not supposed to take place round the whole coast of the Greek Peninsula, for the Phaiakes are supposed to hang as strangers on the outer skirt of the Greek world, not to traverse all its chief waters.[1] It must therefore have been a passage by a supposed northern sea.

(b) When Hermes travels from Olympos to the Island of Calypso, he passes over Pieria, and then sweeps down upon the sea.[2] That sea must therefore have been in the north or north-east. The journey of Here over Pieria to Emathia and Lemnos[3] shows the acquaintance of the Poet with the general direction of those countries.

(c) The Shades of the Suitors, on their way to the Underworld, take a northerly direction, pass the Leucadian rock, in a journey towards the stream of Ocean, and the gates of the Sun.[4] Can there be a clearer declaration than this that they were to pass into the east along the Adriatic — apparently avoiding the known land of Greece on their journey?

Next, Homer appears to have compounded into one group two sets of Phoenician reports concerning the entrance from without to the Thalassa or Mediterranean: one of them referring to the Straits of

[1] Od. vii. 19-20.
[2] Od. v. 43-58.
[3] Il. xiv. 225-230.
[4] Od. xxiv. 11-14.

Messina, with their Scylla and Charybdis; the other to the Bosphorus and its Planctai. It is also very easy to believe, that with each of these narrow passages he associated another strait beyond it at a distance of several hundred miles, namely the Straits of Gibraltar with the first, and the Straits of Yenikale with the second: and the striking resemblance of these last to one another, in the cardinal point of presenting at all times an inward flowing current, would tend to favor the confusion. The Ocean was, in Homer's system, the feeder of the Sea: he tells us in the Odyssey distinctly enough of one sea-passage to the Ocean, but he nowhere glances at the existence of any second access.

This Ocean mouth, to which he conducts Odysseus, is unequivocally placed in the East, near the island of Aiaia, and the rising Sun. To the left and North, lie the people of the Kimmerians hid in fog, for which the Black Sea is even now said to be remarkable. Kirkè is the daughter of Aietes, to whose country Jason had sailed through the Bosphorus. And giving the darkness a place near the dawn is a proceeding necessary to complete the idea of morning. The mouth of the Underworld is farther southward, inasmuch as Odysseus is carried to it by the Wind Boreas, up the Ocean-Stream. The whole of his voyage, up to this point, is accomplished without his being obliged to traverse any dangerous narrows. But, pursued by the vengeance of Poseidon, who rules the outer or Phœnician Thalassa, he eschews returning by the same open, lengthened, and menacing route. Kirkè accordingly apprises him of a short passage, by which he may soon find himself once more within the margin of the Greek or

Ægean waters. This is the Bosphorus; near which
the Poet plants Thrinakiè, an island evidently projected
in his mind on the basis of ideas derived from Sicily,
and with it the Scylla and Charybdis of the Straits of
Messina.

This transportation of western features to the East
is further illustrated by the Homeric treatment of Atlas.
For, associated though he be in general tradition with
the coast of Africa, and the Straits of Gibraltar, he is
with Homer the Father of Calypso, whose island plainly
lies in the northern and eastern waters, since it seems
to be Boreas who brings Odysseus from thence to
Ithaca.

The general result of this blending is, that the supposed Ocean mouth in the Euxine gets the benefit of
the open sea-route which really leads to the Straits of
Gibraltar; and the real Ocean mouth at Gibraltar has
credit for being placed in a northern latitude and a
distant eastern longitude; while the Faro and the
Bosphorus, in consequence of this identification, are
brought near to one another: each group of reports
thus throwing its own separate attributes into the common stock.

The Bosphorus must be considered not as belonging
to the Greek world, but yet as fast linked to it, and
therefore as a point fixed by practical experience, and
not to be removed. And even if we could not give
probable ground for Homer's having placed the Faro
near it, the fact would still be undeniable from the
evidence of the text, and must be recognized in any
transcript of the Outer Geography which we may
attempt.

The island of Calypso, again, must be in the north:

(a) From the direction taken, as we have seen, by Hermes.

(b) Because fire is kept burning there, which indicates a climate requiring it. Kirkè has none in her island.[1]

(c) Because it is the omphalos,[2] or central point of a vast sea, spreading on all sides, with which nothing to the east, west, or south of Greece corresponds either in nature, or in the ideas of Homer.

(d) Because the meaning of her name, the Concealer, and the length of the voyage back to Scherié, indicate her dwelling as belonging to a region wholly untravelled and unknown to the Greeks.

(e) Because Odysseus[3] is apparently carried to it by Notos. And the general rule of the Wanderings is, that southerly winds bear Odysseus away from home, while northerly ones carry him towards it.

Again, the association of Calypso with the Eastern mythology prevents us from placing her in the Northwest, where lies the country of the Laistrugones; and keeps her in relation with the east rather than the west of North.

The island of Aiaié is bound to an eastward position by the name and character of Kirkè; by its relation to Aietes, and thus to Jason, and his voyage; by the names of Helios, the father of Calypso, and of her mother Persé, an appellation savoring, in Homer, of the far East, to which the Persians of that day belonged;[4] by its being the point of Sunrise; and by the residence of Dawn.

---

[1] Od. v. 60; x. 210 seqq.   [2] Od. i. 50.
[3] Od. xii. 426, 447.
[4] Rawlinson, Anc. Monarchies, vol. iv. p. 349.

All particular conjecture respecting any position for these islands is, however, vague: the several points of the scheme of Homer in the Outer Geography were determined by relation to each other broadly conceived, and by directions generally taken, rather than by any attempt at exactitude even in mental measurement.

With these *data*, I now proceed to note the several stages of the Voyage of Odysseus.

1. From Troy to the Kikones on the north coast of the Ægean; in a region strictly belonging to the Inner Geography.[1]

2. From the Kikones, Boreas (N.N.E. wind) carries Odysseus to Cape Malea, prevents him from rounding it, and drives him out to sea, where nine days of bad or plaguy winds (oloou anemoi) bring him to the land of the Lotos-Eaters, which appears to be like an Egypt in a new dress. As five days[2] drive a ship from Crete to Egypt, we must suppose that nine imply some considerable westing, and place the Lotos-Eaters on the African coast along the Syrtis Major. We are now in the Outer Sphere.[3]

3. From the Lotophagoi to the Kuklopes, we have no direct guide afforded by the text, except that it was a voyage onward, and that the Kuklopes live on a mainland,[4] not an island. From this mainland they had, at an earlier date, displaced their neighbors the Phaiakes, who, being a nautical people, passed over and settled in Scherië. Therefore we are probably to place them in Iapugia, the heel of Italy, over against Scherië.[5]

4. From the land of the Kuklopes, perhaps called by

---

[1] Od. ix. 39. [2] Od. xiv. 253. [3] Od. ix. 67, 80-81.
[4] Od. vi. 4-8. [5] Od. ix. 105.

Homer Hupereiê,¹ Odysseus proceeds to the island
Aiolië,² and Aiolos gives him a Zephyr (N.W. wind)
which would carry him home to Ithaca. Therefore the
island of Aiolos (whether related to Stromboli as its
prototype or not) lies to the north and west of Ithaca,
with a clear sea-passage between.³ Then a tempest
drives him back to Aiolië, after nine days of Zephuros,
and when the ships were in full sight of Ithaca.⁴
Thus we have a very good measurement from the direct
evidence of the text: and Aiolië lies at sea and at from
eight hundred to a thousand miles from Ithaca, in a
north-westerly direction.

5. From Aiolië, Odysseus comes, in seven days of
rowing, to Laistrugonië, the city of Lamos, evidently
far north, as it is the land where one day runs into an-
other.⁵ We are now seventeen days from Ithaca in a
direction north and west. There can be little doubt
that the prototype of this place was supplied by a tradition brought from the north-western main. The very
marked description of the harbor, and the epithet
(αἰπυ) applied to the city, correspond closely, I am
told, with one or more of those on the south Devon-
shire and south Cornish coasts. But the site in the
open sea, and the description of the continuous day,
might more properly be taken from the Faro Islands.
The size of the people, especially of the women⁶, suggests a Scandinavian race; the want of cultivation⁷ a
position in the far north, and with a climate suited for
pasture, not for tillage.

6. From Laistrugonië we pass, without indication, to

[1] Od. vi. 4.   [2] Od. ix. 565; x. 1.   [3] Od. x. 25, 46.
[4] Od. x. 28, 54.   [5] Od. x. 80-83.   [6] Od. x. 113.
[7] Od. x. 98.

Aiaiê.¹ I have already shown that this island is absolutely fixed, according to the mind of Homer, in the East, as Aiolié is in the West. It cannot be in the remote North, because no fire is used. It is not very likely to lie to the south of East, because of the neighborhood of Kimmerian fog. This is a difficulty for Homer, since his Dawn ought to be somewhat to the south of East. He tries (it may seem) to escape, like some of his Trojan heroes, in a fog; for he declares that, on arriving here, Odysseus could make out nothing about his position relatively to the Dark and the Dawn, the Sunset and the Sunrise.² This difficulty of course cannot wholly be removed: but it rather bears upon latitudes, than on longitude or distance eastwards. I place Aiaiê at a spot near the Colchis of Aietes; adding that we are by no means to assert positively that the island lies to the northward of East, even though the balance of evidence may lie in that direction.

From Aiaiê, one day's favoring wind takes Odysseus to the Ocean-mouth, hard by the Kimmerian darkness.³ It is Boreas that carries him southward, or up the stream, it is hard to say which.⁴ After landing, the party pursue the course of the shore, in the same direction, to the entrance of the Underworld; we know not at what distance. Thence they return to Aiaiê. No fresh indication is given.

7. From Aiaiê to the Island of the Sirens. No specific indication is afforded us; except that apparently the passage is a short one. We are now within the virtual limits of the eastern and southern Euxine.⁵

¹ Od. x. 133–135. ² Od. x. 189–192.
³ Od. xi. 1–19. ⁴ Od. x. 507.
⁵ Od. xii. 149–154, 165–167; also 39, and xxiii. 326.

8. From the Sirens, by Scylla and Charybdis, leaving the (neighboring) Planctai aside, to Thrinakiê. This evidently is also a short passage.[1] Odysseus is here detained by Notos (S.S.W.) chiefly, but also by Euros; both of them blowing from the southern hemisphere.

9. From Thrinakiê, Notos having ceased to blow, he is able to pursue the homeward route. The ship founders in a violent gale from the North-west.[2] Notos carries him back in one night to Scylla and Charybdis, which he traverses in safety[3] after great peril; and then, drifting on, apparently with the same wind, he reaches, on the tenth day, Ogugiê, the Island of Calypso, the quasi-central point of the great (northern) sea.[4]

10. From Ogugiê to Scheriê; never called an island, but called the land of the Phaiakes, which may be on account of its size, for the Poet appears to have considered it as an island.[5] This is a raft voyage, and the eighteenth day brings him within view of Scheriê. Then comes the storm, with a hurricane of all the winds.[6] The raft founders;[7] and Odysseus drifts, with a wind (Boreas) sent by Athenê, to Scheriê, where he arrives on the third day.[8]

In this passage he is ordered to observe the stars, and to steer with Arctos looking over against, or opposite, his left;[9] that is to say, on his right. The exact phrase used is not a common one in Homer, and it has

---

[1] Od. xii. 201, 261, 262; xi. 106, 167; xxiii. 327-329.
[2] Od. xii. 408. [3] Od. xii. 424, 427-430, 442-446.
[4] Od. xii. 447, 448; xxiii. 333; l. 50. [5] Od. vi. 204.
[6] Od. v. 263, 278, 293, 331, 345. [7] Od. v. 370.
[8] Od. v. 382-398. [9] Od. v. 277.

usually been translated 'on his left.' If this were
correct, the island of Calypso must lie in the north-west.
This would not so well agree with the winds indicated,
though not expressed; namely, Boreas for the passage
home, and Notos for the passage from the Bosphorus to
Ogugiê. Nor would it agree as well with the time
allowed for reaching Ogugiê from the Bosphorus. Besides,
we have to keep in mind the fact, that all other
associations draw Calypso eastward.

11. From Scheriê to Ithaca; a passage of some sixteen
or eighteen hours in the hawk-ship; beginning
early in the day, and ending before the next dawn.[1]

Allowing for the rapidity of the voyage, it is plain
that Homer placed his Scheriê farther north than the
original Corfû, which may be eighty miles from Ithaca.
Eighteen days of raft voyage, with an allowance for
the distance of Scheriê, when first seen, will place
Ogugiê at more than eleven hundred miles from Ithaca.
Ten days of floatage from the Bosphorus will give five
hundred miles, or thereabouts, from that point. We
have already found that Laistrugoniê is near seventeen
hundred miles from Ithaca. All these routes are
over the open sea. Speaking generally, Homer gives to
the voyage of Odysseus all the world he knows of,
lying from South, round by West and North, and then
far to the East of Greece; except only what in terms
of slight outline he gives to the tour of Menelaos,
between the East and South.[2] The two routes diverge
at the Malean promontory.[3] Perhaps it is because the
real Phœnicia lies on the border of the Outer world, in

[1] Od. xiii. 18, 78, 86, 93–95. [2] Od. iv. 80–83.
[3] Od. iii. 318.

the south, that he has given us an idealized Phœnician people upon the border-line towards the north, and the name Scherié is possibly Surié (Syria), travestied for the ear, as the Phaiakes are the Phoinikes.

The general arrangements of Homer show that he thought the Earth and Sea had a great extension northwards, but give no idea of great distances in the longitudinal line, or from east to west. How far he carried it to the south, we have no means of judging. We know that the Shield of Achilles represented the form of the Earth, with the River Okeanos for its rim.[1] Now a shield in general is sometimes compared with the moon by Homer;[2] but he does not say the full moon: and the prevailing epithets for the shield would tend to show an oval form, or one adapted to cover the entire figure;[3] the same form as that indicated in the formula of the Spartan mother for a soldier son: 'bring it, or be brought upon it.' The natural shape of the hide, of which the name is often applied to a shield, likewise seems to favor this belief. And such a form of the shield apparently agrees with the figure which the descriptions of the Outer Geography tend to give to the Earth, in conjunction with the representation of the Shield of Achilles.

The noble conception of a great circumfluent River was probably founded on a combination of a double set of reports; the one, of great currents setting into the Thalassa, or Mediterranean Sea, and seeming to feed it, such as those of Yenikalé, the Bosphorus, Gibraltar; the other, of Outer Waters, such as the Caspian, the Persian Gulf, and probably the Red Sea.

[1] Il. xviii. 606; Il. xix. 374.   [2] Il. xix. 374.
[3] Il. xi. 32; xv. 646; and xiii. 130.

The name Kimmeria is derived by some from the
Arabic *kahm*, black; Maiotis from *maneth*, meaning
death;[1] and Tartaros is taken to be the reduplication
of the *tar* in *tarik*, the Persian word for darkness. The
seeming contradiction of perpetual light and perpetual
darkness in the north is of course removed for us, who
know that both reports are true, but for different seasons
of the year.

[1] Welsford on the English Language, pp. 75, 76, 89. Bleek, Persian Vocab. (Grammar, p. 170).

CHAPTER XIV.

PLOTS, CHARACTERS, AND SIMILES.

SECTION I. *The Plots of the Poems; especially of the Iliad.*

THE works of Homer are not constructed upon speculative models. His is the fresco painting of poetry. He is a man singing to men, and to men immensely his inferiors. He is perhaps more under the conditions of the orator, than of the modern poet. He cannot store up or record his thought; there is but one depository for it, upon the living tablets of the heart, and within its deep recesses. Hence, in both the Iliad and the Odyssey, we have that rush and exuberance of life, which result from the common action between the Bard and his hearers, the separate currents of whose existences seem to be thrown into one great volume, never exhausted, though gently slackened from time to time to meet the conditions of our nature.

He is also an artist, living by his art; addressing himself by his genius to universal nature, but by his circumstances to his country, and to the several squares of that tessellated nation, each with its local patriotism and limited traditions, as well as with its portion in the common inheritance of Hellenism.

Viewed in the light of considerations such as these, the plot of the Odyssey is simple, without knots or breaks of texture, and generally well-devised if not uniformly sustained; but that of the Iliad is, as far as I may presume to judge, in the main a consummate work of art. The mechanism is double throughout. But the train of action on Olympos never clashes with that in Troas, and nowhere impairs the free, natural, and thoroughly human character of that part of the business, which is in the hands of mortals. At the same time, it is so contrived as to assist the Poet in overcoming one of his greatest difficulties; which was, to maintain a clear and ample martial superiority on the part of the Greek chieftains, and yet to give them in Troy a thoroughly worthy and sufficient object for their prowess. What in this respect was lacking in the Trojan leaders, has been supplied by the Theotechny, or divine movement of the Poem.

The most favorite topic of objectors to the plot of the Iliad has been the length of time during which Achilles is kept out of sight. From the Second to the Eighth Book inclusive, and again from the Twelfth to the Fifteenth, he does not appear upon the stage.

Now it is by this withdrawal of Achilles that Homer obtains scope for his other heroes, who were dwarfed by the presence of that colossal figure. The moment he appears they become insignificant; they are almost invisible in the blaze of his light. But, by means of his absence, Diomed, Ajax, Agamemnon, Idomeneus, and likewise Odysseus in the Doloneia, and Menelaos in the Seventeenth Book as well as in the Third, have each their opportunities of distinction. In this manner a double object is gained. First, satisfaction is given to the local sentiment of the parts of Greece, with which these heroes are severally connected. In the second place, by this series of personages, embodying the idea and practice of martial prowess as it was commonly understood, Homer constructs, as it were, a platform, on and from which he can build upwards the astonishing figure of his Achilles, for which the reader has been prepared by a *propaideia*, or preliminary course of greatness, on the scale on which it commonly (as far as it is common at all) appears among men.

But perhaps the most emphatic confutation of such objections is to be found in the total failure of all attempts to combine the ideas of the objectors into anything like one positive sense or view, or to improve the Iliad by the process of excision. While this negative criticism treads its hopeless and dreary circle of doubt without progress or achievement, the Poem itself confirms and enlarges, from generation to generation, its hold upon civilized mankind; and the translations in which it is (of necessity so imperfectly) represented, but which carry it beyond the limited circle of Greek scholarship, multiply in this nineteenth century of ours, and in the very focus of its keenest activity, at a rate beyond all precedent.

The main steps of the action of the Iliad seem to be these. Upon the Wrong perpetrated by Agamemnon arises the Wrath, and thereupon the Secession, of the prime hero, in whose marvellous character the Greek nationality is to find its supreme satisfaction. And this character, not the fate of Troy, is the true central thread of the great epic. On the absence of Achilles, the Greeks, after a panic and recovery, decide upon doing as well as they can without him. Though their superior prowess is fully maintained, they are losers on the whole; and they seek the aid of a rampart, which previously they had disdained. Here is the first marked triumph of the Wrath. Driven back upon their works, they are themselves threatened with a siege. The infirm spirit of Agamemnon gives way, and he a second time utters counsels of flight, to which the chivalrous spirit of the other chiefs will not submit. A mission to the tent of Achilles is substituted, offering splendid gifts and the maid Briseis; a reparation morally imperfect, for there is no confession of the wrong. To the inflamed and inexorable spirit of Achilles they afford matter for fresh exasperation, and the Envoys return baffled in their aim. Here is the second triumph of the Wrath. Not till the ships are about to burn, will he entertain the thought to interfere.

The Greeks fight again; and, a second time, with martial superiority, yet with an unfavorable issue. The rampart is broken by the brave Sarpedon, a chief be it remarked of Greek associations, and apparently the best warrior fighting on the side of Troy. Fire reaches the fleet. But Achilles does not go forth. In his towering pride, he will even now only send Patroclos, a semblance of himself; and this, too, with the vindictive wish that they two, all else having perished, may alone dash down the sacred battlements of Troy.[1]

This, the third great triumph of the Wrath, seems also to mark the point of its overflow into excess; and the moral[2] order must avenge itself, in the divine decrees, and through the persons of men. By divine

[1] Il. xvi. 97-100.
[2] See a fuller discussion on the Plots of the two Poems in Studies on Homer, vol. iii. Aoidos, Sect. 5.

intervention, after acts of might unsurpassed by the other chiefs, Patroclos is slain, and Achilles receives a punishment, in recesses of his nature more profound even than those penetrated and possessed by the Wrath; those recesses, wherein dwelt his intense affection for his friend. That which was to have been the last triumph of his wounded pride, namely, that not he but his deputy should repel the attack which all the other chiefs had failed to baffle, now becomes the cause of an agony so intense, as by far to surpass, both in duration and in intensity, the emotions he had suffered from anger.

The remainder of the fiery current, thus diverted from the Greeks, he turns upon the Trojans. When he goes forth as a warrior, we seem to feel as if we had seen or heard of no warriors before. The King repents, and makes restitution. Hector is slain. The Greeks have been punished for the wrong which they did, or allowed. Achilles has been punished for allowing indignation to degenerate into revenge. The mutilation and dishonoring of the body of his slain antagonist now became to him a second idol, stirring the great deep of his passions, and bewildering his mind. Thus, in paying off his old debt to the eternal laws, he has already contracted a new one. Again, then, his proud will must be taught to bow. Hence, as Mr. Penn has well shown,[1] the necessity of the Twenty-fourth Book, with its beautiful machinery.

On the other side, the death of Hector opens the way for the retribution due to the great guilt of Troy. The recovery of his remains is a tribute to his personal

[1] Primary Argument of the Iliad, pp. 241-278.

piety; and, after the fierce excitement of the action of the Poem, sheds a softened light upon its close. If the plot of the Iliad is to be condemned, where is the epic that can claim either admiration or acquittal?

SECTION II. *Some Characters*[1] *of the Poems.*

1. ACHILLES.

The character of Achilles, as I view it, differs from that of all other heroes of poetry and romance in these respects: it is more intense; it is more colossal in scale; it ranges over a wider compass, from the borders of savagery to the most tender emotions and the most delicate refinements. Yet all its parts are so accurately graduated, and so nicely interwoven, that the whole tissue is perfectly consistent with itself.

The self-government of such a character is indeed very partial. But any degree of self-government is a wonder, when we consider over what volcanic forces it is exercised. It is a constantly recurring effort at rule over a constantly recurring rebellion; and there is a noble contrast between the strain put upon his strength, in order to suppress his own passion, and the masterful ease with which he prostrates all his enemies in the field. The command, always in danger, is never wholly lost. It is commonly re-established by a supreme and desperate struggle; and sometimes, as in the first Assembly after the intervention of Athene,[2] we see the

---

[1] The reader should, on the Greek characters of Homer, consult Col. Mure's History of Greek Literature, vol. I.
[2] Il. i. 219–346.

tide of passion flowing to a point at which it resembles a horse that has gained its utmost speed, yet remains under the full control of its rider.

Ferocity is an element in his character, but is not its base. It is always grounded in, and springing from, some deeper sentiment, of which it is the manifestation. His ferocity towards the Greeks grows out of the intensity of his indignation at the foul wrong done, with every heightening circumstance of outward insult, not merely to him, but in his person to every principle of honor, right, and justice, in the matter of Briseis; as well as to the real attachment he felt for her. His ferocity towards Hector is the counterpart and recoil of the intensity of his passionate love for the dead Patroclos.

Magnitude, grandeur, majesty, form the framework on which Homer has projected the character of Achilles. And these are in their truest forms; those forms which contract to touch the smaller, as they expand to grasp the greater things. The scope of this character is like the sweep of an organ over the whole gamut, from the lowest bass to the highest treble, with all its diversities of tone and force as well as pitch. From the fury of the first Assembly, he calms down to receive with courtesy the pursuivants who demand Briseis. From the gentle pleasure of the lyre, he kindles into the stern excitement of the magnificent Debate of the Ninth Book. From his terrible vengeance against the torn limbs of Hector he melts into tears, at the view and the discourse of Priam. The sea, that home of marvels, presents no wider, no grander contrasts, nor offers us an image more perfect according to its kind in each of its varying moods. Foils, too, are employed with skill to exalt the hero. The half-animated bulk and strength of Ajax (who was also greatly beautiful)[1] exhibit to us the mere clay of Achilles, without the vivifying fire. The beauty of Nireus,[2] wedded to effeminacy, sets off the transcendent, and yet manful and heroic, beauty of Achilles; and the very ornaments of gold, which in Nastes the Carian[3] only suggest Asiatic luxury and relaxation, when they are borne on the person of the great Achaian hero, seem but a new form of tribute to his glorious manhood.

2. Odysseus.

The high quality of Homer's portraitures is in no way better apprehended, than by the clearness of the distinctions between the personages who most approximate. Odysseus receives in the Odyssey a development, which raises him, as a protagonist, almost to the level of Achilles; but in the Iliad, while he is separated from Nestor by some twenty years of juniority, these two characters bear a resemblance which some might mistake for repetition. But, in truth, they are radically distinct, both in speech and action. Nestor's eloquence is gentle and flowing, with a decided flavor of egotism and of garrulity. That of Odysseus is masculine and compressed: when he refers to himself, it is only to enhance his own obligation, in a great crisis, to act as it demands;[4] and he never wastes a word. The sagacity of Nestor is addressed to questions where calm judgment, and the weight given by age and great experience, are alone required; the

[1] Od. xi. 469. [2] Il. ii. 671.
[3] Il. ii. 872. [4] Il. ii. 259-264.

interpositions of Odysseus are in cases, where vehement impulses and strong passions are to be encountered, and where the presence of mind, which can face a crisis, is indispensable. He checks and recalls the whole army from its tumultuous rush homewards; he undertakes the burden of the remonstrance and petition to Achilles. But the interposition of Nestor, in the great Debate of the First Book, is only employed by the Poet when the matter has already, by the direct interposition of Athenê, been reduced to an issue of words alone. To untie a knot is the office of Nestor; to stem a torrent, or scale a frowning barrier, is the business of Odysseus. Again, and more generally, Nestor heals differences by a soothing interposition, and offers suggestions: Odysseus constructs wider plans, but the specialty of his case is this, that he executes what he designs. He has touched that period of life when the faculties of the mind are fully ripened, and the bodily powers are consolidated, but not yet decayed. Nestor belongs to one more advanced; when the mind, without acquiring vigor, in the main retains it, but when the province of bodily action is narrowed by comparative infirmity, and the person becomes as it were a head without a hand, a dependent instead of a self-subsistent organism.

The character of Odysseus, as a whole, is admirably balanced between daring and prudence, both of which are carried in him to the highest degree. The picture is however diversified by two occasions, on each of which he records his having failed in his usual circumspection. On visiting the cave of Poluphemos, his companions advise him to be content with carrying off a supply of cheese, and retiring; but he determines to remain and see the monster.[1] And after the escape from the cave and the re-embarkation, while his men try to keep him quiet, he persists in exasperating the Cyclops with his stinging addresses.[2] In both these cases we may discern a fault; yet not a fault alone, but the irresistible aspiration of genius to measure itself with danger, and to pierce boldly into the unknown.

Odysseus is represented as somewhat wanting in one element of the beauty of the Homeric hero; namely, amplitude of stature. Menelaos is taller by the head and shoulders;[3] and the Cyclops despise him for his deficiency in height.[4] But that his frame was otherwise well developed and powerful is manifest, as he was more majestic than Menelaos when they sate down;[5] and also from his wrestling on equal terms with the huge Ajax,[6] and from his extraordinary feats of strength and endurance in the Odyssey. But it is observable that, amidst the long list of epithets bestowed upon him, none have reference to personal beauty, except when, in Scherié, Athené had endowed him with it in a manner which seems to have gone much beyond mere restoration from his weather-beaten aspect.[7] He seems to speak of himself, even among the Phaiakes, as not possessed of this special gift equally with them.[8] On the other hand, we ought perhaps to set the attachment of Calypso as tending in the opposite direction; and when he returns to Ithaca, Athené disguises him by wrinkling his fair flesh, and by spoiling his hair, now auburn, but elsewhere hyacinthine.[9]

[1] Od. ix. 224.   [2] Od. ix. 492-502.   [3] Il. iii. 210.
[4] Od. ix. 515.   [5] Il. iii. 211.   [6] Il. xxiii. 700 seqq.
[7] Od. vi. 227-235.   [8] Od. viii. 166-175.
Od. vi. 231; xiii. 399.

His age, too, is of course to be taken into account. Perhaps it is on this ground that Homer may have meant to ascribe to him majesty, rather than simple beauty, of countenance.

Although a prudence ever wakeful, and sometimes leaning towards craft, is the most commonly noticed characteristic of Odysseus, and became in after ages the key-note of the character, it is in Homer only one of several features highly distinctive, by means of which the Poet has raised this extraordinary conception to something very near a parity of rank with his Achilles. Though he does not compete with the son of Peleus in his grand prerogatives, in each one of them he is left second to no other hero. He wrestles with Ajax in the Twenty-third Iliad, and beats him in the contest for the Arms of Achilles, thereby establishing for himself the second place among the Greek chieftains. The depth of his passion, and the power of his eloquence, as they are exhibited in the encounter with Eurualos, if they are still behind Achilles in each point, are before those of every other Greek. But by way of compensation for their being only second, Homer has awarded to him a many-sidedness, such as is possessed by no other hero. He is a master not only in war, but in government, and in every industrial pursuit; and the sole approach that we find in the Poems to anything like Fine Art from the hand of a Greek, is in the bed[1] which he had wrought. There is yet another capacity in which Homer has assigned him a clear pre-eminence; the capacity of father and husband, of a model of the domestic affections. After an absence of near twenty years

[1] Od. xxiii. 195–201.

he is still yearning for the day of escape from the arms
of a goddess, that he may return to his wife and child;
and the very smoke of Ithaca would be dear to his
eyes.¹ Of the Odyssey this is the theme. But the
Iliad, too, sustains by its slighter indications the sister
poem; for he alone among the Greek chieftains desires
to be known as the father of his son; and touchingly
sets forth his sense of the hardship of being detained,
even but a single month, away from a wife.²

The faculty of tears is generally ascribed to the
Greek chiefs and soldiery; and the Poet did not think
their susceptibility derogated from their manhood. But
even here Odysseus has a specialty. This man of iron
nerve and soul, who within the Horse's ribs saved the
lives of his comrades by sternly compelling silence; who
in the cave of Poluphemos executed his vengeance, and
then clung beneath the great ram as the blinded monster
felt its back; and who again gave place to a profound
and inexorable wrath, not only against the Suitors, but
even against their helpless and miserable minions;
even this same man it is, who weeps at the recognition
given of his return by the dog Argos in his twentieth
year.³

3. Agamemnon.

The Agamemnon of Homer is described as a good
king and a stout warrior. He shows a natural affection
to his brother, and is not deficient in the courtesy
which, then as now, marked his race; but he is not in
other respects an amiable, nor a decidedly estimable
man: and Homer seems to take care that we shall not

¹ Od. I. 58. ² Il. II. 290, 292. ³ Od. xvii. 304.

love him. His besetting sin is personal; it is an avarice, which seems to make him both cruel in war, with a view to spoil, and niggardly in general conduct. His marked virtue is official; he has a profound sense of responsibility to the army. To this responsibility he greatly defers; and though avarice, appetite, and pride, were alike gratified in the acquisition of Chryseis, he yields her up.[1] And a circumstance, disclosed later in the Poem, shows us that, doubtless from motives of policy, he did not assume an absolute possession of the woman he had taken from Achilles. Yet he has neither the fire of genius, nor any gift of profound political sagacity. On the contrary, while, like so many politicians, he is a practitioner in finesse, he contrives by it to outwit himself. This seems to be, in part at least, the explanation of the unhappy device in the Second Iliad, where he seeks to provoke the people to an attack on Troy, by counselling them to go home forthwith;[2] which they would have done, to his utter confusion, unless the error had been retrieved by Odysseus.

It is a remarkable illustration of the power of the Hellenic anthropomorphism, that the characters of the Olympian and the Pelopid chief have some close resemblances. Zeus, wielding the highest power, is strong in the sense of responsibility, while inferior in intellect to some members of the group around him; and he partially redeems the meaner elements of his character by a strong touch of natural affection for his son Sarpedon, just as that of Agamemnon is in a degree ennobled by his fraternal love for Menelaos.[3] He may be in part the reflection of a human prototype.

[1] Il. i. 117. [2] Il. ii. 139-145. [3] Il. iv. 148; vii. 107.

Whether he be or not, it is in great part true that Zeus is the Agamemnon of Olympos, and Agamemnon the Zeus of Greece.

4. Diomed and Ajax.

In the same manner the characters of Ajax and Diomed, allied by resemblances in action, are profoundly and broadly distinguished. Each is superlative in its degree; but while Diomed is gallant, Ajax is sturdy. Diomed is impassioned, Ajax is calm; Diomed is rapid, Ajax is slow. Diomed can brag; Ajax moves in a simple unquestioning self-reliance. Diomed is not above taking a circuitous advantage, as we find when, in the act of fulfilling the duties of guestship, he makes an extraordinarily profitable exchange with Glaucos: Ajax ever goes direct to his point. With a fine discernment, the Poet selects Ajax and Odysseus as the envoys to Achilles, in the Ninth Book, to attempt a conciliation. The favorable prepossessions of the great warrior are commanded by his sympathy with the powerful intellect of the one, and the straightforward simplicity of the other. A certain vein of craft and of talk in Diomed carried him away from the type of the first without giving him the weighty attractions of the second. And it may also be observed that, although Achilles is in truth incomparable, yet the combination of intellect and spirit with activity and rapid force in Diomed make him the one chieftain of the Iliad, who, if any, would be placed in a direct competition with the hero of heroes. Hence probably there was a latent estrangement. And hence, probably, Achilles selects Diomed for the chief subject of the matchless passage in which, gloating over the miscarriages of the Greeks, he combines bitter taunt with fiery exultation.[1]

Diomed, indeed, possesses every quality necessary to make up a complete Achaian hero. Acute, prompt, intelligent, decided in mind, daring, constant and resolved in spirit, active, strong, and seemingly resistless in strength of body, he is more than able to cope with the brute strength of the god Arès. Of any other poem he might have been the model man. But even the extraordinary composition of his gifts is artfully employed by Homer with a view to the greater glory of that one character, which, in all qualities and all proportions of intellect and soul and body, without deviating from true humanity, is nevertheless colossal.

5. Helen.

The Helen of the Homeric Poems has been conceived by the Poet, himself of peculiar delicacy, with great truth of nature, and evidently with no intention to deprive her of a share in the sympathy of his hearers. He has made her a woman, not cast in the mould of martyrs or of saints, nor elevated in her moral ideas to a capacity of comprehension, and of endurance, beyond her age; but yet endowed with much tenderness of feeling, with the highest grace and refinement, and with a deep and peculiar sense of shame for the offence into which she has been forced or tempted, and from the consequences of which she is unable to escape.

In order justly to appreciate the character of the Homeric Helen, we must begin by casting aside, if we can, all which later times have added, and which poets

[1] Il. xvi. 74–78.

more widely familiar than Homer have conveyed into the modern mind. That she was a willing partner in the crime of Paris at its inception, we are not informed by the Poems; in which, on the contrary, Paris describes himself as having carried her off by violence.[1] We only know that she acquiesced in the consequences of it, by which she became his mate through a series of years, and by which also, on his death, like other widows, she was apparently transferred to another husband, his brother Deiphobos.[2] In this no general baseness or depravity of character is implied, but only the absence of a power of resistance, which would have exceeded that of Penelope, and would have been almost preterhuman at a period, when the condition of a woman withdrawn from the regular family order was one of great, nay total, helplessness.

After the fall of Troy, Helen resumes her place in the palace of Menelaos, as his Queen. The subdued tone of her character, and the absence of self-assertion in her, are still observable; but by her husband, and by all around them, she is treated with the same sentiments, as if nothing had happened to break the original tenor of her married life. Indeed we find in the Odyssey a passage, which seems to indicate a remarkable tenderness on the part of Menelaos, in connection with the most questionable act recorded of the conduct of Helen during the war. When the Greeks were inclosed within the frame of the Horse, the Trojans, suspecting the ambush, brought her down to the spot, and she imitated the voices of the wives of the chieftains, in the hope that they, if there, would reply. This

[1] Il. iii. 443–444. [2] Od. iv. 276.

act, done against the Greeks, savors of that slightness of character, which seems to be represented as the source of her great error. But Menelaos, when he mentions the subject, shifts the blame from her. 'Thither,' he says, 'thou camest; but no doubt it was some deity, favorable to Troy, that prompted thee.'[1]

Helen was the object of much reproach in Troy; not, however, from the mild Priam,[2] nor from the virtuous Hector,[3] but from Hecuba, or from the princes and princesses. This is amply to be accounted for, from their natural sense of the suffering which by her means had been brought upon their family and country, without presuming unfavorably of her beyond what has been already stated. But it could hardly have been the general rule; for when her sister-in-law Laodikè summons her to the Wall in the Third Iliad, she addresses her by the title of 'dear bride.'[4]

Among the Greeks of the War, she is never made the subject of reproach. In one verse of the Iliad, Achilles speaks of her as that dreadful Helen. But this is in the agony of his mind: and in his conference with the Envoys, where it would greatly have enhanced the force of his argument if he could have represented her as worthless, he does nothing of the kind.[5] Penelopè says of her, that the deity impelled her to do an evil deed.[6] But in the context of this very passage, she speaks of Helen simply as deluded, without any malice prepense, and uses the deplorable result to justify her own extraordinary circumspection in the matter of the

[1] Od. iv. 274–279. [2] Il. xxiv. 770. [3] Il. xxiv. 771.
[4] Il. iii. 130. [5] Il. ix. 337. [6] Od. xxiii. 222.

recognition of Odysseus. Compare this with the words in which the Poet describes the sin of Clytemnestra, 'To his home Aigisthos led her, as willing as himself.'[1]

In truth, Homer awards to Helen, when in his own person he speaks of her, an honorable, not a dishonorable treatment. The epithets attached to her name are chiefly descriptive of beauty and birth; but they are never colored with any tint of blame. And when in the Odyssey he compares her to his Artemis,[2] we see on the positive side that favorable bias of his mind, of which we may recognize the negative side of the fact that he never once compares her to Aphrodite. In truth, the only censures of her that we read in the Poems, are those pronounced by herself.

The scene between her and Aphrodite in the Third Iliad exhibits the highest aspect of her character. The goddess endeavors to excite her passions, by a glowing description of Paris in his beauty and his splendid garments, and desires her to repair to him. Struck at first with fear when she perceives who it is that is addressing her, she then kindles into indignation, and makes a bitter and stinging reply; reproaches Aphrodite for interfering to prevent Menelaos from taking her home, and bids her assume to herself the odious character she was seeking to force on another, who had too long borne it. It is only under violent threats, that she at length and with shame complies; and, on arriving in the presence of Paris, she addresses him in terms of scorn and aversion.[3]

Upon the whole, I think that no one, forming his

[1] Od. iii. 272. [2] Od. iv. 122. [3] Il. iii. 390-436.

estimate of Helen from Homer only, could fall into the gross error of looking upon her as a type of depraved character. From the odious Helen[1] of the Second Æneid she is immeasurably apart. Her beauty, grace, refinement, are not contaminated by vicious appetites; they are only not sustained by an heroic, almost a superhuman, firmness. Her fall once incurred, she finds herself bound by the iron chain of circumstance, from which she can obtain no extrication. But to the world, beneath whose standard of morality she has sunk, she makes at least this reparation, that the sharp condemnation of herself is ever in her mouth, and that she does not seek to throw off the burden of her shame on her more guilty partner. Nay, more than this; her self-abasing and self-renouncing humility come nearer, perhaps, than any other heathen example, to the type of Christian penitence.

6. Hector.

The character of the Homeric Hector has been so exaggerated, and so defaced, by the later tradition, that it has lost every distinctive feature of the original, and has come to stand as a symbol of the highest bravery and chivalry. But neither bravery nor chivalry are, in a proper sense, distinctive features of the Homeric Hector.

In the original portraiture itself, which is perfectly simple and intelligible, there is nothing to account for this change. Hector, in the Iliad, is a person of warm domestic affections, of upright purpose, of feeble will, of considerable, but not first-rate, fighting force; with

[1] Æn. II. 567-587.

all the convictions of a good citizen, though without
the light of imagination or the fire of enthusiasm.
He seems to be born in a family of lower tone, and
weaker fibre, than his own; hence upon him is laid
the whole burden of war and government in a terrible
crisis, and his responsibilities are beyond his powers.
Hence, probably, come the discords of his character;
between boastfulness, feebleness, and even shabbiness
on one side, and fundamental rectitude, worth, and
attachment to virtue on another. The contrast seems
to result from an overstrain. And hence it may be
that, though much looked up to in the Poems by his
own family, he does not seem to enjoy the confidence
or respect either of the self-centred Æneas, or of the
circumspect Poludamas,[1] or even of the gallant and
good Sarpedon.[2]

It may be truly said, that Hector is the most inconsistent character in the Iliad. No man is braver than
he is at times: on the other hand, no man shows more
palpable signs of cowardice. No man is more rash;
yet none has a deeper presentiment of the future.
No man is so improvident, it might almost be said so
insolent, in repelling wise counsel tendered to him;
and yet none shows more unequivocal signs of personal
humility. But the faults in his character, though
numerous and glaring, do not form its main tissue.
They are flaws in a delineation essentially good, and
occasionally noble. No act of cruelty or bad faith
or violence, of greed or lust or selfishness, associates
itself with his character; the stream of his thought is
pure; the love he has for his country, his parents, his

---

[1] Il. xii. 211; xiii. 726.   [2] Il. v. 472 seqq.

wife, his child, overflows even in a protective care for Helen.[1] In the measure open to his day and people, he is one who fears God, and regards man; and perhaps the total absence of vice, as it is contradistinguished from infirmity, in his character, co-operated with other causes in bringing about his adoption in the Christian literature of the middle ages, as the model, for the olden time, of the heroic man.

But the very inconsistency of Hector affords a marked testimony to the skill of the Poet. Had he been consistently great, he would have been a real rival to those prime Achaian chieftains, to whom Homer sought to secure an undisputed supremacy of admiration. Had he been consistently mean and small, he would have been a foe so unworthy, that no honor could redound to them from overcoming him. One of these dangers he has avoided by the flaws in the character of Hector; the other by his virtues and his merits. It is not easy to see by what other means he could effectually have attained the ends of his art. And he has further contrived, that the virtues of Hector shall be mainly of a stamp, in which the Achaian chieftains shall not be tempted to compete with him; the affectionate sorrow of his anticipations of the future, the stern rebuke of an unworthy brother, the dignified endurance of misfortune, and that form of resigned heroism, which can only be exhibited in the extremity of disaster.

[1] Il. xxiv. 767-772.

7. Paris.

The character of Paris is as worthy, as any other in the Poems, of the powerful hand and just judgment of Homer. It is neither on the one hand too slightly, nor on the other too elaborately, drawn; the touches are just such and so many, as his poetic purpose seemed on the one hand to demand, and on the other to admit. Paris is not indeed the gentleman, but he is the fine gentleman, and the pattern voluptuary, of the heroic ages; and all his successors in these capacities may well be wished joy of their illustrious prototype. The redeeming, or at least relieving, point in his character, is one which would condemn any personage of higher intellectual or moral pretensions; it is a total want of earnestness, the unbroken sway of levity and of indifference to all serious and manly considerations. He completely fulfils the idea of the *poco-curante*, except as to the display of his personal beauty, the enjoyment of luxury, and the resort to sensuality as the best refuge from pain and care. He is not a monster, for he is neither savage nor revengeful; but still further is he from being one of Homer's heroes, for he has neither honor, courage, eloquence, thought, nor prudence. That he bears the reproaches of Hector without irritation, is due to that same moral apathy, and that narrowness of intelligence, which makes him insensible to those he receives from Helen. No man can seriously resent what he does not really feel. He is wholly destitute even of the delicacy and refinement, which soften many of the features of vice; and the sensuality he shows in the Third Book[1] partakes largely

[1] Il. iii. 437-448.

of that brutal character which marks the lusts of Jupiter. No wise, no generous word ever passes from his lips. On one subject only he is determined enough; it is, that he will not give up the woman whom he well knows to be without attachment to him,[1] and whom he keeps not as the object of his affections, but merely as the instrument of his pleasures. One solicitude only he cherishes: it is to decorate his person, to exhibit his beauty, to brighten with care the arms that he would fain parade, but has not the courage to employ against the warriors of Greece.

Paris, though effeminate and apathetic, is not gentle, either to his wife or his enemies; and, when he has wounded Diomed, he wishes the shot had been a fatal one. The reply of Diomed cuts deeper than any arrow when he addresses him as

'Bowman! ribald! well-frizzled girl-hunter!'[2]

Again, the Poet tells us, as if by accident, that when, after the battle with Menelaos, he could not be found, it was not because the Trojans were unwilling to give him up, for they hated him with the hatred which men feel to dark Death.[3] And again we learn, how he uses bribery to keep his ground in the Assembly; how he refuses to recognize even his own military inferiority, but lamely accounts for the success of Menelaos by saying that all men have their turn;[4] and how he causes shame to his own countrymen, and exultation to the Greeks, when they contrast the pretensions of his splendid appearance with his miserable performance in the field.[5]

[1] Il. III. 428. [2] Il. xi. 385. [3] Il. III. 454.
[4] Il. vi. 339. [5] Il. III. 43, 51.

The immediate transition, in the Third Book, from the field of battle, where he was disgraced, to the bed of luxury, is admirably suited to impress upon the mind, by the strong contrast, the real character of Paris. Nor let it be thought, that Homer has gratuitously forced upon us the scene between him and his reluctant partner. It was just that he should mark as a bad man him who had sinned grossly, selfishly, and fatally, alike against Greece and his own family and country. This impression would not have been consistent and thorough in all its parts, if we had been even allowed to suppose that, as a refined, affectionate, and tender companion, he made such amends to Helen, as the case permitted, for the wrong done her in his hot and heady youth. Such a supposition might excusably have been entertained, and it would have been supported by the very feebleness of the character of Paris, and by his part in the war, had Homer been silent upon the subject. He, therefore, though with cautious hand, lifts the veil so far as to show us that, in our variously compounded nature, animal desire can use up and absorb the strength which ought to nerve our higher faculties, and that, as none are more cruel than the timid, so none are more coarse than the effeminate.

SECTION III. *The Similes of the Poems.*

The detailed similes of the Iliad are about 194 in number; besides near sixty comparisons without any detail or varied ornament.

They are very unequally distributed. The First Book has none; the Sixth only one. In both these the action is of highly sustained and varied interest. On the other hand, the Books occupied exclusively with battle are largely embellished with them. The Fifteenth has sixteen similes, the Sixteenth has eighteen, and the Seventeenth has nineteen. In the Second there are thirteen, all of them intended to set off the gatherings and array of the Army.

In the Odyssey, the greater or detailed similes become very much fewer. They are only forty-one; and this not only before the arrival in Ithaca, where the action is highly varied, and the movement quick; but also in the latter half of the Poem, after the arrival of Odysseus in Ithaca, when it is more relaxed: since the lower tone of the diction and of the subject does not call for, or perhaps even admit, this kind of gorgeous ornament; perhaps also, according to a very natural and reasonable supposition, because those books were composed in the declining years of Homer, as they certainly indicate, with some noble and brilliant exceptions, a lower standard of power.

The character, too, of the greater similes in the Odyssey entirely changes. The lion appears but four times,[1] the vulture once,[2] war never, storm never. Industry, domestic life, the phenomena of outward nature when she is tranquil, now supply the materials to the hand of the Poet.

The similes of the Odyssey, then, have the same harmonious relation to the Poem they embellish, as we find in the Iliad. And we should bear in mind, that in nothing has Homer more emphatically established a type of his own, than in the matter of similes. This

[1] Od. iv. 335, 791; vi. 130; xxii. 402.   [2] Od. xxii. 303.

being so, a treatment so remarkable and characteristic, found in each of the two Poems, furnishes of itself one among the very large number of particulars, which go to make up an inductive argument for the unity of their authorship.

The similes of Homer may in one sense be considered as a miniature of the Poems themselves. Accompanying the movement of the action, they sweep the entire round of human life. There is in them the same elasticity and variety, as in the thought and the style: these they follow over hill and dale, as the faithful dog follows the step of his master. Their tone changes in precise proportion to that of the subject, and of the effect that the Poet seeks to produce.

The similes afford, as I conceive, one among the incidental proofs that, if Homer was indeed blind, he was blind not from his birth, but from subsequent failure of the organ, or calamity. The experience of hunting in the woods and among the mountains, for example, is detailed with a vivid exactness which implies a knowledge founded on experience, just as experience in this case seems probably to imply vigorous limbs, hardy habits, and the perfection of the organs of sense.

CHAPTER XV.

MISCELLANEOUS.

SECTION I. *The Idea of Beauty in Homer.*

THE conception of beauty in the Poems of Homer is alike intense and chaste. He never associates Beauty with evil in such a manner, as to attract our sympathies towards a bad or contemptible person. This is markedly shown by his treatment of Aphroditè, of Nireus, and of Paris, on whose personal beauty he never dwells as he does on that of Nausicaa[1] or of Euphorbos.[2] Only on the one occasion when he has shown some sense of shame and duty, and is going forth full-armed to battle, is this prince allowed to appear for a moment otherwise than despicable.[3] It is not by a didactic morality, but by a genuine impulse and habit of nature, that Homer thus joins and severs, as far as in him lies, what ought to be joined and severed respectively. The legend of Ganymede,[4] which was afterwards perverted to the purposes of depravity, is in Homer perfectly pure, and indeed seems to re-

[1] Od. vi. 149–169.
[2] Il. vi. 832, 505.
[3] Il. xvii. 50–60.
[4] Il. xx. 233–235.

call, though it is in a lower form, the tradition of Enoch, who 'was not, for God took him.'[1]

We may, however, mark the downward course of these traditions, following the lapse of time. Two generations after Ganymede, Tithonus, of the same family, is appropriated by the goddess Eōs as a husband.[2] One generation more gives us the lawless love of Aphroditē and Anchises;[3] and the same goddess, in the next generation, promises to Paris a beautiful wife, whom he was to obtain by treachery and violence as well as adultery. Priam seems wholly without rule on this subject; he charges the fall of Helen[4] on the gods, and, even when reviling Paris inclusively with his surviving sons, makes no reference to his peculiar crimes.[5]

It would appear that in ascribing so much beauty to the royal family of Troy, Homer may have been following tradition. When treating of the Greeks, he appears to award it in pretty close proportion to general excellence. Achilles, the greatest hero of the Greeks, is the most beautiful;[6] and Thersites, their basest wretch, is loaded with ugliness and deformity.[7] Odysseus, the counterpart, without being the rival, of Achilles, has undoubted beauty of a different kind, although without lofty stature;[8] and Ajax, the second of the army in strength, is in the Odyssey called second in beauty also.[9]

We may trace the value set by Homer on personal beauty not only in the loving spirit of passages such as

[1] Gen. v. 24. [2] Il. xi. 1. Od. v. 1. [3] Il. ii. 821.
[4] Il. iii. 164. [5] Il. xxiv. 250.
[6] Il. ii. 674; xxiv. 629. Od. xi. 470. [7] Il. Il. 216-219.
[8] Il. iii. 193. [9] Od. xi. 470.

those that relate to Euphorbos and Nausicaa, and in his assignment of the gift to his two protagonists, but also in some notes appertaining to the two nations respectively. No Trojan is allowed the glory of that auburn hair which is ascribed to Achilles,[1] in one place to Odysseus,[2] and habitually to Menelaos. Nor are they ever adorned collectively with epithets of personal attractiveness such as those given to the Greeks of the flashing eye (ἑλίκωπες),[3] of the flowing hair (καρηκομόωντες),[4] and of the admirable beauty (εἶδος ἄγητοί).[5] And while, in the case of Nireus, Homer has carefully discriminated between mind and body, he has so marked his perfection of form that no reader of the Iliad, however careless, can fail to be impressed by the record. Manifestly, too, he delivers his own sentiments from the mouth of Odysseus at the Court of Alkinoos, where he speaks of beauty, the power of thought, and the power of speech, as the three great gifts of the gods to the individual man.[6]

Stature, as well as form, entered very much into the conception of beauty among the ancients; and this for women as well as men. Yet he was sensible, at least with respect to women, that tallness might pass into excess. Accordingly, among the Laistrugones, when two comrades of Odysseus met the queen, 'they found her big as a mountain's top, and loathed her.'[7]

Homer had a profound perception of the beauty of animals, at least in the case of the horse, as to color, form, and especially movement. We trace in him a

---

[1] Il. I. 197.   [2] Od. xiii. 399.   [3] Il. I. 389, et alibi.
[4] Il. II. 11, et passim.   [5] Il. v. 787; viii. 228.
[6] Od. viii. 167–177.   [7] Od. x. 113.

commencement of the pedigrees of this animal.¹ It is
with an intense sympathy that the Poet describes the
lordly creature and his motions, which he has idealized
up to the highest point by the tears of horses, their
speech, and their scouring the expanse of sea and the
tips of standing corn.² The whole series of passages
relating to the horse in the Iliad is noble and emphatic
throughout; and in no parts of the Poems can we more
distinctly trace, by the slower or quicker movement of
his verse, his adaptation of sound to sense. Space
does not permit me here to exhibit in detail the proofs
of Homer's admiration for the beauty of the horse.³

The appreciation of landscape was a faculty less
highly developed in Homer; yet it surely existed.
The mountainous country of Lacedæmon, which he
calls hollow, he also calls lovely;⁴ the epithet employed
(erateinos) being the same which he uses to describe
Hermione, the daughter of Helen, a person endowed
with the beauty of golden Aphrodite.⁵ Corfu, to which
he applies the same descriptive word,⁶ is in our day of
the highest fame for the beauty of its scenery.

Again, Telemachos apprises Menelaos that Ithaca
is a goat-feeding island, without meadows, and more
eperatos than a horse-feeding country.⁷ The epithet
is equivalent to the one last before mentioned; and
as the meaning is that a hill-country is more beautiful
to the eye than champaign, we seem here to have a
distinct appreciation of the beauty of scenery. The
famous simile of the watch-fires and the sky by night

¹ Il. v. 265-273; xx. 221.   ² Il. xx. 226.
³ See Studies on Homer, iii. 410-416.
⁴ Il. ii. 581; iii. 239. Od. iv. 1.   ⁵ Od. iv. 13.
⁶ Od. vii. 79.   ⁷ Od. iv. 606.

appears to carry something of a like interpretation.[1] And as regards the more limited combinations of what may be termed home-views, we have at the least two great instances in the Odyssey: one of them the garden of Alkinoos;[2] the other the grotto of Calypso, of which he closes his description by saying that 'even an Immortal, on beholding it, would be seized with wonder and delight.'[3]

At the same time, I do not doubt that life, and not repose, is the grand and vital element of beauty in the conceptions of Homer, whether they are applied to nature, or to the animated world.

SECTION II. *The Idea of Art in Homer.*

The Homeric Poems give us a view substantially clear of the state of art in the time of the Poet. They also contain conceptions of the principle of art, so vivid as perhaps never to have been surpassed. And, unless I am mistaken, they indicate to us the source from which the specific excellence of Greek Art, in its highest form, proceeded. By the term Art, I understand the production of beauty in material forms palpable to the eye; whether associated with industrial purposes or not.

First, then, there are many works of art mentioned in Homer: but, in the whole of them, it is associated with some purpose of utility. The greatest of them all is the Shield of Achilles. Next to which, perhaps, comes the armor of Agamemnon;[4] various bowls, men-

---

[1] Il. viii. 557.   [3] Od. vii. 112-132.
[2] Od. v. 68-75.   [4] Il. xi. 15-40.

tioned in different places;[1] the baldric of Heracles;[2] and the golden clasp of the mantle of Odysseus.[3] In all of them, living form is represented. There are other objects of a less defined class, but belonging rather to mere decoration. Such are the necklace of gold and amber, carried by the Phoinikes to Surië;[4] the couch or chair of Penelopë, with a stool to match;[5] and the burnished sheets of copper in the palaces of Alkinoos and Menelaos.[6] There are also works of simple mechanical skill, such as the airy net of metal worked by Hephaistos.[7] We find in the Poems no production of what is termed pure art: everything, to which art is applied, has an object beyond itself: utility aspires to be decked with beauty; and beauty is never dissociated from utility.

Next, as to the material of art. We have in Homer no sign of the use of any material, except metal, for the production of beautiful forms; and, specifically, the metals of gold, silver, tin, and copper. It seems probable that there were, at least in Troy, statues of the gods. But probably also these were rude images of wood, such as Pausanias describes under the name of xoana, in which Homer would find nothing answering to his conception of beauty.

As to the range of art in point of subjects, we must consider it, in all likelihood, as almost entirely confined to the exhibition of form, and of form too, in the solid. Of painting proper, and therefore of colors as connected with painting, we have no sign; though we

[1] Il. xxiii. 740–750. Od. iv. 613–619.
[2] Od. xi. 609–614.
[3] Od. xix. 225–231.
[4] Od. xv. 459.
[5] Od. xix. 55–58.
[6] Od. iv. 72; vii. 86.
[7] Od. viii. 279.

have one case of the use of a single color, in the staining of ivory.[1] But the use of the sheets of copper, already mentioned, is a step in that direction; and the intermixture of varieties of metal, especially on the Shield of Achilles, and in the armor of Agamemnon, show what was perhaps the fullest resort to the principle of color that the limited command of material permitted.

As to the seat of art, we cannot affirm that it had as yet for any purpose been practically established in Greece. No single operation is recorded in the Poems which gives an indication of high metallic skill as having been attained anywhere in that country. By far the most considerable is the bedstead of Odysseus, which is adorned with gold, silver, and copper: but then Odysseus is a master in every art, almost a magician: and we are not told that even his art included the representation of living form.[2] The coloring process, to which reference has been made, is supposed to be carried on, not by a Greek, but by a Meonian or a Carian woman. And in most of the cases where a true work of art is mentioned, it is referred directly to Sidon or the Phœnician; in one or two instances to Thrace, on the shore of which the Phœnicians seem to have had settlements. In other cases it is referred, like the Shield, to Hephaistos, a god of Phœnician associations. In the case of the bowl, presented by the king of the Sidonians to Menelaos,[3] we are told expressly that it was the work of Hephaistos. The gold-beater and the $\chi\alpha\lambda\kappa\epsilon\acute{u}\varsigma$, or smith, are known to Homer; but only, as far as appears, for

[1] Il. iv. 141.   [2] Od. xxiii. 195–201.   [3] Od. iv. 615–619.

the simplest operations; the former simply attaches a plate or band of gold to the horns of the sacrificial ox, and it appears from the passage that he did not ply a separate trade, but was merely the copper-smith engaged in beating gold,[1] inasmuch as he is called chalkous, as well as chrusochoos. All that related to the execution of works of art, so far as we can judge from the Poems, the Achaian Greeks had yet to learn.

But as in other points, so in this, the Poet opened the way for his countrymen, and taught them how they should walk along it in the after-time. As his perception of beauty in living form was most keen, so his idea of art in forms inanimate, copied from nature, was alike powerful and simple: it was that which brought them up to life. In the nature of things, we perhaps may say, it cannot be carried farther. The chairs of Hephaistos moved spontaneously.[2] The porter-dogs of Alkinoos, wrought in gold and silver,[3] were of an immortal youth. The metallic handmaids of the god himself were endowed with thought as well as motion.[4] In the ploughing scene upon the Shield, as the furrow is turned, the earth darkens, though it is of gold.[5] And in the battle compartment, the sculptured warriors fight, and the dead are dragged off the field, with actual movement as in a scene of war.[6] Such is the bold delineation by which the oldest poet of Art has given the challenge to his successors, and bids them excel him if they can.

But all these representations, however raised into

[1] Od. iii. 432-438. [2] Il. xviii. 375. [3] Od. vii. 91.
[4] Il. xviii. 417. [5] Il. xviii. 549. [6] Il. xviii. 533-540.

sublimity by genius, must have had a basis in fact; and it seems difficult to resist the conclusion that Homer, and the Greeks of his time, must have seen, though they had not yet learned to make, art-works of a high order, imported, without doubt, in general from Phœnicia, and produced either there or further eastwards.

The Sidonian works themselves, if executed, as Homer commonly represents, in gold and silver, were doomed without doubt to perish, so soon as the time should arrive when men might come to prize the workmanship less, than the application of the mere material to other uses. But if we may judge from the testimony of such remains as are now accessible, there were two great schools, with which Phœnician artists must have been in relation, alike from their political and their geographical connections: the Egyptian and the Assyrian. It is not, I suppose, too much to say, that we perceive, in a portion at least of the actual remains of these schools, the attainment of high excellence in intention and design, with no inconsiderable progress in execution. They seem, however, to me to represent different principles: the Assyrian appears to embody the principle of life and motion; the Egyptian, the principle of repose. If this be true, there can be little doubt, I presume, that the ideas of Homer had their base and fountain-head much more in the former than in the latter. But in any case, it would really seem probable, from the vivid and stirring descriptions of Homer, that these Phœnician importations supplied patterns, and suggested ideas, which might well, in process of time, become the nucleus of the first great efforts of Greek art.

When that nucleus was once supplied, and when the new life began to grow, then the Olympian system of religion provided it, through the union of the divine nature to the human form, with that lofty aim, which braced it to a perpetual effort upwards, and so conveyed to it the pledge and the talisman of all transcendent excellence. Every idea appertaining to deity was held capable of representation in matter; but it could only be matter moulded according to the shape of man. Thus Greek art was a perpetual untiring pursuit of the highest standard of the ideal, while it seems to have had for its starting-point foreign models which, though not similarly inspired, were of such high merit as to suggest to Homer that imitation might run no unsuccessful race with nature. This happy union of the most fundamental conditions of design and execution was seconded by the lights of a fine climate, by the possession of the purest marbles, and by the corporal perfection of a race abounding in the noblest models. We cannot wonder that, with these advantages, Greece, within her limits of knowledge and experience, should have held down to our own day the throne of Art.

Section III. *Physics of Homer.*

Homer's ideas of physics were extremely simple, as well as apparently few. He perceived that rivers were fed by rain and snow; and therefore he calls them διιπετεῖς, Zeus-fallen, which we should probably understand to mean 'coming from the realm of Zeus.' Fire is the single element which he seems in any direct mode to identify with an Olympian Deity, and this only in one undoubted instance, where he calls it Hephaistos. He considered the human body to be composed of the elements which make up earth and water, for he treats it as resolvable by Death into these substances.[1] It is not easy to arrive at a positive conclusion about his conception of the figure of the Earth, beyond the fact that he considered it to be oblong, which may be probably shown from a comparison of many passages in the Poems. The land, as known to his experience, was limited. A circle, of from 350 to 400 miles in diameter, would have comprised more than all the places, that were within the limits of ordinary Greek knowledge and experience. All his ideas of vastness were connected with the sea. From his placing the River Ocean at all points of the compass, and his making it flow round the Earth, together with the general disposition of objects on the Shield of Achilles, he may be imagined to have conceived of our planet as a flat surface. On the other hand, he seems to connect the extreme East with the farthest West, Sunset with Sunrise, as if he thought it were a surface wrapped (so to speak) round a cylinder. For, placing in the far east the Island of Thrinakiè and the Oxen of the Sun, he makes that deity declare that with these animals he amused himself not only when he rose, but when he returned from heaven to earth; that is to say, at the time of his setting. To this idea there is a partial approximation in the formation of a shield, such as it appears either uniformly or commonly to have been in the time of Homer, namely an oval, or oblong. The Homeric shield is called ἀμφιβρότη, as

[1] Il. vii. 99.

covering the human figure. But it is also called εὔκυκλος. Does this refer to a rounding at the top and bottom? or does it more probably mean that an horizontal section of the shield represented a segment of a well-drawn circle? If the latter be the meaning, the two epithets are placed in thorough harmony. For, the more the shield is rounded horizontally, the more does it shelter the warrior who uses it. And this form might agree with the passage in Od. xii. 380,[1] where the 'return' of the Sun may mean his passing from the point at which men lose him in the West, to his bed or place of rising (ἀντολαί) in the East.[2]

The amusing threat of the Sun, that he will go down to Hades and shine there, is not so strange or far-fetched, relatively to Homeric ideas, as might at first sight appear. For, while he set and rose in the περικαλλὴς λίμνη,[3] the exceeding beautiful expanse of Okeanos, as he had to make his way from the Okeanos of the West to the Okeanos of the East, he might easily be thought, in doing this, to pass through, or near, that underground region, in which dwelt the Gods-Avengers, and which was the realm of Aïdes and Persephonê. Aïdes, says Poseidon, obtained by lot the ζόφος ἠερόεις.[4] Now zophos in Homer is used to signify the West: and yet Odysseus enters the realm of Aïdoneus in the East, near the Sunrise. With all that dark subterranean space between, the Olympian Immortals had no concern: for them, as for us, the light of the Sun both

---

[1] We might be tempted to treat as Phœnician this piece of cosmology. But we should then perhaps be pushing to an extreme the doctrine of a Phœnician origin for the Theotechny of the middle Odyssey, which would hardly reach so far into details.

[2] Od. xii. 4.   [3] Od. iii. 1.   [4] Il. xv. 191.

came and went; 'He rose on gods and men, over the teeming earth.'[1] The change threatened to be made may have been only this, that the Sun, instead of passing through or round the dwelling of Aïdes, would remain there. Zeus therefore takes his menace as perfectly serious, and replies in effect, 'Do as heretofore, and all shall be right.'[2]

Section IV. *Metals in Homer.*

Archæological inquiry is now teaching us to investigate and to mark off the periods of human progress, among other methods, by the materials employed from age to age for making utensils and implements. And the Poems of Homer have this among their many peculiarities; they exhibit to us, with as much clearness perhaps as any archæological investigation, one of the metallic ages. It is moreover the first and oldest of the metallic ages, the age of copper, which precedes the general knowledge of the art of fusing metals; which (as far as general rules can be laid down) immediately follows the age of stone, and which in its turn is probably often followed by the age of bronze, when the combination of copper with tin has come within the resources of human art.

The grand metallic operation of the Poems is that of Hephaistos in the production of the Shield. The metals used[3] were gold, silver, tin, and chalcos, which has been by more license of translators interpreted as brass, for there was no brass till long ages after Homer had rolled away: which has been more plausibly taken

---

[1] Od. iii. 8.   [2] Od. xii. 384–388.   [3] Il. xviii. 474.

to mean bronze: but which, after a good deal of inquiry, I am satisfied can only mean copper, either universally and absolutely, or as a general rule, with very insignificant exceptions.

The discussion would be too long for this place. But the passage immediately before us of itself affords almost sufficient instruction.

In the formation of the Shield, there is no mixture or fusion of metals. The same, and all the same, which are put into the roaring fire, reappear, each by its original name, in various portions of the Shield. There is indeed one passage, where a trench is represented, and this is called kuaneé, a word meaning either made of kuanos, or like kuanos in color. There are two reasons for giving the latter signification to the word. One, that it commonly bears that sense in Homer; the other, that though kuanos may have been a mixed metal, yet there is no sign of founding or casting in this great masterpiece of Hephaistos.

He could only mix by melting; and had he melted metals, we must have heard of moulds to receive them. Instead of this, the only instruments which he makes ready for the work[1] are

1. The anvil.
2. The hammer in his (right) hand.
3. The pincers in his left.

It is plain, then, that he was supposed not to melt, but only to soften the metals by heating, and then to beat them into the forms he wished to produce.

Had Homer been conversant with the fusing or casting of metals, this is the very place where we must

[1] Il. xviii. 476, 477.

have become aware of it; especially as his works of skilled art are all of Phœnician origin or kin, and his Hephaistos is a god of Phœnician associations.

If chalcos be not copper, then copper is never mentioned in Homer. But, in an early stage of society, copper was commonly by far the cheapest and most accessible of metals; and it is quite impossible to suppose, that we never once hear of copper from an author, who incessantly makes mention (so it is argued) of another metal, whereof it is by far the largest component part.

One of Homer's epithets for chalcos is eruthros, red; and this it is impossible under any conditions to apply to bronze.

There is abundant evidence of a correspondence between the seven metals of Homer, and the seven metals of the ancient planetary worship of the East: but one of these is copper, and from it Cyprus was named; and Homer introduces Mentes sailing to a port of Cyprus (Temesè) for chalcos.[1]

We find chalcos in Homer a very cheap and common metal; tin a very scarce and rare metal, only used in very small quantities, and even approaching in some degree to the character of what we now term a precious metal. It is very improbable that the defensive armor, and all the meaner utensils, in Homer could have contained an eighth part, or thereabouts, of tin.

So Hesiod, in his age of chalcos, represents not only the arms and implements, but the dwellings as made of that material.[2] This could not have been bronze.

[1] Od. l. 184.   [2] Opp. 143-155.

* And I have high metallurgical authority for stating, that the sheathing of chalcos on walls as already mentioned must, for mechanical reasons, have been some material other than bronze.

It is said that chalcos cannot be hardened so as to make a cutting tool; whereas this material is named in Homer as used for peeling bark, and cutting twigs and young branches, as well as for making weapons of war.[1] We have, however, in at least one place its imperfection by reason of softness noticed.[2] But, as portions of tin are found in some copper ores, may it not be that there were also small portions of it in virgin copper used for these purposes? I find, moreover, that ancient nails have been discovered, containing 97¾ per cwt. of copper, and only 2¼ of tin: and surgical instruments made of copper alone have been discovered recently in a tomb at Athens.[3]

But although it seems clear that chalcos in general means copper, this may not compel us absolutely to exclude from its signification all compositions of the nature of bronze. In later times the word appears to have included both senses. The Latin æs without an epithet described a compound metal; with the epithet cyprium it meant copper. Some bronzes with a polish are not wholly unlike copper, though they want its redness. Possibly some sharp instruments of this composition might be imported into Greece, without at once leading to a distinction of name, especially if there were native copper, or kinds of copper, in use, which had some slight natural admixture of tin.

---

[1] Il. i. 236; xxi. 37.   [2] Il. xi. 237.
[3] Göbel, Einfluss der Chimie auf die Ermittelung der Völker der Vorzeit, pp. 25, 85.

But these cases must have been exceptional, so far as the use of the word in the Poems is concerned.

— Kuanos is generally the type of a very dark color in Homer, and the word may possibly mean bronze. The Greeks had it in small quantities: it was more valuable than copper, but apparently less prized than tin. In the planetary worship of the East, six deities were connected with six pure metals, and one with kuanos. In Homer we find the six metals, and the kuanos. Now as the septiform system was apparently represented in the seven gates of Thebes, and as the Greeks evidently depended on the Phœnicians for imported metals, I conclude that kuanos is the seventh metal, a mixed one; and I know no conclusive reason why it should not be bronze. It was used only for ornamentation, and in small quantities: if we except the cornice of kuanos in the quasi-Phœnician palace of Alkinoos.[1] Metals in those days seem to have been the great basis of commerce, when there was no apparatus available for storing, sheltering, or distributing with rapidity, perishable materials.

The metals of Homer, then, are —

1. Gold.
2. Silver.
3. Tin.
4. Kuanos.
5. Iron.
6. Chalcos or Copper.
7. Lead.

Silver appears to have been rarer than gold: as might be expected, considering that it is chiefly obtained by scientific means. It came but from one place,[2] Alubē in Asia Minor. We do not hear of it as used in ex-

---

[1] Od. vii. 87.   [2] Il. ii. 857.

change, nor, I think, in stored wealth; but, in plating only, and in works of art.

The respective order of value for the metals is, I believe, that in which I have just placed them. Not so their quantities. Of lead we hear very little indeed. Iron was greatly more esteemed than copper, and was very rare, though seemingly more abundant than tin or kuanos. We hear of it, together with gold and copper, as an article of stored wealth.[1] It was only used for cutting instruments; and chiefly, as far as appears, for woodmen's axes. The quantities of all the metals would seem to have been very limited, except of chalcos only.

Gold was employed in plating, for works of art; it appears also as stored wealth, and moreover, as in the Suit on the Shield, with a slight approach to the character of a measure of value.[2]

Tin was used in small quantities for ornament, and was plated on copper.[3] The only articles entirely made of it were the greaves of Achilles; and these proceeded from a divine, not a human, workman.[4]

SECTION V. *The Measure of Value in Homer.*

Although the Greek of the heroic age was eminently temperate, and abhorrent of excess, the spirit of acquisition was already strong within him. Not only were the crude elements of wealth carefully stored, but works of art had begun to be prized; and beautiful armor, garments, and even personal ornaments,

---

[1] Il. vi. 48, et alibi.
[2] Il. xxiii. 561; xx. 271.
[3] Il. xviii. 507.
[4] Il. xxi. 582, 590-594.

were in use among the great. We have, however, no distinct case recorded of inland commerce as among the Greeks; and the business of exchange had not passed beyond the form of barter.

Yet it appears that gold had begun to be used as a convenient material for the requital of service, and probably also for the liquidation of penalty. On the Shield, the most approved Judge was to receive two talents of that metal [1] for his sentence. And as we hear of the payment of fines on various occasions [2] (distinguished, in the terms of the Pact, from the restitution of the stolen property), it is probable that there is a reference to a precious metal. The epithets τιμήεις and ἐρίτιμος or 'priceful,' [3] applied to gold, and to that only, may have a relation to this custom. In the Twenty-second Odyssey, we have a τιμή or fine of gold and copper.[4]

But a measure of service is one thing, and a measure of value for exchange is another; and we have no sign that gold or silver was used as a common standard, to place commodities in any definite relation of value to one another; although the hoarding, of gold in particular, was a step towards this further development. Another initial sign was the division of the metal into fixed and equal quantities, which is recorded on the Shield.

The only commodity which approximates, in the actual usage exhibited by the Poems, to a measure of value, is the ox; for in this alone other commodities are priced. The arms of Diomed are worth nine oxen;

---

[1] Il. xviii. 507.
[2] Il. ix. 632-634; xiii. 669. Od. ii. 192.
[3] Il. xviii. 475; cf. ix. 398.
[4] Od. xxii. 57-59.

those of Glaucos are worth a hundred.¹ The tripod, which was the first prize for wrestlers in the Twenty-third Iliad, was valued at twelve oxen; the woman captive, skilled in works of industry, at four.² This case does not probably exhibit the normal relations; for in the camp women-captives would be cheap, and oxen dear. Accordingly we find that, when Eurucleia was brought to Ithaca, she was purchased by Laertes for twenty oxen, or for the value of them.³

When Euneos sent ships laden with wine to trade with the Greek army, his men took in return — (1) copper, (2) iron, (3) hides, (4) slaves, (5) oxen. Probably the demand for wine was universal: each paid for it with what he had to spare, in the different kinds of booty acquired. It is not likely that oxen would be sent away from the camp; but it may be intended that the men of Euneos took them from those who had them beyond their wants, as a commodity which they could easily dispose of to others of the chiefs or soldiery less amply supplied.⁴

And we have seen from Æschylus, in the Agamemnon, that the figure of the ox was the sign first imprinted upon a coin; doubtless one intended to represent the equivalent in the metal of the animal.⁵

Section VI. *The Use of Number in Homer.*

The idea of number is one which, up to a certain point, is readily grasped by an average adult of the present day. Persons with a special gift apprehend the idea, with the same clearness, on a larger scale.

¹ Il. vi. 236.   ² Il. xxiii. 702-705.   ³ Od. 1. 431.
⁴ Il. vii. 472-475.   ⁵ Agam. 87.

Children fall short of those who are grown up, and in early youth have no distinct conception beyond a very few units. It seems that, in the childhood of the world, men even of the capacity and grasp of Homer had no definite idea of numbers beyond a very narrow range. By a definite idea of numbers I mean that, which grasps the whole without losing the separate conception of the parts.

We find in Homer as round numbers the sums of ten thousand, and nine thousand. An accomplished person knows ten thousand things.[1] The shout of Ares was like that of nine thousand or ten thousand men.[2] These expressions are evidently altogether vague.

Erichthonios had three thousand horses.[3] Euneos, who came to trade with the Achaian army, presented the two Atridai with a thousand metres of wine.[4] At the Trojan bivouac, a thousand watchfires were kindled on the plain.[5] Iphidamas, having given a hundred oxen to gain a wife, promises a thousand goats and sheep.[6] Some of these instances are obviously figurative: and it is even possible that all are so; for we find the rough and indefinite use of the numeral descending as low as to the single hundred. It is plain, from many passages in the Poems, that the hecatomb does not mean a hundred oxen, but only a batch of oxen, sufficient for one of the more solemn sacrifices. Crete has in one passage a hundred cities, in another ninety.[7] Lucaon says, that Achilles sold him in Lemnos for the value of a hundred oxen.[8] But

---

[1] Od. li. 16. [2] Il. v. 860. [3] Il. xx. 221.
[4] Il. vii. 471. [5] Il. viii. 562. [6] Il. xi. 244.
[7] Il. ll. 649. Od. xix. 174. [8] Il. xxi. 79.

though a prince by birth, he could only be worth a very
small fraction of that number of oxen, when sold as a
slave from the Greek camp. Every gold drop or tassel
of the Aigis of Athené was worth a hundred oxen.[1]
This, if taken literally, would assign to the Aigis itself
a weight of perhaps not less than a ton and a half,
which is inadmissible, since she carries it in the field
among the Greeks, and must be in a certain relation
of stature to them.[2]

The negative evidence of the Poems is in consonance with these instances of the positive class. The Poet nowhere states the numbers of the Greek Army; not even of any of the separate contingents. And when he gives the number of ships for each contingent, it is in every instance, except a very few, of which the highest is twenty-two, a round number. In two cases he states the crews; they are 120 and 50 respectively. These numbers have been taken as a key to an exact computation. But it is impossible that all the chief contingents should have been in round numbers; and we are told that Agamemnon's division was by far the first in number of men,[3] whereas in number of ships it was but very little beyond some others.

Homer has clearly shown us how weak he felt himself in the use of numbers, by the curious passage in which he compares the relative numbers of Greeks and Trojans proper. Were they to be counted, says Agamemnon, the Greeks in tens, and the Trojans appointed singly to serve them with wine, many a party of ten would be without a cup-bearer.[4] Had he been in any manner familiar with the use of numbers on a large

[1] Il. ii. 448.   [2] Studies on Homer, vol. iii. p. 430.
[3] Il. ii. 580.   [4] Il. ii. 123–128.

scale, he could not, on a point of such interest, have
been contented with so slight and vague an approximation. We may therefore be sure that when he
speaks of the thousand watchfires of the Trojan bivouac, and adds that by each fire there sat fifty warriors,[1]
he had never performed the mental process, to us so
simple, of reckoning the force in arms at fifty thousand.

The largest number which I find in the Poems with
any sign of definite use, is that of the fat hogs under
the care of Eumaios. They are 360;[2] and, as one is
daily sent down to the banquet of the Suitors, they
correspond with the days of the year; of which it is
probable that, with the help of the months as an intermediate step, a real computation had been made.[3]

Except where aided by the revolutions of the seasons,
or by some fixed usage, Homer is extremely vague in
the specification of periods of time. Odysseus describes as 'yesterday and the day before,' which we
may take as the equivalent of our 'a day or two ago,'
what had happened at a distance of time between a
fortnight and three weeks back. The periods of years
which go beyond a generation are never mentioned;
but time is always computed, and with a remarkable
accuracy, by the genealogies of notable persons. The
generation, or γενεή, appears to have been conceived
by the Poet as equal to thirty years; and yet here we
ought probably to say, to thirty years more or less.
The age of Nestor was evidently about or over seventy;
he was bearing the kingly office in his third γενεή or
generation.[4] And it seems as if the ten years of the

[1] Il. viii. 563. [2] Od. xiv. 20.
[3] Od. xiv. 93. [4] Il. i. 252.

war, with ten of preparation preceding them, and ten of wanderings which follow, were intended poetically to make up this whole, so that an entire generation should be spent upon it. Yet the first of the three terms would appear incapable of a literal interpretation. We may be sceptical as to the other two; but it seems clear, that the Poet could hardly have intended us to believe that ten years were expended in gathering the force.

Only in one place does Homer refer to any actual process of reckoning. He describes Proteus counting his seals by the word pempassetai.[1] I understand this to mean no more than that he reckoned them on his five fingers. It is however somewhat remarkable, that this only reference to any part or element of the decimal scale, which we are still supposed to derive from the East, should be found upon an Eastern scene, and in connection with a personage of purely Phœnician associations.

Section VII. *The Sense of Color in Homer.*

In the 'Studies on Homer,' I have considered at some length the manner in which Homer handles the subject of color. I can in this place only lay down certain propositions without attempting the proof of them in detail.

To us of the present day, color, and its broader distinctions, are familiar from childhood upwards. But, in the first place, it is to be borne in mind, that the acquired knowledge of one generation becomes in time the

---

[1] Od. iv. 412, 451.

inherited aptitude of another. In the second place, much of our varied experience in color is due to chemistry, and to commerce, which brings to us the productions of all the regions of the world. Mere Nature, at any one spot, does not present to us a full and well-marked series of the principal colors such as to be habitually before the mind's eye. Thirdly, the curious investigations[1] of late years have shown us that, even now and in our own country, no inconsiderable proportion of persons are without the faculty of perceiving some of the primary distinctions of color.

With respect to Homer, my main conclusions are

1. That his perceptions of color, considered as light decomposed, though highly poetical, are also very indeterminate.

2. But that his perceptions of light not decomposed, as varying between light and dark, white and black, were most vivid and effective.

3. That accordingly his descriptions of color generally tend a good deal to range themselves in a scale (so to speak) of degrees, rather than of kinds, of light.

The primitive experience of the prismatic colors must have been principally drawn from the rainbow. But Homer only once mentions the rainbow,[2] and here he compares it with the snakes of dark metal on the breastplate of Agamemnon; of which comparison I can discern no other ground than that they would flash a varying light as the chieftain moved.

His goddess Iris is in evident relation to the rainbow. Yet he never gives her an epithet of color;[3]

[1] See Wilson on Color Blindness. [3] Il. xi. 27.
[2] Il. vlii. 398.

though he calls her golden-winged. I think these facts go some way towards proving my main theses.

There are no words in Homer which can with any certainty be held to mean any one of these three colors: orange, green, and blue. His word kuaneos, which is more like indigo, does not seem to have been clearly separated in his mind from black;[1] while he also applies it to wet sand.[2] His word porphureos for violet, runs into his word eruthros for red. His word xanthos for yellow is applied to auburn or red hair, to the ears of corn, to a chestnut horse, to a river (apt to be swollen I suppose, and darkened by mud). In truth, there is not one single epithet of color which we can affirm to be thoroughly defined. The word phoinix, which seems to intermix with xanthos, is also used as the equivalents of the words which would be rendered purple and red. Only a minute examination could collect the whole evidence in the case; but I will close with observing that oil is once called rosy,[3] iron and wool violet, and oxen wine-colored. But in the use of the words white and black, light and dark, which is abundant, Homer's eye seems rarely or never to go astray.

[1] See Il. xxiv. 94.   [2] Od. xii. 243.   [3] Il. xxiii. 186.

INDEX.

A

ACHAIANS, who, 66; epithets applied to, 61; local force of the Achaian name in the historic ages, 65; distinction between them and the other inhabitants of Greece, 66; Achaian race in Crete, 67; closely related to the Pelopids, 161; the Achaian 'succumbs to the half-savage Heraclid,' 174.

Achaic Argos, 48.

Achaïs, force of the word, 40 et seq.

Achilles, lands occupied by his contingent, 110; his powerful denunciation of falsehood, 389; and elevation of character, 389; his singular courtesy, 395, 426; general survey of his character in Homer, 600–602.

Actoridai, house of the, 137.

Adultery, crime of, held in abhorrence, 398; fine imposed upon the adulterer, 411.

Advent of our Lord, previous history a preparation for that event, 377.

Æneas and the title 'Anax Andrōn,' 162; case of his birth, 872.

Agamemnon as Anax Andrōn, 155; account of his sceptre, 150; and of his extraction, 157; unjust and rapacious, 820; his threat in regard to Briseis, 411; his suzerainty over other princes, 420; his succession hereditary, 427. See *Polity, Kings*, &c. Description of Agamemnon in Homer, 500.

Aidoneus, 253; obscurity of his figure, 253; particulars concerning, 254, 255; Homeric adjustment regarding the anterior and the present Olympian dynasty, 257.

Aiguptioi, the, visited by Menelaos, 128. See also *Egypt*.

Aiguptos, an Ithacan noble, 120.

Aiolids, the question of their Phœnician origin discussed, 136.

Aiolos, a Phœnician, 140; force and derivation of the name, 141.

Ajax, 608.

Anax Andrōn, 151; to whom applied, with facts relating to the phrase, 153; the term disappears from use after Homer, 155; title applied to Agamemnon, 155; to Anchises and Æneas, 163; title a sign of affinity between the Greeks and the Trojans, 166; applied to Augeias, 167; to Euphetes, 170; to Eumelos, 171; a title probably drawn from a more patriarchal state of so-

ciety, 178; what it specially denoted was some primitive chiefship or superiority, 174.
Anchises and the title 'Anax Andrôn,' 162.
Animal-worship, 361; oxen of the sun, 361; immortal horses, 362; assumption of the forms of birds by deities, 362; animal sacrifice, 363.
Anthropomorphism, Zeus the type of, 214; the principle of Greek religion, 363.
Aphroditè, 313; her position, and circumstances concerning her, 313; superintends marriage in its physical side, 314, 315; referable to the mythology of Assyria, 317.
Apollo, dignity of, 271; uniform identity of his will with that of Zeus, 275; the defender and deliverer, 276. See also Athenè and Apollo.
Appellatives, the Three Great, 31; evidence of chronological succession among, 34.
Approximation, modes of, between the divine and the human nature, 363.
Arcadians, the Swiss of Greece, 51.
Arès, 296; 'compound of deity and brute,' 296; the representative of animal force, 299; Homeric evidence concerning, 298, 299; probably of Pelasgian and elemental origin, 300.
Argos, significance of the name, 34; Achaïc Argos, 48; Iasian Argos, 49; name applied to three settlements, 50; a plain country, 51; put sometimes for Greece at large, 51; recapitulation of its four uses, 52; used adjectively, 54; force of the word 'Argeioi,' 35; poetic and archaic name, 43; its possible local use, 45.
Army, 432 et seq.; ranks traceable in, 433; privates of, 433; nature of the arms employed, 433; two modes of fighting, 434.

Art, works of, obtained from Phœnicia, 124; idea of art in Homer, 525; works of art, 525; materials thereof, 525; range of, 526; seat of art, 528; Egyptian and Assyrian schools of, 529.
Artemis, 305; a reflection of Apollo, 305; relation of to the elemental system, 306, 307; great inferiority of to Apollo, 309; ministry of death, 320; rival of Aphroditè in matter of beauty, 320.
Assemblies, Homeric, 432; centre of the life of the community, 438; opposing factions in the, 439; Trojan Assembly, 461.
Atè, the temptress, 356; eldest daughter of Zeus, 357; resemblance between this Greek allegory and the representation of the Serpent in Scripture, 357; examples of her agency, 358.
Athenè, highest intelligence of Olympian deities, 211; relation of rank between Herè and her, 270.
Athenè and Apollo, 268; their position explained by Hebrew tradition, 269; their sanctities superior to that of Zeus, 272; never deceived or put to shame, 273; epithet 'dear' applied by Zeus to them, 274.
Augeias, and the title 'Anax Andrôn,' 167.
Autochthonism, or birth from the soil, 38.

B.

BALANCE of forces, political, unknown to Homer, 419.
Basileus, as a designation of dignity, 152; use of the term in the Odyssey, 445. See King, Polity, &c.
Beauty, admiration of the poet for, 402; moral purity of the idea, 402; idea of Beauty in Homer, 521.
Blood, recognition of the tie of, 402.

INDEX.

Boulé, or Council, 434.
Briareus, 339.
Briseis, 409, 410.

C.

Calypso, situation of the island of, 480.
Cannibalism, 399.
Catalogues, the, 171–174.
'Chorizontes'— those who maintain a separate authorship — 14 et seq.
Chruses, 64.
Color, sense of in Homer, 544.
Concubinage of rare occurrence, 411.
Conscience, voice of recognized, 386.
Courtesy, fine example of in Achilles, 395, 425.
Crete, Pelasgian character of its population, 90; races inhabiting, 90; base of Achaian warlike effort against Egypt, 148.

D.

Danaos, 40 et seq.: Danae, 40; Danaoi, 30; military character of the epithets applied to, 86; probable conclusions respecting the name, 42.
Data for constructing Map of the 'Outer Geography,' 482.
Date of Homer, 3; of the fall of Troy, 2.
Debate, Homeric, 437.
Delicacy of Homer, 403.
Demeter, 262; epithets and Homeric evidence, 263 et seq.; etymology of, 266; a figure partly Hellenized, partly Pelasgian, 266.
Demiurgoi, the, 443.
Demodocus, 2, 5.
Destiny, binding efficacy of, 850. See *Fate.*
Diomed, Homer's description of, 408; exchange of arms with Glaucos, 402.
Dioné, 266; of the family of Nature Powers, 267.

Dionusos, 819; slight and obscure traditions concerning, 319; recency of his worship, 821; Dionusian orgies, 822; within the circle of Phœnician traditions, 822.
Distances, Homer's measures of, 483.
Doom, ministers of, 849, 858.
Dorian conquest, effect of, 4.

E.

Egypt, somewhat narrow direct notices of in the Poems, 126; Egyptian Thebes, 126; drug presented to Helen, 126; Egyptians, 127 et seq.; Egyptian chronology, 143; Achaian invasion of Egypt, 146; zenith of the Egyptian power, 147.
Elysian Plain, the, 374.
Ephuré, 161.
Erinues, 218, 350; action and functions of, 352 et seq.; derivation of the name, 356.
Ethics of the Heroic Age, 381; connection between duty and religious belief and reverence, 384.
Eumelos, 171.
Euphetes, 270.

F.

Fate or Doom, 858; explanation of the words (Kér, Moira, &c.) expressing this idea, 858–861.
Filiation, Divine, 867.
Food, 129.
Fraud, element of in Homer, 212; tenderness for fraud the weakest point in Homer, 388; case of Diomed and the oxen of Glaucos, 389.
Future State, Homeric view of, 873; its threefold division, 874.

G.

Genealogies of the Catalogue, 172.
Geography of Homer, 471; Ho-

meric division of the Greek territory, 172; Geography of the Plain of Troy, 174; 'Outer Geography,' 179; data for constructing an Homeric Map of the Outer Geography, 182.
Gods, classification of, 218, 219. See also the deities under their several headings. Consult also *Religion*.
Greek life in the Heroic Age, sketch of, 405.
Greeks of the Iliad, their ordinary appellations, 83; moral character of the Homeric Greeks, 381.

H.

Here, 327; office exclusively Olympian, 328; probably a purely ideal conception, 328.
Hebrew idea of a Deliverer reflected in Homer, 210; story of Joseph and the Greek legend of Bellerophon, 203; concerning the punishment of Rebellious Powers, 342; concerning the Serpent and the Greek Atè, 357.
Hebrew traditions concerning the Messiah, 205, 206.
Hector, 613–616.
Helen, 502–513.
Helios, a person, 821; appears with more marked effect in the Odyssey rather than in the Iliad, 823; oxen of the Sun, 324; an Eastern god, incorporation of the Sun with the Trojan Apollo, 325.
Hella, 110; its derivatives, 110.
Hephaistos, character, functions, and instances of his operation, 291 *et seq.*
Heracles, character of, 283.
Herè, 230–243 *et passim*.
Hermes, 201; secondary part played by, 301; functions point to a Phœnician source, 303; an agent rather than a mere messenger, 304; connected with the East by Welcker, 305.

Hesiod and Homer, comparative antiquity of, 27; contrast between the theologies of, 171.
Homer, influence of his works, 1; his blindness, 2; date at which he lived, 3; place of his birth and residence, 6; his poetry historic, 7; historic also with regard to his chief events and persons, 7; theurgy of his Poems self-subsistent, 9; special feature of his Poems in the delineation of personal character, 10, 11; obscurity respecting the Iliad and Odyssey, 12; discussion of the question of the unity of his Poems, 13 *et seq.* Consult also *Iliad*, and cognate headings. Text of the Poems, 23; plots, characters, and similes of the Poems, 495.
Homicide, 387.
Houses, pedigree of the ancient Greek, 368.
Hymns, the Homeric, discussed, 12; their inferiority, 13.

I.

Iliad, influence of on modern life, 1; plot of compared with the plot of the Odyssey, 17; careful preservation of the text, 23; plot of, 430; main steps of his action, 427. See various headings: *Homer, Sense of Beauty in Homer, Use of Number*, &c. &c.
Ionians, 81, 85 *et seq.*
Iris, 332; her office, 333; the rainbow, 334; instances of her action, 334 *et seq.*

J.

Justice, sense of, 391.

K.

Kadmos, 123; etymology of his name, 136.

INDEX.   551

Kephallenes, 116.
Kimmeria, derivation of the name, 494.
King of kings, or Suzerain, the position of Agamemnon, 433.
Kings, Homeric, personal reverence for, 418; a distinct class, 420; stand in a special relation to deity, 421; personal vigor of, 422; skill in the games, 423; gifts of music and song, 424; manual employments of, 424; Judge, General, and Priest, 424; succession of hereditary, 425; testimony of the Olympian arrangements to the higher dignity and authority of the elder brother, 428; King as priest, 428; Judge, 429; as a great proprietor, 430; hospitality expected from, 431; might obtain private property, 431; lax law of kingly succession in Troy, 466, 467.
Kudones, of Pelasgian origin, 90.

L.

Larissa, 77, 78.
'Law,' no word for in Homer, 449; substitutes for, 447; fivefold basis of society, 452.
Leleges, who, 91.
Leto, 259; epithets ascribed to her, 259; her action circumscribed, 259; high ascriptions of her dignity, 260; etymology of her name, 261; a record of the Hebrew tradition regarding the Deliverer, 262.
Logos, the, 210.

M.

Marriage. No clear instance of a married deity, save Zeus, 210; Homeric marriage, 409-415; strictness of the law concerning, 410; restraints imposed upon, 412.
Medium of exchange, 460.
Memnon, an Egyptian, 149.

Menelaos. See *Helen*, *Paris*, *Marriage*.
Messiah, The, Hebrew tradition respecting, 205; the Deliverer, 210.
Metals in Homer, 532; those used in the shield, 533; Homer ignorant of the fusing or casting of metals, 535; chalcos, 535; kuanos, 537; list and value of the metals, 538.
Minos, his Phœnician character, 120 *et seq.*
Moderation, the base of a model man in Homer, 336.
Music probably introduced by the Phœnicians, 134.
Myrmidons, of Hellenic and Achaian race, 101.

N.

Names applied to the Greeks of the Iliad, 31; derivation of national or tribal names, 37; derivation of names of countries and places, 63; names, Greek and Trojan, 104; local concatenation of names of places, 118.
Nature, modes of approximation between the divine and the human, 303; four main channels of approach, 373.
Nature Powers, 340; communication of the human Dead with, 376; worshipped in Troas, 456. See *Religion*.
Nemesis, 386.
Nereus, the sea-god, 245, 347.
Nestor, 9, 85, 436; his age, 643.
Number, use of in Homer, 640-644.
Nymphs, 348.

O.

Oath, peculiar importance of, 446.
Odysseus, 68; Phœnician element in his fictions, 126, 127; notices concerning, 128, 140,

823, 824; his characteristic virtue of patience, 892; his self-command, 896; his filial sentiment towards Laertes, 401, 403, 422, 424; his profound refinement, 425; eloquence of, 436; state of society in Ithaca, 445; several stages of the voyage of Odysseus, 458; Homer's portraiture of Odysseus, 502.

Odyssey. See other headings: *Homer, Chorizontes, Iliad, &c.* Plot of the Odyssey characterized, 495.

Olympian system, 176, 846; classification of various preternatural personages, 846 *et seq.*: see *Religion, Approximation, Animal-Worship, Future State:* Results of the Olympian system, 377; its character, 378.

Oratory, Homeric, 437.

'Outer Geography,' the, 479; data for constructing map of, 482.

P.

PAIAN, hymn to Apollo, 332.

Paleon, Egyptians of the race of, 125, 330; singular relation between Paleon and Apollo, 332.

Panachaioi, 70.

Panhellenes, force of the word, 114.

Parents and children, profound natural attachment between, 400.

Paris, 389, 402; Homer's character of, 510–513.

Patience, exalted view of, in the Homeric ethics, 892.

Pelasgians, epithet 'dioi,' 76; direct notices concerning, 78–78; other heads of Homeric evidence relating to them, 78 *et seq.*; etymology of the name, 94; words common to the Greek and Latin languages are Pelasgian, 96; lists of these words, 97 *et seq.*; extra-Homeric evidence touching the wide extension of the Pelasgoi, 107.

Pelasgicos, the archaic name of Zeus, 74.

Penelopê. See *Odysseus.*

Persephonê, 311; epithets applied to her, 311; co-ruler with Aidoneus, 312; representative of the old Pelasgian tradition, 312; etymology of, 312.

Phaiakes, people of Scheriê (Corfu), were Phœnicians, 133.

Phœnicians (the) and the Egyptians, 119; Minos a Phœnician, 120; Kadmos, Daidalos, 123; Phœnician works of art, 124; Greeks dependent on Phœnicians for intercourse with the outer world, 125; points of contrast between the Phœnician and Hellenic world, 128; meaning of the word 'Phœnicia' in its widest sense, 130; building, use of hewn stone, &c., a Phœnician art, 132; art of music probably introduced by the Phœnicians, 134; Phœnicianism of the Aiolids, 138; some Phœnician personages also called Sidonian, 144; intercourse of the Phœnicians with the Jews, 202; tales of the Odyssey having a Phœnician origin, 203; Poseidon a Phœnician god, 250; Phœnicians brought into Greece the Assyrian planetary worship, 316; dependence of the Greeks on the Phœnicians for metals, 637. See also *Voyage of Odysseus* and *Art.*

Phthiê, significance of the territorial name, 112.

Physics of Homer, 625–628.

Plots, characters, and similes of the Poems, 495.

Polity of the Heroic Age, 417; resemblance between the Homeric and our own ideas, 417; personal reverence for sovereigns, 418; qualifications preventing excesses, 418; no 'balance of forces,' 419; reciprocal duty, 419; Homeric kings, 420; leading political ideas exhibited in the Poems, 452. See

also *Kings, Army, Assembly, Council.*
Polygamy of Priam, 455.
Poseidon, 243; his character, 243; not an elemental deity, 245; prayer how addressed to him, 246; functions of, 247; Greek legends respecting, 248; instances of his action, 249; his working supremacy in the Odyssey, 250; prevalence of his worship among the Phœnicians, 251; special attributes, 252.
Priam, 455; his sons, 466; suzerainty over subordinate districts, 468.
Priests, no professional, 428; king as priest, 428, 429; the Trojan priesthood, 460.
Proitos, 131.

R.

Rainbow in Scripture and in Homer, 210.
Rebellious Powers, the, 249.
Recensions (state) of Homer, 21.
Recitations (state) of the Homeric poems, 22.
Religion of Greece, its variegated aspect, 178; conflict of religions, and conflict between Nature-worship and the Homeric system, 179; the two religions: instances of amalgamation or expulsion of deities, 180; character of the Olympian system, 181; its debasement, 182; devoid of authority, 183; had no priesthood, 183; its prevailing character humanitarian, 184; influence of the popular and of the philosophic mind upon the system, 184; two simultaneous processes of a speculative ascent and a practical decline, 186; Plato's reproaches against Homer's treatment of the gods baseless, 187; principal materials of the Homeric religion, 188; Homer's mode of dealing with the older Nature Powers, 189; vestiges of the earlier system, 191; relation between the older and the younger schemes, 194; Homeric mythology to be severed also from the Roman mythology and the mythology of classical Greece, 195; the polity of the system framed on the human model, 195; heterogeneity discernible among members of the Olympian court, 196 *et seq.*; classification of the Olympian personages, 200; limitations and liabilities among the gods, 201; marked correspondence between certain legends and the Hebrew traditions conveyed in the books of Scripture, 202; Hebrew tradition respecting the Messiah, 205, 236; origin of Pagan religions: opinions of St. Paul, Eusebius, and others, 206; machinery of the Homeric poems, 207; idea, in Homer, of a Deliverer and tradition of an Evil Being, 210; grand distinction between Homeric and later systems, 214; collective and individual action of the gods, 214; distinction between the Greek and Trojan religions, 455. See *Olympian system,* and the deities under their several designations.
Resemblances and differences between the Greeks and the Trojans, 455.
Reverence, the formative idea of Greek society, 453; reverence for parents, for kings, for the poor, &c., 454.
River, Homer's notion of a great circumfluent (Okeanos), 491.
River-worship, 192. See *Religion;* also *Nature-worship.*

S.

Sacrifices, animal, 803.
Sanscrit, names of Hellenic deities derivable from, 345 note.
Scherie (Corfù), 70.

Sellos, Selloi, explanation of the words, 116.
Sidon, 144.
Similes of the Poems, 513–521.
Sin, 310.
Sketch of Greek life in the Heroic age, 405.
Slavery, not a prominent feature of Greek society in Homer, 448; war and kidnapping the two sources for supplying slaves, 448; mitigated character of Homeric slavery, 449.
Society, five-fold basis of, 449.
Sun. See *Helios*. Oxen of the sun, 188, 323.

T.

TARTAROS, 370.
Text of the Poems carefully preserved, 21.
Thebes, the, of Kadmos, 124; Egyptian Thebes, 125.
Themis, 329; deification of an impersonated idea, 330; Hahn's derivation of the word, 330.
Thetis, 330; of elemental origin, 336; her rank, 338; marriage to Peleus, 338; principal particulars concerning her, 342; epithets applied to her, 344; character of the later traditions concerning, 344.
Tis, the Greek Public Opinion, 441; primary ancestor of the famous Greek Chorus, 442.
Tradition. See *Hebrew Tradition*.
Trinity, 210; and the trident of Poseidon, 251, 252.
Trojans, religious system of the, 459 *et seq.*; excelled the Greeks in religious observance, 462; inferior to the Greeks in morality, 462; polygamy of Priam, 465; lax succession of their kings, 465; Trojan Assembly, 469.
Troy, Geography of the Plain of, 474–479.

U.

UNDERWORLD, the, 375.
Unity of authorship, 14.

V.

VALUE, measure of, in Homer, 538–540.
Voyage of Odysseus, several stages of the, 488.

W.

'WILL and Ought,' 217, 350, 351.
Wolf, Professor, his argument, 14.
Woman, her position, 409; marriage, 409–416; whether capable of political sovereignty, 415; domestic employment of, 415, 416.

Z.

ZEUS, 221; formed in many points upon the conception of the One and Supreme God, 221; his five capacities, his epithets and verbal ascriptions, 222; the Pelasgian Zeus, 223; the Divine Zeus, 225; the Olympian Zeus and Lord of Air, 228, 229; Zeus, the type of anthropomorphism, 204.

www.ingramcontent.com/pod-product-compliance
Lightning Source LLC
Chambersburg PA
CBHW031935290426
44108CB00011B/559